THE OXFORD INTERNATIONAL RELATIONS IN SOUTH ASIA SERIES

SERIES EDITORS
Sumit Ganguly and E. Sridharan

After a long period of relative isolation during the Cold War years, contemporary South Asia has grown immensely in its significance in the global political and economic order. This ascendancy has two key dimensions. First, the emergence of India as a potential economic and political power that follows its acquisition of nuclear weapons and its fitful embrace of economic liberalization. Second, the persistent instability along India's borders continues to undermine any attempts at achieving political harmony in the region: fellow nuclear-armed state Pakistan is beset with chronic domestic political upheavals; Afghanistan is paralysed and trapped with internecine warfare and weak political institutions; Sri Lanka is confronted by an uncertain future with a disenchanted Tamil minority; Nepal is caught in a vortex of political and legal uncertainty as it forges a new constitution; and Bangladesh is overwhelmed by a tumultuous political climate.

India's rising position as an important player in global economic and political affairs warrants extra-regional and international attention. The rapidly evolving strategic role and importance of South Asia in the world demands focused analyses of foreign and security policies within and towards the region. The present series addresses these concerns. It consists of original, theoretically grounded, empirically rich, timely, and topical volumes oriented towards contemporary and future developments in one of the most populous and diverse corners of the world.

Sumit Ganguly is Professor of Political Science and Rabindranath Tagore Chair in Indian Cultures and Civilizations, Indiana University, Bloomington, USA.

E. Sridharan is Academic Director, University of Pennsylvania Institute for the Advanced Study of India, New Delhi.

'Nicolas Blarel's book offers a uniquely comprehensive account of India's Israel policy since even before both countries became independent states. It is a fascinating entry point in the transformation of the attitude of New Delhi vis-à-vis the Middle East and its conflicts. Blarel shows that if the Palestinian cause remains dear to India, the mainstream political parties—the Congress as well as the BJP—have shifted towards Israel for strategic reasons. This masterpiece is a major addition to the literature and a must-read at a time of recomposition of the region.'

—CHRISTOPHE JAFFRELOT, Senior Research Fellow at CERI-Sciences Po/CNRS, Paris, Professor of Indian Politics and Sociology at King's India Institute, London; non-resident scholar at the Carnegie Endowment for International Peace , Washington D.C.

'*The Evolution of India's Israel Policy* fulfils a crying need amongst policy-makers, academics and practitioners to unravel the near mysterious ways in which India charted its course on relations with Israel... Blarel's analysis of the evolution of these events in a broader historical and comparative context gives his writing unique distinction. It has not been attempted [earlier] on any specific aspect of India's foreign policy. It may have set up a model worthy of emulation... India's policy towards Israel demonstrates the inevitability of gradualism ingrained in Indian foreign policy-making as a whole.

I recommend Blarel's book to anyone seriously interested to understand how India's policy on Israel came to be made and the factors that lie behind its policy-making as a whole.'

—AMBASSADOR RAJENDRA ABHYANKAR, Professor of Practice of Diplomacy and Public Affairs, School of Public and Environmental Affairs, Indiana University, Bloomington

irsa

THE OXFORD INTERNATIONAL RELATIONS IN SOUTH ASIA SERIES

The Evolution of India's Israel Policy

Continuity, Change, and Compromise since 1922

Nicolas Blarel

OXFORD
UNIVERSITY PRESS

UNIVERSITY PRESS

Oxford University Press is a department of the University of Oxford.
It furthers the University's objective of excellence in research, scholarship,
and education by publishing worldwide. Oxford is a registered trademark of
Oxford University Press in the UK and in certain other countries

Published in India by
Oxford University Press
YMCA Library Building, 1 Jai Singh Road, New Delhi 110 001, India

ISBN-13: 978-0-19-945062-6
ISBN-10: 0-19-945062-5

Typeset in Adobe Jenson Pro 10.5/13
by The Graphics Solution, New Delhi 110 092
Printed in India by G.H. Prints Pvt. Ltd, New Delhi 110 020

Contents

Tables and Figures

Tables

Figures

Acknowledgements

WHY DID INDIA recognize Israel only in September 1950 and why did it establish diplomatic relations with Tel Aviv only in January 1992? Why did India deliberately refuse to revise its position for 42 years? What led to a new strategic thinking in the early 1990s? Investigating these questions has been my professional concern for the past decade. If I have been able to craft an empirical and theoretical answer to these queries in the form of this book, it is because of the exceptional support of certain individuals and institutions. I would be negligent if I did not acknowledge the several people who have contributed to this work at various stages of the research project and ensured its completion.

A number of key institutions and individuals supported me while I researched and wrote this book. The earliest seed of this project was sown over a decade ago when I worked as a research assistant for Christophe Jaffrelot at the Center for International Research and Studies (CERI) at Sciences-Po in Paris. Jaffrelot first introduced me to this relatively unknown but particularly interesting research topic. At the time, I was already struck by the lack of general knowledge about this burgeoning relationship, which had started merely a decade after the two countries had normalized their diplomatic relations. The idea of systematically exploring the origins of India's drastic policy change vis-à-vis Israel in 1992 became the topic of my BA thesis. With the support of Jaffrelot, and of Denis Rolland at the Institute of Political Science in Strasbourg, my short thesis was published in France in 2006.

However, I quickly realized that I had only scratched the surface of this study. For the second stage of this research project, I owe a profound debt of gratitude to Sumit Ganguly at Indiana University (IU) who encouraged me to continue working on this topic and to expand my research project. When I was only a first-year doctoral student, Ganguly gave me the opportunity to write a chapter on the evolution of India–Israel relations for his seminal volume on India's foreign policy. That fateful request led me to pursue the research that culminated in this book. Ganguly challenged me to not only solve the empirical puzzle behind the absence of ties between India and Israel for 42 years but also to reflect on the broader theoretical implications of this radical foreign policy change. He also provided me with my first contacts in the field, and I thank him immensely for introducing me to people and institutions that proved to be consequential as I conducted my research in New Delhi. As a result, the argument advanced within these pages was critically augmented thanks to Ganguly's steadfast support and insightful questioning.

I found myself equally ensconced in a highly productive and stimulating scholarly community within the Department of Political Science at IU. Among the faculty, Karen Rasler and William Thompson's support came in manifold forms, perhaps most clearly in urging me to develop rigorous methodological skills and in helping me build a strong theoretical argument to explain the empirical puzzle presented in this book. Other friends and colleagues at IU have contributed to this project in various ways. In particular, Manjeet Singh Pardesi shared with me his vast knowledge about India's diplomatic history and critically appraised my interpretation of historical events in ways that have immeasurably improved the final result. Manjeet also painstakingly read the very early drafts of this book and gave me invaluable feedback. My regular discussions with Adrian Florea, who shares an interest in the study of foreign policy change, forced me to reconsider and improve my theoretical model. Hicham Bou-Nassif helped me develop a sophisticated understanding of the international relations of the Middle East. Jean-Bertrand Ribat took an early interest in this project and enthusiastically read and commented upon many chapters. I also thank Jean-Bertrand for always giving me his particularly honest perspective on my work. For insightful comments at various stages of writing and presenting at IU, I would also like to thank Vasabjit Banerjee, Jacob Bower-Bir, Nick D'Amico, Janice Clark, Nick Clark, Prashant Hosur, Vera Heuer, Shahin Kachwala, Michael Lee, Brian McFillen, Kentaro Sakuwa, Jason Stone, Anjali Vithayathil, and Josef Woldense.

This project was also formed during the 18 months I spent immersed in research and interviewing in India. To the many dozens of academics, civil servants, journalists, military officers, and other experts who so generously accepted to help me and share their insights, I am deeply grateful. My fieldwork would not have been possible without the generous assistance of Madhusudan and Kiran C. Dhar and the Dhar India Studies Program at Indiana University-Bloomington that provided me with two generous fellowships to travel to India. In India, I would like to thank Krishnappa Venkatshamy, Narendra Sisodia, and Arvind Gupta for providing me a visiting fellowship and with an incredibly stimulating academic atmosphere to work within the Institute for Defence Studies and Analyses (IDSA), New Delhi. IDSA has been particularly supportive of this project as I have worked with the Institute on various occasions on the issue discussed in this book. I would particularly like to thank Krishnappa who encouraged me to look more closely at the historical sources of India's Israel policy which largely predated the 1992 decision to normalize relations. At IDSA, I would also like to thank Ruchita Beri, Vivek Chadha, Laxman Kumar Behera, Smruti S. Pattanaik, P. K. Pradhan, Samuel C. Rajiv, Richard Toppo, Bhavna Tripathy, and Amali Wedagedara for their invaluable feedback on my work and for their unfaltering support during my stay. I would also like to acknowledge Basudeb Chaudhuri and the Centre de Science Humaines (CSH) for providing me with office space during a visit to New Delhi. Finally, I owe a debt of gratitude to Fanny Amman, Jerome Buchler, Michelle Celerier, Debarshi Dasgupta, Suraj Gopal, and Anita Sharma for always helping me feel at home in New Delhi and for facilitating my research in many more ways than they know.

Various versions of the ideas and arguments discussed in this book were presented at several conferences and were, in consequence, refined and improved. For these opportunities, I am grateful to the Center on American and Global Security (CAGS), the Center for the Advanced Study of India (CASI), CERI-Sciences-Po, IDSA, the German Marshall Fund, and the Norwegian Institute for Defence Studies (IFS). This book has also been moulded and improved by the inputs from a broader scholarly community. Kanti Bajpai, Rajesh Basrur, Uday Bhaskar, Thomas Cavanna, Hannes Ebert, Valerie Hudson, Efraim Inbar, Dhruva Jaishankar, Gaurav Kampani, Devesh Kapur, Raphaelle Khan, P. R. Kumaraswamy, Jeff Legro, Tanvi Madan, David M. Malone, Manjari Chatterjee Miller, Dinshaw Mistry, Sebastien Miraglia, C. Raja Mohan, Anit Mukherjee, Rahul Mukherji, Vipin Narang, Martin Quencez, Srinath Raghavan, Iskander Rehman, Stephen Rosen, Rahul Sagar, Isabelle de Saint-Mezard, Eswaran Sridharan, Paul Staniland, Harrison Wagner, and Constantino Xavier are all to be thanked for generously giving their time at various stages of the writing and the presenting of this manuscript. Special thanks are extended to Ambassador Rajendra Abhyankar who has always taken out the time to share with me his first-hand knowledge of many of the events described in this book, and who has always offered me unique feedback. Of course, all the remaining errors of fact and interpretation are mine alone.

I am also grateful for the patience and encouragement of my editors at Oxford University Press, new Delhi. They were unfailingly competent and encouraging as they steered this manuscript to its completion. I also wish to thank the two anonymous reviewers of this manuscript for their valuable comments and suggestions.

I would like to thank my fiancée Eve Huchon for her steadfast support in this enterprise. Her challenging questions on initial drafts of my chapters helped me flesh out and structure my argument, which originally looked too complex and abstruse for the unfamiliar reader. Her emotional support in the development of this project and her unconditional love were essential to the completion of this manuscript.

Finally, I also owe to my family the love for Indian culture and for animated political debate, which ignited my interest in the topic of this book. In fact, there is a long and ongoing love story between India and the Blarel family. My brother, fellow PhD student, roommate in Delhi, confidante, and colleague Olivier Blarel, deserves a special note of gratitude for his informed comments on previous versions of my argument and for keeping me closely up to date with the latest diplomatic developments in New Delhi. In the context of his own research in diplomatic archives, Olivier also referred me to little-known but key historical developments in India–Israel relations. The constant support of my parents, Sabine and Jean-Francois, and of my sister, Anais, has made it possible for me to write this book. My interest in Indian foreign policy dates back to my parents' decision to move to and reside in New Delhi in the early 1980s. Their shared memories and their fascination for India have marked me as a child and young adult. I owe to them the aspiration to travel back and to reconnect with India in personal and professional ways. But for their love and support, this project would never have seen the day. That is why I dedicate this book to them.

Abbreviations

ADL	Anti-Defamation League
AEW	airborne early warning
AEW&C	airborne early warning and control
AICC	All India Congress Committee
AJC	American Jewish Committee
AMD	anti-missile defence
APG	All Palestine Government
ARC	Asian Relations Conference
ARO	Asian Relations Organization
ASC	Asian Socialist Conference
ATGM	anti-tank guided missile
AWACS	airborne warning and control system
BJP	Bharatiya Janata Party
BJS	Bharatiya Jana Sangh
BSF	Border Security Force
CBI	Central Bureau of Intelligence
CCS	Cabinet Committee on Security
CII	Confederation of Indian Industry
CPI	Communist Party of India
CPI (M)	Communist Party of India (Marxist)
CWC	Congress Working Committee
DRDO	Defence Research and Development Organisation
FDI	foreign direct investment
FICCI	Federation of Indian Chambers of Commerce and Industry
GCC	Gulf Cooperation Council
HAL	Hindustan Aeronautics Limited
IAEA	International Atomic Energy Agency
IAF	Indian Air Force

IAI	Israel Aerospace Industries
IB	Intelligence Bureau
ICJ	International Court of Justice
IDF	Israel Defence Forces
IDSA	Institute for Defence Studies and Analyses
IFS	Indian Foreign Service
IMA	Israel's Manufacturers Association
IMF	International Monetary Fund
IMI	Israel Military Industries
INC	Indian National Congress
ISRO	Indian Space Research Organisation
JKLF	Jammu and Kashmir Liberation Front
JSG	joint study group
JWG	joint working group
LoC	Line of Control
LR-SAM	long range surface-to-air missile
LTTE	Liberation Tigers of Tamil Eelam
MEA	ministry of external affairs
MFA	ministry of foreign affairs
MoU	memorandum of understanding
MTCR	Missile Technology Control Regime
NAM	Non-Aligned Movement
NDA	National Democratic Alliance
NPT	Non-Proliferation Treaty
NSA	national security advisor
PA	Palestinian National Authority
PHD	Progress Harmony Development Chamber of Commerce and Industry
PTA	preferential trade agreement
OAPEC	Organization of Arab Petroleum Exporting Countries
OFB	Ordnance Factory Board
OIC	Organisation of Islamic Conference
PLO	Palestine Liberation Organization
PMO	Prime Minister's Office
PNC	Palestine National Council
PRC	People's Republic of China
PSP	Praja Socialist Party
RAW	Research and Analysis Wing

SAARC	South Asian Association for Regional Cooperation
SAM	surface-to-air missile
SIBAT	Foreign Defense Assistance and Defense Export Organization (Israel)
UAE	United Arab Emirates
UAR	United Arab Republic
UAV	unmanned aerial vehicle
UF	United Front
UN	United Nations
UNCHR	United Nations Commission on Human Rights
UNEF	United Nations Emergency Force
UNGA	United Nations General Assembly
UNHCR	United Nations High Commission for Refugees
UNRWA	United Nations Relief and Works Agency
UNSC	United Nations Security Council
UNSCOP	United Nations Special Committee on Palestine
UNSCR 242	United Nations Security Council Resolution 242
UPA	United Progressive Alliance
USO	United Socialist Organization
WHO	World Health Organization
WJC	World Jewish Congress
WTO	World Trade Organization
WZO	World Zionist Organization

Introduction

IN SEPTEMBER 1950, after two years of intense debates, Indian Prime Minister Jawaharlal Nehru decided to recognize the newly created state of Israel while deferring the establishment of full diplomatic relations. However, it was not until January 1992 that India became the last major non-Arab and non-Islamic state to establish full and normal diplomatic relations with Israel (Gargan 1992). For decades, Israel's repeated diplomatic overtures did not receive any positive answer from the Indian leadership. The absence of any substantial exchanges during 42 years is surprising as both countries apparently lacked any direct conflict of interest. Paradoxically, there was no major reappraisal of India's neutral and sometimes critical posture towards Israel until the early 1990s.

For the last two decades, however, trade and economic relations have taken an upward swing. The signing of various trade agreements paved the way for an enormous increase of the volume of bilateral trade from $200 million in 1992 to $6 billion today.[1] Although both governments are still reluctant to talk openly about cooperation in this sensitive area, arms sales are another major component of this flourishing partnership. India has become Israel's largest arms export market in the world over the last decade (replacing China); and Israel is today India's second-largest arms supplier (behind the traditional Russian partner) (*Economic Times* 24 September 2012; Inbar and Ningthoujam 2012). This fast-burgeoning relationship revealed an unexploited potential for fruitful and complementary cooperation between the two nations. Some analysts have also cited India's new engagement with Israel as an example of a more pragmatic foreign policy following 1991 (Cohen 2001; Kapur 2006; Malone 2011; Mohan 2005; Pant 2008a; Raj Nayar and Paul 2003).

These recent developments raise some key empirical and theoretical questions. Given the now visible strategic benefits of Indo-Israeli cooperation, how can we explain India's deliberate policy of not establishing official diplomatic relations with Israel for more than 40 years? Can the absence of bilateral relations be judged as a 'hypocritical' policy, an 'aberration', an 'embarrassment', and an 'anomaly' in the history of India's foreign policy, as some have argued?[2] India's relationship with Israel has been one of the most sensitive and controversial issues in New Delhi's foreign policy. For example, India's decision to recognize Israel without establishing formal diplomatic links in the early 1950s remains a unique political move with no parallel in its diplomatic history (Brecher 1963; Misra 1966). As a point of comparison, over the same time period, India kept or re-established diplomatic relations with Pakistan and China, two countries with which it has had armed conflicts and with which it has ongoing border disputes. In spite of these inconsistencies, why did India refuse to reassess its position? Similarly, why did India refuse to engage Israel while other Asian nations like Burma and Turkey managed to develop relations with Israel without damaging their parallel relations with Arab countries (Thakur 1994: 289–90)? What was the strategic thinking behind the foreign policy decisions taken in 1950 and 1992 to first recognize and then to finally establish full diplomatic relations with Israel? How can we account for the timing of these key decisions?

This empirical paradox relates to a broader theoretical debate on foreign policy change in the international relations literature (Checkel 1997; Hermann 1990; Holsti 1982; Legro 2005; Rosati et al. 1994; Welch 2005). What are the conditions under which we are most likely to observe a modification of a certain foreign policy? Why are governments generally reluctant to change their foreign policy orientation despite sometimes negative or, to the least, ambiguous feedback? Are policy changes immediate reactions to overwhelming international and domestic pressures? Or are these changes the result of an accumulation of more discrete long-term and incremental adjustments? Likewise, are the reasons and interests invoked to sustain a certain foreign policy (such as the absence of relations with Israel) always consistent over the entire period? In other words, under an impression of foreign policy continuity, is it possible to identify points of tensions and transition that can augur future comprehensive policy changes?

Despite a growing literature on the subject, these questions have mostly been left unanswered. Current accounts of Indo-Israel relations have mostly concentrated on the major international and domestic changes of 1990–2 such as the end of the Cold War, the domestic economic reforms, and the Israeli–Palestinian talks following the Madrid Conference as leading to the reappraisal of India's Israel policy (Aaron 2003; Blarel 2009; Cohen 2001; Dixit 1996; Inbar 2004; Kapila 2003a; Kumaraswamy 2010; Naaz 2005; Nair 2004; Pant 2004). India's decision to establish full diplomatic relations and to build a strong defence partnership with Israel was subsequently interpreted by some as a pragmatic redirection of India's policy.[3] But what led to this new thinking in India's West Asia policy? What was the specific causal path linking these important events and a renewed debate on the merits of engaging Tel Aviv? These mostly descriptive studies have, for the most, emphasized the coincidence of the aforementioned 1990–2 events and India's decision to normalize relations with Israel without clearly specifying any causal mechanisms leading to this foreign policy change.

As a consequence, the focus on 1992 as the sole benchmark in Indo-Israeli relations has made it methodologically complicated to identify and separate continuities and actual changes occurring in Indian foreign policy decision-making vis-à-vis Israel. This static narrative has overdetermined the impact of the 1992 events in transforming this relationship and neglected other long-term and less visible factors which have equally influenced and shaped this bilateral relationship *before and after* 1992. This is an important issue in the theoretical literature on policy change as most studies still have a binary or dichotomous perspective of policy change (foreign policy change occurs or not). Because of this exaggerated focus on the 1992 decision, there has been a general assumption in the existing literature that India's no-relationship policy with Israel and its policy of consistent support for the Palestinian cause had been continuous and consensual from 1948 to 1992. Likewise, there has been an impression that the sudden change in India's Israel policy after January 1992 has been complete and unchallenged. This is a constant problem in the international relations literature where many theoretical frameworks still privilege exogenous shocks—such as an unexpected and abrupt change in environmental conditions either at the international, domestic, or policy level—as necessary catalysts to bring about radical re-evaluation of foreign policy behaviour. However, this dependence on the unanticipated conjuncture of different factors to explain change in Indo-Israeli relations overlooks other longstanding and dynamic factors. As a consequence, the evolution of Indo-Israeli relations has remained a puzzle to many analysts. The persistence of ambiguities in India's Israel policy has yet to be theoretically treated by the existing literature. Rather than to analyse change in Indo-Israeli relations in binary terms (no relations vs normal relations), I find it more productive in this book to focus on gradations of change in India's Israel policy over the last 65 years. This analysis aims to offer a new theoretical framework to understand the nature of the current Indo-Israeli partnership.

My objective in this book is to look at how India's Israel policy was actually contested from the start and evolved over time to adapt to new domestic and international circumstances and interests. Rather than one continuous and unchallenged Israel policy, my contention is that there were different policies vis-à-vis Israel and the Palestine issue which can be explained by the interplay of contextual determinants and the thinking of actors in charge of defining India's national and international interests. While existing studies have identified some important variables to explain India's Israel policy, they have yet to specify satisfactory causal mechanisms explaining India's Israel policy over time. Building on work in the public policy literature and theories of policy change (Baumgartner and Jones 2009; Hirshi and Widmer 2010; Kingdon 1984; Sabatier and Jenkins-Smith 1993), as well as on recent explanations of foreign policy change (Checkel 1997; Legro 2005; Welch 2005), this book offers a new theoretical framework which can better account for the type of gradual changes we observe in the Indo-Israeli case, and which can help unveil the causal connections between the identified variables and the actual policy outcomes.

In this book, I argue for a broader historical perspective to understand the formation of India's Israel policy in the pre-independence period, and most especially when the Indian National Congress (INC) made its first statements on the Israel–Palestine issue in the 1920s and 1930s.[4] In fact, some scholars have argued the INC's position on Palestine was the first illustration of an emerging independent Indian foreign policy (Ahmad 1973; Prasad 1960; Rajkumar 1952). This policy was quickly undermined by the partitions of South Asia and Palestine in the late 1940s. Right from the creation of Israel in May 1948, there was an important domestic debate on India's position vis-à-vis the new Jewish state that eventually led to a first important policy modification with the partial recognition of Israel in September 1950.[5] For the next decades, Israel continued to figure prominently in foreign policy debates in Delhi. This book identifies different periods and debates which undermined and altered the existing policy before 1992. Rather than looking at India's Israel, Arab, or West Asia policy as a long continuous and coherent policy until 1992, this analysis looks at a dynamic evolution of India's position in reaction to major crises and other pivoting events in the region.[6]

I also contend that Indo-Israeli relations cannot be interpreted just through dyadic lens but that regional and international considerations must equally be considered in a systematic manner to understand how specific decisions were taken at certain conjunctures. For instance, a neglected but decisive factor is the study of how the fate of independence movements in India and West Asia was intertwined and mutually dependent (Heptullah 1991: x). These pre-independence considerations strongly shaped India's initial position over the Israel–Palestine dispute. Following independence, India's Israel policy must also be considered in light of the development in the complex and fluctuating geopolitics of the West Asian region in the immediate post–World War II context. Present literature has looked at a wide range of factors to explain the absence of bilateral relations. Part of the existing scholarship has emphasized domestic factors like the need to accommodate an important Muslim population. Other studies have considered international factors such as the Cold War and the emergence of strong ties between post-independence India and the Arab states. Finally, some authors have studied the influence of political personalities like Mohandas Karamchand Gandhi and Nehru who opposed the Zionist project in Palestine (Brecher 1963; Mudiam 1994; Rao 1972; Shimoni 1977). But these studies have often had a static understanding of these factors, which are presented as constant irritants to the improvement of bilateral relations until 1992. This book will argue that the salience of certain domestic, regional, and international determinants has, in fact, evolved over time and that India's position has correspondingly changed. Similarly, India's Israel policy today must be interpreted in a larger policy outlook towards West Asia as India is trying to secure and advance its diverse energy, economic, and geopolitical interests in a constantly evolving political landscape.

In examining different turning points, my study seeks to bring a greater historical and political background to understand specific decisions which have structured India's Israel policy over the long term. Certain policy decisions which were taken in the context of the partition of Palestine, in reaction to the Suez conflict, during the different West Asian crises of the 1960s and 1970s, and following the Indo-Pakistani wars of 1965 and 1971, must not be judged from the standpoint of 1992 or of 2012, when the strategic benefits of Indo-Israeli cooperation have become evident. This work does not intend to judge past decisions in light of current developments and is more interested in tracing and explaining the decision-making process leading to certain policies (George and Bennett 2005). Likewise, this book is not an effort in reinstating individual leaders by rationalizing their policies and by arguing that they were facing a unique historical context. While this study does look in a very detailed manner into specific critical junctures to understand particular policy outcomes, it also aims to compare and to demonstrate how international, regional, and domestic factors either varied and/or were interpreted differently by different Indian leaders over time. By looking at these linkages, it is possible to determine and evaluate what was consistent and changing in India's Israel policy. Through this comparison of different policy decisions taken vis-à-vis Israel, it will also be possible to control for various actors' definitions of India's national interest, especially in the West Asian context. It is also important to emphasize that this is a study of India's Israel policy, which concentrates on India's foreign policy-making process vis-à-vis Israel and West Asia, and not a study of Indo-Israeli relations.[7] While Israel's position and actions vis-à-vis India are also assessed, they are observed here mostly as they influence the Indian decision-making process and Indian actors' perceptions. For instance, this book analyses how Indian leaders perceived certain Israeli diplomatic overtures and how Israeli actions in West Asia were interpreted by Indian political actors.

The relevance of this project must be understood in the light of a growing presence of China and India in West Asia. Today, as a result of India and China's emergence as global economic powers, the strategic implications of increasing and unprecedented exchanges between these two powers and West Asia are closely monitored (Alterman and Garver 2008; Calabrese 2009; Davidson 2010; Kemp 2010; Olimat 2012; Pigato 2009; Simpfendorfer 2009; Wakefield and Levenstein 2011). India has historically been involved in West Asian politics through centuries-old commercial ties with the Gulf States and through a more recently shared colonial history. Today, as India again becomes an important political player in the region, it is interesting to study the extent to which it will be drawn in the complicated geopolitics of West Asia. India's muted reaction to the Arab Spring revolts demonstrated how its policy vis-à-vis West Asia is still in flux (Ahmad 2013; Chatterjee 2012; Fontaine and Twining 2011; Kumaraswamy 2012). India's obligation to secure its energy imports coming from the region has kept it from making any 'sharp choices' (Khilnani *et al.* 2012: 24). In the context of this evolving political landscape, India is trying to develop a more explicit and coherent strategy, by engaging 'more widely in the region' to secure its strategic and economic interests (Khilnani *et al.* 2012: 23). Where does Israel fit in this wider regional policy reassessment? Looking back at the context of decision-making vis-à-vis Israel and West Asia over the last 60 years, it is possible to read some long-term determinants behind India's Israel policy.

Reviewing the Existing Literature

Surprisingly, there have been few books and analyses that have concentrated on this paradoxical relationship until recently.[8] This stands in contrast to a more important corpus of publications on the equally complex evolution of diplomatic relations between Israel and China (Brecher 1974, 1976; Chen 2012; Ehrlich 2008; Goldstein 1999; Kumaraswamy 1999; Suffot 1997). A first limited wave of academic studies in the 1950s and 1960s were particularly interested in Israel's first contacts with Asian countries and analysed the original efforts from Israeli diplomats to develop relations with the newly independent Asian states (Brecher 1963; Jansen 1971; Kohn 1959; Laufer 1972; Levi 1958; Medzini 1972; Rivkin 1959). Among these scholars, some attempted to explain Nehru's decision to recognize Israel and to delay the establishment of diplomatic relations (Agwani 1963b; Brecher 1963; Jansen 1971; Kozicki 1958; Levi 1958; Schechtman 1966). There were also interesting factual accounts of this period and of preliminary Indo-Israel contacts which can be found in the autobiographies and memoirs of Israeli diplomats like Walter Eytan (1958), David Hacohen (1963), and Gideon Rafael (1981).

However, the bulk of the scholarship on Indo-Israeli relations emerged in the post-normalization phase, and especially in the last decade, as strategic benefits from this bilateral partnership had become manifest and publicized. This new literature has mostly viewed India's Israel policy in two phases. The first phase went from roughly 1947 to 1992 where 'nonrelations' was considered to be the 'hallmark' of India's foreign policy (Kumaraswamy 2010: 163). The second period, going from 1992 to today, has been characterized by burgeoning defence and trade relations that developed following normalization (Aaron 2003; Berman 2002; Bitzinger 2013; Blarel 2006; Gopal and Sharma 2007; Gerberg 2008; Inbar 2004; Inbar and Ningthoujam 2012; Kandel 2009; Kapila 2003a; Kumaraswamy 1998, 2004a, 2010; Naaz 1999, 2000, 2005; Nair 2004; Pant 2004; Pant 2008b: 131–50). Before addressing how these studies have specifically explained the two 'phases' of Indo-Israeli relations, the first obvious flaw of the existing literature is the arbitrary periodization. The focus on the events of 1992 has encouraged the development of a static narrative of Indo-Israeli relations overlooking many historical contacts and discussions, which actually occurred despite the absence of formal diplomatic ties. This periodization also fails to grasp the important internal debates which had emerged in the late 1940s, before India officially recognized Israel. Following the recognition, Nehru held discussions with Israeli leaders over the possibility of officially exchanging diplomats until 1956 (Eytan 1958; Gopal 1979: 169–70). In the conflicts of 1962, 1965, and 1971, India also asked for and received military equipment from Israel.[9] In the late 1970s and in the late 1980s, two of India's prime ministers—Moraji Desai and Rajiv Gandhi—met with Israeli officials to discuss potential cooperation (Dayan 1978: 26; Kumaraswamy 2002). These are only a few of the many examples of bilateral contacts that existed and anticipated the normalization of relations in 1992. Similarly, this book will demonstrate how the immediate post-1992 developments do not seem to support the image of a sudden and uncontested improvement in Indo-Israeli relations.

When looking at the first identified phase of Indo-Israeli relations (1947–92), there is an ongoing and sometimes passionate debate over the causes of India's no-relationship policy (see Table I.1). Although different factors have been identified to explain the absence of bilateral relations, there has yet to be any consensus on which explanation was the most pertinent. In fact, most studies have often presented a laundry-list of potential causal variables which seemed to have an impact on India's Israel policy, without really comparing and qualifying their explanatory leverage. Some have, for instance, insisted on the role of certain political personalities like Gandhi or Nehru in shaping the foundations of India's no-relationship policy (Abadi 1991; Brecher 1961, 1963: 129–30, 1968;

Table I.1 Alternative Approaches

Authors	Approach
Brecher (1963), Schechtman (1966), Nanda (1976), Shimoni (1977), Heptullah (1991), Kapila (2003b), Kumaraswamy (2010)	Ideas from eminent political figures (Gandhi, Nehru)
Jansen (1971), Cohen (2001), Naaz (2005)	Ideological opposition to a state conceived on religious principles (analogue to Pakistan)
Rajkumar (1952), Prasad (1960), Heptullah (1991), Rubinoff (1995), Nair (2004)	Traditional sympathies with Arab nationalist leaders
Cohen (2001), Kumaraswamy (2004a, 2010), Mohan (2005)	Nehruvianism
Eytan (1958), Brecher (1963), Nair (2004), Kumaraswamy (2010)	Presence of an important domestic Muslim population
Jansen (1971), Gordon (1975), Ward (1992), Rubinoff (1995), Dixit (1996), Pant (2004)	Need for energy resources
Brecher (1963), Misra (1966), Mudiam (1994), Dixit (1996), Rao (1972), Rubinoff (1995), Pant (2004), Nair (2004), Baba (2008), Kumaraswamy (2010)	Need for diplomatic support from Arab and Muslim countries
Rao (1972), Cohen (2001), Pant (2004), Mohan (2005), Kumaraswamy (2010)	The Cold War

Source: Author

Gordon 1975; Kumaraswamy 2010; Nanda 1976: 74–7; Shimoni 1977). Their personal refusal to support Zionist territorial claims in Palestine was explained by a lack of familiarity and understanding of Jewish history and nationalism,[10] by their distorted view of the Palestine dispute through an Islamic prism (Kumarawswamy 2010: 68–84), or by their ideological opposition to the idea of religion being a legitimate basis for state-formation.[11] Personal factors were important in the pre- and immediate post-independence years, when the leader of the INC and later prime minister, Nehru, was by all accounts the primary architect of India's foreign policy.[12]

However, the responsibility of individual actors needs to be qualified. First, as with much of the foreign policy literature on individual psychology and leadership traits, it is difficult to argue that individual and cognitive factors are capable of *independently* causing foreign policy outcomes as many other variables can influence policies (Hudson and Singer 1992; Jervis 1976; Legro 2000). Leaders evolve in material and ideational settings that often constrain and influence their preferences and actions. Leaders' cognitive predispositions need to be more modestly interpreted as *key intervening variables* in the decision-making process. Second, the emphasis on leaders' responsibility overlooks other decisive international and domestic factors that often entered India's foreign policy calculations without systematically being included in the rhetoric of Indian leaders. This book will argue that Indian leaders', and especially Nehru's, position dramatically evolved following independence and the creation of Israel in 1948.

Ideational arguments have also often been used to explain India's strategic thinking, especially in the early post-independence years. Some scholars have argued that in the last 60 years, some competing 'visions' of India's place in the international system have successively or concurrently shaped the formulation of India's foreign policy (Bajpai 2010, 2014; Cohen 2001: 36–65; Engelmeier 2009). While none of these 'schools' have completely dominated India's decision-making apparatus, the conventional wisdom was that India's foreign policy was first dominated by a Nehruvian or moralist school inherited from the freedom movement and shaped by India's first Prime Minister Nehru, and was later contested by more realist, neo-liberal, and even Hindu nationalist perceptions of international politics (Bajpai 2002; Mehta 2009; Sagar 2009). These strategic 'paradigms' have notably been used to explain India's decision to neglect Israel after 1948 on anti-imperialistic and moral grounds (Gordon 1975; Kozicki 1958). From this viewpoint, Indian nationalists did not support the Zionist movement, which they considered as exclusively based on religion and at variance with India's professed secular form of nationalism. Nehru was sympathetic towards the Arabs as well as the Palestinian cause and made it a central theme of Indian foreign policy. According to this argument, Nehru defined the ideational foundations and parameters for India's West Asia policy for 40 years (Heptullah 1991: xi). Path dependence can therefore explain why successive Indian leaders did not deviate from an entrenched Nehruvian interpretation of the Israel–Palestine conflict. By contrast, India's decision to establish full diplomatic relations with Israel in 1992 was interpreted as a pragmatic reassessment of India's West Asia policy.[13]

However, assessing the causal determinacy of foreign policy ideas and ideological motivations is empirically difficult. Invoking these factors as structurally inducing certain behaviours is even problematic as it is complicated to directly link them to specific policy actions (Kowert and Legro 1996). Different actors feel more or less constrained by such ideational considerations. Some key players might actually frame and use such factors to rationalize their own foreign policy decisions and to serve their own interests. Given the complexity of India's national interests, the changes in political leadership, and an evolving feedback from policies, it is not possible to identify a continuous and linear ideational narrative. For instance, Prime Minister Indira Gandhi invoked her father's opposition to the creation of Israel to justify her own position but it can be argued that her policies towards West Asia were considerably different.

Many scholars have attributed the absence of bilateral relations between India and Israel to the existence of domestic and international constraints. It is conventional wisdom in International Relations theory that individual leaders see their choices limited in the face of structural factors (Waltz 1979). In the post-independence years, the new Indian government was perceived to be trying to accommodate both its internal domestic Muslim population, which had just experienced the trauma of partition,[14] and its Arab partners in West Asia, in order to obtain their support in its diplomatic disputes with rival Pakistan (Agwani 1973b; Levi 1958; Mudiam 1994: 12–15; Rubinoff 1995). Following the partition of the subcontinent between India and Pakistan, the priority for the Indian leadership was to reassure Muslims who had stayed in India and to guarantee their loyalty to the new nation-making process that had begun (Heptullah 1991: 160–1). Any overture towards Israel could have had adverse effects on the supposedly fragile legitimacy of the newly established regime within the domestic Muslim population. At the diplomatic level, non-engagement with Israel was aimed at neutralizing Pakistani efforts in seeking assistance from Muslim and Arab countries against India, notably in their territorial dispute over Kashmir. These pressures, at both the national and international levels, limited India's diplomatic leverage in the region and can explain India's reluctance to openly engage Israel.

However, just like when considering individual leaders' influences or ideational influences, it is very difficult to actually weigh these international and domestic factors' explanatory leverage over time. The existence of structural constraints must only be seen as a good starting point to delimit the domain within which leaders can decide. Within these limits, leaders still possess some agency to choose among different foreign policy choices. As a result, most of these studies fail to explain the actual evolution of India's Israel policy. For instance, why were these constraints salient for 42 years and then suddenly less decisive after 1992? In fact, accommodating the Muslim community in the 1990s should have become more of a political priority for Congress as the Indian political system moved durably in the 1990s into a period of unstable coalition governments where every electoral support became decisive (Sridharan 2012). The fallacy of 'the Muslim factor' has often been used by politicians, journalists, and analysts to criticize India's foreign policy whether it is vis-à-vis Israel or the US.[15] There have yet to be any rigorous studies measuring the actual impact of Indian Muslim communities on India's West Asia policies. Recent studies, which concentrated on domestic Indian politics, have demonstrated the heterogeneity of India's Muslim community and debunked the myth of any cohesive Muslim vote bank.[16] Furthermore, as Pakistan was renewing its attempts to get support from West Asian states on the Kashmir issue in the early 1990s, it was also considered to be in India's interest to not antagonize Arab states by engaging Israel (Baba 2008).

In spite of these adverse domestic and international conditions, India decided to normalize relations with Israel in January 1992. The decision to change India's Israel policy leads to question the utility of systemic-structural explanations which treated the Indian state as a black box and implied direct causal relationships between existing irritants and specific policy outcomes vis-à-vis Israel. These deterministic approaches have also been at a loss to explain when and why Indian decision-makers actually chose a new foreign policy between different substantive choices. The objective of this book is to therefore nuance and evaluate the causal determinacy of these structural factors and to understand why some of these domestic and international variables, though still present, were not as decisive in the mind of Indian decision-makers in 1992.

Other factors cited to explain the absence of Indo-Israel relations like the economic and energy factors and Cold War dynamics have only had a sporadic and limited impact. For instance, some analysts have argued that Cold War divisions explained the prolonged estrangement between Delhi and Tel Aviv until 1992 (Cohen 2001; Kumaraswamy 2004a; Mohan 2005). The two countries were considered to be more or less integrated in the two rival Cold War blocs. This argument fits nicely the pre- and post-1992 story as the abrupt end of the Cold War and the disappearance of the USSR seemed to have encouraged India to diversify its relationships and to change its Israel policy (Blarel 2009). However, the Cold War did not directly affect South Asia and West Asia in the immediate post-independence phase. In fact, both India and Israel originally opted for an autonomous foreign policy approach, refusing any diplomatic entanglement in Cold War politics. Israeli diplomats even originally tried to point out similarities between India's non-alignment posture and their own efforts to not side with any great power.[17] However, these similarities in foreign policy approach did not last beyond the late 1950s and the emergence of the Afro-Asian movement which officially excluded Israel after the Bandung Conference.[18] The creation of the Non-Alignment summit in 1961 in Belgrade without Israel further distanced the two countries. The influence of Cold War politics on India's foreign policy only became significant in the 1960s when India started engaging the USSR while Israel became more and more dependent on US aid.[19] According to this argument, the integration of both countries into different blocs excluded any direct dialogue until the early 1990s.

The economic and trade factor in Indo-Israeli relations has rarely been mentioned in the literature but has been an underlying factor in early policy-making vis-à-vis Israel. Some analysts have, for instance, observed a degree of regularity in policy-making vis-à-vis West Asia, from British India to independent India, on matters such as facilitating trade through guaranteeing access to sea-lanes and to the Suez Canal, the 'highway to India.'[20] Just like the former Raj government,[21] Indian leaders were particularly concerned about the security of key strategic points such as the Strait of Hormuz, the Suez Canal, and the Strait of Babel Mandeb (at the entrance to the Red Sea) and adjusted their regional policy in order to preserve India's economic and trade interests. These economic priorities for a newly independent India indirectly influenced its Israel policy. For example, in the 1940s and 1950s, Indians leaders were very cautious in their dealings with Israel to avoid antagonizing Egypt which controlled the access to the Suez Canal (Bishku 1987; Mudiam 1994: 37–58).

The trade factor progressively lost its relevance as the Canal was closed for long periods of times following the different West Asian crises of the 1960s and 1970s. At that time, India started importing energy and oil from West Asia. Some scholars argue that the oil factor was decisive after 1972 in consolidating India's already existing pro-Arab policy (Ward 1992; Kumaraswamy 2010: 174). India became vulnerable to the oil embargoes and rapid oil prices increases, and lost all leverage to embark in an important regional policy change (Ward 1992: 36). The lower oil prices of the early 1990s following the Gulf War reduced India's dependence on oil from the Arab countries and can be an explanation for the normalization of relations with Israel. However, India's oil dependence vis-à-vis the Gulf States is still important today, even as it has an open and strong economic and military relationship with Israel. How can India manage these different partnerships today while it appeared that it could not do so a few decades earlier?

There has also been an important strand in the literature looking at the development of economic and military relations between the two countries during the second post-1992 phase. Most of these studies have been descriptive and have merely enumerated the new areas of cooperation between the two countries.[22] These studies have either listed the different defence deals signed between India and Israel over the last 20 years (Inbar and Ningthoujam 2012), or discussed the growing bilateral trade figures (Feiler 2012). Within this literature, a body of scholarship has analysed an ideological rapprochement between the Hindu right, which came to power in the late 1990s, and the Likud in Israel as an explanation for the emergence of a strong strategic axis (Berman 2002; Jaffrelot 2003; Tillin 2003). However, the ideological argument was empirically invalidated when the traditionally pro-Palestinian Congress party came back to power in 2004 and unambiguously resumed important defence and economic relations with Tel Aviv (Blarel 2014).

As a result, with a few exceptions, this literature on the second phase of India's Israel policy has often tended to be overly descriptive and atheoretical. These studies have failed to account for the lack of real progress in bilateral relations until the late 1990s when trade figures and military exchanges drastically increased.[23] Most studies have also failed to explain how the Indian government has managed to develop its relations with Israel while also maintaining a strong pro-Palestinian stand in multilateral fora like the United Nations (UN) (Desai 2012; Rajiv 2011). To explain the evolution of India's Israel policy, one must develop a cohesive theory that goes beyond a laundry-list of potentially relevant variables. As a consequence, the current state of Indo-Israeli relations remains a puzzle to many analysts. Most publications on this subject have brought interesting factual evidence to our attention but lacked a strong theoretical argument to explain how India's Israel policy came to consolidate itself over the last two decades.

The Central Argument

While most existing studies have identified and isolated some crucial variables, they have yet to specify satisfactory causal mechanisms explaining the formation and stability of a no-relationship policy before 1992 and the emergence and consolidation of a new Israel policy over the last two decades. It is tempting to read this ambiguous policy as a unique historical 'aberration' that evades rational foreign policy thinking, and as an outlying phenomenon which cannot be explained by traditional International Relations (IR) theories. Breaking with the descriptive nature of the literature, this book offers a conceptual framework that can account for the formation of India's Israel policy as well as for its evolution and transformation as it was confronted with changing circumstances, different leaders, and varying ideas.

By employing this new theoretical approach, this book intends to facilitate a comparison between different decisions taken vis-à-vis Israel that have usually been studied in isolation because they were considered to be different and unique historical periods. Additionally, the theoretical concepts presented in this study may also be applied to other similar cases of dynamic and gradual foreign policy change to test the theory's explanatory scope. This book indeed argues that (i) this case is actually symptomatic of Indian foreign policy-making over the last 60 years, and that (ii) other seemingly inscrutable Indian foreign policy decisions could be explained by this new theoretical framework.

The objective of this manuscript is not to prioritize one theoretical lens over others but rather to stress the overlaps in their efforts and the current lack of dialogue in combining different explanations to offer a more complete and dynamic understanding of the evolution of India's Israel policy over the last 60 years. Simply listing variables of interest cannot satisfactorily explain the changes and continuity in Indo-Israeli strategic relations. These one-dimensional interpretations have often overlooked the dynamic interaction over time between international, domestic, and individual/small group-level factors in shaping India's Israel policy.[24] Similarly, the evolution of India's Israel policy cannot be interpreted in a stylized idealpolitik vs. realpolitik narrative.

While international and domestic changes have certainly had an impact in the reassessment of India's position, these arguments are not theoretically satisfying as they do not offer specific mechanisms explaining the collapse of the old thinking and the emergence of a new consensus on India's strategic priorities vis-à-vis Israel and West Asia. They have also tended to simplify some of the more complex (and still evolving) debates within India's strategic community over its position vis-à-vis West Asia. What are the specific causal links between the fall of the USSR, the internal economic crisis, the change of leadership in government (and within the Congress party), and the developments in West Asia like the Gulf War and the normalization of relations with Israel?

Foreign Policy Change

The study of change in foreign policy is fairly recent. The discipline of international relations has long concentrated on discerning and explaining continuous patterns of foreign policy (Buzan and Jones 1981; Gilpin 1981). The constant search for general, parsimonious international relations theory and generalizations accounting for a large number of phenomena can explain this initial neglect for the problem of foreign policy change (Waltz 1986). First, many scholars of international relations thought that phenomena of political change concerned only a small number of exceptional cases. Additionally, foreign policy deviations only seemed to concern peripheral actors and not the great powers that mainly preoccupied international relations scholars (Gilpin 1981: 5). Because of this small-n problem, scholars never considered the theoretical challenge of understanding foreign policy change to be of any importance. Most accounts of discontinuities in foreign policy behaviour such as India's Israel policy were treated as anomalies and led to mostly descriptive studies with few theoretical contributions.

Only recently has there been some effort to account for instances of foreign policy change, notably after traditional IR theories failed to anticipate the turbulence and changes in world politics in the late 1980s and early 1990s (Hudson 2007). It is in this new context that some scholars began to question the utility of structural explanations to understand the foreign policy of specific states, and concentrated on the circumstances under which states displayed 'deviant' behaviours from the structurally induced and stabilizing patterns that dominant approaches (neo-realism and neo-liberalism) had concentrated on until then (Goldmann 1988; Hermann 1990; Holsti 1982; Rosati et al. 1994; Rosenau 1981). These new multi-causal models moved away from treating the state as a black box and insisted on the need to look at the interplay between international and domestic factors (systemic shocks and domestic decision-making processes) as well as into leaders' views and/or predisposition to arrive at a better understanding of the drivers of foreign policy change. At the same time, there were signs of a departure from the dominant binary perspective—foreign policy change occurs or not—towards a more continuous and dynamic view that looked at gradations or degrees of foreign policy change (Rosati et al. 1994: 236). However, no strong causal mechanisms evaluating the links between these different variables emerged and most of these scholars continued to rely on exogenous shocks as the main reason for change.[25]

A more recent body of literature has offered more rigorous and useful theories to explain foreign policy change. These approaches looked closer at institutions, ideas, and human psychology as key determinants of foreign policy change. The ideational turn of part of the foreign policy change scholarship was an innovative way to link demand for change provoked by certain material factors to the decision to opt for a particular set of policy solutions (Mark Blyth 2003; Goldstein and Keohane 1993; Hall 1993; Lieberman 2002). Breaking with the traditional bias in the international relations literature that states are individual unitary actors, the ideational literature looked at the definition of states' strategies as the result of debates between the most powerful groups (Snyder 1991; Moravcsik 1997; Checkel 1997; Legro 2005; Narizny 2007; Dueck 2008; Taliaferro et al. 2009, 2012). Within this literature, Jeffrey Legro introduced a useful two-step model assessing the process of changing dominant orthodoxies in defining foreign policy (Legro 2005: 8). Legro argues that the old pro-status quo dominant orthodoxy must first collapse. This usually happens following a shock linked to major failures of policies that were expected to succeed. This shock enables partisans of an alternative (new orthodoxy) to offer their perspectives. Second, there is a second stage through which new orthodoxies must be consolidated and ideally reinforced by success (Legro 2005: 13–16). Foreign policy change will not happen if there is not a prominent alternative to the pre-existing ideas.

In my opinion, Legro's two-stage framework is probably the most synthetic account, combining factors from different levels of analyses, that has emerged from the foreign policy change literature. Legro identifies multiple variables but also explains how they come together and interact in particular and regular ways to influence continuity and change (see Figure I.1) (Legro 2005: 161, 179–80). Enterprising agents, environmental feedback (perception of success or not of new policies), and collective ideas come together to maintain or change foreign policy (Legro 2005: 162). According to Legro's model, it seems that change will ultimately depend on the distribution of replacement ideas and how united the opposing new orthodoxy is. The group solving the 'collective ideation' problem will manage to influence the policy process (Legro 2005: 14–15).

Is the Legro framework useful to understand India's Israel policy? If the process postulated by Legro's model is indeed at work, an exogenous shock would first serve as a catalyst for a questioning of the efficacy of the existing policy vis-à-vis Israel (i.e., to collapse of 'old thinking' in Legro's jargon). Events in 1991–2 such as the disappearance of the USSR (and therefore of India's major arms supplier) and the beginning of the West Asia peace process negotiations (legitimizing Israel as a potential partner

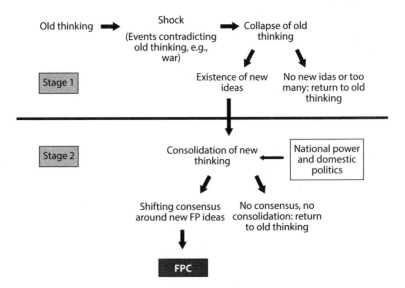

Figure I.1 Legro's Two-Stage Model of Foreign Policy Change

Source: Adapted from Legro (2005)

Note: FP—foreign policy; FPC—foreign policy change.

in that region) could be interpreted as such change-inducing shocks. The problem is that this approach only concentrates on rapid discontinuous transformations, discarding other more moderated and incremental types of change (Legro 2005: 181).

I argue in this book that the evolution of India's Israel policy is a more dynamic and gradual phenomenon. There had already been a series of shocks which had discredited and encouraged policy adjustments before 1992. Following the change-inducing shock, Legro talks about a need for a period of consolidation for new foreign policy ideas, but does not clarify when exactly the consolidation process ends. One limitation of Legro's model is that both collapse of old ideas and consolidation of new ideas are seen as difficult, protracted processes. It is not clear when India's new post-1992 Israel policy actually 'consolidated'. To explain the specific issue of India's Israel policy, this book intends to build on Legro's model but also to bring in other useful theoretical insights from the public policy literature.

India's Israel Policy as a Subsystem

Building on work in the public policy literature and theories of policy change, this book argues for an observation of India's Israel policy as a policy subsystem. Since the foreign policy field is very complex, and political decision-makers have incomplete knowledge of numerous foreign policy issues, cognitive limitations, and a restricted attention span, it is safe to say that they can only focus on a limited number of policies (Stein and Welch 1997). Decision-makers at the highest level only sporadically get involved in specific issues. Some academics have argued that these cognitive limitations are partly compensated by the recourse to strategic ideas, values, or norms that act as roadmaps to limit their universe of possibilities for action or reaction when in a context of uncertainty (Goldstein and Keohane 1993: 13–17; Narang and Staniland 2012). While political leaders are certainly guided by certain principles, it nevertheless seems improbable that a set of broad strategic principles can provide decision-makers specific guidelines in every possible policy area. For instance, Nehruvianism is an important ideational reference point for Indian decision-makers but it does not offer practical guidelines for foreign policy-making in the particular context of West Asia.

I argue that the foreign policy process is not one monolithic decision-making apparatus with only one national debate including solely governmental-level actors. To give a more accurate picture of policy change, the subsystem approach looks exclusively at informed and interested actors (whether they are governmental actors, experts, interest groups, and/or institutions) directly involved in the policy-making process in a specialized foreign policy area like India's Israel policy. Within this subsystem, a more limited set of actors (both public and private) are actively involved with a policy problem or issue and regularly seek to influence policy in that domain. Policy-making can be seen as an amorphous set of sub-governments or subsystems (Baumgartner and Jones 2009: xxiii–xxvi; Haas 1992). Usually subsystems are characterized by what political scientists Frank Baumgartner and Bryan Jones have called 'policy monopolies' which are the dominant political understandings about a policy issue.[26] The monopolies are structured around two elements.

First, there are the formal or informal institutional rules of access, which limit the participation of 'outsiders,' or actors that are not traditionally involved in this specific policy process. These policy monopolies are therefore characterized by a 'lack of interference by broader political forces in subsystems, and deference to the judgment of experts.'[27] Second, a policy monopoly is also structured around a prevalent understanding of the policy that is so positive that it evokes only support or indifference by those who are not directly involved (thereby ensuring their non-involvement). A policy with perceived effective results and a positive image will be difficult to reverse. Every actor interested in a certain policy and involved in a policy subsystem has a primary interest in establishing a monopoly, in defining the political understandings of this policy, and establishing institutional arrangements reinforcing that understanding and limiting interferences from other actors (Baumgartner and Jones 2009: 6).

In contrast to foreign policy change approaches, this subsystem framework allows for more adaptability and adjustments which can happen under the appearance of policy continuity. It helps account for a lot of activity, debate, and change actually happening at some important crucial phases, before the policy consolidates itself. Small networks of foreign policy specialists and advocacy coalitions interact to deliberate specific issues, set agendas, and formulate policy alternatives, and they also serve as brokers for introducing new ideas into the decision-making circles of bureaucrats and elected officials (Kingdon 1984; Sabatier and

Jenkins-Smith 1993). Within the more narrow confines of a policy subsystem, there are fewer institutional and ideational constraints for policy entrepreneurs and/or advocacy coalitions promoting change to oppose the policy monopolies in these subsystems. The micro-dynamics at the subsystem level will be able to better tell us how this foreign policy vis-à-vis Israel first emerged and then evolved into a series of different 'policy monopolies' over the last 60 years.

Shocks, Policy Compromises, and Gradual Policy Change

Building on Legro's model and theories of policy change in a subsystem, this book offers a new conceptual framework (Figure I.2). According to Legro, you first need the collapse of the existing dominant orthodoxy when its policy ideas lose legitimacy following a shock. At that stage,

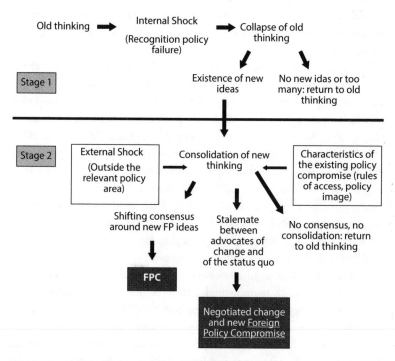

Figure I.2   Model of Policy Change in a Subsystem
Source: Author (model adapted from Legro 2005).
Note: FPC—foreign policy change.

the definition of the foreign policy position is fluid and open to debate. Legro justly argues that there needs to be a second stage of ideational change (a consolidation phase) when a new orthodoxy competes with the dominant orthodoxy (Legro 2005: 29–38). It is often impossible for the advocates of different policy ideas (pro–status quo coalition vs. pro-change coalition) to agree on objective standards on which to judge in favour of a certain policy over another. This study will therefore build on Legro's emphasis on a political (rather than the technical) process leading to policy change (Legro 2005: 31). The movement from one policy idea to another will ultimately entail a set of judgements that is more political in tone, and the outcome will depend not only upon the arguments of competing coalitions but also on their positional advantages within institutions, on the resources they can command in the pertinent debates, and on external factors affecting the power of one set of actors to impose its policy prescriptions over others. As a result, policy-making is as much an attempt to offer solutions to existing foreign policy problems as a struggle for power and influence between different actors or groups of actors.[28]

The literature on policy change rightly discusses the need for a shock that leads to the collapse of old strategic ideas and to destabilize the previous dominating policy consensus. Shocks are decisive to demonstrate anomalies within prevailing policy paradigms, to push for a search for alternatives, and to shift the locus of authority over policy (Dueck 2004; Legro 2005: 29–32). Shocks are therefore important policy windows of opportunity for pro-change actors. Following these shocks, policy entrepreneurs and/ or advocacy coalitions can elucidate the cause-and-effect relationships for decision-makers and provide advice about likely results or various courses of action (Haas 1992; Kingdon 1984). But in the context of the division of foreign-policy making, this book argues for a distinction of external and internal shocks to the policy subsystems.

Internal shocks originate within a policy area, and are more likely to be the result of monumental policy failures. Crises highlight the inappropriateness of current policies, triggering their re-evaluation and providing impetus for change. An intense sense of urgency associated with a search for new information or new interpretations and issue definitions can lead to change (Baumgartner and Jones 2009: xxiv). By contrast, external shocks originate outside the relevant foreign policy area. These external shocks are open opportunities for those opposing the existing policy within the subsystem. The policy will not change unless the pro-change actors use this open 'window of opportunity' to link these external shocks with their own replacement ideas inside the policy subsystem (Kingdon 1984: 165–95). This is a way to mobilize traditionally apathetic actors (with no direct interest in or access to this specific policy subsystem) to join their advocacy coalition (Baumgartner and Jones 2009: 238–9). A combination of both shocks increases the likelihood of a new orthodoxy taking over the policy subsystem.

Here, I build on the public policy literature to evaluate how different sets of actors manage to enter, influence, and change foreign policy debates like India's Israel policy. Subsystems are traditionally structured around a 'policy monopoly' which is the way in which the policy issue is perceived. The consequence of policy monopoly is foreign policy stability. However, I prefer move away from calling these understandings and arrangements 'monopolies' and suggest a different appellation: 'policy compromises'. This book will demonstrate how various groups have interests in changing or preserving the existing policies but for very different reasons. These groups do not always congregate into well-structured and coordinated advocacy coalitions. They might agree on opposing the existing policy and ask for adjustments, but they do not innately have a clear or unified conception of the direction of change.[29] Here, I define the term 'coalition' largely as consisting of members who share policy beliefs such as the benefit of engaging Israel. The coalition does not necessarily engage in a planned and concerted cooperation but in an indirect and nontrivial degree of coordination to push for a new policy direction. Similarly, the old orthodoxy which supports the status quo might remain strong and unified enough to counter-mobilize and resist full scope policy change. Instead of arguing that this deadlock leads to a return to old ideas, there might be a negotiated agreement. To borrow from the international conflict resolution literature, a 'hurting stalemate' can push the different pro-change and pro–status quo groups to opt for negotiations and a 'policy compromise' (Zartman 1991). The pro–status quo group could be willing to make some policy concessions by including some propositions from the challenging groups without changing the entire policy. Such policy adjustments result in partial and negotiated policy change, short of complete foreign policy change.

Complete foreign policy change only happens when a sufficient number of actors are mobilized towards a new policy direction and have access to decision-making. This can happen through 'conflict expansion', a dynamic associated with a change in intensities of interest.[30] The content of ideas will matter in refining the basic dimensions of conflict to attract previously uninvolved actors (Baumgartner and Jones 2009: 35–7). Hence, the old orthodoxy has an interest in limiting the scope of the foreign policy debate and in maintaining their niche policy, while the new orthodoxy has an incentive to enlarge the dimensions of the conflict, to mobilize larger constituencies on their behalf. Conflict expansion can therefore have important consequences for the distribution of force between advocacy coalitions within the subsystem. The introduction and presentation of replacement ideas with a potentially larger receptive audience makes policy compromises unstable in the long run.

But how can these entrepreneurs and coalitions attract new actors to the policy debate? They need to demonstrate to diverse interests that they all share similar concerns for a new foreign policy direction. They can attempt to link shocks, problems, and solutions from different policy areas and broaden the stakes of the policy they seek to influence. The rhetorical strategy of conflict expansion used by advocacy coalitions to attract more people to support their own policy ideas is a more observable factor than the traditional emphasis on the alleged 'skills' of a 'good' policy entrepreneur. In the foreign policy literature, these studies looking at 'successful' entrepreneurs have mostly relied on post-hoc biographical accounts and idiosyncratic and personality-related features to explain the decisive role of these specific actors in explaining foreign policy change (Byman and Pollack 2001; Hermann et al. 2001). In this study, successful entrepreneurship is strictly evaluated through how they can attract the attention of actors usually uninvolved or excluded from the policy subsystem.[31]

This study therefore outlines a new causal mechanism that attempts to explain why and how new ideas and events inform governmental actors and state behaviour on certain foreign policy decisions like the opportunity to engage Israel (Figure I.2). The interplay between internal and external shocks to the policy subsystem, the balance of force between pro-change and pro–status quo actors, and the nature and characteristics of the existing policy compromise over time explain the continuity or change of a certain foreign policy. This new theoretical framework will be used to present a new narrative of India's Israel policy over the last 60 years.

Methodology and Case Selection

In this book, I concentrate on five critical junctures to trace and compare the decision-making processes which lead to diverging outcomes. Indo-Israeli relations have a long history which can be traced back to the early twentieth century. In fact, even before independence, some of the first statements on foreign affairs made by the INC were directly linked to the Palestine issue. Since this is a relatively long period to analyse, it is more meaningful to understand the evolving process towards the normalization of Indo-Israeli relations and the subsequent development of an Indo-Israeli strategic partnership through five critical junctures.

To test my theoretical framework on these five cases, there is a need for a careful historical reconstruction of the relevant elements of the political setting, of the context under consideration such as the era of political history, the nature of the policy debate, and the relevant units of analysis. This study is concerned not merely in correlation and strength-of-association measures but also in teasing out the dynamics and causal mechanisms through detailed process-tracing. Data collection needs to look at how and when the type of factors my approach has identified have influenced specific actors involved in foreign policy debates. Only such an approach, looking at the different steps of the decision-making process, can help determine actors' motivations and preferences as well as their situational incentives. The method of process-tracing is particularly helpful in this context as the complex and multivariate phenomenon of foreign policy change involves the convergence and interplay of various conditions, independent variables, and causal chains (George and Bennett 2005: 212–13).

The empirical reconstruction of the cases under investigation draws on two qualitative analytic techniques: the systematic analysis of documents (primary, archives, and secondary sources, governmental and non-governmental) and semi-structured interviews. As a result, most of the empirical material used to support this argument comes from archival research and interviews with key Indian foreign policy analysts and decision-makers. This book will draw on various kinds of sources. In all five cases, it is possible to identify primary sources such as statements, speeches, and writings from decision-makers as well as political parties' resolutions, Constituent Assembly and parliamentary debates, that can help reveal the issues and factors which influenced the decision-making process. This study has also analysed original articles from newspapers that covered Indo-Israeli relations over the past 60 years. In addition, there are many secondary sources such as biographies of important decision-makers. I have supplemented this research by interviews with different analysts and a number of retired Indian diplomats and senior military officers who had been based in West Asia, West Asia, especially in Israel, or who had directly interacted with Israeli officials . In short, this book will combine primary documents, secondary sources, and interviews to develop a methodologically grounded and theoretically engaged account of India's Israel policy. Paradoxically, despite the absence of diplomatic relations and the controversial nature of this specific policy, there is an important corpus of unexploited sources. Such material gave me the opportunity to carefully process-trace India's Israel policy at the critical policy junctures.

This study identifies 1922–47, 1948–56, 1967–74, 1984–92, and 1992–2012 as five critical junctures because these time periods correspond to phases when the existing policy arrangement vis-à-vis Israel was contested and in flux (Table I.2). These five foreign policy debates are illustrative case studies of the strategic thinking that occurred prior to India's policy decisions. During these periods, the Indian leadership settled on new understandings which defined India's Israel policy over the last 60 years. The comparison of these cases, where there is a variation either at the level of international, domestic, and individual factors and/or at the level of the outcome (as in the policy decision), can help determine what were the necessary and/or sufficient conditions for the normalization of Indo-Israeli relations and for the development of a strategic partnership.[32] The comparison is also important to discern what the constraints to change were (such as leadership predisposition, bureaucratic inertia, and international and/or domestic constraints). The study of a series of decision points finally helps tease out some of the more enduring determinants of India's Israel policy as well as the primary motivations for normalizing and developing strategic relations with Israel.

Overview of the Book

Following the introduction, the book begins in Chapter 1 with an analysis of India's first position vis-à-vis Israel. The question of Palestine had been a concern for Indian leaders long before independence in August

Table I.2   The Different Phases of India's Israel Policy

Time periods	Subsystem status	Key actors/institutions debating/defining the policy	Parameters of the policy compromise
1922–47	First policy	• British Foreign Office • India Office • British government • Government of India (British) • INC • Nehru • Muslim League	• Independence from British rule (both for South Asia and Palestine) • Federal solution for Palestine • Opposition to partition of Palestine (especially two-state solution on religious grounds) • Ensure religious rights of the Jewish minority • Appease domestic Muslim sensitivities
1948–56	Policy in flux	• Nehru • Close advisors (Azad) • First-generation Indian diplomats • INC	Policy in definition: • Progressive acceptance of Israel as political reality • Desire not to antagonize Arab states • Appease domestic Muslims sensitivities • Secure access to Suez Canal
1956–67	First policy compromise	• INC • MEA	• No relationship with Israel while refugee problem not resolved • Cairo-centric policy • Appease domestic Muslim sensitivities • Play an important role in Non-aligned movement

(Cont'd)

Table I.2 (*Cont'd*)

Time periods	Subsystem status	Key actors/institutions debating/defining the policy	Parameters of the policy compromise
1967–74	Policy in flux	• INC • MEA • Parliamentary opposition (BJS, PSP, Swatantra party) • Indian media	Policy in redefinition: • Move away from Cairo-centric policy • Courting Arab and Muslim states to counter Pakistani influence • Need to maintain energy supplies coming from Gulf
1974–92	Second policy compromise	• INC • MEA	• No relationship with Israel while Palestinian territories occupied (1967 borders now part of the policy), refugee problem not resolved, UN Resolution 242 not applied • Opening to Gulf States, and move away from Cairo • Recognition and engagement with PLO • Appease domestic Muslim sensitivities
1992–2004	Policy in flux	• Congress • MEA • BJP • Defence establishment • Governments of Indian States • Private economic actors	Policy in redefinition: • Need to find alternative sources for weapon procurement • Need to liberalize economy and attract FDI • Need to engage the US • Need to counter Pakistani influence in OIC on Kashmir issue • Need to appease domestic Muslim sensitivities

(*Cont'd*)

Table I.2 *(Cont'd)*

Time periods	Subsystem status	Key actors/institutions debating/defining the policy	Parameters of the policy compromise
2004 to present	Third policy compromise	• Defence establishment • Governments of Indian states • Private economic actors • Congress	• Military–technical cooperation and acquisitions for 'security requirements' (defensive/surveillance capabilities, development of self-sustaining military industry) • Economic–industrial collaboration in certain niche fields (investments, coproduction, joint research) • Multi-engagement in West Asia

Source: Author

Notes: INC— Indian National Congress; MEA— Ministry of External Affairs; BJS— Bharatiya Jana Sangh; PSP— Praja Socialist Party; BJP— Bharatiya Janata Party; UN—United Nations; PLO—Palestine Liberation Organization; FDI— foreign direct investment; OIC— Organization of the Islamic Conference.

1947 and the proclamation of the state of Israel in May 1948. Chapter 1 will detail and trace the process leading to the definition of India's initial policy towards Israel in 1947. At the time, the Indian national movement, represented by the INC, decided to oppose the partition of Palestine and the creation of the state of Israel. As the INC eventually formed the government of independent India, this became India's official position in the immediate post-independence years. This initial debate and its outcome remained an important institutional and ideational precedent for all of the prime ministers of India who followed Nehru.

The next two chapters deal with two phases of contestation and debate over the existing policy. While both periods are characterized by a state of policy flux and redefinition, they did not end with a complete reversal of India's original position. As a result, the literature has usually discounted these cases as irrelevant in the continuity of India's no-relationship position. But these cases are very instructive to better understand the nature of change in India's Israel policy. Looking at these policy debates also helps determine which factors played against change and why actors had interests in preserving the status quo. Policy reversal is impossible to assess without an understanding of the calculations and constraints that shaped leaders' opinion before 1992. Short of a complete foreign policy change, both periods ended with a new policy arrangement satisfying the altered circumstances.

Chapter 2 starts with the independence of Israel in 1948. India had to deal with two new political realities in 1947–8: the partition of the South Asian subcontinent and Israeli statehood. These two events can be construed as exogenous shocks that served as powerful catalysts for a reassessment of New Delhi's policy in West Asia. During this period of policy instability, there was an important debate on the opportunity to recognize Israel. After two years, India cautiously decided to recognize Israel in September 1950 but did not establish diplomatic relations. Nehru and the Indian leadership were open to instituting diplomatic relations with Israel and originally kept a prudent approach when dealing with Israel and the Arab states. This situation lasted until 1956 and the Suez crisis, when the window of opportunity for a rapprochement closed. After that date, the question of normalization was not officially considered for more than a decade.

The third chapter discusses a much-neglected phase of India's Israel policy. India's no-relationship policy came under serious criticism after the West Asian crisis of 1967. This is a 'most likely' case for policy change study where there were important conditions for a possible reassessment of India's Israel policy.[33] During this period of 1967–74, the bases of India's West Asia policy were undermined by the lack of positive diplomatic results from the traditional pro-Arab policy. India had not received explicit support from the Arab states in its military disputes with China in 1962 and Pakistan in 1965. In fact, some Arab states even supported Islamabad. There was also a growing domestic pressure for a different policy in the region. Finally, it became clear that there was a potential for cooperation with Israel, after India had asked for and obtained limited military assistance from Israel in the Indo-Pakistan wars of 1965 and 1971. Despite these pressures and incentives for policy change, the Indira Gandhi government deliberately refused to publicly acknowledge Israeli help and did not normalize its relations with Tel Aviv. I demonstrate in this chapter that this debate ended in a new policy compromise after 1974.

The fourth and fifth chapters deal with a much discussed but also much misunderstood phase of India's Israel policy: the 1992 decision by the Narasimha Rao government to normalize relations with Israel and its immediate aftermath. Chapter 4 analyses the process towards normalization and explains why a drastic change in India's Israel policy happened at that specific historical juncture and not in the previous two cases. The theoretical framework will help understand how the unique interaction of certain variables was different and more favourable for normalization in 1992. At the same time, this book will also demonstrate how past debates over Israel have also informed the 1992 decision. However, despite the 1992 decision, I will demonstrate in Chapter 5 that the new orientation did not consolidate itself until 2004 and the return of Congress in power. Past works have concentrated on the sudden and abrupt changes in 1992 and the decision to normalize but have rarely analysed the immediate post-normalization years, when the Indian government was prudent in publicly discussing its new Israel policy. Trade and defence ties were insignificant until the late 1990s.

In the fifth chapter, I will concentrate on the overlooked consolidation phase of India's new Israel policy during the last decade and how different governments have managed the apparent contradictions between engaging Israel in important economic and defence deals while maintaining a pro-Palestine rhetoric in parallel. Despite initial doubts about the endurance of the Indo-Israeli partnership, when the traditionally pro-Palestinian Congress party came back to power in 2004, relations with Tel Aviv have continued and increased. The chapter stresses how the present literature has not yet theoretically addressed the consolidation of India's new Israel policy. The new theoretical argument helps demonstrate how the policy-making process in the 1990s was progressively opened to new types of actors in the military and economic sectors that have redefined India's Israel policy to their advantage.

In Chapter 6, I conclude the book by summarizing the findings and then exploring further implications. I explain how one needs to look at India's Israel policy more like a segmented foreign policy-making process with different actors, levels of analysis, and niched interests. At the political-state level, there has always been an impression of policy continuity, because the Indian government followed its pro-Palestinian policy to satisfy historically held ideological principles, domestic constituencies, and its Arab and Muslim allies in the region. While this rationale has usually been presented by the literature as the main explanation for the absence of policy change, it did not cover all the dimensions of interactions between India and Israel. Likewise, India's current Israel policy is not an overarching plan decided by a few key political players at the top but the aggregate outcome of debates and bargaining between different groups. The new policy compromise in the Israel policy subsystem is now defined by an emerging 'coalition' of technical-military experts who appreciate the Israeli military industry's unique expertise and assistance, and by domestic political and economic actors who benefit from specialized joint ventures (in irrigation technology, for example) with Israeli private actors. Their expert input deeply affects the image of this policy and the current positive feedback. This explains the intention of successive governments to support the current state of bilateral relations despite the ideological and diplomatic ambiguities this policy has created at the public level. In the final chapter, I will also discuss possible directions for future research and notably of ways to test this new theoretical approach in different settings.

Notes

1. These figures do not include defence ties. See 'India-Israel Trade Rises to $6 Billion in 2012-13', *The Hindu Business Line*, 7 July 2013.
2. Respectively, Kumaraswamy (2010: 2, 242); Thakur (1994: 289).
3. See, for example, Mohan (2005: 47, 224–7); Kumaraswamy (2004a).
4. The Indian National Congress (INC) was founded in 1885 and became the organization leading the Indian independence movement. After independence in 1947, it became the dominant political party.
5. K. P. Misra noted, for instance, there were four questions raised over the issue of the recognition of Israel by members of the Constitutional Assembly to Nehru and the provisional government from 1948 to 1950. It was the most discussed foreign policy issue in the Assembly. Even the issue of the recognition of the People's Republic of China (PRC) did not attract as much public attention. See Misra (1966: 52–3).
6. Rejecting the Eurocentric terms 'Near East' or 'Middle-East', Prime Minister Jawaharlal Nehru had a more Asia-centric worldview and therefore referred to this region as 'West Asia'. The West Asian region extends from Turkey to Southern

Yemen and from Egypt to Iran. Some scholars had a broader interpretation of West Asia which included Sudan and Afghanistan. See Ward (1992: 15); Kozicki (1958: 162–72). This book will henceforth be using the expression of West Asia when discussing India's position vis-à-vis the Middle East.

7. For theoretical purposes and because of the depth of information needed to trace and understand certain foreign policy decisions, I made a deliberate decision to concentrate on the Indian point of view.

8. The only notable book-length study in a major academic press has been P. R. Kumaraswamy's *India's Israel Policy* (2010). Two other works offer many historical details: Gopal and Sharma (2007) and Gerberg (2008). The latter covers the Israeli side of the relationship. Gerberg was a former consul-general of Israel in Bombay (Mumbai) after the establishment of diplomatic relations in 1992.

9. Given the limited access to official sources regarding these different conflicts, there has been much debate and speculation on the exact nature and quantity of assistance provided by Israel. In Chapter 3, this book will recollect different existing accounts of these wartime military exchanges.

10. The Israeli scholar Gideon Shimoni probably provided the most detailed description of the visit of Zionist emissaries to India before independence to establish contacts with Gandhi and Nehru. He also analysed the frustration experienced by the Jewish leadership in Palestine because of India's determination to avoid antagonizing the Indian Muslim community as well as their consistent support of the Arab cause (Shimoni 1977). For a similar argument about the absence of knowledge of Judaism among Indian nationalists, see also Glucklich (1988), Gordon (1975), Schechtman (1966). Kumaraswamy (2010: 3–4) also argued that India's initial refusal to engage Israel was even contradictory given that Hinduism and Judaism could easily coexist. This cultural argument is problematic because, while Hinduism was the majority religion in independent India, religious considerations did not and do not dictate foreign policies in India's secular political system. Furthermore, one must not confuse the lack of anti-Semitism in India for a support for a Jewish national home. Gordon (1975) even argued that the absence of anti-Semitism made the Zionists' attempt to convince Indian leaders of the urgency of a Jewish state even harder.

11. These scholars likened the INC's rejection of the religious nationalist project behind the Zionist movement with the INC's own domestic opposition with the Muslim League's two state solution. See Naaz (1999), Kumarawswamy (2010: 8).

12. Brecher (1957) was the first to argue that India's foreign policy in general and towards Israel in particular, until the mid-1960s, was the product of Prime Minister Nehru who enjoyed the overwhelming support of the Indian public

and was not contested within the Indian Congress structure on foreign affairs. Nehru's decisive role was confirmed by an extensive literature: Bandyopadhyaya (1970); Cohen (2001); Dixit (2003); Kapur (2009: Chapter 1); Kennedy 2012; Mittchell (2007); Schottli (2012).

13. See, for example Mohan (2005: 47, 224–7).

14. Brecher (1963: 129–30). Even Nehru's biographer, Sarvepalli Gopal, admitted the important influence of Indian Muslims in Nehru's decisions (1979: 169).

15. For example, the former foreign minister in the Bharatiya Janata Party (BJP) government Jaswant Singh, while visiting Israel, had criticized the fact India's Israel policy had become tied to 'Muslim vote bank politics' and 'captive to domestic policy' (quoted in Malhotra 2000). On the 'Muslim factor' and India's foreign policy, see also Ghildiyal (2008); Suroor (2011). However, most studies discussing this argument have never presented conclusive evidence to back up the claim that India's Arab policies had enjoyed a strong domestic support from Indian Muslims. For instance, Kumaraswamy (2010: 16, 157–8) makes a comparison between India's Muslim community and the Israel lobby in the US domestic political context but does not offer clear evidence to justify this analogy.

16. Gayer and Jaffrelot (2012); Yadav (2009). However, there are some exceptions. Both Kanchan Chandra (2004) and Steven Wilkinson (2004) have argued that the Muslim factor mattered in more localized elections where Muslims can serve as a crucial voting bloc. But foreign policy issues such as India's Israel policy are not particularly salient in this context. For example, the reference to Israel in the 2012 Uttar Pradesh elections by Rahul Gandhi in an attempt to discredit his adversary did not procure any visible electoral dividends. See Ganguli (2012).

17. See the memos from Walter Eytan and Abban Eban pointing out the initial similarities between India and Israel's diplomatic approaches, quoted in Kumaraswamy (2010: 164–6). For a discussion of India's non-alignment posture, see Nehru (1961). On Israel's attempt at maintaining an independent foreign policy, see Decalo (1967); Brecher (1972); Bialer (1981).

18. The exclusion of Israel from the Bandung Conference was not initially supported by India. See Chapter 2.

19. On relations between India and the Soviet Union, see Robert C. Horn (1982); Thakur and Thayer (1992); Nadkarni (forthcoming). On relations between Israel and the US, see Ball and Ball (1992); Bass (2003).

20. Adams (1971); Gordon (1975); Ward (1992: 30). India, for example, advocated during the 1956 Suez crisis the maintenance of the Convention of Constantinople of 1888 which had been negotiated by the British and which had declared the Canal a neutral route. The Suez Canal is still considered a strategic gateway today; see 'India, Britain Discuss Security in Suez Canal', *Times of India*, 1 February 2011.

21. The British Raj was the British rule in the Indian subcontinent between 1858 and 1947. The region was also called the Indian Empire by the British.

22. See, for example, the books and memoirs of J. N. Dixit, India's former secretary of the Ministry of External Affairs (MEA), who played a significant role in the establishment of diplomatic relations with Israel: Dixit (See also Kumaraswamy (1998; 199); Naaz (1999, 2000, 2005); Berman (2002); Inbar (2004); Pant (2008a); Khemlani (2010).

23. For instance, in an earlier article, Kumaraswamy (1996b) was sceptical about the actual development of bilateral relations. Only in the last decade have Israeli defence sales surpassed $10 billion; see '$10 Billion Business: How Israel Became India's Most Important Partner in Arms Bazaar', Economic Times, 24 September 2012.

24. For an argument analysing India's Israel policy as a reaction to evolving international, domestic, and individual-level factors, read Blarel (2009).

25. Gerberg's attempt to use Herrmann's 1990 model in his dissertation to account for the evolution of Indo-Israeli relations is a good example of the initial problems encountered in this literature. Building on Hermann's multi-causal model, Gerberg identifies a multitude of independent factors at different levels of analysis but does not compare and weigh the relative explanatory leverage of these different variables over time. See Gerberg (2008).

26. Baumgartner and Jones (2009). Policy monopolies could be considered to be close to Jeffrey Legro's (2005) concept of 'dominant orthodoxies'.

27. Baumgartner and Jones (2009: 7). In international relations theory, the epistemic unities literature also emphasized the important role of advice and ideas provided by informed foreign policy experts. See Haas (1992).

28. Motivations of advocacy coalitions are mixed. Their expected returns of promoting foreign policy change can take the form of policy outcome they favour, or personal aggrandizement in form of increased reputation and/or better career prospects. See Kingdon (1984: 122–3).

29. The most important illustration of that situation was in 1967 when there was a widespread opposition to India's pro-Arab policy but this new orthodoxy failed to mobilize collectively to demand for the establishment of diplomatic relations with Israel. See Chapter 3.

30. Cobb and Elder (1983). The concept of conflict expansion is also closely related to the notion of 'frame extension' found in the social movement literature. See Tarrow (1994: 109–10).

31. Obviously, successful entrepreneurs or advocacy coalitions must also offer credible and feasible policy options that can also master necessary political support and that can tackle old deficiencies, but this is a necessary and not sufficient condition for change.

32. For a discussion on the role of case studies in identifying variables as necessary and sufficient conditions for a certain outcome, see George and Bennett (2005).

33. In a most-likely case study, the variables posited by a theory are at such a value that intuitively suggests a certain extreme outcome. For an extended discussion on methods of case selection and the usefulness of identifying 'most likely' cases, see George and Bennett (2005).

1 Conflicting Nationalisms

The Gradual Formation of India's First Israel Policy (1922–1947)

INDIA DID NOT WAIT until independence on 15 August 1947 and the creation of the state of Israel on 14 May 1948 to shape its position on the Jewish state. Historical accounts of India's foreign policy have traditionally neglected the pre-independence period.[1] In a practical and formal sense, India did not have an autonomous foreign policy until 1947. Before independence, British India's position on West Asian affairs was decided by the British Foreign Office and by other actors like the India Office and the British Government of India (which had different, and sometimes conflicting, concerns than London). Despite this particular decision-making structure, the foundations of independent India's West Asia policy can be located between the two World Wars. During this period, Indian leaders started developing their own foreign policy positions and acquired diplomatic experience. The Indian nationalist movement consciously decided to distance itself from British India's position on West Asia before 1947.[2] In fact, the Indian National Congress (INC), which would eventually form the first independent government in 1947, made its first statement on the Palestine question in 1922 (Zaidi and Zaidi *Encyclopedia of the INC*, 1977: Vol. 8, p. 542). It is therefore legitimate to look at statements and positions made in India's pre-independence phase to trace the gradual formation of a principled and cohesive foreign policy (Prasad 1960: 1).

Most studies looking at early clues of an Indian position towards Israel have concentrated on the views of the two marking figures of the

Indian nationalist movement, Gandhi and Nehru. Their perceptions on Zionism, expressed in early writings in the 1930s (before the actual creation of Israel), are often interpreted as having influenced India's policy after independence. But their positions have evolved in view of shifting circumstances in Europe, and after meetings with Jewish acquaintances and Zionist emissaries. This study offers to integrate and evaluate the historical context that influenced the positions of both Gandhi and Nehru over the Palestine issue and their actual policy implications.

The existing literature on Indo-Israeli relations has often highlighted that there had not been any direct conflict of interest between India and Israel. This judgement was based on two assumptions. First, some authors argued that there was no direct political or military dispute between India and Israel, and that there had not been evidence of anti-semitism in India.[3] This literature also emphasized the fact that both countries emerged as democracies after a protracted anti-colonialist struggle against the British Empire and that their initial governments and ruling elites shared similar socialist ideals (Gordon 1975; Schechtman 1966). However, this is only a partial reading of the nationalist trajectories of both countries. There was in fact one neglected conflict of interest which opposed both nationalist movements.[4] The INC fought for a secular and united India while the Zionist movement aspired for the opposite solution: a partition of Palestine on religious grounds following British withdrawal. The Jewish nationalist movement was arguing for a solution similar to the one the Muslim League was defending in the subcontinent. The INC's domestic struggle with the Muslim League is another decisive background condition which helped explain the nature of India's initial Israel policy.

Consequently, I identify and assess in this chapter the international and domestic factors as well as the various actors that influenced the debate over India's Israel policy from 1922 to 1947. Far from being an ambivalent approach, the formation of India's policy on the Palestine issue must be reconsidered in the context of the debates in British India and Palestine before independence.

Historical Background

India has very old ties with West Asia and Palestine. Some historians date Indo-Arab relations back to 2500 BC. Archaeological evidence demonstrates the existence of trade links between the Indus valley civilization and the civilizations of Mesopotamia, Babylonia, and Sumeria (Ahmad 1969; Ratnagar 2004). Cultural and commercial ties were reinforced by the settlements of Indians in the Arab world and of Arabs on the western coast of the Indian subcontinent. India was brought in direct contact with the Arab world with the emergence and expansion of the Achaemenid Persian Empire (549–525 BC) which extended from Greece all the way to the current Punjab (Ahmad 1969). The construction of the Nile Canal further helped exploration of the India Ocean and commercial exchanges with the Indian coast (Hasan 1928). Later, the Mauryan kings exchanged ambassadors with West Asian kingdoms such as Egypt and Syria (Ahmad 1969: 67). Political links between the two regions were very ancient and therefore predated Islam.

The medieval period was marked by more direct and confrontational contacts between the Arabs and the Indian rajas. The concurrent rise of Islam as a religion and political force and the decline of the Mauryas and Guptas led to direct military oppositions and the annexation of Sindh in 711–12 AD (Keay 2000: Chapter 9). By contrast, relations with Arab merchants remained cordial in the south, where they were welcomed by the Rashtrakuta Empire of the Deccan.[5] As this time, there were also many Arab colonies on the western Indian coast, in Malabar or Gujarat. West Asian rulers sent envoys and emissaries for the purpose of establishing cultural contacts and to learn more about religious and political conditions in the East (Ahmad 1969: 70). Arab rulers were equally interested by Indian scientific contributions, notably astronomy, mathematics, and medicine (Wasey 2003). Given its geographical location, the Indian subcontinent was the centre a sophisticated network of commerce between Arab and South Asian merchants. These exchanges created an impression of quasi-unified system of regional interdependence across the Indian Ocean (Robert Blyth 2003; Bose 2006; Kaplan 2010).

During this period of sustained exchanges, there were early links between the Indian subcontinent and Jewish merchants. During the time of King Solomon, the port of Ezion Gerber was built at the head of the Gulf of Aqaba and from there trade was reportedly carried on between Africa and India (Allen 1974: 22). According to some scholars, a Jewish navy travelled east to the port of 'Ophir' (which is believed to have been on the southwestern coast of India) every three years and brought back gold, silver, apes, peacocks, Almug trees, and precious stones.[6] The fact that Hebrew words to define these mercantile products are believed to have Indian origins has been interpreted as evidence of the existence of ancient commercial links.[7] There is also evidence that Jewish traders from Egypt were very active in the commercial exchanges between West Asia and the southern part of the Indian west coast.[8] Attracted by the naturally rich Malabar Coast, Syrian Christians and Jews settled in the region that is today the state of Kerala in south India. The Cochini or Malabar Jews, who are considered to be the oldest Jewish communities in India, most probably arrived after the fall of Jerusalem in 70 AD.[9] However, the earliest reference to the Jewish community in India was made by the king of the Cheras, Ravivarman, in the tenth century, who allegedly gave lands and privileges to a Jew named Joseph Rabban (Thapar 2002: 368–9).

The religious and political linkages between the subcontinent and the Gulf expanded again rapidly after Islam spread into northern India. Indian Muslim leaders, like the Arab rulers of Sindh and the Delhi Sultans, found it indeed politically convenient to obtain recognition from the Arab Caliphs of Baghdad and then of Egypt. The Caliphs of Baghdad exercised a strong political and religious influence on South Asia because, until the thirteenth century, they were still considered to be the legitimate representatives of the Prophet Muhammad by the more orthodox Muslims of the subcontinent (Ahmad 1969: 70–1). The legal blessing by the Caliphate integrated these Muslim kingdoms within the broader political Islamic structure and comforted their own local rule.

However, political and religious fractionalization in the Islamic world destabilized the status of the Caliphate. The religious rift in West Asia was also to some degree reflected in the rivalries between the Arab rulers of Sindh and the sultans of Delhi (Ahmad 1969: 70–6). The Muslim dynasties in Delhi, whether it was the Ghoris (1173–1206), the Khaljis (1290–1320), the Tughlaqs (1320–1413), or even the Lodis (1451–1526), kept some loose political and religious allegiance to the Caliphate despite a decline in diplomatic relations with Egypt where the Caliphate had moved (Khosla 2009: 14). The arrival of the Mughal rulers in the sixteenth century definitely broke with this traditional hierarchical link with a foreign Caliphate. The new Mughal Empire refused to recognize the Ottoman Sultans of Turkey as Caliphs.[10] After this period, relations between West Asia and Mughal India were different. There had already been a commercial fallout linked to the decline of the Baghdad Khilafat which moved to a more distant Cairo. However, the greatest setback was the arrival of European powers in the Indian Ocean which competed with Arab–Indian naval links (Bose 2006). It was also around this time that a second wave of Jewish immigrants came to India. The Baghdadi Jewish community moved from Iraq to Surat (Gujarat) and Bombay to escape religious persecution in West Asia. Jews from all over the Ottoman Empire joined that community. The Baghdadi Jews contributed a lot to the development of Bombay's manufacturing and commercial houses.[11]

Many Indian diplomats and politicians refer to these very ancient commercial, cultural, and political links between the subcontinent and West Asia as background evidence indicative of the potential of an important relationship between the two regions in the future. It is also evident that the rich and mixed culture of India today is the result of repeated waves of cultural influence emanating from West Asia. However, given the political and cultural fragmentation of both regions over time, it is complicated to study these interactions as taking form in a continuous way between two stable and consistent geopolitical identities. This book is not attempting to make any long-term argument over India's modern West Asia policy based on these ancient links. The only conclusion from this historical background is that the two regions have been interlinked in an almost interdependent system and that West Asia had always kept an important position in political and commercial designs for successive rulers in the subcontinent.

A greater argument can, however, be made about the influence of the British Empire's policies on contemporary India (Prasad 1965). The decline of the Mughal Empire and the emergence of the British Empire in South Asia established a new type of relationship with West Asia. Starting in the second half of the eighteenth century, the British East India Company built on pre-existing trading networks and adapted them to its own commercial and strategic needs, notably by connecting these trade lanes with the larger British Empire (Robert Blyth 2003). However, with the growth in scale of British political control of India,[12] the spread of direct British influence over West Asia became necessary to protect the 'crown jewel' of the Empire from other European powers (Darwin 2009: especially Chapter 5). The British were suspicious of French, German, and Russian intentions in West Asia, which had the potential to disrupt the direct access to the eastern part of its international empire. To establish a firm control over India and to safeguard trade links with the metropole, Britain created a series of outposts and buffer zones in

West Asia (Heptullah 1991: ix; Ward 1992: 22). As long as India was subjugated politically, the West Asian region would suffer the same fate.

Within this new context, and for practical reasons, British Indian policymakers had a strong autonomy from London (Kumar 1966; Metcalf 2007; Onley 2007). The need to quickly react to events in West Asia made it neither possible nor desirable for London to control the minutiae of British Indian diplomacy in the Gulf. As a result, it was the British Indian government which directly handled treaty negotiations with Arab states, which developed commercial and security policies in the region, and which performed small-scale naval operations to ensure the security of sea-lanes of communication (Robert Blyth 2003: 2–3). This was confirmed by the fact that responsibility for the Persian Gulf region was delegated from London to the British Viceroy in India, an arrangement that was maintained until 1947 (Ansari 2007: 277). While there were some structural limits imposed by London, the British Indian government effectively managed to develop its own regional policy.

The first objective of this regional policy was the pacification and supervision of the Gulf. The territorial expansion along this extended maritime frontier was considered compulsory as the establishment of a foreign naval base in the Persian Gulf could become a direct threat to British interests. This led British India to become closely associated with the internal affairs of Gulf countries. It established consular missions and placed British Residents across the region (Onley 2009). Occasionally, this policy also led to the annexation of political and commercial protectorates around the Gulf of Aden (Curzon 1907: Part 4; Robert Blyth 2003: 4; Onley 2007). To preserve the safety of the route to India and an access to the Suez Canal, Britain also decided to occupy Cyprus in 1878 and Egypt in 1882.[13] Following World War I, the British Empire again expanded in the region as Britain was given the mandate to administer Iraq and Palestine in 1922 by the League of Nations. Interestingly, to control these new territories, the British Empire used Indian administrators to run the local governments and the Indian Army to suppress opposition to British rule.[14]

Progressively, British India created its own sub-Empire stretching from the Gulf to Eastern Africa. This study will demonstrate in the next chapter how this concern to maintain long-distance contacts with western Europe and to guarantee access to West Asian sea-lanes of communication would be shared by post-independence India. India remained dependent on access lines like the Suez Canal for decades after independence. But in the pre-independence phase, there were two immediate adverse consequences of the imperial overreach of the British Raj in West Asia. The first one was the domestic repercussion of being directly involved in West Asian politics. The Government of India opposed the London Foreign Office's designs in the region, notably its role in the dissolution in the Ottoman Empire, as it created unrest among Indian Muslims over the fate of the Turkish Caliphate.[15] The official British attitude towards the Ottoman Empire was therefore criticized by the British Government of India which had to consider the sensitivities of its Muslim subjects. The Indian nationalist movement also exploited Muslim concerns to unite Hindus and Muslims in their opposition to British rule in the subcontinent. Rival players in Palestine, Zionists like Chaim Weizmann as well as Palestinian nationalists, took early note of this indirect influence of the important Indian Muslim minority on British policies towards the region and started looking towards India for the necessary political support for their movements. The other consequence was the progressive realization that nationalists in both regions shared a common enemy in British imperialism. The Indian nationalist movement gradually established contacts with movements in Egypt and Palestine. As a consequence, a new competing West Asia policy (and Palestine policy) started to emerge in the nationalist Indian mindset following 1917.

Congress Leaders and Israel: Thoughts, Debates, and Actual Policy Impact

Mahatma Gandhi and Jawaharlal Nehru were the most articulate Indian nationalist leaders on the subject of Palestine. Their perceptions of Zionism, expressed in early writings in the 1930s have often been interpreted as having decisively influenced India's post-independence Israel policy (Kumaraswamy 2010: 25–43, 47–53; Shimoni 1977). Much has, for instance, been said about Gandhi's position on Israel because he had regularly discussed the question of a Jewish national home between 1906 and 1947.[16] The problem is that his (as well as Nehru's) opinions were never fixed and definite. As Gandhi and Nehru debated the issue with Jewish acquaintances and Zionist representatives, their views changed and became more sophisticated as they learned more about the intricacies of the Palestine question. The evolution of India's struggle for independence and events in Palestine also shaped their thinking over time. Their interpretation of the situation in Palestine was shaped by a mixture of ideological and practical considerations. Consequently, it is difficult to charge both Gandhi and Nehru with either a complete incomprehension of Zionist arguments or an unquestioning trust in the Arab stand. One must therefore be very careful when attributing causality in India's Israel policy to statements from both Indian leaders.

In addition, Gandhi's opinion has never had an actual impact on policy-making vis-à-vis Israel. Unlike Nehru, Gandhi had never held a position of direct influence on foreign policy matters after independence. This relates to a problem in the literature on India's Israel policy which has interpreted Gandhi and Nehru's statements as having guided India's position after independence. Their quotes have often been used as rhetorical references to rationalize policies in the region. However, the actual impact of their ideas has rarely been evaluated and problematized. How did these two leaders shape India's Israel policy?

Gandhi and Zionism

Gandhi's experience in South Africa led him to learn about the Jewish religion and about the demand for a Jewish national home at a very early stage. Gandhi made many Jewish acquaintances during his 21 years in South Africa, including two of his oldest friends, Hermann Kallenbach and Henry Polak (Chatterjee 1992; Gandhi, *Collected Works*, 48: 105; Lelyveld 2011: 94–5, 278–82; Panter-Brick 2008; Shimoni 1977: 4–11). These relations were decisive during what is considered to be a formative period in his politico-moral philosophy (Guha 2013; Lelyveld 2011). Talking about his connections with Jews in South Africa in a 1931 interview with the *Jewish Chronicle* in London, Gandhi said he had great sympathy towards the Jews and that he admired their 'spirit of comradeship' as well as the fact that they were a 'people with a vision' (Gandhi, *Collected Works*, 48: 105–6). A few years later, Gandhi also explained how he had learned about the 'long persecution' of the Jews through his interactions with his Jewish friends in South Africa (Gandhi, *Harijan*, 26 November 1938, in *Collected Works*, 68: 137). Gandhi also expressed sympathy towards the Jews following their persecution in Germany in the late 1930s. In a famous and oft-quoted 1938 article in *Harijan*, Gandhi drew a direct parallel between the treatment of Jews in Europe by Christians and the conduct of Hindus with untouchables

(Gandhi, *Harijan*, 26 November 1938, in *Collected Works*, Volume 68: 137). Given the unique historical persecution of Jews in Germany, he also argued that war against Germany would be justified (Tendulkar 1961, Volume 4: 380–2). But he also explained in this article that his sympathy did not blind him to the 'requirement of justice' and that the 'cry for the national home for the Jews' was not legitimate for him (Gandhi, *Harijan*, 26 November 1938, in *Collected Works*, 68: 137).

Three factors have mainly shaped Gandhi's critical attitude towards Zionism.[17] These factors were not fixed and their saliency evolved over time given the changes in international and domestic conditions and the efforts made by the Jewish Agency to persuade Gandhi to support their cause in Palestine.[18] First, Gandhi was thoughtful of the concerns of India's Muslim community which he considered to be supportive of Arab demands and opposed to the creation of a Jewish state in Palestine. Following the inception of the British mandate over Palestine in 1922, Gandhi, for instance, cited arguments generally advanced by Muslim members of the Khilafat movement. He observed the unrest among Indian Muslims over the issue of Palestine and empathized with their Pan-Islamic anxieties. Repudiating the Balfour Declaration in 1921, he declared that Palestine could not be given to the Jews as a result of World War I and criticized the British for making this promise to the Zionists. In parallel, he appealed to the Zionists to 'revise their ideal about Palestine' (Gandhi, *Young India*, 23 March 1921, in *Collected Works*, 19: 530). He notably called on his 'Jewish friends' to consider the concerns of 'seventy million Muslims of India' (Gandhi, *Young India*, 23 March 1921, in *Collected Works*, 19: 530). In a follow-up article, Gandhi referred to Palestine as a country destined to remain under Muslim custody because the country had been ruled for centuries by Muslims. According to him, this did not mean that the Jews and Christians could not freely go to Palestine as a place of worship or even acquire their own lands. What non-Muslims could not do was to acquire sovereign jurisdiction over Palestine (Gandhi, *Young India*, 6 April 1921, in *Collected Works*, 19: 530). In the specific context of the Khilafat movement, Gandhi decided to unconditionally back religious claims of Arab Muslims by refusing to allow non-Muslim sovereignty over Jerusalem and Palestine.[19] The motivations behind his support for the Khilafat movement were not only principled but strategic as he hoped for the INC to gain support and legitimacy among Indian Muslims in their struggle against the British. After 1922 and the dissolution of the

Khilafat movement, Gandhi, however, moved away from looking at the Palestine issue from a religious angle.

A second factor which explained Gandhi's critical attitude was his strong ideological opposition to political Zionism. From 1922 to 1931, Gandhi shied away from making any further statements on the Palestine issue. In 1931, Gandhi, however, started making a very different argument when talking about Palestinian sovereignty. In his interview to the *Jewish Chronicle*, Gandhi judged Zionism as a 'lofty aspiration' which should only be realized internally and spiritually and not politically and territorially.[20] In a letter written to Albert Enstein, Gandhi said he understood the desire for Jews to return to Palestine and Jerusalem as a religious ritual but he backed away from supporting their political aspirations in that region (Sorkhabi 2005). Gandhi argued that the connection of the Jews with Zionism was first and mainly spiritual and could therefore be realized everywhere where Jews were based and not exclusively in Palestine (Gandhi, *Collected Works*, 48: 105–6; Sorkhabi 2005).

In his interpretation of Zionism, Gandhi clearly dissociated religious and political claims, and refuted Zionist territorial claims over Palestine. This was later confirmed in his 1938 *Harijan* article when he explained that 'the Palestine of the Biblical conception' was not a 'geographical tract' and that it gave no base to Jews for a 'national home' in modern Palestine (Gandhi, *Harijan*, 26 November 1938, in *Collected Works*, 68: 136–8). He notably criticized basing citizenship on religion, and highlighted the problems of dual nationality and allegiance that the creation of Israel would generate. By contrast, Gandhi believed that Arab nationalist claims over Palestine were more legitimate. He famously said that 'Palestine belongs to the Arabs in the same sense that England belongs to the English or France to the French'. It was therefore 'wrong and inhuman to impose the Jew' on the Arab majority (Gandhi, *Harijan*, 26 November 1938, in *Collected Works*, 68: 136–8). Instead of demanding a national home on illegitimate grounds, Gandhi advised the Zionists to appeal to the 'Arab's goodwill' for a just treatment of their religious rights in Palestine (Gandhi, *Harijan*, 26 November 1938, in *Collected Works*, 68: 136–8). Gandhi's position had therefore evolved in the 1930s: his opposition to a Jewish national home was henceforth grounded in an ideological opposition to the Jewish nationalist project. The Zionist projects stood now clearly in contrast to his more secular conception of nationalism.

A third and final factor explaining Gandhi's reluctance to support Zionism is his rebuttal of Zionist methods. Early on, Gandhi had criticized Zionist efforts to obtain British support in their territorial designs in Palestine. The INC was fighting the British Empire in the subcontinent and therefore could not discuss with a Jewish national movement which was cooperating with London. Gandhi also criticized the Jewish nationalist movement's resort to violent methods to fulfil their aspirations. In a 1931 interview, Gandhi opposed the use of military force to support territorial ambitions in Palestine. Gandhi's reference to British 'bayonets' also aimed at highlighting and criticizing the Zionist movement's overreliance on British political and military support in Palestine against the Arabs (Gandhi, *Collected Works*, 48: 105–6). Gandhi instead advocated peaceful methods and friendly cooperation with the Palestinian Arabs. In his 1938 article, he criticized both Arab and Jewish excesses and regretted that both communities had not resisted British occupation through non-violent methods. When referring to the Jewish national movement, Gandhi also reiterated that a 'religious act cannot be performed with the aid of the bayonet or the bomb' (Gandhi, *Harijan*, 26 November 1938, in *Collected Works*, 68: 136–8). In the 1940s, some discontented elements of the Zionist movement radicalized their actions and committed multiple terrorist attacks against the British administration. Gandhi criticized this resort to terrorism which he judged to have damaged the Jewish case which he considered to be 'proper' (Gandhi, *Collected Works* 87: 417). He later told an American journalist that any solution to the Palestine dispute rested on the Jews' rejection of 'terrorism and other forms of violence' (Gandhi, *Collected Works* 88: 48). If it were not for the escalation of violence in Palestine and the terrorist methods used by some actors, Gandhi seemed to have been open to accept (although not to support) the political legitimacy of Zionist demands. Why did his position evolve?

Gandhi had consistently opposed the Zionist political project in Palestine. His opposition had mostly prevailed despite multiple efforts from the Jewish Agency to convince him to speak favourably of their cause in Palestine (Kumaraswamy 2010: 31–5; Shimoni 1977; Ward 1992: 13–14). The Jewish Agency had attempted to establish contacts with Gandhi whom they considered to be an influential personality of international fame and whose moral character evoked sympathy amongst Jews worldwide. By the early 1930s, the Jewish Agency also realized that it needed to counter Pan-Islamic propaganda circulated in India through the Mufti al-Hussayni.[21] This effort to persuade individuals rather than organizations like the INC serves as an example of the enduring difficulties for the Jewish nationalist movement to identify itself with other Asian movements. There was therefore a deliberate strategy under Moshe Sharett, the head of the political department of the Jewish Agency, to individually engage Gandhi and to inform him of the Zionist perspective on the Palestine question (Jansen 1966; Shimoni 1977: 27–8).

The Jewish Agency also tried to use Henry Polak and Hermann Kallenbach's friendly relations with Gandhi to their advantage.[22] Polak was, for instance, instrumental (through a letter of introduction) in putting Gandhi in touch with Selig Brodestky and Nahum Sokolov, both members of the World Zionist Organization (WZO) in October 1931 in London. However, Gandhi was mostly preoccupied with the London negotiations over India's own freedom struggle and was not ready to discuss the Palestinian issue at the time (Kumaraswamy 2010: 32–3). In 1936, Immanuel Olsvanger, a Sanskrit scholar, was sent to Delhi as an official Zionist emissary to meet with Gandhi.[23] Kallenbach was also sent by the Jewish Agency to persuade Gandhi of the legitimacy of the Zionist cause. Kallenbach tried for two months to obtain Gandhi's understanding and sympathy. He stressed the urgent need for a national homeland in Palestine for persecuted Jews in Europe. Kallenbach's visit did not change Gandhi's critical attitude towards Zionism but the Indian leader became more sensitive to the problems in Europe. Apparently, Gandhi confided to his friend of his willingness to help Jews and Arabs cooperate but did not want to make this offer public. In a letter to Kallenbach in July, he reportedly said that he understood the Jewish demand for a national home but qualified his eventual support to prior Arab approval (Shimoni 1977: 33, 36).

Repeated efforts from the Zionist movement to get Gandhi to publicly express himself about the Palestine issue proved finally fruitful in 1938.[24] However, his statements on Palestine belonging to the Arabs and his condemnation of Zionist collaboration with imperialist Britain in his 1938 Harijan article revealed the difficulties of the Jewish Agency's efforts in swaying the Indian nationalist leader and their failure in changing his original position. Zionists strongly criticized the article and abandoned the idea of convincing Gandhi.[25] Martin Buber, the Austrian Jewish philosopher, and Judah Magnes, the then rector of the Hebrew

University, replied to Gandhi's statements in two open letters (Buber and Magnes 1939; Shimoni 1977: 40–7). While Buber admitted in his 1939 open letter that Jewish settlers had not always respected the 'Arab way of life', he nevertheless rejected the validity of Gandhi's claim that Palestine belonged to the Arabs (or to the least that they had a more legitimate claim than the Jews).[26] Buber also criticized Gandhi's recommendation of 'non-violence' (Satyagraha) as a method of resistance for the Jews in Germany.[27] However, there is no evidence that Gandhi read the letters.

After World War II, Gandhi's position seemed to have evolved to some degree. Gandhi met Kallenbach again in March 1939, who urged him to publicly express his views on the Arab–Jewish question in Palestine, and to condemn the persecution of the Jews in Germany, but Gandhi was reluctant to do so. A. E. Shohet, an Indian Jew from the Baghdadi Jew community, who conducted the affairs of the Zionist office in Bombay, used the occasion of Kallenbach's visit to interview Gandhi for the *Jewish Advocate*. According to Shohet's report, Gandhi viewed the Palestine question as a purely Muslim question; nevertheless Shohet recommended that contact with Gandhi should be maintained.[28] On 22 March 1939, Kallenbach organized a meeting in India between Gandhi and Joseph Nedivi, the representative of the political department of the Jewish Agency in Palestine. Nedivi explained to Gandhi the many contributions to the economic and agricultural development of Palestine by the Jewish settlers. The meeting did not change Gandhi's views, and he refused to make a public statement on the Jewish–Arab conflict (Shimoni 1977: 51). At first, the outbreak of World War II and the revelations about the Holocaust did not seem to have changed Gandhi's opinion. In 1942, although he condemned the persecution of the Jews in Europe in strong terms, he insisted that restoring Palestine to the Jews, partly or wholly, as their national home would be a crime against humanity, as well as against the Muslims (Shimoni 1977: 39, 51). Gandhi then became reluctant to make public statements as he argued he had not enough 'knowledge' about the situation (Shimoni 1977: 55–6).

In spite of that statement, Gandhi still agreed to meet the American pacifist John Haynes, who had been sent by Rabbi Stephen Wise, and Sidney Silverman, a strong promoter of India's independence in the British Parliament. Silverman tried to explain to Gandhi that the terrorist methods were only used by a minority (Shimoni 1977: 58–9; Ward 1992: 13). Gandhi's meeting in 1946 with his biographer, the journalist Louis

Fischer, was a decisive step as Gandhi for the first time conceded that the Jews had a 'prior claim' to Palestine.[29] In a later article in *Harijan* in July 1946, Gandhi clarified his position: he now thought the Jews had been 'wronged by the world' but he also criticized their reliance on American and British help as well as on terrorist methods (Gandhi, *Collected Works* 84: 440–1). In an interview with Don Campbell of Reuters in May 1947, Gandhi again argued that the Jews had a 'proper case' that had been squandered by their resort to terrorist methods. However, Gandhi equally added he believed that the problem had become 'almost insoluble'. (Gandhi, *Collected Works* 87: 417)

These various statements demonstrate that Gandhi did not have a fixed opinion of the Palestine issue but instead a complex and evolving perception of the situation.[30] While he did not officially change his position, he stressed a new justification for his reservations regarding Zionism. Gandhi now referred to the violent methods used by the Jewish movement in Palestine, which, in his opinion, were in complete contradiction with his Satyagraha philosophy. Gandhi died a few months before the creation of Israel, and did not therefore have any direct impact on India's Israel policy. It is, however, interesting to note that Indian diplomats and academics have consistently quoted his 1938 statement on Palestine belonging to the Arabs to justify India's policy and overlooked his other statements on Zionism made in 1947.[31] This is why it is important to analyse how and why actors selectively cited Gandhi to support their own agendas, rather than to look at Gandhi's ideas as an immediate causal factor in the development of India's Israel policy after independence.

Assessing the Role Played by Nehru in Shaping India's Israel Policy

Nehru's position on Palestine in the inter-war period is critical to analyse for three reasons. First, contrary to Gandhi, Nehru had a central foreign policy-making role after independence as both prime minister and minister of external affairs. He had to deal with the creation of Israel and the question of recognition of the Jewish state after May 1948. Prime Minister Narasimha Rao (who normalized relations with Israel in 1992) said in 1991 that Nehru was 'responsible for forging the modern relationship between India and West Asia' after independence and 'laid the foundations' of India's extensive political and economic ties with the region.[32] Second, his position was not rigid and evolved over time. He first progressively defined his position on the Palestine issue during the nationalist struggle against Britain from 1927 to 1947. In the next chapter, I will show how circumstances such as the creation and survival of the Jewish state led him to rethink his policy. Nehru's sentiments towards some of the Zionist leaders were also mixed. While he opposed their conception of a national home based on religion, he shared ideological affinities and socialist leanings with some eminent Jewish leaders like Chaim Weizmann and David Ben-Gurion. Nehru notably commented in a letter in 1933 how the 'greatest socialists and communists' had been Jews.[33] Third, the 'Nehruvian' framework of foreign policy has regularly been invoked as an explanation for the absence of relations with Israel until 1992. Some Indian political leaders criticized the normalization of relations after 1992 as a 'betrayal' of India's Nehruvian foreign policy.[34] It is therefore crucial to examine how Nehru's stance on Palestine was fashioned.

Nehru only started expressing himself on the Palestine issue in 1933 in a letter he sent from prison to his daughter Indira. Like Gandhi, he shared sympathy with the plight of the Jews in Europe, and he seemed impressed by Jewish accomplishments in science, finance, business and politics (Nehru 2004 [1934]: 886). Nehru later acknowledged in 1938 that Jewish immigrants had helped improve Palestine by introducing new industries and by raising standards of living (Nehru 2004 [1934]: 891). However, again like Gandhi, Nehru opposed the concept of a Jewish national home. He moved away from Gandhi's initial religious understanding of the issue in the specific context of the Khilafat movement. In fact, he argued against the Pan-Islamic nature of the Khilafat which had little to do with Indian nationalism (Nehru 2004 [1934]: 832–3). Nehru felt a greater sympathy with what he described as Ataturk (Kemal)'s 'pure' Turkish nationalism in opposition to a 'looser international ideal of Islam' (Nehru 2004 [1934]: 821). In 1938, he rejected any claims of the Palestine issue being a religious one (Nehru 2004 [1934]: 886).

When commenting on the Balfour Declaration in 1933, Nehru criticized the British of having made contradictory promises to the Arabs and the Jews. He especially condemned Britain's betrayal of Arab interests after soliciting their support during World War I. Palestine for him was not to take because it was not a 'wilderness, or an empty, uninhabited place' but it was 'already somebody else's home'. Nehru deplored Zionist efforts to establish a Jewish state in the territory of Palestine, especially given their collaboration with the British to achieve this objective (Nehru

2004 [1934]: 885–7). In a letter to the editor of the newspaper *The Jewish Advocate* in 1937, he argued that Palestine was a predominantly Arab country but also judged that Jews were also an integral part of Palestine. Consequently, Jewish religious rights would have to be respected in an independent Palestine (Jawaharlal Nehru in Gopal [1972], Series I, 8: 714). Nehru promoted the creation of one united Palestine just as he defended the notion of one secular and undivided India.

According to Nehru, the problem of Palestine was primarily an Arab nationalist struggle against British imperial control. By contrast, the Jewish issue was a minority problem that had mainly been fostered by British policies. Nehru highlighted the growing socio-economic differences between the Arab residents and the immigrant Jews which increased tensions between the two communities. For Nehru, Palestine was unable to absorb new immigrants. As a consequence, the Jewish issue was a minority problem encouraged by Britain's elastic immigration laws. In addition, comparable to the divide-and-rule tactics used in South Asia to create a rift between Hindus and Muslims, the British also pitted 'Jewish religious nationalism against Arab nationalism' (Nehru 2004 [1934]: 885–6). These tactics made Britain's moderating presence seem indispensable to preserve the peace both in the subcontinent and in Palestine. Like Gandhi, he admitted Jews had a right to look at Jerusalem as their Holy Land, and that they should have free access to it. However, these were religious rights which did not give them any legitimate base for the creation of a Jewish state (Prasad 1960: 129–30; Ward 1992: 8).

Expressing himself again on the Palestine issue in 1938, Nehru criticized the partition solution, suggested by the Peel Commission report (Smith 2010: 138–40). Nehru said that Arabs should not be 'crushed and suppressed' in what he considered to be their 'homeland' (Nehru 2004 [1934]: 890–1). Nehru sympathized with the Jews in their 'trials' in western Europe at the time, notably the pogroms and their ghettoization in Europe (Nehru 2004 [1934]: 886, 890–1). Just like Gandhi, he was affected by the growing persecution of Jews in Germany that he witnessed first-hand while travelling in central Europe in 1938. Following this visit, Nehru advocated for India to become an asylum for European Jewish refugees in the late 1930s.[35] He was instrumental in facilitating the entry of Jewish refugees in India in the late 1930s despite the opposition from the British Government of India and from elements of the INC.[36] Nehru also encouraged both communities to cooperate against the British 'imperial scheme' of divide-and-rule and to build a large 'Arab federation with a Jewish autonomous enclave' (Nehru 2004 [1934]: 891). Addressing the Peace and Empire Conference in London in July 1938, he again held the British Empire as responsible for the divisions. Nehru, however, conceded that the nationalist struggle would not be an easy task given the geostrategic importance of Palestine, 'being on the sea and air route to India and the East' (Nehru 1942: 274). Nehru therefore associated the trajectories of both independence movements within the larger British imperial structure. Hence, Zionist collaboration with the British seemed like a major variable inhibiting any support from Nehru's side.

Like Gandhi, Nehru was approached by Zionist emissaries who were looking for his understanding and/or support on the creation of a Jewish state. Nehru was admired among Zionist political leaders for being a progressive and modern leader (Brecher 1963: 129). His autobiography, translated in Hebrew in 1936, was widely read by Jews in Palestine (Brecher 1976: 222; Jansen 1971: xi). Nehru also shared some socialist ideals with many of the Zionist leaders. The first approach was during the Brussels International Congress against Colonial Oppression and Imperialism in 1927. However, it did not lead to any observable change in Nehru's thinking about Zionism.[37] Nehru then met Olsvanger, a Zionist representative, twice in 1936. While Olsvanger failed to modify Nehru's position, he managed to forge personal ties and prolonged their dialogue through a correspondence (Shimoni 1977: 30). Chaim Weizmann also tried to convince Nehru of the legitimacy of the Zionist cause in a meeting in London organized by the WZO in July 1938. The two nationalist leaders kept a correspondence after the meeting (Weizmann 1983, 18: 206, 18: 458–9). However, Nehru's position did not evolve despite these repeated interactions.[38]

Nehru was a key player in the emergence of India's Israel policy as he was the president of the INC when it passed multiple resolutions on the Palestine issue in the late 1930s. Through his writings, it is possible to delineate a position which was supportive of Arab nationalism but not hostile to Jewish religious interests in Palestine. Nehru was conscious of the oppression of Jews in Europe and of the subsequent refugee problem. Nehru even offered to welcome many of these refugees to India. He also suggested a federal arrangement which would guarantee Jewish religious rights in Palestine. However, because of domestic considerations and his principled convictions on secularism and state-making, he could not support the Zionist project in Palestine. Furthermore, Nehru consistently condemned collaboration between the Jews and the British occupation forces. It is therefore useful to evaluate Nehru's position in light of the evolution of the national struggle for independence.

The INC's First Major Foreign Policy Initiative: Riding the Khilafat Wave

Despite originally being loyalist and content to follow the lead of the British government on most matters, the INC progressively began to develop its own position on foreign affairs.[39] At first, the INC only opposed British interventions in West Asia because these operations involved Indian resources and led to increased taxation on British India (Prasad 1960: 38–9). The INC then gradually started denouncing London's colonial expansion in the region as imperialism (Prasad 1960: 49). The Muslim factor entered the INC's calculations only when Indian Muslims became disturbed by the British policy towards Turkey and Persia. Although Islam evolved very differently in both regions, with entirely independent Muslim kingdoms emerging in the subcontinent, there was a visible Pan-Islamic revival among middle-class Indian Muslims by the end of the nineteenth century (Landau 1990). The rise of Pan-Islamic sympathies was illustrated by the growing influence of political activist and Islamic ideologist Jamal al-din al-Afghani.[40] Al-Afghani argued that the collapse of Islam could be averted by reuniting all Muslim countries under one political structure and by launching an intellectual renaissance of Islam (Agwani 1963c; Aziz 1967: 123–6; Keddie 1968: 47–51; Niemeijer 1972: 36). Having studied in British India and then moved to West Asia, he argued that European imperialism that had conquered South Asia was threatening West Asia by the end of the nineteenth century (Niemeijer 1972: 36).

Sultan-Caliph Abdul Hamid II was interested in exploiting this rising Pan-Islamic ideology to salvage his own rule from external attacks from European powers and from internal pressures coming from a growing secular-nationalist movement. He notably invited Al-Afghani to Constantinople in 1892 in order to use his influence in South Asia to rehabilitate the Caliphate to its past international stature (Ahmad 1973; Mishra 2012: 94–5, 111–2). Interestingly, this call for Islamic solidarity found an important echo among Indian Muslims.[41] During the Greco-

Turkish war of 1897, a conflict in which the British supported Greece, Indian Muslims rejoiced when the Turks won a victory in Crete (Ahmad 1973). At the time, the INC did not pay particular attention to foreign affairs and did not comment on these distant events. Indian Muslims were also particularly suspicious of the Young Turks' secularizing agenda and wanted guarantees that the Caliphate institution would remain unscathed by the revolution of 1908–9 (Oliver-Dee 2009). During the Balkan wars the Ottoman Empire (pitted against other super powers) was supported by Indian Muslim journals like *The Comrade*, edited by Mohammad Ali, who was a rising prominent Indian Muslim leader in the early twentieth century (Prasad 1960: 51). Ali also opened a relief fund for Turkish victims of the wars (Niemeijer 1972: 56). Since Britain was not directly involved in the Balkan wars, the INC did not take an official position on the matter. It did, however, express sympathy with Turkey in its 1912 session as a gesture towards its Indian Muslim constituents. At the next session in 1913, the INC again made reference to the Ottoman Empire's problems and to the concerns of Indian Muslims (Prasad 1960: 51–2).

Since the 1857 mutiny, the British had considered that Indian Muslims represented a key internal threat to imperial security. In response to this rising internal problem, the British chose a policy of accommodating Indian Muslims, notably by giving them separate electorates through the Minto–Morley reforms of 1906–9 (James 2000: 3–79). However, the outbreak of World War I accelerated Muslim mobilization in India against the British. This was actually encouraged both by the Sultan, who had called for a religious 'jihad' to support the Caliphate, and by the British themselves, who attempted to exploit the rising Pan-Islamic sentiment to their own advantages against the Ottoman Empire. World War I amplified the discrepancies between the different West Asian policies followed by the Foreign Office, the Government of India, the Arab Bureau in Cairo, and the Colonial Office. This resulted in a policy of conflicting objectives and mixed signals to Indian Muslims. In its effort to defeat the Ottoman Empire, the British Foreign Office offered in October 1914 to support an Arab Caliphate without consulting the India Office and the Government of India. Both strongly complained about the implications of this new policy for Indian Muslims who perceived the Sultan to represent the Caliphate institution.[42] After being alerted of the strong Indian Muslim feelings on the issue, the British Foreign Office adopted a more cautious position on the Caliphate question.[43] The INC again did not take a position on this issue as it supported Britain during the conflict, notably by backing the dispatch of Indian troops on the Western Front and to fight against the Ottoman Empire in West Asia.[44] The major preoccupation of the British (or to the least of the India Office and Government of India) through the rest of the conflict was the opinion of the Indian Muslims, especially as the peace treaties were being negotiated and as the new nationalist government in Turkey moved towards abolishing the Caliphate.

The dismemberment of the Turkish Empire, required by the Treaty of Sevres, troubled Indian Muslims who were concerned with the fate of the Caliphate. Article 139 of the treaty stipulated that Turkey would formally renounce any rights of sovereignty over Muslims (Oliver-Dee 2009: 93). Indian Muslims' grievances took the organizational form of the Khilafat movement which was created to protect and preserve the Caliphate.[45] The movement had three important spokesmen. The first one was Mohammad Ali, an Aligarh- and Oxford-educated Muslim activist who was a founding member of the All-India Muslim League. His brother Shaukat Ali also became an important leader of the Khilafat movement. The other key leader was Maulana Abul Kalam Azad who was the Khilafat movement's principal theoretician.[46] Azad built on al-Afghani's idea that the Caliphate was a cohesive force which united the Islamic society against the British, and that the Caliph was a necessary instrument through which solidarity could be maintained among Muslims.[47] Finally, British rejection of Indian Muslim demands to maintain the Caliphate resulted in the Khilafat conference of November 1919 which united the Ali brothers and Azad to form the Khilafat committee which directed Muslims all over India to protest and boycott the government (Ahmad 1973; Oliver-Dee 2009: 112–3; Prasad 1960: 58).

Given the rising Pan-Islamic anxieties about the fate of the Jazirat al-Arab, the INC under Gandhi saw a new opportunity to reach out to the Indian Muslim population and to broaden the appeal of his first 'all India' agitation.[48] In order to further mobilize against the British, the INC decided to widen its demands by incorporating grievances expressed by the nascent Khilafat movement. Indian Muslims had mostly abstained from participating in the INC and from joining INC actions against the British because of their concerns that they would be a threatened minority within an autonomous or independent India with a clear Hindu majority (Hasan 1994; Niemeijer 1972: 50). By the end of 1919, Gandhi and the INC had expressed disappointment over the Montagu–Chelmsford reforms that did not go far enough to guarantee Indian autonomy.[49] The economic stresses of World War I and of the Rowlatt Act added to the INC's frustrations.[50]

Gandhi, who had assumed a leadership position within the INC, saw Muslim indignation over the treatment of the Caliphate issue as an opportunity to demonstrate the INC's solidarity with their struggle. He sought an alliance with the Ali brothers as a way to gather support for the INC's bid for Home Rule (Azad 1989 [1959]: 9–11; Hasan 1994: 112–17). Speaking very candidly about his political intentions, Gandhi admitted his intention to 'buy' the Indian Muslims' friendship at a 'critical moment of their history' (Gandhi, Young India, 23 March 1921, in Collected Works 19: 530). Hindu–Muslim unity on this issue could strengthen Gandhi's movement and legitimize him as a leader both within the INC leadership structure and in the popular opinion. Gandhi believed that a mass movement following both the Jallianwala Bagh massacre and the dismemberment of the Turkish Empire could affect the British government. Despite the explicitly religious nature of the Khilafat movement, Gandhi and the INC marked their solidarity with their demands. The political imperative of the nationalist struggle therefore shaped Gandhi and the INC's first reaction to the West Asian region.

In March 1920, a Khilafat delegation, led by Mohamnmad Ali, met with British Prime Minister Lloyd George in London to express their fears about the dismemberment of the Turkish Caliphate and the fate of the Turkish Sultan (Oliver-Dee 2009: 109–17). Ali argued that the dismembered state of the Ottoman Empire had complicated the possibility for the Caliph to perform his traditional functions (Niemeijer 1972: 44–5; Oliver-Dee 2009: 111–12). Additionally, Ali suggested a constitutional reform in Turkey to guarantee the 'security of life and property and opportunities of autonomous development of all communities, whether Moslem, Christian, or Jewish...'.[51] Two months after this meeting, Muslims in India learned about the terms of the Treaty of Sevres and were upset to see that none of their concerns had been taken into account by the British (Hasan 1994: 132–3). In reaction, Gandhi cooperated with the Ali brothers to organize the All-Indian Caliphate Committee in August 1920 in Bombay. Under the leadership of Gandhi, the Khilafat committee adopted a programme of non-cooperation, without even asking for the INC's approval. Gandhi himself gave up his titles and decorations he had received from the British government because of the 'wrong done' to the religious sentiments of his 'Muslim countrymen' (Hasan 1994:).

The INC followed suit and officially called for a settlement of the Caliphate issue in accordance with the sentiments of Indian Muslims and on the bases of the promises made by Britain.[52] In a special session in Calcutta in September 1920, the INC also adopted a non-cooperation plan which called for the renunciation of titles and honorary offices and the boycott of functions held by government officials (Zaidi and Zaidi, *Encyclopedia of the INC*, 11: 400). The Congress Working Committee (CWC) also asked Indian soldiers present in West Asia to stop cooperating with the British army in the occupation of Mesopotamia (Prasad 1960: 70–1). The non-cooperation movement lasted throughout the rest of 1921. Officially, the new mobilization had two objectives: the traditional goal of the INC which was to obtain self-government, and a new objective which was the restoration of the Turkish Caliphate. Both movements framed their ambitions in a way that they could effectively find common ground and cooperate. However, in all practical sense, both movements only agreed on their opposition to the British Empire.

This specific context of coalition-building led Gandhi and the INC to originally frame their position on Palestine and the Balfour Declaration through an anti-British and Islamic lens.[53] It is also important to note that both the India Office and the Government of India, preoccupied by the Indian Muslim agitation, also opposed the British Foreign Office and supported restoration of the Sultan's suzerainty over the holy places of Islam.[54] Their input seemed to have had an initial impact as the British Cabinet Committee on Palestine kept vacillating, as far as its policy on Palestine was concerned, by stating that 'We have, in fact, to choose between the possibility of localized trouble with the Jews in Palestine and the virtual certainty of widespread disturbances among the Arabs throughout the Middle East and possibly among the Muslims in India... the latter represents a military commitment twice or three times as great as does the former.'[55] The British were concerned that the Muslim community in India would reject their policy on Palestine, and that this would have implications for British security in India.

In November 1921, the All India Congress Committee (AICC) officially declared its independence from British foreign policy and started developing an autonomous position. The INC strongly criticized the British participation in the mandate system which Gandhi described as 'sinful imperialism' (Prasad 1960: 76). Following the lead of Mohammad Ali, the INC formally demanded in 1921 and 1922 that effective guardianship of Islam and Jazirat-al-arab, the holy places of Islam, be freed from non-Muslim control.[56] This statement also targeted Jewish immigration to Palestine (Prasad 1960: 76). According to Gandhi in 1921, Jews could freely go to Palestine and 'even reside there and own properties' but could not acquire sovereign-jurisdiction over these lands (Gandhi, *Collected Works*, 19: 530). In November 1923, Palestinian Arab delegations were also welcomed in India to collect funds to restore the Al Aqsa mosque in Jerusalem (Chawla 1981: 47). In 1923, Mohammad Ali, who had now become the INC president, urged Indians to make common cause with the struggle of the Palestinians.[57] As a result, the INC now formally opposed the Balfour Declaration and the concept of a national home of the Jews in Palestine.

However, the Khilafat mobilization began to wane in 1922 and ended in 1923. In February 1922, with many of the movement's leaders in prison, Gandhi decided to call off the non-cooperation because of the violence that accompanied the movement. Following the communal rioting in Kohat in December 1923, Gandhi and the Ali brothers definitely decided to suspend their cooperation (Ward 1992: 4). The Congress party modified its official position and only asked—for what would be its last resolution on the Khilafat issue in the Amritsar session of 1924—for the 'removal of alien control from the Jazirat al-Arab'.[58] The decision in March 1924 by the nationalist leader Mustafa Kemal, who became the first president of Turkey, to abolish the Caliphate, gave the final blow to the Khilafat movement in India.

The tactical alliance between the INC and the Khilafat against the British proved short-lived. While the India Office and the Government of India had taken Indian concerns into account and had pressured London to accommodate their demands, efforts to influence British policies in West Asia proved ultimately ineffective.[59] In the end, the British dismantled the Ottoman Empire and took control of Palestine and Iraq through the mandate system in 1922. Finally, the aims of the Khilafat movement proved to be at odds with the ground realities as Arab and Turkish nationalists in West Asia moved away from the conception of an Islamic political system. Kemal, for instance, repudiated Pan-Islamism as a basis to establish a new Turkish republic and abolished the Caliphate.

The Khilafat movement was decisive in the sense that it shaped the INC's first official statement on the Arab–Jewish dispute in Palestine. The need to garner support against the British helps explains the initial Islamic perspective taken by the INC. Following 1924, both the INC and Muslim leaders adapted their positions in accordance with an evolving geopolitical landscape in West Asia. The INC framed its West Asia policy in more secular-nationalist terms and engaged Arab nationalist movements in the region. In parallel, Muslim leaders from the defunct Khilafat movement moved away from discussing Pan-Islamic themes to promoting a more restricted South Asia-centered Muslim nationalism.

The INC's Perception of the Palestine Issue as a Secular-Nationalist Struggle

Following 1924, the INC began to think about its relations with other countries and especially with other independence movements across the world. As early as 1923, Maulana Azad, who was president of the INC at the time, suggested that India make common cause with the struggle of Arabs in Egypt, Syria, and Palestine.[60] The reference to the guardianship of Jazirat-al-arab was dropped from INC resolutions and the INC only referred to the successful settlement of Turkey's war for independence after 1924 (Rajkumar 1952: 45). Further moving away from the Caliphate issue, the AICC adopted in December 1924 a resolution on the Egyptian crisis (Nehru 2004 [1934]: 863–70; Zaidi and Zaidi, *Encyclopedia of the INC*, 8: 681). The INC was gradually developing a foreign policy based on the suppression of political and economic imperialism and the cooperation of free nations (Prasad 1960: 278). There was a realization among Indian nationalists that as long as India was subjugated politically, West Asian nations would also stay under British control. The fate of these anti-colonialist movements was then intertwined and it created a sense of fellowship and of shared purpose in the two regions (Agwani 1966). There was also an assumption among leaders of the INC that India could take a leadership position in this nascent freedom struggle (Prasad 1960: 278). The INC was indeed the oldest and most organized of all the existing nationalist movements, and could serve as an organizational and ideological model. In spite of this aspiration for closer cooperation, there were only limited exchanges and institutionalized contacts (Prasad 1960:

Appendix, 'Jawaharlal Nehru, "Report on the International Congress against Imperialism"').

The INC only started acting on these preliminary linkages when Jawaharlal Nehru took a central position in the party architecture. Nehru had stayed for over a year and a half in Europe in 1926–7 and had represented the INC at the International Congress against Colonial Oppression and Imperialism held at Brussels in February 1927.[61] Nehru played an important role in the deliberations of the conference and was elected member of the Presidium. He met with many Arab nationalists during the conference, and especially with Palestinian leaders Kader al-Husseini and Djomal Effendi (Syed 1964: 18). At his return in 1927, Nehru played a key role in establishing institutional links with other movements by creating the foreign department of the INC. Nehru worked to publicize and promote the INC's message on leading issues in Asian and world affairs. He especially encouraged sending delegations to various international forums where anti-imperialist movements met to foster direct contacts and coordination. These initiatives established a dialogue between an entire generation of Indian and Arab nationalists which thrived despite travel restrictions imposed by the British for many of the movement leaders (Prasad 1960: 84; Heptullah 1991: 3). 'Fraternal' Arab delegations from Egypt, Syria, and Palestine were invited to attend INC sessions (Kumar 1982; Prasad 1960: 8–9; Ward 1992: 9–10). Nehru established personal relations with important Arab leaders such as Mustafa Nahhas Pasha from the Wafd party in Egypt, the Syrian nationalist Faris al-Khoury, and Kamil al-Chadirchi of the Iraqi Istiqlal (Independence) party (Prasad 1985, 3: 814–5). In its official discourse, the INC now identified itself with Asian nationalism and especially with Arab nationalist movements in West Asia (Zaidi and Zaidi, *Encyclopedia of the INC*, 11: 478; Nehru 1958: 284–6; Agwani 1973a; Prasad 1979).

As a result, in the late 1920s, the INC began to publicly voice its support for Arab nationalism. At its 1927 session in Madras, the INC demanded the withdrawal of Indian troops from Mesopotamia and Persia (Prasad 1960: 82). In January 1928, the INC expressed its sympathy and support to the 'people of Egypt, Syria, Palestine and Iraq' in their 'struggle for emancipation from the grip of Western Imperialism' (Zaidi and Zaidi, *Encyclopedia of the INC*, 9: 538). This was the first time the INC passed a resolution in favour of Palestinian Arabs. But this statement was mostly condemning the British occupation of Palestine and did not make any direct reference to the Zionist efforts to establish a Jewish national home. As president of the INC, Nehru further compared India's nationalist struggle to other similar movements in West Asia like in Egypt, Turkey, or Persia. He argued that India was part of a 'world movement' and that it had to collaborate with other movements.[62] He, however, did not refer to the specific Palestine issue.

Nehru started expressing himself on the Palestine question in the 1930s. As mentioned previously, Nehru perceived the Palestine issue as an Arab nationalist struggle against British colonial control. Within this dyadic opposition, he considered that the British had pitted the Jewish minority against the Palestine national movement (Nehru 2004 [1934]: 885). The INC followed this line as Nehru became president and looked at the Palestine issue as a struggle between the nationalist Arabs and British imperial control. This position was officially articulated in a series of resolutions voted by Congress in the second half of the 1930s. At the meeting at Wardha in June–July 1936, the Congress Working Committee (CWC) sent its 'greetings to the Arabs of Palestine in their struggle for Independence against British Imperialism'.[63] The committee also emphasized the need for Arabs and Jews to directly collaborate to establish a democratic state in Palestine (Zaidi and Zaidi, *Encyclopedia of the INC*, 11: 153, 487). The Congress then observed 27 September 1936 as Palestine Day by holding meetings and demonstrations across the subcontinent in solidarity with the Palestinian Arabs in their revolt against the British (Prasad 1960: 131). On this occasion, Nehru referred to Zionism as an artificial phenomenon created by the British.[64] He equally linked the situation in Palestine to India by saying: 'We are trying at present to explain to the Muslims here that the fight in Palestine is not between Jews and Arabs but between both and British imperialism and they should not protest against the Jews but against the British Government who hinders the development of peaceful resolution' (Shimoni 1977: 30). The AICC meeting in October 1937 passed another resolution which protested against the British 'reign of terror' in Palestine and assured the Arabs of the 'solidarity of the Indian people in their struggle for national freedom' (Zaidi and Zaidi, *Encyclopedia of the INC*, 11: 260).

At the Haripura session of February 1938, the INC condemned the plan for partition of Palestine which had been recommended by the report of the Peel Commission in July 1937. The INC again expressed its full sympathy with the Arabs in their struggle for national freedom against British imperialism. In addition to this traditional support, the INC suggested an 'amicable settlement' between Arabs and Jews which was perceived as the 'proper method of solving the problem' (Zaidi and Zaidi, *Encyclopedia of the INC*, 11: 427). They appealed to the Jews not to seek the protection of the British mandatory administration, and not to be used as an instrument in the continuation of British imperialism in Palestine. The new president of the INC, Subhas Chandra Bose, pursued Nehru's argument that the British had made contradictory promises to the Jews and the Arabs in Palestine, and notably to the latter in an effort to reassure Muslims in India (Zaidi and Zaidi, *Encyclopedia of the INC*, 11: 400). A mass meeting held in Calcutta on 26 August condemned the Peel Commission report and articulated an alternative solution: a termination of the British mandate with an independent Palestinian state with adequate safeguards for the Jewish minority. An all-India Palestine Day was again observed to support the Palestinian Arabs against British occupation (Gopal and Sharma 2007: 105). At the following meeting of the AICC in Delhi in September 1938, the INC again condemned the partition policy (Zaidi and Zaidi, *Encyclopedia of the INC*, 11: 445–6).

There was a slight policy change in December 1938 when the CWC met in Wardha and started openly talking about 'self-determination' for Palestine (Zaidi and Zaidi, *Encyclopedia of the INC*, 11: 497). The persecution of Jews in Germany led Nehru to discuss again the Jewish question at length. Nehru openly sympathized with the situation of the Jewish minorities in Europe in the 1930s However, he still thought Palestine to essentially be an Arab homeland (Nehru 2004 [1934]: 890–1). As discussed previously, Nehru encouraged both Jews and Arabs to jointly oppose British occupation in order to build a broad 'Arab federation with a Jewish autonomous enclave' (Nehru 2004 [1934]: 891). Building on this interpretation of the Palestine issue, the CWC sympathized with the plight of the Jews in Europe but also criticized their overreliance on British political and military support to obtain concessions in Palestine. Building on the earlier Haripura resolution, the CWC argued that only Arab–Jewish cooperation could lead to a free Palestine with 'adequate protection of Jewish rights' (Zaidi and Zaidi, *Encyclopedia of the INC*, 11: 497). In March 1939, at the Tripuri session, Congress passed another resolution expressing support for Palestinian Arabs in their struggle and demanding full independence for Palestine with the protection of Jewish religious rights (Zaidi and Zaidi, *Encyclopedia of the INC*, 12: 159–60).

This was to be the last important INC resolution to be voted on the Palestine question before World War II. The INC sympathized with the Arab nationalists but was also conscious of the Jewish grievances and the need accommodate them in a type of federal framework. As a result, this became the INC's official position after independence when the question of Palestine was discussed at the United Nations in 1947.

Conflicting Nationalisms: Opposing Goals, Distinct Strategies of the INC and Zionist Movements

While the INC under Nehru developed relations with Arab nationalist movements in West Asia and especially in Palestine, it only had limited contacts with the Zionist movement and the Jewish Agency for Palestine.[65] Nehru played a key role in promoting solidarity and cooperation between the INC and other movements in West Asia but never considered the Zionist movement as a genuine national liberation movement. When expressing solidarity with different movements fighting Western imperialism, the INC never quoted any Jewish organization. This happened in spite of the efforts by some eminent Zionist leaders like David Ben Gurion who directly supported the Indian national movement.[66] The absence of relations with the Zionist movement can be explained by five factors.

First, Nehru and the INC promoted a secular type of nationalism after 1922 and did not adhere to the religious rationale of the Zionist movement (Nehru 2004 [1934]: 886). Influenced by the events in the subcontinent and by its own debate with the Muslim League, the INC argued that the Jews in Palestine were a religious minority and did not have legitimate grounds to create their homeland in Palestine, essentially populated by Arab Muslims. The only solution was a pluralistic state or a federation with constitutional guarantees for the Jewish minority.[67] Second, as discussed earlier, the INC strongly condemned, through different resolutions, the Zionist movement's reliance on British support. Nehru regretted that the Jewish national movement had preferred to 'take sides with the foreign ruling power', while Gandhi lamented that the Jews of Palestine had not discarded the 'help of the British Bayonet' (Nehru 2004 [1934]: 888; Gandhi, *Harijan*, 26 November 1938, in *Collected Works*, 68: 137). Third, the influx of Europe-based Jews into Palestine strengthened the image of the Jew as an alien on Asian soil in the Indian nationalist mind.[68] Because of the mainly European and North American origins of this recent immigration to Palestine (mostly from Britain, Eastern Europe, and the US), Indian intellectuals identified Zionism with its countries of origin (Glucklich 1988). The fact that the Zionist movement drew most of its support from European and US sources did not engender Indian sympathy and the INC leaders viewed Zionism as a movement that was directly under the protection of British power. The Zionist movement saw no immediate profit in offending Great Britain by publicly aligning its cause with that of the INC. The major priorities for the Zionist movement were arms procurement, fund raising, and facilitating Jewish immigration in Palestine. The INC was not in a position to support these pressing objectives. Fourth, INC leaders like Gandhi had issues with the violent methods used by some of the Jewish nationalists. Gandhi, for instance, strongly criticized the Jewish resort to terrorism.[69] Finally, the Zionist movement was also to blame for not actively trying to establish links with the INC during the inter-war period. The Zionist movement voluntarily avoided identifying itself with other nationalist movements in Asia (Brecher 1976). It made a tactical choice to concentrate its diplomatic attention on British and American material and political support. The absence of a politically and economically influential Jewish population in India (and by contrast the presence of an important Muslim community) led the Jewish nationalist movement to initially neglect the INC as a major diplomatic partner.

Nevertheless, in the late 1930s, there were sporadic attempts by the Jewish community to get support from Gandhi and Nehru for the Zionist cause. Reportedly, some early contacts were established in the late 1920s and early 1930s between Indian representatives and Zionist members but these limited interactions did not have any long-term consequences on the INC's approach.[70] The Jewish Agency decided only in the 1930s to send emissaries to develop contacts with Indian nationalist leaders.[71] However, it was not until the Arab riots in Palestine in 1936, following which some prominent Indian leaders, including Nehru and Gandhi, started openly speaking out in favour of the Arabs, that Moshe Sharett and the Jewish Agency decided to send a high-level emissary, Olvsanger, to India. During his trip, in 1936 Olsvanger met with many Indian political personalities from the INC other than Gandhi and Nehru, such as Sarojni Naidu, Vallabhai Patel, G. B. Pant, and from other political organizations, like B. R. Ambedkar.[72] Olsvanger failed to reverse the pro-Arab position of the INC.[73]

Eliyahu Epstein, the head of the Arab desk in the political department in the Jewish Agency, recommended to launch an information campaign in India and to develop contacts with Indian leaders. As discussed previously, Kallenbach was also sent by the Jewish Agency to meet with Gandhi. Joseph Nedivi, the representative of the Jewish Agency in Palestine, met with Nehru, on 20 March 1939, but failed to change Nehru's pro-Arab position. Nedivi also met Patel, chairperson of the Parliamentary Sub-Committee of the INC and Gandhi's trusted associate, G. D. Birla, one of the biggest industrialists and supporters of the INC (Shimoni 1977: 28, 49–50). The Jewish Agency was more successful in its efforts to establish trade links with some of the princely states.[74] Preliminary trade links between the Jewish Agency and the Diwan of Cochin were, for instance, discussed. The princely state of Bikaner also contacted the Jewish Agency to obtain technical assistance in dry farming (Kumaraswamy 2010: 64). K. M Panikkar, who represented the interests of various princely states in the 1930s, as secretary to the chancellor of the Chamber of Princes,[75] was instrumental in establishing these early diplomatic connections with the Jewish Agency.[76]

However, efforts to convince Indian nationalists of the validity of their cause came too late, after the INC's position had been definitively shaped. This assessment was notably made by Olsvanger two years after his India visit, as he argued that Nehru should have been engaged at an earlier time when his thinking on the Palestine issue was still in formation. A year later, Olvsanger encouraged more diplomatic efforts to engage not only Congress but also Indian Muslims and the Bene Israel community.[77] Another problem was that the Jewish Agency ultimately failed to send high-level Zionist personalities to meet with INC leaders. This situation contrasted with the close relations that existed between Arab nationalist leaders and Indian leaders. The only notable exceptions were a meeting in London in 1938 between Nehru and Chaim Weizmann, and the correspondence during World War II between Ben-Gurion and Gandhi.[78] However, neither Weizmann nor Ben-Gurion managed to modify Nehru and Gandhi's positions.[79] The absence of substantial contacts prior to 1947 was highlighted in a memorandum written by the Israeli diplomat Walter Eytan in 1948, who criticized the fact that the Jewish National Fund had largely neglected India before World War II.[80] Beyond the lack of contacts between the two movements, the INC also had to take domestic politics into account in the late 1930s, and most especially it had to deal with the rise of the Muslim League.

The Congress/Muslim League Rivalry and the Palestine Question

There is an interesting comparison to be made between the political situations in South Asia and Palestine in the inter-war period. Both colonies were part of the British Empire and witnessed the rise of anti-colonial movements fighting for independence.[81] In both contexts, the independence movement was divided. In Palestine, Arab and Jewish nationalists had competing goals and failed to cooperate towards a united Palestine. In South Asia, after a short period of cooperation during the Khilafat movement, the INC and the Muslim League parted ways. While the INC had the ambition to represent a united nationalist movement and promoted a secular sovereign India, the Muslim League defined itself as the more exclusive spokesman of the Muslim interests in the subcontinent. Progressively, the Muslim League argued that the defence of Muslim rights could only be guaranteed through the formation of a separate nation. The domestic rivalry between the two movements was also visible on the Palestine issue. While the INC tried to keep an approach that was pro-Arab but not hostile to the Jews, the Muslim League was explicitly pro-Arab and pro-Islamic. Their position on Palestine was less an ideological position than a propaganda strategy in their competition with the INC for the adhesion of Indian Muslims.[82] Taking a strong position in support of the Muslims in Palestine was considered as an important rallying point for Indian Muslims at home. Past scholarship has neglected to look at how the INC's position on Palestine was indirectly influenced by the Muslim League's view. In its domestic competition for broad national support with the Muslim League, the INC felt it had to reassure Indian Muslims and was pressured to take a clear position on the Palestine issue at times when it would have preferred to stay cautiously silent or noncommittal.

Very early, the Muslim League took an aggressive anti-Zionist position. It criticized the Balfour Declaration in December 1917 by condemning the occupation of the holy places by non-Muslims, including Christians and Jews (Pirzada 1970, 1: 442). It hardened its position in 1919 when the existence of the Caliphate was threatened, and warned that any dismemberment of the Ottoman Empire would lead to agitation and the boycott of the British Army by Indian Muslims (Pirzada 1970,1:

537). In 1921, as some of its members, like the Ali brothers, cooperated with the INC, the Muslim League demanded that Palestine be freed from all non-Muslim influence (Pirzada 1970, 1: 662). As the alliance between the Khilafat and Congress crumbled in the context of the communal riots of 1921–2, the Muslim League was weakened and divided (Hasan 1994: 191–3, 203–38). One of its eminent leaders, Mohammed Ali Jinnah moved back to London and a faction broke away from the movement. In addition, many other important Muslim personalities from the Khilafat movement like Maulana Azad joined the Congress. These organizational problems kept the Muslim League from making strong statements on the Palestine issue for some years.

In the late 1920s, Amin al-Hussayni, the Mufti of Jerusalem, began to directly court Indian Muslims to obtain their support against the British mandate and the Zionist efforts to create an independent state in Palestine. Mufti Hussayni wanted to frame the Palestinian issue as a larger Pan-Islamic struggle to enlist support from Muslims worldwide (Porath 1971). In this diplomatic effort, British India was an interesting prospect: it had the largest Muslim population and had previously expressed solidarity with Palestinian Muslims during the Khilafat movement. As a result, Hussayni developed contacts with the Ali brothers and a number of Indian Muslim rulers like the Nizam of Hyderabad who contributed an important donation to restore the Al Aqsa mosque (Chawla 1981). Following the death of Mohammed Ali in early 1931, Hussayni offered to Shaukat Ali to bury his deceased brother in Jerusalem. Following their meeting, Hussayni and Shaukat Ali decided to organize the Jerusalem Islamic Conference in 1931 (Kramer 1986: Chapter 11). The conference was mainly devoted to the preservation of Muslim holy places in Jerusalem. The Government of India allowed Shaukat Ali and Indian Muslim delegates to travel to Jerusalem and advised the India Office and the Colonial Office against banning the conference to avoid discontenting Indian Muslims (Kramer 1986: 125–6). The indirect impact of the Mufti's approach on British policies drew the attention of the Jewish Agency towards the subcontinent.

Zionist leaders had become aware at a very early stage of the decisive influence of Indian Muslims on British policy vis-à-vis Palestine. They established early contacts with representatives of India's Muslim population in order to obtain their support. In the late nineteenth century, Waldemar Haffkine, a Russian Jewish biologist, travelled to India where he collaborated with the Aga Khan to fight the bubonic plague of 1897. While in India, he asked the Aga Khan to help him convince Ottoman authorities to let Jews resettle in Jerusalem. The Aga Khan was originally sympathetic and met other eminent Zionists, including Baron Edmond de Rotschild, during a trip to Paris. However, he failed to persuade Sultan Abdul Hamid of a resettlement project in Palestine (The Aga Khan 1954: 150–1). In the 1930s, the WZO and the Jewish Agency made other concerted efforts to court Indian Muslims. Weizmann, for instance, met with Shaukat Ali in 1931.[83] During his trip to India, Olvsanger also met with Muslim leaders like Khan Abdul Ghaffar Khan, Muhammad Iqbal, and Maulana Azad (Gopal and Sharma 2007: 84; Kumaraswamy 2010: 63; Shimoni 1977: 31). In spite of these efforts to engage India's Muslim community, the Muslim League still opposed the creation of a Jewish national home.

The Muslim League decided to act on the renewed interest in Palestinian affairs among Indian Muslims in the 1930s. When Mufti Hussayni called for an international Palestine Day, the Muslim League decided to organize the first Palestine day on 16 May 1930 in India (Mattar 1992: 57). In November 1933, the Muslim League officially demanded the abrogation of the Balfour Declaration (Pirzada, 2: 225–6). There was further unrest among Indian Muslims following the Peel Commission report and the discussion of partition of Palestine. An All Palestine Conference was organized in September 1937 to convey India's solidarity with the Arabs in their struggle against British occupation. The president of the Conference, A. R. Siddiqi, urged Indian Muslims to unite with the rest of the Muslim world against the division of Palestine. He also warned the British that they would push 80 million Indian Muslims to a choice between loyalty to the Empire or to their faith. The Conference also suggested sending the Aga Khan to represent the sentiments of Indian Muslims before the Assembly of the League of Nations (Gopal and Sharma 2007: 102–3).

This attention of the Muslim League to events in Palestine coincided with the return of Muhammad Ali Jinnah as its undisputed leader in 1937. Jinnah realized how this Pan-Islamic concern could be used for domestic purposes. By taking a strong position in favour of Arab Muslims and for the protection of the holy places in Jerusalem, Jinnah wanted to project himself as a defender of Islamic interests internationally and at home. As a result, the Palestine question took centre stage at the All-India

Muslim League session in Lucknow in October 1937. In his presidential address, Jinnah expressed the support of Indian Muslims for the Arabs in their 'just struggle' carried 'against all odds' (Pirzada, 2: 272). He criticized the British for not respecting their original promises made to Palestinian Arabs during World War I and condemned the recommendations of the Peel Commission. Following these declarations, the Muslim League decided on a resolution condemning the British policies in Palestine and demanding that the holy places should not be placed 'under non-Muslim' control and freed from the 'enslavement of British imperialism backed by Jewish finance' (Pirzada 2: 277–8). The League recognized for the first time the legitimacy of the Supreme Muslim Council and of the Arab Higher Committee, two Palestinian organizations headed by Mufti Hussayni.[84] Finally, the League warned Britain that it would become an enemy of Islam if it persisted in its 'pro-Jewish policy in Palestine' (Pirzada, 2: 278).

The Muslim League adopted a similarly aggressive resolution in the December 1938 session in Patna and cautioned the British that its support for the 'Jewish usurpation' in Palestine could lead to a Pan-Islamic coalition against British interests (Pirzada 2: 315–16). Jinnah lauded the 'heroic fight' led by the Palestinian Arabs against the British and assured them of the support of Indian Muslims (Ahmad 1952: 72–3). After World War II started, most Congress leaders were incarcerated and the Muslim League became the only dissenting voice against the British on the Palestine question. During the Lahore session of 1940, the League again reminded the British of their earlier promises to Arab Muslims (Pirzada, 1970 2: 346). In November 1939, Jinnah addressed the British government requesting them to meet the 'national demands of the Arabs in Palestine' (Menon 1957: 70). The Viceroy in India gave a conciliatory reply on 23 December 1939, in which he stated that the British government was conscious of the 'importance of the position of the Muslim community in India' and that it would take their views into account (Menon 1957: 70). The Muslim League took a stronger anti-Zionist view at the Delhi session of 1943 by criticizing Jewish finance and the US pressure to create a Jewish state in Israel (Pirzada, 1970 2: 439–40). In its last session in Karachi before Partition, the League called for the end of all mandates in West Asia and the prompt establishment of a sovereign Palestine (Pirzada, 1970 2: 3489–90). Jinnah also sent a telegram to Prime Minister Attlee in November 1945 informing Britain 'that any surrender to appease Jewry at the sacrifice of Arab demands' would be resisted by Muslims in India (Bethell 1979: 220).

The Muslim League was a key player in the emergence of the INC Palestine policy in two ways. First, the Muslim League's vocal support for the Arab cause in Palestine indirectly pressured the INC into taking a strong pro-Arab position in Palestine. Both parties were competing in India for the allegiance of Muslims (who numbered approximately 95 million out of a total population of about 388 million before Partition) (Government of India, Census of India, 1941) and the INC needed to frame its statements in a way that would accommodate the Muslim minority's interests. The INC never made explicitly religious arguments (with the exception of the Khilafat period) nor did it make strong anti-Zionist statements like the Muslim League, but it exclusively supported Arab territorial demands in Palestine and refused to accept the possibility of a Jewish national home. Any other open-ended position accommodating Zionist demands would have been exploited and framed by the Muslim League as pro-Zionist and anti-Muslim. Gandhi explained, for instance, to both Shohet and Nedivi in 1939 that any statement in support of the Jewish objectives in Palestine would be exploited by the Muslim League (Shimoni 1977: 49–51). As a consequence of this competition for the allegiance of Indian Muslims, the INC itself decided to organize various Palestine Day demonstrations. It also led Nehru and Congress to express solidarity with a religious figure, Mufti Hussayni, in his 'struggle for Palestine independence' in 1937 (Sarvepalli Gopal, ed., *Selected Works of Jawaharlal Nehru*, Series I, Vol. 8: 723). The Muslim League indirectly pushed the issue of Palestine to the forefront of the INC's annual sessions and resolutions, and induced the INC into taking a strong and unambiguous stand on the issue. By contrast, the INC was more elusive on other foreign policy issues.

Second, the Muslim League also indirectly shaped the INC's position vis-à-vis Zionism because both these religious nationalist movements were ideologically at odds with the INC's own state-making project.[85] The INC opposed the Muslim League's argument that South Asian Muslims were a distinct nation and also the two-nation theory which led to the eventual partition of the subcontinent.[86] By resisting partition in Palestine and a separate independent Jewish state, the INC was indirectly challenging partition as a political option on the Indian subcontinent. When framing its own secular nationalist project in contradiction with the more narrow and exclusive religious nationalist project promoted by the Muslim League, Congress was also indirectly arguing against the Zionist plan. Congress leaders could not support a state-making project where religion was the basis of citizenship. The INC persisted in its political belief that the questions of minorities, including the Muslim and Jewish issues in India and in Palestine respectively, had to be settled within the framework of a pluralistic state and not by partition. To uphold ideological consistency, the INC refused to recognize Jewish nationalist demands. The INC was opposed to a partition on religious grounds in both South Asia and Palestine and advocated for a federal arrangement with respect for minority rights in both cases.[87] As a consequence, the Muslim League and internal politics were important contextual determinants which shaped India's Palestine policy following independence.

Many Actors, One Israel Policy in 1947

The gradual formation phase of an early policy on Palestine is rarely discussed in the literature. The rare studies looking at the pre-independence period have concentrated on the personalities and writings of Gandhi and Nehru. This book offered to qualify and to contextualize the role of these two political actors. These leaders hardly had static understandings of the Palestine problem, and their positions changed depending on the evolution of the independence struggle in India, events in West Asia, and interactions with other important policy actors such as the British administration, the Muslim League, and representatives of the Zionist movement. Furthermore, Gandhi and Nehru's positions of influence and of leadership within the Indian national movement have also changed overtime. As a result, every one of their statements must be carefully put in a temporal and situational perspective. Their positions, just like the INC's, were in flux for much of that period, and progressively consolidated over a policy compromise by the end of the 1930s, which would become India's first Israel policy.

There were multiple actors involved in the formation of India's future Israel policy in 1947. As a result, there were multiple floating ideas and alternative foreign policies towards the Palestine issue. Before independence, the official position on matters regarding West Asia was dictated by the British Foreign Office but also by the India Office and the British Government of India. As demonstrated in this chapter, these last two actors followed London's line which was to maintain the control of the Palestine mandate, which was an essential geopolitical link between Britain and British India. However, these two actors had slightly divergent interests because they were concerned with stability in the British Indian Empire and with the unrest among Indian Muslims caused by British designs in West Asia. These actors attempted to bring their own input on matters which frustrated Indian Muslims, notably during the Khilafat period. The India Office was therefore instrumental in warning the Foreign Office against directly supporting Zionist aspirations in Palestine because of the opinion of Indian Muslims. In the 1940s, for instance, based on a report from the Viceroy of India, Archibald Wavell, the British Foreign Office supported a restricted policy of Jewish immigration to Palestine to prevent Muslim agitation in India. In a joint memorandum released in London on 19 November 1940, by the British secretary of state for foreign affairs and the secretary of state for the colonies, concern was expressed about the influence of disturbances in West Asia on the British control over the Muslims in India (Sofer 1998: 521).

The Muslim League was another neglected but important actor with its own interests. The movement was at the origin of the unrest in British India from 1917 to 1922 when the fate of the Ottoman Caliphate was being decided in London, Paris, Sevres, and Lausanne. The Muslim League played an important role in bringing the fears of Indian Muslims to the attention of both the British Government of India and the INC. While the former warned London of the strong internal opposition to the dissolution of the Caliphate, the INC decided to join the Khilafat movement and to support the concerns of Indian Muslims. This cooperation did not last and the Muslim League lost some of its influence on this policy debate until the late 1930s. At that time, the Muslim League began to actively exploit the Palestine issue to its own advantage in its domestic rivalry with Congress. Support for Muslims in Palestinians was a useful rallying point for South Asian Muslims and a clear division line with the INC. This indirectly pressured the INC into taking a strong stand against Zionism.

The Jewish Agency only gradually recognized India's importance. Links with the INC were not a priority despite intermittent efforts to convince Gandhi and Nehru to the Zionist cause. There was only a gradual recognition of India's central position in the broader Asian decolonization movement. However, efforts to engage the INC came too late and did not salvage a failing diplomatic strategy. The Zionist movement failed to respond to and rectify Indian political perceptions regarding the Palestine issue which were determindely pro-Arab by the late 1930s. In addition, not much effort was made to publicize relevant information amongst the Indian public about Zionist objectives in Palestine. The Zionist movement's overtures did not have a decisive impact on the formation of the INC's policy on Palestine.

The INC was the most decisive actor of this period as it was directly involved in foreign policy decision-making after independence. Events in West Asia and Palestine were the first opportunity for the INC to craft an alternate foreign policy to the one fashioned by London. The position of the movement evolved depending on the leaders spearheading it and on the domestic circumstances in British India. The INC first expressed itself in the context of the Khilafat and its first resolutions on the Palestine question originally validated a pro-Islamic interpretation of the situation. This was mainly the result of concerted efforts on the part of Gandhi and the INC to ride the Pan-Islamic wave against British meddling in Ottoman and West Asian affairs. The objective was to rally Indian Muslims to the broader national struggle for Indian self-government. After the failure of this strategy, the INC opted for a different position. It then favoured direct negotiations with secular-nationalist Arab movements in West Asia. Under the leadership of Nehru, the INC framed the problem in Palestine primarily as one of a national Arab struggle against foreign rule. There was also humanitarian sympathy for the Jews but no support for a Zionist political project in Palestine. The best solution to the Palestine problem was the creation of a federal state with constitutional guarantees for the Jewish minority. However, even before independence, the INC had to compromise its position due to domestic and international factors. Its rivalry with the Muslim League at the domestic level led it to take a strong and clear stand against Zionism and to refuse any public recognition of Jewish aspirations in Palestine. Discussions with Zionist emissaries were kept secret and no public support was given. The indirect influence of the Muslim League kept the INC from just pushing for a vague and open-ended policy which could be adjusted after independence in the light of unfolding events in the region. The opposition to the Muslim League also inhibited any rapprochement with the Zionist movement as any endorsement of religious self-determination would have created a negative precedent with implications for South Asia.

Progressively, a new alternative policy was shaped by the INC which only had an indirect access to foreign policy-making in India. Even before independence and foreign policy autonomy, it is possible to outline some pressures on and compromises to the INC's position which would be further tested by the evolution of the situation in Palestine and South Asia. How did this emerging Israel policy fare when faced with exogenous shocks such as the creation of the Jewish state in 1948? Did the partition of the subcontinent have an impact on India's policy? How did this policy evolve given the new regional and international conditions? What was the new policy compromise which emerged in the 1950s?

Notes

1. The notable exceptions being Prasad (1960) and Prasad (1979).

2. However India did share some of British India's concerns after independence such as energy security and free access to sea-lanes of communications in West Asia.

3. However, the absence of any authoritative history of southern India, and especially of Cochin, prior to the fourteenth century makes this claim impossible to verify. For instance, some have claimed that Tipu Sultan attacked the Jewish kingdom of Cranganore (Kodungallur, in today's state of Kerala) and began a massacre. As a result, 10,000 Jews apparently ran away and converted to Christianity. Another account is that the Bene Israel were taken captive by Tipu Sultan and that his mother intervened to have them released. See Nandy (2002: 169); Kapadia (2008).

4. I want to thank Ambassador Rajendra Abhyankar for highlighting this historical issue.

5. The Rashtrakuta Empire was a royal dynasty ruling large parts of the subcontinent between the sixth and the tenth centuries; Ahmad (1969: 69–70).

6. Majumdar (1968); Ahmad (1969: 3–4). Ahmad argued that the port of Ophir could be located in the area of modern-day Sopara, situated next to Bombay.

7. For instance, the Hebrew word 'koph' (monkey) is argued to have come from the Sanskrit 'kapi', and 'tukki' (peacock) from the Tamil word 'togai'. See Basham (2005 [1954]: 232).

8. According to the historian Romila Thapar, the Cairo Geniza records contain letters written by Jewish traders who traded with the Indian subcontinent. See Thapar (2002: 369).

9. The arrival of Jewish settlers in Cochin parallels the chronological uncertainty of the arrival of Christians in the same region. Most Cochini Jews

have now left India and moved back to Israel after its formation in the 1950s. See Thapar (2002: 369). Goldberg (1995); Katz (2000).

10. Ahmad (1969: 75–6). The only Muslim ruler to maintain contacts with the Caliphate up to the late eighteenth century was the Tipu Sultan of Mysore. See Qureshi (1945).

11. Naaz (1999). The majority of them immigrated to the US and Britain after 1947.

12. British authorities replaced the East India Company after the Mutiny of 1857.

13. This happened soon after the India sepoy mutiny which had given the impression that the British rule in India was now fragile. The control of the Canal and therefore of Cairo was considered necessary. See Darwin (2009: 73–4).

14. During World War I, the British government sent an Indian army unit to seize oil refineries in southern Persia and in the nearest port of Basra (now in present Iraq). Units of the Indian Army were also permanently stationed in Iraq to prevent dissent. See Barr (2011: 18, 219).

15. For a detailed discussion on the tensions between the Foreign Office, the India Office, and the Government of India, see Oliver-Dee (2009).

16. The formation of Gandhi's attitude towards Jewish nationalism can be dated back to his years in South Africa. In 1906, in his publication *Indian Opinion*, he criticized South African Jews for not helping another persecuted minority, the South African Indians. He felt there should have been a sense of solidarity as he compared anti-Semitism in Europe to the treatment of Indians in South Africa. See Shimoni (1977: 13); Ward (1992: 13).

17. Here I partially build on Ward and Rao who have identified a series of factors to explain Gandhi's opposition to Zionism. See Ward (1992: 13); Rao (1972: 42).

18. The Jewish Agency was an organization created in 1929 for the purpose of advising and cooperating with the British Administration of Palestine in economic, social, and other matters as may affect the establishment of the Jewish national home and the interests of the Jewish population of Palestine.

19. Gandhi, *Young India*, 23 March 1921, in *Collected Works* 19: 530. For more on Gandhi and the Khilafat movement, see the relevant section in this chapter.

20. Gandhi, *Collected Works*, 48: 105–6. This statement from Gandhi was severely criticized by *The Jewish Chronicle* in their editorial for being contradictory: Gandhi argued that Jews should not think of their own rehabilitation in national terms, but he was himself in London to demand national self-determination for India (*The Jewish Chronicle*, 2 November 1931). One month later, Rabbi Stephen Wise criticized Gandhi, also in *The Jewish Chronicle*, for his negative attitude regarding the Jewish national homeland, while he himself had supported national self-determination for India. See Gerberg (2008: 204).

21. Haj Mohammed Amin el-Hussayni was a Palestinian Arab nationalist and Muslim leader. The concern with anti-Zionist propaganda in Indian Muslim communities was, for instance, conveyed by Zionist leader Hayim Greenberg, editor of the US-based *Jewish Frontier* newspaper, in a letter he sent to Gandhi in 1937; see Schechtman (1966).

22. Both were Jewish South Africans whom Gandhi had known during his stay in South Africa; see Lelyveld (2011: 79–104).

23. In 1936, Moshe Sharett, head of the political department of the Jewish Agency, had decided to send Immanuel Olsvanger to meet Nehru and Gandhi in India. Olsvanger was a doctor of philology with some knowledge of Sanskrit and an official of the South African Zionist Federation through which he met Hermann Kallenbach. After his meetings, Olvsanger judged that the political influence of Gandhi on the Indian nationalist movement was limited and it would therefore be a better strategy to engage other political personalities. Olsvanger also met with other Indian political actors. See Shimoni (1977: 30–1).

24. Gandhi himself admitted he had received multiple letters asking him to declare his views on the questions, in Gandhi, *Harijan*, 26 November 1938, in *Collected Works*, 68: 136–8.

25. For example, A. E. Shohet, the editor of the *Jewish Advocate* in Bombay, criticized Gandhi for being pro-Arab and biased. Shohet felt that Gandhi had applied double standards in his judgement of the Palestine issue. Quoted in Shimoni (1977: 49). Hayim Greenberg, the editor of the *Jewish Frontier* newspaper, also wrote a letter to Gandhi, in which he accused Gandhi of being biased and unfair towards the Jews. He added that Gandhi had overlooked the imperative existential need for a Jewish homeland. Gandhi responded to this accusation in a column in *Harijan* and even reproduced an abridgement of Greenberg's letter, pointing out that he saw no reason to change his opinion. See Shimoni (1977: 49). Only Moshe Sharret had not lost hope to convince Gandhi. Quoted in Kumaraswamy (2010: 35).

26. Ramana Murti (1968). In fact, Buber had moved away from organizational Zionism because he argued for the formation of a bi-national confederation which he considered to be a more adequate fulfilment of Zionism than an exclusive Jewish state. See Buber (2005 [1954]).

27. Buber (1999 [1957]: 140–3). Henry Polak also disagreed with Gandhi's opinion that the Jews should practice Satyagraha against Nazi persecution. Polak wrote to Gandhi looking for reassurance that there was a misunderstanding. Gandhi replied, in another *Harijan* issue, that his point was that the Jews were not non-violent. Polak replied in strong terms and challenged Gandhi to prove his statement or to withdraw it unequivocally. As a consequence, Gandhi made a public retraction in a later *Harijan* issue: 'I did not realize the importance of the rebuke and I only hope that my observation did not harm any single Jew.' See

Shimoni (1977: 47–9). See Gandhi, "No Apology." *Harijan*, February 18, 1939, available at: http://www.gandhiserve.org/information/writings_online/articles/gandhi_jews_palestine.html; and Gandhi, "Withdrawn," *Harijan*, May 27, 1939, available at: http://www.gandhiserve.org/information/writings_online/articles/gandhi_jews_palestine.html#Withdrawn

28. The interview was never published as Gandhi did not approve it for publication; see Shimoni (1977: 49–50); Gerberg (2008: 206).

29. Gandhi also told Fischer he had mentioned this to Silverman; see Fischer (1947: 42).

30. It also discredits the argument that Gandhi's perception of Judaism was shaped in a particular context of exposure to Christian influences in London. See Shimoni (1977: 15–16, 18, 20); Glucklich (1988). Shimoni further argued that Gandhi's early perception of Judaism was not re-evaluated and therefore precluded any kind of sympathy for a Jewish homeland (1977: 19–20).

31. See, for example, India, Ministry of External Affairs (1968).

32. Quoted in the preface to Heptullah (1991).

33. Nehru (2004 [1934]: 885). This ideological connection helped the first generation of Israeli leaders to find common language with Asian socialist leaders like Nehru and the Burmese Prime Minister U Nu in the 1950s. These ties also led to the organization of the first Asian Socialist Conference in 1953 in Burma which Israel co-sponsored. See Jansen (1971).

34. For instance, the human resources minister and deputy prime minister in 1992, Arjun Singh, was concerned that the establishment of diplomatic relations with Israel could be interpreted as a departure from the Nehruvian framework of India's foreign policy. See Dixit (1996: 311).

35. See Nehru's correspondence with Subhas Chandra Bose who opposed such a move in 1939, in Sarvepalli Gopal, ed., *Selected Works of Jawaharlal Nehru*, Series I, Vol.9: 53 ; Rao (1972: 4); Sareen (1999).

36. Jewish refugees from Central and Eastern Europe but also from Iraq and Afghanistan travelled to India during World War II. See Sareen (1999).

37. Jansen (1971: 30). The World Zionist Organization did not join the international congress against imperialism following the 1927 Brussels Conference.

38. Nehru also met Nedivi in 1939, but the meeting did not lead to any change in his position. See Shimoni (1977: 49–50).

39. Originally, the Congress party was primarily a pressure group of local notables seeking no more than colonial self-government but its position escalated in the early century towards more radical demands for autonomous rule and then for full independence. See Weiner (1967).

40. For an analysis of the influence of al-Afghani's ideology on Muslims in India, see Jalal (2000: 188–9); Mishra (2012: Chapter 2).

41. Ironically, a few years earlier, when the Ottoman Empire and Britain were allies against Russia, the Sultan had called on Indian Muslims to stay loyal to the British during the mutiny. See Niemeijer (1972: 39). However, not all Indian Muslims supported the Pan-Islamic authority of the Ottoman Sultan. The famous Indian Muslim activist Sir Sayyid Ahmad Khan argued that the Ottoman Sultan was not the Caliph of Indian Muslims and rejected Ottoman calls for Pan-Islamic solidarity. As a consequence, Al Afghani and Khan became fierce intellectual rivals in the 1880s. See Niemeijer (1972: 45–6); Mishra (2012: 91–4).

42. Surprisingly, the perception of the opinion of Indian Muslims on the question was based on a reported meeting between the Aga Khan III and the British undersecretary of state for foreign affairs in 1915. The Aga Khan is the hereditary title of the Imam of the Nizari Ismaili community and therefore could not be considered as the sole and legitimate spokesman of the Muslims of the subcontinent. Nevertheless, he warned the undersecretary against interfering in the Caliphate question because Indian Muslims would not support the idea of an Arab Caliphate. Despite the lack of real evidence of widespread support for the Ottoman Caliph among Indian Muslims in general, the undersecretary decided to support a policy of non-involvement. However, other officials also dismissed his views as exaggerating the international repercussions of the Caliphate question. See Niemeijer (1972: 64–5); Oliver-Dee (2009: 48, 55–6).

43. The mutiny by Indian Muslim troops in Singapore also served an important warning against the dangers of manipulating Muslim politics. See Oliver-Dee (2009: 48–56).

44. Even Mohammad Ali Jinnah, an INC member who would become the leader of the Muslim League, wholeheartedly supported the British Empire. See Prasad (1960: 53–6); James (2000: 439–45).

45. The Khilafat movement was a protest campaign organized by Muslims in British India after World War I. The movement, which lasted until 1924, arose out of fears of prominent Indian Muslim leaders about the integrity of the caliphate. This movement was particularly concerned with the status of the Caliph after the Armistice of Mudros of October 1918 with the military occupation of Istanbul and the Treaties of Versailles (1919) and Sèvres which officially disbanded the Ottoman Empire. They wanted the Turkish Sultan (Khalifa) to retain control over the Muslim sacred places and demanded that Syria, Iraq, and Palestine remain under Muslim sovereignty. The purpose of this book is to specifically discuss the Khilafat movement's influence on the INC's position on Palestine and later on Israel. For more detailed historical accounts of the Khilafat mobilization, see Niemeijer (1972); Minault (1982); Qureshi (1999).

46. Maulana Azad was a symbol of the important religious connections between the two regions. He was born in 1888 in the Mecca. His mother was of

Arab descent, the daughter of Shaikh Muhammad Zahir Watri; and his father, Maulana Khairuddin, lived with his family in the Bengal region until he left India during the Mutiny and settled in Mecca, where he met his wife. See Niemeijer (1972: 59); Gandhi (1986: 219).

47. Azad was, however, more of a reformist than Mohammad Ali and believed the Caliph should be elected. If an election was impossible, then power should be legally invested in a 'de facto Caliph'. He had both a religious and political conception of the Caliphate. See Niemeijer (1972: 59–60).

48. There are different geographical definitions of Jazirat al-Arab. According to some Muslim scholars in India, Jazirat-al-Arab extended 'from Aden to the Mountains of Syria—From Jeddah and the sea coast to the agricultural lowlands of Iraq', (in Hasan [1994: 136]). In other Indian accounts, Jazirat al-arab also included Constantinople and Jerusalem. Gandhi, for example, supported the claim that Palestine was an integral part of Jazirat al-arab in *Young India* (26 April 1921) (Gandhi, *Collected Works* [1958, 19: 472]).

49. The Montagu-Chelmsford Reforms were recommendations about political reforms made after World War I by the Viceroy of India Lord Chelmsford and the Secretary of State for India Sir Edwin Samuel Montagu. Chelmsford and Montagu suggested the introduction of some degree of self-governance in India. Their report was ultimately adopted as the Government of India Act of 1919.

50. The Rowlatt Act was a legislation passed on March 10th 1919 by the Imperial Legislative Council, which was the legislature of British India. The Act allowed the British Indian authorities to imprison suspects of terrorism without trial for periods of up to two years. The object of the Act was to extend the repressive provisions of the Wartime Defence of India Act of 1915. The Act was based on the recommendation of a committee presided by British Judge Sir Sidney Rowlatt.

51. Quoted in Oliver-Dee (2009: 112; emphasis added). This is the first time an Indian politician interpreted the Jewish problem in West Asia as a minority group issue.

52. Prime Minister Lloyd George had initially declared that the British had no intention of dismembering the Ottoman Empire. See Zaidi and Zaidi, *Encyclopedia of the INC*, 11: 260; Hasan (1994: 132–3).

53. The Balfour Declaration was a letter from the British Foreign Secretary Arthur James Balfour to Baron Walter Rothschild, a leader of the British Jewish community. It favoured the establishment in Palestine of a national home for the Jews. It was later incorporated in the Treaty of Sevres and the Mandate for Palestine. See more in Schneer (2010).

54. The India Office also had an important input in the redaction of the Lausanne Treaty which replaced the Sevres Treaty. Given the agitation of Indian Muslims, the India Office recommended the Lausanne agreement to be more

favourable to the Turks and to find an arrangement to preserve the religious authority of the Caliphate. See Ahmad (1973); Oliver-Dee (2009: 125–37).

55. Quoted in Cohen (1982: 23).

56. Zaidi and Zaidi (*Encyclopedia of the INC*, 8: 478 and 8: 542). Muhammad Ali's position seemed to have evolved during his negotiations with the British in London. Gradually, he seemed to argue more for the requirement of Arabia to stay under 'Muslim' control rather than under Ottoman control; see Oliver-Dee (2009: 114). The second meeting between Lloyd George and the Khilafat delegation in March 1921 did not alleviate Indian Muslims' grievances on these issues. See Oliver-Dee (2009: 117–19).

57. He also supported the anti-colonialist struggle of Egypt and Syria. Quoted in Dastur (1988).

58. It is important that it is no longer question of 'non-Muslim' control of Jazirat-al-Arab. See Zaidi and Zaidi (*Encyclopedia of the INC*, 8: 673).

59. The Khilafat delegation, for example, met twice with British Prime Minister Lloyd George on the insistence of the India Office and the Government of India in 1920 and 1921.

60. Quoted in Levi (1952: 22).

61. This conference is sometimes also called the Congress of Oppressed Nationalities. See Prasad (1960: 79); Mudiam (1994: 3–4).

62. See Nehru's presidential address at the forty-forth session of the INC in Lahore in December 1929, in Zaidi and Zaidi, *Encyclopedia of the INC*, 9: 602.

63. This was the first time the INC explicitly expressed its support to the Palestinians since 1928 and the first time it was an exclusive reference to the Palestine issue; see Zaidi and Zaidi (*Encyclopedia of the INC*, 11: 153).

64. Rao (1972: 19). On this occasion, Golda Meir, of the political department of the Jewish Agency in Jerusalem, sent a letter of protest to the INC explaining that the people of India misunderstood the socialist Zionist work in Palestine (quoted in Gerberg [2008: 188]).

65. The Zionist movement was a Jewish nationalist movement supporting the creation of a Jewish nation state. It took the organizational form of the World Zionist Organization (WZO) in 1897 and later founded smaller bodies like the Jewish National Fund and the Anglo-Palestine Bank. By contrast, the Jewish Agency was officially created during the 16th Zionist Congress in Zurich in 1929. Its goal was to collect funds to enable Jewish settlement in Palestine. It was originally not a political association and did not directly advocate for a Jewish state. The organization merged with the WZO in 1947. After 1948 it formed the provisional government of Israel. For more, see Laqueur (2009).

66. Quoted in Singh (1979 : 387–88).

67. See, for example, the resolutions cited in Zaidi and Zaidi (*Encyclopedia of the INC*, 11: 497 and 12: 159–60).

68. Nehru (2004 [1934]: 886) even referred to the recent Jewish immigration to Palestine as a 'colonizing movement'. See also Gordon (1975).

69. Gandhi (*Collected Works of Gandhi*, 87: 417). Nehru equally discussed Jewish terrorism but interpreted it as an escalation and reaction to Arab terrorism (2004 [1934]: 890).

70. Indian journalist and former diplomat G. H. Jansen, for instance, said that Nehru met Zionist members within the context of the Brussels International Congress against Colonial Oppression and Imperialism as early as 1927 but did not talk in detail about their discussions; see Jansen (1971: 30). According to Kumaraswamy, there were also contacts between Zionist representatives and Indian delegates at the Assembly of the League of Nations in 1931 but nothing came out of these talks since the Indian delegation did not represent India or the INC but British Indian interests at the time. See Kumaraswamy (2010: 64).

71. For instance, the journalist Gershon Agronsky was sent to India in April 1930. Following his visit, Agronsky recommended that the Zionist organization start engaging Asian nationalist movements. Shimoni (1977: 27–8).

72. Ambedkar was a jurist and politician. He was at the head of the Independent Labour Party. After independence, he became India's first law minister in the new provisional government and was appointed chairman of the Constitution Drafting Committee. For more on these meetings, see Shimoni (1977); Kumaraswamy (2010: 62).

73. Olsvanger reportedly received personal (but not official) support from Naidu and Ambdekar. He also met with Rabindranath Tagore and a number of Indian academics, and suggested possible institutional links and exchange of students between the Banaras Hindu University (BHU) and the Hebrew University of Jerusalem. See Shimoni (1977).

74. The princely states were nominally sovereign entities of the British Indian Empire that were still governed by Indian rulers but under a form of indirect rule subordinate to the British crown which found it advantageous to maintain these political structures in the Empire. For more, read Menon (1956).

75. The Chamber of Princes was an institution established in 1920 which provided a forum in which the rulers of the Indian princely states could discuss their needs with the government of British India. It was dissolved in 1947.

76. K. M. Panikkar also served as foreign minister of the states of Patiala and Bikaner which established economic links with the Jewish Agency. On 1 June 1937, David Ben-Gurion, the chairman of the Jewish Agency, met with Panikkar in London in order to discuss the Zionist cause in Palestine. Gerberg (2008: 89).

77. Quoted in Kumaraswamy (2010: 65–6).

78. Weizmann was the president of the Zionist Organization and was to become the first president of the state of Israel. In the early 1940s, David Ben-Gurion, in his capacity as chairperson of the Jewish Agency, maintained a

correspondence with Gandhi. Ben-Gurion was an admirer of Gandhi and wanted to gain Gandhi's support for the Zionist cause. See Gerberg (2008: 191).

79. See Weizmann's letters to Nehru in 1938 and in 1947, in Weizmann (*Letters and Papers of Chaim Weizmann*, 18: 206, 18: 458–9, 23: 31–2, and 23: 42–3).

80. Quoted in Kumaraswamy (2010: 66)

81. Palestine was only officially integrated in the British Empire in 1922 and had the status of a mandate.

82. Paradoxically, while arguing that South Asian Muslims constituted a distinct nation and therefore a separate state, the Muslim League refused to accept the Zionist rationale in Palestine.

83. There was a historical link between Weizmann and India as he was offered a teaching position at the University of Calcutta in 1909 but he eventually refused it as he became more involved in the Zionist movement in Palestine. See Weizmann (*Letters and Papers of Chaim Weizmann*, 5: 135–6).

84. By contrast, the INC never officially recognized the Mufti as representing Palestinian interests.

85. The Muslim League was itself inconsistent when defining its position vis-à-vis Zionism. In spite of the similarities between the Muslim League's and the Zionist movement's nationalist projects, the Muslim League opposed the existence of a Jewish national home. Partition in South Asia on religious terms was justified whereas it was not acceptable in Palestine. Zafarullah Khan, Pakistan's first ambassador to the United Nations (UN), made a famous statement on the question explaining that Pakistan did not regard 'partition as inadmissible in principle but each problem had to be studied on its own merits' (quoted in Mudiam [1994: 219]). Almost 40 years later, Pakistan's president Zia ul-Haq stated that 'Pakistan is like Israel, an ideological state. Take out the Judaism from Israel and it will fall like a house of cards. Take Islam out of Pakistan and make it a secular state; it would collapse' (*The Economist*, 12 December 1981). For comparisons between the ideational foundations of the two nations, see also Burke (1973: 66); Cohen (2004: 35); Devji (2013).

86. Similarly, the INC opposed the creation of a Hindu state, which was a solution promoted by the Hindu Mahasabha.

87. Interestingly, the rivalry between the two parties on the Palestine issue was prolonged after independence when both India and Pakistan competed for diplomatic support from the newly independent Arab states.

2   Reality Check?

Recognition of Israel and the Limits of Indo-Israeli Rapprochement (1948–1956)

Any action that we may take must be guided not only by idealistic considerations but also a realistic appraisal of the situation. Our general policy in the past has been favourable to the Arabs, at the same time not hostile to the Jews. That policy continues. For the present, we have said that we are not recognising Israel. But this is not an irrevocable decision and the matter will no doubt be considered afresh in view of subsequent developments...

—Jawaharlal Nehru[1]

I DISCUSSED IN THE PREVIOUS CHAPTER how India had already laid out some of the foundations of its post-independence foreign policy. As the Indian National Congress (INC) became the leading political force in independent India and formed the country's provisional government, its pre-1947 statements and policies had a lasting influence on India's domestic and foreign policies. However, this did not mean India was bound by these positions. During its nationalist struggle, the INC preached moral principles without considering how these statements might adversely affect relations with other countries. Following independence, a rectification of the balance between ideational and practical factors in the formulation of India's foreign policy became necessary. Prime Minister Nehru argued that India's foreign policy had to be 'idealistic' and 'in keeping with the traditional background and temper of the country' but also at the same time 'realistic' and not 'adventurist and wholly ineffective' (Brecher 1959: 217). For example, while the INC previously demanded nothing short of full sovereignty, it finally settled down on becoming a member of the Commonwealth of Nations upon independence on 15 August 1947 (Singh 1995). The Congress also decided to remain a member in December 1948 despite the fact India had become an independent republic. This decision was made in order to facilitate a smooth transfer of power (Brecher 1975). Another important foreign policy change was the recognition of Israel in September 1950.

The INC resolutions voted during 1936–9 were the only references to Zionism and defined India's initial position. However, even if scholars and practitioners often refer to these texts to see a continuous and consistent Congress policy on the question, in this chapter I argue that post-independence India strongly deviated in practice from these initial statements. The pre-independence period created a policy consensus on which Nehru and the INC had to build on. Policy change was complicated because of this existing policy compromise which had emerged after years of deliberations within the INC. A coalition of actors defended the relevance of this policy compromise. However, the bases of the existing policy were gradually contested by evolving circumstances. The two partitions in 1947–8 in South Asia and in Palestine pressured Indian policymakers to come to terms with the new political realities. In addition, one of the main architects and supporters of the policy compromise on Israel, Nehru, was more open-minded than the literature stipulates. Nehru adapted his position in face of international changes in the late 1940s. I therefore argue that India's Israel policy was in flux following independence. After a decade of debate and fluctuating situations in India and in West Asia, a new policy compromise on Palestine and Israel only emerged in 1956.

As discussed in the Introduction, policy change only happens through a series of steps. We can identify three stages in India's position vis-à-vis Israel from 1947 to 1956. First, the literature on policy change rightly discusses the need for a shock for the collapse of old ideas, and to destabilize the previous dominating policy consensus. Originally, India pursued the Palestine policy which had been shaped in its pre-independence struggle. It maintained its emotional interest in the decolonization of the West Asian region, and accordingly continued supporting the political and economic rights of Arab nationalists. In the pre-independence period, Nehru and the INC had interpreted the Palestine struggle as a manifestation of the wider problem of decolonization. This had led the Congress to oppose the imposition of a Jewish national home on Palestinian Arabs. These foundations still broadly defined New Delhi's approach in 1947–8 when the Palestine question was considered at the United Nations (UN).

In a second stage between 1947 and 1950, India progressively embraced two new realities: the partition plan for Palestine and the proclamation of the Jewish state in 1948, and the partition of British India into two states, India and Pakistan. These two events can be construed as exogenous shocks that served as powerful catalysts for a reassessment of New Delhi's Palestine policy. Other new considerations also emerged during that period such as the Cold War, security and economic requirements (notably the need for foreign aid coming mostly through naval lanes in West Asia and the Suez Canal), territorial integrity (with the Kashmir issue), and rivalry with Pakistan. These new factors led to a renewed debate over India's Israel policy from 1948 to 1950. On September 17 1950, India recognized Israel but did not establish diplomatic relations with the Jewish state. This chapter will demonstrate that this was a policy compromise to satisfy diverging interests, and to cope with evolving circumstances at the international and regional levels. This policy compromise had tangible results at first as it ensured political material support from Western powers while also consolidating links with the Arab world, and it countered any possibility of a Pan-Islamic bloc around Pakistan (Blarel 2014). At the domestic level, it was also a compromise between an old orthodoxy supporting the pre-independence position, and a new orthodoxy asking for change and adaptation to geopolitical events in West Asia at the turn of the decade.

A third phase from 1950 to 1956 is characterized by an ensuing debate between defenders of the status quo and advocates of changes vis-à-vis Israel. This is a neglected but key period of Indo-Israeli relations. There is ample evidence to demonstrate that Nehru and India were open to establishing diplomatic relations and to normalizing bilateral relations. There were also important efforts from the Israeli diplomatic side to obtain normalization. However, events in the subcontinent and especially in West Asia progressively constrained Nehru's choices. While Nehru had managed to make a very strategically weighted decision in 1950, any further diplomatic step in direction of Israel was perceived as threatening India's interests in West Asia. This section will concentrate on the international, regional, and domestic factors which gradually limited Nehru's options until the Suez crisis of 1956. This section will also analyse how the old orthodoxy, which defended India's pre-independence position, managed to prevent a complete policy reversal vis-à-vis Israel.

The literature has often discussed the imprint of a personality like Nehru in the early days, and how his political legacy has authoritatively determined India's policy vis-à-vis West Asia for decades (Nanda 1976: 77). This study concurs that Nehru's position was important as the ultimate foreign policy decision-maker following India's independence. During most of his tenure as prime minister of India, Nehru was his own minister of external affairs and practically all decisions on foreign affairs were taken by him.[2] However, his policy evolved from 1947 onwards. Two years after Israel was created, Nehru went back on his original position and decided to recognize the new Jewish state. The following years, he also made statements hinting at the acceptance of Israel as an international and bilateral partner. In spite of positive statements made vis-à-vis Israel in the late 1940s, Nehru never established diplomatic relations with Israel of his living. Rather than concentrating exclusively on Nehru's role and responsibility (with the risk of misunderstanding his actual objectives), it is important to understand the domestic and international factors at stake as well as the policy debates confining Nehru's choices.

1947–8: An Attempt to Implement India's Original Palestine Policy

In 1947, before independence, India had its first interactions with the future Israeli leadership, and even made its first policy decisions at the UN. These initial positions indicated a loyal continuation of its pre-independence policy. India was supportive of Arab nationalism but not hostile to Jewish religious interests in Palestine. That is why it supported a dialogue between Arabs and Jews towards a federal arrangement accommodative of all interests. While events were unfolding in South Asia and Palestine, the Indian provisional government stood strong on its original positions on the Palestine question at the Asian Relations Conference (ARC) in New Delhi in March–April 1947. However, the first key test of India's Palestine policy was in the summer of 1947 when India was appointed at the UN Special Committee on Palestine (UNSCOP).

The Asian Relations Conference of 1947

By the end of World War II, the Jewish Agency had begun to actively engage India, which was progressively becoming an autonomous political actor on the international sphere. For example, India sent an independent delegation to participate in the constitution of the UN in June 1945 (Baghavan 2012; Kember 1976). Before the conference, Eliahu Epstein, in his capacity as head of the Jewish Agency's political department in Washington, met Sir Firoz Khan Noon, a member of the Indian delegation, but the meeting did not produce any tangible results.[3] In November 1945, F. W. Pollack, the secretary of the Central Jewish Board in Bombay,[4] wrote to the Jewish Agency in Jerusalem to suggest a new action plan for India.[5] However, the Jewish Agency was concentrated in lobbying Western powers, and the budgets allocated to the Bombay office for political activities were limited. Only in January 1947 did the political department of the Jewish Agency recognize the need to forge closer ties with Indians in London and in India. Moshe Sharet himself stressed the growing diplomatic importance of India in Asian politics (Gerberg 2008: 192).

This was the context when the New Delhi Conference of the Asian Relations Organization (ARO) took place between 23 March 1947 and 2 April 1947. The ARC was an international conference during which the INC convened different Asian nationalist movements fighting for independence. It was a way for Nehru—who had become the head of India's interim government since September 1946—to institutionalize the emerging links between Asian nationalists and to promote understanding and cooperation regarding their common problems. India invited 32 delegations, including both an Arab and a Jewish delegation from Palestine. According to some authors, there was a strong opposition within the INC against inviting a Jewish delegation (Kumaraswamy 2010: 64; Shimoni 1977: 57). The pressure from both Sarojni Naidu and Vijaya Lakshmi Pandit (the latter was India's representative to the UN and Nehru's sister) was decisive. Pandit had discussed the issue with a pro-Israel Congressman of the US, Emmanuel Celler, in Washington.[6] The invitations were also consistent with the INC's traditional policy of supporting Palestinian Arab nationalism while also accommodating Jewish religious concerns. It was a strong symbolical move from the INC because it was the first time a Jewish delegation had been invited to a conference uniting Asian movements (Kochan 1976).

The 10-member Jewish delegation (sometimes also called the 'Hebrew University delegation') was headed by Professor Hugo Bergman from the Hebrew University in Jerusalem, and was composed, among others, of Olsvanger and diplomats Yaacov Shimoni and David Hacohen. During the conference, the delegation met key Indian leaders, including Gandhi. Hacohen, an eminent member of the political department of the Jewish Agency, called on Gandhi to express himself in favour of the persecuted Jewish people in Europe, but Gandhi preferred to remain neutral. He again condemned the resort to terrorism in Palestine (Gerberg 2008: 66). The delegation also met with Nehru. At the delegation's request, Nehru agreed to extend by 6 months the duration of the stay of a few hundred Jewish refugees from Afghanistan who were stranded in Bombay and waiting to migrate to Palestine (Kumaraswamy 2010: 186). During the meeting, Hacohen brought up the option of partition in Palestine, arguing that only the establishment of a 'Jewish commonwealth' in West Asia could solve the Jewish persecution issue.[7] He again insisted on the important Jewish contributions to 'nation building' in Palestine (Gerberg 2008: 202). Nehru, who opposed the idea of partition both in Palestine and South Asia, refused to support the idea of a Jewish state both during this meeting and in his later correspondence with Hacohen. The delegation also reportedly established contacts with Indian socialist leaders, like Jaya Prakash Narayan, Ashok Mehta, and Rammanohar Lohia, who expressed an interest in social enterprises such as the Kibbutz and the Moshav, as well as in Jews' experiences in agriculture in Palestine.[8] The delegation also met with Panikkar, who was prime minister of the princely state of Bikaner at the time and who participated in the ARC as an India delegate.[9]

The participation of the Jewish delegation at the ARC created a diplomatic incident which proved to be the first major test of India's Palestine policy. While the Arab League was present, six other Arab countries (Syria, Lebanon, Transjordan, Saudi Arabia, Yemen, and Iraq) declined their individual invitations. The only Arab participant, Egypt, apparently associated the refusal of Arab countries to attend to the presence of a Jewish delegation (Gopal and Sharma 2007: 219; Kumaraswamy 2010: 184). The absence of most Arab states was the first opportunity for a Jewish delegation to establish formal contacts with other Asian nationalist movements and with India's leadership. It was also possible for them to publicly convey their case for a Jewish homeland. Bergman and Shimoni were able to make speeches during the conference, and Hacohen was elected chairman of the economic round table group (Gerberg 2008; Kumaraswamy 2010: 185–6). Bergman's speech was conciliating: he referred to an aspiration for a Jewish 'old-new homeland' in Palestine while also explaining that their aim was not to dispossess Palestinian Arabs (Jansen 1971: 191–2). The speech was however contested by the Arab League and Egyptian delegations which did not want British rule to be replaced by the domination of 'European Zionists' (Jansen 1971: 191–2). The Egyptian representative welcomed Jewish settlers, but reasserted that Palestine belonged to the Arabs. Bergman demanded a right to respond to the statement but it was denied. This led the Jewish delegation to walk out in protest (Appadorai 1948: 281; Jansen 1971: 192). The delegation was persuaded by Indian delegates to return so the session could resume.[10] Nehru later referred to this incident in his ARC closing speech and apologized (Gopal, Sarvepalli, ed., Nehru, *Selected Works*, Series II, 2: 511).

The clash with Arab delegates was a new factor for Indian diplomacy in the region. For the first time, India had to balance its relations with both the Arab and Jewish nationalist movements. Nehru tried to fulfil a mediating role during the conference, especially in his two speeches at the opening and closing of the ARC. In his inauguration speech, Nehru avoided any direct reference to the Jewish delegation, although he individually welcomed other delegations (Gopal, Sarvepalli, ed., Nehru, *Selected Works*, Series I, 1: 302–3). In his closing speech, Nehru again expressed the sympathy of the Indian people with the suffering of the Jewish people in Europe, but he also reiterated India's position that Palestine was mainly an Arab country and that no national settlement could be made without the consent of Arabs. Nehru also hoped that the issue could be resolved through discussions between the two movements following the withdrawal of the British (Gopal, Sarvepalli, ed., Nehru, *Selected Works*, Series II, 2: 511). Through his compromising speech, Nehru confirmed India's pre-independence policy vis-à-vis Palestine: India continued to support Arab nationalism while also empathizing with Jewish concerns.

Although the Jewish delegation failed to obtain explicit support for the creation of Israel, it managed to communicate its case to the Indian public and to establish some long-term contacts with the Indian socialists. The participation in the ARC also raised strong hopes among the Jewish movement that they could establish bilateral relations with India in the long term. After the conference, the Jewish delegation recommended the creation of a permanent political representative of the Jewish Agency to India, of a desk for Indian and Asian affairs within the political department of the Agency, and to use US politicians who had supported both Indian nationalism and Zionism (like Congressman Celler). Following these recommendations, the political department of the Jewish Agency decided to open a permanent office of the Jewish Agency in Bombay on 16 May 1947 (Gerberg 2008: 192–3). On 9 July 1947, a Hebrew Palestinian Unit of the new ARO was effectively created in Jerusalem, and a cable, giving information on the inauguration of the new local unit, was sent to Nehru in New Delhi. In return, Nehru's secretary cabled back to welcome the creation of the Hebrew Palestine Unit.[11] However, when the next meeting of the ARO was held in New Delhi in January 1949, the Hebrew Palestinian Unit was not invited. India decided this time to not invite the Jewish delegation because of Arab pressure and the threat of a boycott (Kochan 1976). This happened after negotiations were held at the UN on the partition of Palestine in 1947 and the creation of the Israeli state in 1948. India had agreed to invite a Jewish delegation, representative of the Jewish religious minority in Palestine, but it refused to recognize a Jewish state as indicated through its vote against the partition of Palestine at the UN.

India at the UNSCOP: Taking a Stand

Between 1945 and 1947, Britain had to face increased opposition from both the Arab and Jewish communities in Palestine. After suggesting different solutions towards independence, which were rejected, Britain finally decided to place the Palestine question before the first special session of the UN General Assembly (UNGA) in April 1947. Placing great confidence in the mediation of dispute through international institutions, India supported the British proposal for the UN to deal with the Palestine question.[12] Nehru nominated Asaf Ali, India's ambassador in Washington, as India's first representative to the Special Session at the UN. Ali was given very specific guidelines from Nehru. He had to support a termination of the Mandate and to ensure that India would be part of any fact-finding committee on Palestine. But Ali was also warned not to commit the government to any position without prior approval from Delhi, and to avoid raising issues which might 'affect' India's relations with other countries.[13] These two instructions demonstrated that India's position was not completely fixed and remained open to change. India was itself in a crucial period of its own history: the position on the Palestine question at the UN would be the first official expression of India in the capacity of a an independent political entity in an international forum. This also meant that India would have to formally take sides in an international debate for the first time. Henceforth, India's decisions would be scrutinized by its regional and international partners.

At the Special Session, Ali argued against the influence of Great Power politics and of economic interests on the matter, and stressed the need for justice.[14] After an intense debate which lasted until 15 May 1947, it was decided that the five major powers (also the permanent members of the United Nations Security Council [UNSC]) would be excluded from membership of the specialized committee created to study the Palestine issue. Following Nehru's instructions, Ali filed for India to be a member of the UNSCOP. However, India had problems integrating the original list of neutral members of the Committee suggested by US representative Warren Austin. India did not even make it to the second list of two additional members suggested by Chile.[15]

There was a general perception that Ali pursued a pro-Arab stand despite Nehru's explicit recommendation to not take any unequivocal stand on the issue. Ali first unsuccessfully attempted to include the Arab proposal, which demanded the immediate termination of the Mandate and the proclamation of the independence of Palestine, in the Agenda of the Special Committee.[16] While Ali managed to get the Arab Higher Committee, represented by Mufti Hussayni, to talk before the Special Committee, he also supported inviting the Jewish Agency to testify.[17] Ali's overt pro-Arab position led him to clash with British delegates and drew disapproval from other representatives. On 8 April 1947, both Moshe Sharett and Eliahu Epstein met with Asaf Ali and were under the impression that Ali was totally committed to the Arab cause. One month later, Ben-Gurion met Ali and refused to consider his suggestion to suspend Jewish immigration to Palestine for five years (Gerberg 2008: 193).

Nehru was disappointed with Ali's performance, which was in contradiction with his specific instructions to avoid controversy (Gopal, Sarvepalli, ed., Nehru, *Selected Works*, Series II, 2: 494). Nehru was concerned that Ali's stance could affect relations with India's Western partners and sent two letters cautioning him against raising divisive issues such as the Arab proposal for immediate independence. Nehru explained he had heard 'adverse comments' in New Delhi following Ali's statements and he recommended making 'fewer commitments' on the issue.[18] While Nehru wanted India to maintain its sympathy for Arab grievances, he also preferred maintaining a cautious and open-ended policy. Finally, the UNGA decided to appoint a more representative UNSCOP. Membership was extended to two other members from the South Pacific and Asian regions, which were underrepresented in the initial nine-member committee.[19] The expansion opened the door for India, which won the vote against Siam (Thailand).[20] Because of an overall perception that India was partial on the issue, New Delhi had to painfully negotiate its membership in the UNSCOP in May 1947.

It became a priority for Nehru to reframe India's position as a more balanced observer of the dispute. One first move was to nominate Sir Abdur Rahman as India's representative to the UNSCOP.[21] Just as he did with Asaf Ali, Nehru gave specific instructions to Rahman. Nehru wanted Rahman to support a federal solution which had to gain Arab approval. However, given the strong divisions on this issue and the uncertain outcome of the deliberations, Nehru also suggested to keep a 'vague' position and remain 'friendly' to both parties (Gopal, Sarvepalli, ed., Nehru, *Selected Works*, Series II, 2: 474–5). This was a confirmation of India's original policy, but it also marked a new willingness to be flexible if the context evolved. Nehru did not want Rahman to make the same mistakes as Ali and to rhetorically commit India in one direction. Nevertheless, Nehru's letter to Rahman was ambiguous in regards to the authority to which he was ultimately accountable. While Nehru said Rahman was a representative of the UN organization and that he was free to make his own judgements, he equally ordered Rahman to refer back to Delhi as he was a representative of India (Gopal, Sarvepalli, ed., Nehru, *Selected Works*, Series II, 2: 474–5).

The coming partition of India further complicated Rahman's loyalty concerns.[22] Rahman began to express doubts about the continuing legal status of India in the UN structure following the partition. Consequently, Rahman defended India's federal solution at the UNSCOP, but also offered a dissenting note on 14 August 1947 (just as the subcontinent was being divided). Rahman agreed with Nehru's position that partition was not a viable solution as it would not lead to a lasting peace between Arabs and Jews (UN [UNSCOP] 1947: Vol. 1, Ch. IV, 44). However, in his personal note, he rejected the federal solution which he judged equally impractical as it was opposed by all parties.[23] Rahman explained that the creation of a federation presupposed the prior existence of two nations and could only come into being when both the parties accepted such an institutional arrangement (UN [UNSCOP] 1947: Vol. 1, Ch. IV, 46).

These two conditions were not present in 1947. Rahman, for instance, explained that the only two areas where Jews and Arab cooperated in 1947 were in the Potash Company and the oil refinery (UN [UNSCOP] 1947: Vol. 1, Ch. IV, 13). Consequently, Rahman personally supported a unitary state where a clear Muslim Arab majority (three-fourths) had a right to self-determination. A partition scheme would, in the view of Rahman, be opposed to the principle of self-determination (UN [UNSCOP] 1947: Vol. 2, A/364, Add. 1, 9 September 1947, 44); he, however, also argued that religious, cultural, linguistic, and educational rights should be defended by the constitution, and that there should be proportional quotas for Jewish participation in government and other public offices. After the partition, India's ministry of external affairs (MEA) condemned the note and instructed Rahman to only support the federal plan.

The Jewish Agency closely followed the disputes between Delhi and its representative to the UNSCOP and was concerned that Rahman would support (along with the Iranian representative) the Arab case within the UNSCOP. In July 1947, Ben-Gurion testified twice before the UNSCOP as the committee was visiting Jerusalem.[24] Ben-Gurion criticized what he perceived as Rahman's 'open pro-Arab approach' during the meeting.[25] To remediate this problem, there were various Zionist efforts to inform Nehru of Rahman's bias. American Congressman Celler expressed his own concerns about Rahman in a cable he sent to Nehru. In his response, Nehru explained he had given instructions to Rahman that highlighted the quasi-judicial character of the inquiry and that insisted on Rahman's need to remain completely impartial. In July 1947, Nobel laureate Albert Einstein wrote to Nehru to praise the abolition of untouchability and to urge him to support another group of victims of persecution by backing the partition plan. Nehru reportedly replied by reaffirming India's position of support to the Arabs (Gerberg 2008: 209–12).

The UNSCOP final report was presented to the UNGA on 1 September 1947. Within the recommendations, there were 11 principles agreed on unanimously among the UNSCOP members, including the termination of the British Mandate in Palestine. In addition, the majority of the committee recommended that Palestine should be partitioned, whereas a minority report, supported by India, Iran, and Yugoslavia, proposed the creation of an independent federal state of Palestine which would consist of Jewish and Arab states. Both states would enjoy internal autonomy. There would also be constitutional safeguards for minorities (UN [UNSCOP] 1947: Vol. II, A/364, Add. 1, 9 September 1947, 47– 58). The federal plan was the continuation of India's longstanding position on the Palestine issue. After the report was submitted, the UNGA met to vote on its recommendation. The discussions lasted from 25 September to 25 November 1947. Vijaya Lakshmi Pandit, who headed the Indian delegation at the UNGA, publicly explained India's stand on Palestine on 11 October 1947. She argued that peace in Palestine was vital because of its geographical proximity with India. She also reiterated that Palestine was predominantly an Arab country. In an independent Palestine, Pandit suggested that the Jews should be given strong autonomy in the areas where they had a clear majority.[26] She also refused to link the questions of displaced Jews in Europe and of Palestine (UN [UNGA] 1948: A/AC.14/SR.11).

There were attempts by the Jewish Agency to convince the Indian delegation at the UNGA to modify its policy. The Jewish Agency tried notably to get in contact with Panikkar who had joined the Indian delegation at the UNGA in September 1947. In New York, Panikkar met Weizmann, Sharret, and Epstein several times from September to October to discuss the partition plan (Gerberg 2008: 74, 207; Weizmann 1949: 570). Panikkar reportedly told Epstein that the Indian delegation would not defy Nehru's specific instructions to vote against the partition plan (Gerberg 2008: 194). On Panikkar's advice, Weizmann also met with another member of the delegation, Sir Bengal R. Rau, in November 1947. To convince Rau to the Jewish proposal, Weizmann suggested scientific cooperation between the two future countries, a proposal Rau transmitted to Nehru (Rao 1972: 40).

In October 1947, Celler attempted to influence the Indian voting on the partition plan by directly appealing to Vijaya Lakshmi Pandit. Pandit clearly had her reservations with Nehru's position. Just like Abdur Rahman, she had warned the MEA through a letter on 8 October 1947 that the federal plan had little support and legitimacy because both contending parties, including the Arabs, rejected it.[27] However, Celler's efforts again proved unfruitful, as Pandit could not directly defy Nehru's instructions from New Delhi (Gerberg 2008: 207). The disagreements between Pandit and her brother were not lost to the Jewish delegation. A report was apparently sent to Ben-Gurion stressing the fact there had been a debate within the Indian delegation on the voting and that Mrs

Pandit had suggested to Nehru to abstain from voting on the partition plan.[28] The Indian delegation nevertheless stood by the federal plan.

On 29 November 1947, the UNGA rejected the Indian federal plan to adopt an amended partition plan in Palestine. A majority of 33 states supported the partition plan while India was one of the 13 delegations (and one of the seven non-Arab countries) which voted against the partition solution.[29] A few months after the partition of the subcontinent, India also refused the two-nation theory in Palestine. This is why after the resolution was passed, India (along with the Arab Higher Committee, Pakistan, and the Arab delegates) declared it did not feel bound by the decision and reserved its right to take whatever decisions it judged adequate (Rao 1972: 27). Nehru explained India's official position on the matter on 4 December 1947 before the Constituent Assembly, just days after the partition plan was voted and five months before the creation of the state of Israel (India, *Constituent Assembly Debates*, Vol. 1, Session II, 4 December 1947, 1261). This was a reply to Professor N. G. Ranga's motion which was asking for a withdrawal of support for a federal solution (Mehrish 1972: 422–3). This was the first time a foreign policy issue was discussed in a parliamentary session in India.[30] Nehru defended a federal state with autonomous regions, even if it was opposed by the 'major powers' and the two parties to the conflict (India, *Constituent Assembly Debates*, Vol. 1, Session II, 4 December 1947, 1261). Nehru believed the Indian proposal was 'not only a fair and equitable solution of the problem, but the only solution of the problem' (India, *Constituent Assembly Debates*, Vol. 1, Session II, 4 December 1947, 1261). Nehru thought that any other solution would lead to conflict. He also regretted the belated Arab support for India's federal plan after partition was voted.

After initially rejecting India's federal plan, the Arab states showed a new willingness to consider it after the 29 November vote.[31] Given the violence that erupted immediately after the UN vote, Nehru secretly hoped that the federal solution would be reassesed. India first supported the US, at the second Special Session of the UNGA in April 1948, when it suggested a suspension of the partition plan. India was even included in a 12-member subcommittee which met to formulate a provisional regime for Palestine. Nehru then charged the diplomat B. R. Rau to find a new solution which would conciliate both communities. Rau suggested an intermediary institutional solution between partition and federation which seemed to have gained Weizmann's interest (Kumaraswamy 2010:

105–7). But the proposed new plan never was considered as the state of Israel was proclaimed on 14 May 1948, just a day before the British pull-out of Palestine. Between November 1947 and May 1948, India unconditionally maintained its pre-independence policy in spite of an adverse context and few prospects of success. The eventual proclamation of Israel in May 1948 led to a reconsideration of India's longstanding policy.

Shock and Renewed Debate over India's Israel Policy (1948–50)

India had to deal with two new political realities in 1947–8: the partition of the South Asian subcontinent and Israeli statehood. Both Pakistan and Israel had now become irrevocable *faits accomplis* that India had to cope with. These two shocks started a new policy debate among different actors from the INC and the MEA over the benefits and costs of recognizing the new state of Israel. The question of recognition was frequently brought up in the Constituent Assembly debates, demonstrating an early domestic interest in this issue in India. The frequent questions forced Nehru to publicly articulate his position. When looking at Nehru's various statements over 1948–50, it is possible to observe a gradual change in India's position and to identify what factors were salient and considered by Nehru and other policymakers at various periods.

After trying to prevent and then to delay the partition, Nehru could not ignore the new political fact that was Israel which had almost immediately been recognized by the US and the USSR.[32] Before independence, India consistently supported Palestinian nationalism and defended their right to self-determination. The creation of Israel revealed the absence of any viable Palestinian Arab leadership. The Arab–Israel conflict, which immediately followed the creation of Israel, revealed strong inter-Palestinian and inter-Arab rivalries. During the next few years, India did not have any legitimate interlocutor on the Palestinian side. Its traditional partner of the pre-independence period, Mufti Husseyni, was deprived of power by the Arab states which were fighting Israel for their own political and territorial interests. Husseyni also decided at that time to side with India's new rival, Pakistan. For the next two years, India's Palestine and Israel policies paralleled the fluctuating situation in the region. There was an internal debate which explained the delay and the final outcome of September 1950 with the partial recognition of Israel.

This section will explain the subtle and progressive policy change which occurred between 1948 and 1950.

India is the Prize for Israeli Diplomacy

After independence, the primary goal of the Israeli political leadership was to ensure its survival as a full-fledged state. One effort was military and involved countering the Arab offensives. The other was diplomatic: Israel needed to receive international recognition from a majority of states, and especially from the most influential powers. In the post–World War II context, statehood became an important asset to ensure legal protection, access to loans and aid, and to facilitate security assistance. If the US and the USSR were the priority for Israeli diplomats, India was also an emerging key player in both the international system and the Asian region. One of the first goals of Israeli diplomacy was to receive de jure recognition from India. In spite of Indian opposition to the partition plan at the UN, the Jewish Agency had maintained diplomatic contacts with the Indian government.[33]

On 17 May 1948, three days after Israel proclaimed its independence, Moshe Sharett, who became the minister of foreign affairs in the provisional government of Israel, sent a cable to Nehru asking him for India's formal recognition of the newly born state of Israel.[34] There was initially no response from India. As a result, on 19 May, Eliahu Epstein, the representative of Israel's provisional government in Washington, gave a letter to the Indian chargé d'affaires notifying India of the proclamation of the state of Israel (Kumaraswamy 2010: 109). India did not take any immediate action towards recognizing Israel or even officially acknowledging the Israeli request. On 23 May 1948, the new president of Israel, Chaim Weizmann, himself sent a request for India to recognize the state of Israel but India again withheld its recognition (Rao 1972: 39). India's position at the time of Sharett's request was summarized in Nehru's letter to the chief ministers on 20 May 1948. Nehru preferred not to take any 'action in this matter at present' and to prudently monitor how events on the ground would unfold, in the case there was an opportunity for India play a mediatory role (Parthasarthy, *Letters to Chief Ministers*, p. 128). In May 1948, the continued existence of the Jewish state was not yet clear, and India did not want to make any rushed decisions. However, Nehru also recognized that events like the partition of Palestine and the ensuing Arab–Israel conflict made it difficult for

India to maintain its existing policy. He realized that the prospects for the survival of the state of Israel were strong given the involvement of the US and the USSR. Both great powers had no interest in seeing the state of Israel 'crushed'.[35]

In August 1948, the question of the recognition was brought up for the first time at the Constituent Assembly. Nehru was asked by a representative of the Central Provinces, H. V. Kamath, about the Government of India's position on the creation of Israel.[36] Nehru acknowledged for the first time the existence of the Sharett letter and that the question of recognition was being considered. Nehru said that a 'new State was formed and we had to wait' (India, Constituent Assembly Debates, 20 August 1948, Vol. 6, Session 1, 380–1). When pressed further on the issue, Nehru said that any decision needed to be deferred until the Indian government knew the exact 'international position' on the question (India, Constituent Assembly Debates, 20 August 1948, Vol. 6, Session 1, 380–1). Despite this seemingly cautious approach, there were some new signals which revealed divisions in or, to the least, different interpretations of the future policy direction. For instance, in June 1948, the new Indian ambassador to Egypt, Dr Syed Hussain, said that Israel had not yet fulfilled 'the fundamental principles of international law' concerning new states and that therefore India had not replied to its demands for recognition (The Hindu, 17 June 1948). Two months after the birth of Israel, the secretary of the Central Jewish Board in Bombay, F. W. Pollack, created in Bombay the publication India and Israel. A message from Nehru, which was written by his secretary M. O. Mathai, expressed hope for Jews around the world. In the same publication, the minister of finance and minister of industries, and the speaker of the legislative assembly greeted the birth of Israel (India and Israel, 1: 2, August 1948 : 2–3).

Factors Constraining India's Policy in West Asia

In spite of the political shock that was the creation of Israel in May 1948, India refrained from reversing its old policy and from recognizing Israel immediately because of two main factors. The first was that the situation in the region was still in flux with an outbreak of hostilities following the proclamation of the state of Israel. A second factor was the presence of an important Muslim population who had just been through the trauma of partition and who could have misinterpreted a rushed diplomatic overture to Israel (Brecher 1963: 129–30).

In his letter to the chief ministers in May 1948, Nehru had already suggested not taking any action on the matter because of the developments in West Asia. A good indicator of India's prudent approach is its position vis-à-vis the new Palestinian political authority. Following the partition vote at the UN, the Palestinian nationalist movement was divided and in disarray.[37] In February 1948, the Arab League sponsored the creation of a Palestine Committee. While the movement was reinforced in material and military capabilities, there were important questions about its national legitimacy as the traditional Palestinian authorities like the Arab Higher Committee and the Mufti Husseyini were sidelined by the Arab League. On 22 September 1948, an All Palestine Government (APG), under the leadership of Prime Minister Ahmed Hilmi Pasha, was created. The Republic of Palestine was proclaimed five days later with Mufti Husseyni as its president (Jbara 1985: 189). Hilmi Pasha informed Indian leaders of the formation of the APG and sought India's diplomatic recognition on 30 September (Kumaraswamy 2004a). There were concerns in India about the actual territorial sovereignty of the APG as vast areas of Palestine were controlled by Egypt and Jordan. India was also prudent in regards to the degree of political autonomy of this new political entity. As a result, India decided not to take any action. This non-decision started a policy tradition in India to not directly interfere in inter-Arab conflicts. In addition, with the exception of Pakistan, no non-Arab country recognized the new Palestinian regime. India had also issues with the position of the Mufti Husseyni who was increasingly becoming an open supporter of Pakistan, especially on the Kashmir issue.

India was concerned that recognition of Israel would alienate its Arab partners and particularly Egypt. Any opening to Israel would have to be handled subtlety to not be interpreted as a hostile act towards the Arabs. India was increasingly worried about attempts made by Pakistan to support and promote the efforts of the Arab states in their international campaign against Israel. Pakistan was indirectly using the anti-Israel cause to try to forge a Pan-Islamic alliance. Islamic solidarity was a way for Pakistan to gain Arab sympathies in its own disputes with India. In practical terms, Pakistan attempted to revive the defunct World Muslim Congress that had been supported by Shaukat Ali and Husseyni in the early 1930s (Baba 2008; Bahadur 1998). Pakistan also established the new headquarters of the World Muslim Congress in its capital, Karachi. Finally, Pakistan organized a third conference (after the Mecca and

Jerusalem sessions) which was presided by Mufti Husseyni in Karachi in 1949. India progressively realized that an essential prerequisite to obtain the sympathy of Arab countries was the extension of support in their dispute with Israel. In practical terms, the pre-independence rivalry which existed between the INC and the Muslim League for the ideological and institutional support of Arab nationalists continued after 1947 between the governments of India and Pakistan. India's position was again being framed in reaction to Pakistan's policies.

India's Israel policy was also influenced by another domestic factor: the presence of a significant domestic Muslim population. After independence, 30 million Muslims remained in India. This Muslim minority was recovering from the fresh trauma of Partition. The Indian government believed that Indian Muslims supported the cause of Palestinian Muslims. There were, for instance, reports of Muslim mobilization, notably from important Muslim leaders like the Nizam of Hyderabad, to collect money and volunteers in support of Palestinian Arabs after the creation of Israel (Kumaraswamy 2010: 150–1). The concern about the repercussions of an Indian recognition of Israel among the domestic Muslim population was also publicly expressed in the Constituent Assembly debates. A member of the Assembly, Begum Aizaz Rasul, asked if Nehru would take into account domestic sensitivities on the question of recognition. Nehru implicitly referred to this factor when he insisted on the fact that the government of India would keep in mind 'all the factors', including the 'national and international situation' when considering extension of recognition to Israel (India, *Constituent Assembly Debates*, Vol. 6, Session 1, 19–31 August 1948, 381). The position of Indian Muslims was also conveyed to Nehru and Indian decision-makers through influential Muslim personalities holding gubernatorial as well as important political positions after independence, such as Maulana Azad, who was minister of education but also a close confidante and advisor to Nehru. The domestic Muslim factor justified a longer and slow path towards recognition of Israel in order to minimize domestic concerns.

Costs to Maintaining India's No-Recognition Policy

By the end of 1948, Israel had managed to push back the Arab offensive and was progressively becoming a viable political reality which was now recognized by many international actors. New Delhi's decision to indefinitely defer the question of recognition was increasingly criticized by a group of Indian diplomats who were frequently interacting with their Israeli counterparts. As Israel was becoming a political reality in the new international order, there was now the impression among these diplomats of an increasing diplomatic cost for India's bilateral and multilateral relations. In September 1948, after the second Arab–Israeli ceasefire was signed, India's ambassador to the US, B. N. Rau, had mentioned the possibility of normalization of bilateral relations to his Israeli counterpart, Eliahu Epstein, in Washington.[38] In February 1949, Nehru stated that the 'recognition of Israel would be guided not only by idealistic considerations but also a realistic appraisal of the situation'.[39] He also added that non-recognition was not 'an irrevocable decision' and that the issue would no doubt be 'considered afresh in view of subsequent developments' (Parthasarathy, *Letters to Chief Ministers*, 275). In March 1949, Nehru acknowledged that Israel was 'undoubtedly a state which [was] functioning as such' and that India's policy probably needed to be corrected (India, *Constituent Assembly Debates*, 9 March 1949, 1400).

These latest statements from Nehru revealed a realization that non-recognition created many practical problems. Despite the absence of diplomatic relations, Nehru had sought agricultural and technical assistance from Israel. This demand followed the first discussions which had taken place between Weizmann and Rau at the UNGA in November 1947. The Indian minister of agriculture asked H. Z. Cynowitz, who was the representative of the Jewish Agency in India, if Israel could send agricultural experts to assist India (Gopal and Sharma 2007: 23; Kumaraswamy 2010: 113). Despite these discussions, there is no record of any such cooperation, which was probably complicated by the absence of formal relations between the two governments. There were also operational problems at the diplomatic level. In April 1949, the Indian embassy in Prague demanded clarification from New Delhi on how it should deal with the local Israeli legation. Because India had not yet recognized Israel, the MEA told the embassy to ignore communications from the Israeli diplomats (Kumaraswamy 1995a). Despite the absence of official relations, Indian diplomats in 1949–50 still had regular contacts with their Israeli counterparts and generally encouraged dialogue. There were frequent meetings between Rau and Abba Eban, then Israeli ambassador to the US, in New York; between Eliahu Epstein and Vijaya Lakshmi Pandit in Washington; and between Eliahu Sasson, the Israeli envoy to Turkey, and C. S. Jha, the Indian ambassador to Turkey, in

Ankara (Gopal and Sharma 2007: 92). Panikkar also maintained regular contacts with his old acquaintance Elath despite being posted in China. These repeated diplomatic interactions developed a new understanding between the two countries, or to the least between these diplomatic elites. By the middle of 1949, there was growing support at the diplomatic level for change.

However, this indirect pressure from Indian diplomats was not sufficient to induce a complete policy change. On 11 May 1949, the UNGA was asked to vote on Israel's admission as the fifty-ninth member of the UN. In a first phase, India voted positively (along with Pakistan) to include the question of Israel's admission to UN membership in the UNGA agenda. It, however, voted against Israel's membership to the UN.[40] India did not take the floor to express its views but its delegate, M. C. Setalvad, justified India's negative vote to the press as completely consistent with India's past political views on the Palestine issue. Setalvad explained that the Indian government could not recognize Israel as it had achieved its territorial and political objectives through armed force and not through negotiations.[41] This vote could indeed be interpreted as a loyal continuation of India's 1947 policy. However, Nehru's statements to the Assembly and to chief ministers seemed to prepare a progressive acceptance of the new geopolitical realities in West Asia. According to Nehru's biographer, Sarvepalli Gopal, India had in fact initially opted for abstention but then decided to vote against Israeli admission to the UN (Gopal 1979:169). There were profound disagreements within the UN delegation about the voting decision as Israel was now a functional state.

Some scholars have made a direct causal connection between the UN membership vote and the Kashmir issue which had come before the UNSC in January 1948 (Kumaraswamy 2010: 168; Ward 1992: 49, 75). Following the partition of the British Raj in 1947, both India and Pakistan claimed the former princely state of Kashmir as part of their territory.[42] The territorial dispute resulted in the first armed conflict between the two countries which began in October 1947 and lasted until India moved the issue to the UNSC in 1948. As New Delhi could not resolve the problem militarily or through bilateral negotiations, it opted for international mediation. India urged the UNSC to demand an evacuation of Pakistani troops from Kashmir. Pakistan denied the charges, refused to withdraw, and condemned what it described as India's campaign of 'genocide' against Muslims (UN Security Council 1948: Annex 6, S/646 and corr. 1, 67–

75). Pakistan tried to broaden the issue beyond the Kashmiri territorial dispute to a religious conflict where it could acquire the support of the Muslim world, and more specifically of the Arab states.

In this campaign to gain Islamic solidarity, Pakistan found allies in the APG and Mufti Husseyini who became a militant champion of Pakistan's cause against India. The Karachi World Congress in February 1949, presided by the Mufti, was dominated by two issues: Kashmir and Palestine (Schechtman 1966). Kashmir was not the only controversial issue which affected India at the time. There was also a concurrent vote on the forceful integration in India of another princely state, Hyderabad, which was being discussed at the UN.[43] There was therefore a sentiment that India did not want to upset Arab susceptibilities at the time when the Kashmir and Hyderabad votes were live issues at the UN. There were indeed six Arab votes in play at the UNGA.[44] Vijaya Lakshmi Pandit reportedly acknowledged the Kashmir factor in a discussion with Elath in May 1949 in Washington. She assured the Israeli diplomat that recognition would happen soon after the Kashmir issue was resolved (Avimor 1991: 172).

It is, however, doubtful that the Kashmir issue directly influenced India's stand on Israel for three reasons. First, the timing of the votes does not seem to support that argument. Syria, for instance, refused to accept Kashmir's accession to India at the UNSC only after November 1948. Second, India, and not Pakistan, initially brought the issue to the UN. If India had anticipated a possible Muslim sanction vote against its position, its government would not have asked the UN to arbitrate. Nehru believed the UN to be an 'impartial tribunal' (India, *Constituent Assembly Debates*, 25 November 1947). Third, Pakistan had originally little success in forming a Pan-Islamic group to support its position in the Kashmir dispute. At the time, West Asia was mainly dominated by secular-nationalist regimes with which India had developed strong diplomatic relations. At that time, Kashmir was not a decisive factor to explain India's position towards Israel. However, Pakistan's propaganda efforts at enlisting Muslim support against India in Islamic conferences probably pushed India to delay any drastic change in its position.

In May 1949, the partition of Palestine and the creation of Israel had now been recognized by two-thirds of the UNGA. Some immediate statements following the May 1949 vote revealed a new understanding that India's old position was no longer tenable. A few days after the vote,

Foreign Secretary K. P. S. Menon conceded that Israel's recent admission to the UN had altered the situation and that question of recognition was now being 'reconsidered'.[45] Later, in June 1949, Rau, who now represented India at the UN, told Abba Eban that there was no conflict of interests between the two countries.[46] In June 1949, Nehru also conceded that India would have to re-evaluate its policy in light of Israel's new UN membership (Parthasarathy Vol 1, 1947–49 : 363). The Israeli membership created a sort of dilemma for Nehru who believed in the transformative role of international institutions like the UN to hamper inter-state conflict in the post–World War II context. For the UN to effectively work as a forum for nations to peacefully discuss and resolve their disagreements, Nehru supported universal membership as an essential requirement (Baghavan 2012; Mazower 2009: Chapter 4). Now that Israel had been accepted as official member of the UN and interacted directly with the Indian delegation, Nehru had to prepare a policy change. In September 1949 in Washington, Pandit assured her counterpart Elath that India was gradually moving towards recognition (Kumaraswamy 2010: 112).

Israeli diplomats also used the international recognition of Israeli statehood as a means to pressure India to accept the new situation. In October 1949, during a visit to Washington, Nehru met with Ambassador Elath and Congressman Emanuel Celler. Elath mentioned notably that Turkey had recognized Israel in March 1949. Nehru reportedly replied that Indians were not anti-Semitic and that India could learn much from Israel's achievements in science and agriculture. Nehru also explained that the non-recognition of Israel was due to internal opposition which had to be treated carefully. Nehru did, however, concede that recognition of Israel could not be postponed indefinitely (Avimor 1991: 172; Gerberg 2008: 230–1). In a letter to the Israeli Minister of Foreign Affairs Moshe Sharett, Elath also said that Nehru had directly discussed the impact of the 'painful' Partition on the '30 million Indian Muslims' and that the Palestine question was a 'constant source of agitation' for this community (Gerberg 2008: 230–1). This explained why the Government of India had taken a prudent and gradual approach to recognition.

While Nehru referred to internal opposition to the recognition of Israel, there were also domestic political actors supporting a policy change. As discussed earlier, there was a strong existing interest within the Constituent Assembly on the Palestine question. The representative H. V. Kamath had already questioned India's position on Israel in August

1948 by arguing that the Jewish state was now a political reality (India, *Constituent Assembly Debates*, Vol. 6, Session 1, 20 August 1948, 380–1). The nationalistic party Hindu Mahasabha passed a resolution condemning the discriminatory policy of the Nehru government in regards to Israel.[47] The resolution urged India to take steps to build an 'intimate relationship' with the Jewish state (Schechtman 1966). Israel also received a strong vocal support from Master Tara Singh, the prominent Sikh religious leader and Akali Dal president.[48] However, supports from the Mahasabha and from Tara Singh were strategic decisions, as they respectively supported the establishment of a Hindu-majority state and a Sikh-majority state. The creation of a Jewish state was an interesting nation-building precedent to legitimate their domestic projects. Furthermore, these two peripheral political groups had limited impact on India's foreign-policy making at the time.

Towards Recognition in September 1950

As international pressure for recognition was growing, Nehru indicated that it could not be postponed for long. In front of the Constituent Assembly in December 1949, Nehru publicly acknowledged Israel was now a member of the UN and that its recognition by 'other member states' could not be 'indefinitely deferred' (India, *Constituent Assembly Debates*, 4 December 1949, Vol. 4, Session 7, 233–4). However, despite these pledges, Nehru was still very careful about the impact that the recognition of Israel would have on India's relations with Arab states. Nehru referred to the recognition issue as a subject of 'controversy among nations with whom we have friendly relations' and that therefore he wanted to avoid 'misunderstanding or ill-feeling' when making a decision. He nevertheless concluded that a 'satisfactory decision' would be possible in the 'near future' (India, *Constituent Assembly Debates*, 4 December 1949, Vol. 4, Session 7, 233–4). This ambiguous statement even led to speculation that recognition was imminent (*New York Times*, 5 December 1949). There were other signals of a changing position from India's diplomatic community. On 4 December 1949, A. A. A. Fyzee, India's ambassador to Egypt, said at a press conference in Cairo that India wanted to 'retain the friendship' of Egypt and other Arab states: but was also thinking about 'coming to terms' with Israel (*The Hindu*, 6 December 1949).

The regional context was also evolving. Most of the neighbouring Arab states in open military conflict with Israel (Egypt, Lebanon, Syria, and Transjordan) had signed armistice agreements with the Jewish state in 1949 (Morris 1993). This was not an official end to the Arab–Israeli dispute: the Arab states still refused to recognize Israel and the armistice lines as territorial agreements. Nevertheless, the conflict had clearly lost some of its intensity. The APG had also lost most of its relevance with the annexation of the West Bank and East Jerusalem by Jordan (Morris 2003). Because of these conditions, India did not develop a relationship with any Palestinian movement until the emergence of the Palestine Liberation Organization (PLO) in the 1970s. The Government of India did, however, pursue its policy of sympathy towards the Palestinian people by helping to solve the important refugee problem created by the first Arab–Israeli conflict. India actively supported the UN Relief and Works Agency (UNRWA) which worked to help the thousands of Palestinian refugees. Israel had survived and established a seeming modus operandi with most Arab states and there was no competing Palestinian nationalist movement courting India's favour. These regional developments created a new opportunity for India to change its policy vis-à-vis Israel.

Beyond the permissive regional and international environments, there were growing pressures on Nehru and the INC to recognize Israel. India had to deal with the practical problems of seating at the UNGA alongside an Israeli state which it had yet to acknowledge. India was increasingly isolated on this question: six countries in Asia—Burma, Iran, National China, the Philippines, Thailand, and Turkey—had recognized Israel between 1948 and 1950. Turkey and Iran were also the two first Muslim-majority states to recognize Israel. This development weakened the INC's traditional argument that its domestic Muslim population would oppose recognition. Similarly, in December 1949, India decided to extend recognition to the new communist regime in China, just a few weeks after it had taken power in Beijing (Misra 1966: 57). India had delayed recognition to Israel because it judged the Jewish state's existence, functional status, and international acceptance to not be certain by 1949. By contrast, it immediately recognized the People's Republic of China (PRC). Consequently, the Indian government was accused of adopting different criteria when it came to state recognition both in the Constituent Assembly and in the Indian media (India, *Constituent Assembly Debates*, 28 November 1949, 20; Misra 1966: 53; Schechtman 1966; Srivastava 1967). The legitimacy of India's position on Israel was increasingly being undermined at both the international and domestic levels.

There was a subsequent frustration in Israel, especially in the ministry of foreign affairs (MFA). Although a great supporter of India, the diplomat Walter Eytan was disappointed in 1950 by this awaited and 'belated recognition', at a time when 60 countries had recognized Israel, and after two years of efforts invested in establishing contacts with 'high-ranking Indian personalities' who had made 'many promises and demonstrations of friendship' (Eytan 1958: 169–70). There had been many lobbying efforts from Israel, especially from its diplomats in Washington and New York, who had maintained regular contacts with Indian diplomats. Israeli diplomats also tried to use India's close links with the US to pressure Delhi into changing its policy. Congressman Celler was regularly invited to meetings between Israeli and Indian diplomats to help persuade the latter (Gerberg 2008: 77, 209–10, 215). Since the US and UK aid at the time was considered necessary for the success of India's first five-year plan, diplomatic pressure (or to the least a perception of such) from these countries affected Delhi's calculations (McGarr 2013, Chapter 1).

This led Nehru a step closer to recognition in February 1950 when he announced to the new provisional Parliament that 'the fact that the state of Israel exists is of course recognized' by the Government of India (India, *Provisional Parliament Debates*, 27 February 1950, Vol. 1, 495). This was a de facto recognition of Israel.[49] Nehru added that that 'formal recognition' (de jure recognition) which involved an 'exchange of diplomatic missions' would have to be considered in connection with a number of other factors (India, *Provisional Parliament Debates*, 27 February 1950, Vol. 1, 495). Nehru's statement was ambiguous: for the first time, he publicly recognized the state of Israel but did not specify any moves to formalize this new position. India did not publish any official document recognizing Israel nor did it start discussing the establishment of diplomatic relations. It is possible that Nehru contemplated the idea of an ambiguous de facto recognition which would have the advantage of satisfying all interests, both at home and in the region.

Nevertheless, in spite of these apprehensions, India granted recognition to Israel on 17 September 1950, 28 months after the official Israeli request. The Government of India made a brief announcement deciding to accord recognition, and then published a press communiqué which clarified that Israel in September 1950 was now 'here to stay' and an 'established fact' just like communist China (communiqué published by *The Hindu*, 18 September 1950). The communiqué further explained that both India and Israel had now been 'working together at the UN for two years'. According to the communiqué, Israel was 'now collaborating with other members of the United Nations for furthering the cause of world peace and establishing better economic and social conditions in all parts of the world'. Non-recognition was now considered 'inconsistent' with India and Israel's 'overall relationship' (communiqué published by *The Hindu*, 18 September 1950). Recognition had become a necessary response to the concerns of Indian diplomats, as Israel had obtained de facto statehood and was now communicating and cooperating with Indian delegates at the UN.

It was also a required step as India was increasingly isolated in the international community on this issue. After the UN, most Western states and many Asian states, including Iran, had now accepted this fait accompli. In fact, Iran's recognition of Israel in March 1950 was considered as a rebuttal of India's policy for two reasons. First, the fact that it was a Muslim-majority state which now had diplomatic relations with the Jewish state undermined India's argument about its own domestic Muslim minority's concerns. Second, Iran had been the most obstinate pro-Arab actor in the UNSCOP deliberations along with India. Iran also supported alongside India the federal plan in the November 1947 vote.[50] If Iran had managed to radically change its positions in spite of its own domestic and international constraints, India's own position was increasingly difficult to defend. As a result, the Indian communiqué published in September 1950 emphasized that two Muslim states, Turkey and Iran, had also taken similar steps (*The Hindu*, 18 September, 1950).

The main obstacle to India's recognition of Israel was the fear among Indian policymakers of a diplomatic backlash from the Arab states. The Arab states were still pressuring India to not change its position. In its communiqué, the Government of India revealed that a memorandum had been sent by the government of Egypt insisting that recognition should not be granted to Israel. India's foreign secretary had also warned Indian diplomats stationed in West Asia to prepare for the diplomatic repercussions of an 'impending recognition of Israel' by India.[51] India accorded de jure recognition to Israel only after it had assured its Arab partners that this act did not mean India endorsed the Israeli position regarding the boundaries and the status of Jerusalem. These remaining questions would have to be judged in the future on their specific merits and with due regard given to Arab claims. The communiqué explicitly stated that this new step did in no way harm India's 'friendship of Egypt and other Arab states'. The Government of India stated it would continue to work for 'full justice and humane treatment of Arab refugees'.[52] Two weeks after recognition, Nehru acknowledged the Arab factor when explaining to the chief ministers that the recognition of Israel would have happened earlier but there was a desire at the time to not offend the 'sentiments of our friends in the Arab countries' (Parthsarathy, *Letters to Chief Ministers*, 1 October 1950, 2: 217).

In spite of these conciliatory statements, Nehru also wanted to show the Arab states through the recognition of Israel that India's support on the Palestine issue was not unconditional. The Indian government supported the Arabs on a principled basis, but it also wanted reciprocity in exchange. According to his biographer, Nehru was disappointed by King Farouk's Egypt vote against India on the Hyderabad issue at the UN.[53] India was also not happy with Egypt's abstention on a resolution on the Korean crisis which India had supported (Kozicki 1958: 165). The lack of Arab support on these two votes inclined Nehru towards a modification of his position on the Palestine issue. India also judged that non-recognition would limit its effectiveness as a 'possible intermediary between Israel and Arab states' (*The Hindu*, 18 September, 1950). This latest statement was consistent with India's commitment, since the pre-independence years, to play a mediating role in the regional dispute.

However, contrary to common diplomatic practice, the recognition of Israel did not lead to the immediate establishment of full diplomatic relations between the two countries. The official statement was ambiguous in the sense that it did not specify the type of recognition granted. This led some observers to argue that the Government of India had made a distinction between the legal act of recognizing the state of Israel and the political act of establishing diplomatic relations with the Government of Israel (Misra 1966: 60; Singh 1968: 75–6). Nevertheless, this decision was clearly meant to signal a new formal step in Indo-Israeli relations which went beyond the de facto recognition that Nehru had given to Israel in his original February 1950 statement. Furthermore, the official exchanges between Nehru and Indian diplomats with their Israeli counterparts in the following months marked a formalization of the new political links between the two countries. Nehru sent a cable to Moshe Sharett conveying the decision of the Government of India to accord recognition to the Government of Israel as of 18 September. The political recognition was explicit in this new statement. On the same day, Sharett replied in an official note expressing his satisfaction with the new state of affairs (*Jerusalem Post*, 18 September 1950). Ben-Gurion also stated that he saw 'a new era in the fraternal relations' between the two countries which he described as 'the largest and smallest of the free Asian nations.'[54]

The Israeli press interpreted India's recognition as a possible rapprochement of outlook in international affairs between the two countries (*Jewish Agency's Digest* 3 [1950]: 46–7). The Indian press also generally welcomed the decision and hoped that normal diplomatic relations would be established following the 1950 statement (*The Hindu*, 19 September 1950; *The Hindustan Times*, 19 September 1950; *The Times of India*, 20 September 1950; *The Statesman*, 19 September 1950). The magazine *India and Israel* published by F. D. Pollack in Bombay also had a special edition which included many enthusiastic letters from members of Parliment (MPs), governors, the Socialist Party (which had strong ideological connection with Israeli socialist leaders), the Hindu Mahasabha, and other organizations and personalities (*India and Israel* [Bombay] 3:2, 1950).

The cryptic September 1950 statement about Israel's recognition can be interpreted as a policy compromise. In Nehru's view, this partial recognition policy was a favourable compromise that allowed India to have good relations with both Arab and Western states. Change had become necessary given the increasing diplomatic costs linked to the position India had taken in 1947. Israel had become a geopolitical reality: it had won the war against its Arab neighbours, it had become a UN member, and it was now recognized by many states, including Muslim-majority countries. Non-recognition was also becoming impractical as the two countries were now working side by side at the UN. Non-recognition also limited any possible mediating role India could have played between Israel and the Arab states. Change is usually only possible under conditions of crisis or urgency as the choice for change often carries with it the risk of even greater loss. The recognition decision seems to have resulted from a rational assessment of costs and benefits for each alternative course of action: non-recognition would have incurred substantial diplomatic costs, while recognition would have antagonized the domestic Muslim population. In the end, international imperatives weighted more heavily than domestic concerns.

However, Nehru only opted for a partial change with the limited recognition policy. At the domestic level, it was a palatable decision for both the 'old orthodoxy' (the staunch defenders of the traditional policy of supporting the Palestinian cause and accommodating the domestic Muslim concerns) as well as the 'new orthodoxy' (the supporters of a more pragmatic foreign policy posture). Here, Legro's model is useful to see the different groups defining and constraining the parameters of Nehru's policy choices. India was willing to accept reality rather than to insist on a purely 'ideological' position.[55] In the end, there was little or no outcry from the Muslim community and from the Arab states which did not choose to sever ties with India. The question over the next few years would be to see if India would move to the next step and normalize its diplomatic relations with Israel.

1950–6: Towards the Normalization of Indo-Israeli Relations?

In the process of reversing India's original policy, the Nehru government had managed to take a first decisive step by recognizing Israel and by formally accepting the partition of 1947–8. However, the 1950 recognition was a policy compromise which emerged after two years of a gradual and prudent debate. The post-recognition period can be identified with what Legro has termed as a 'consolidation' phase, a second stage through which the 'new orthodoxy's' control of the policy agenda must be consolidated and its policy option reinforced by success (Legro 2005: 13–16). My model helps identify the forces at stake during the next six years. Originally, the advocates of change had an important success with the September 1950 recognition, and started working for normalization of relations with Israel. Many signals demonstrate that important bilateral steps were taken for an exchange of diplomatic missions. However, actors in support of the status quo were an obstacle to complete foreign policy change. Moreover, a series of events in the 1950s, such as the signing of the Baghdad Pact and the Bandung Conference, put under strain the opening of relations with Israel. These regional developments progressively limited any window of opportunity for full policy change vis-à-vis Israel.

Early Positive Signs

Existing studies have rarely discussed India's original and sincere intention to establish diplomatic relations in the early 1950s. Because India did not have any diplomatic relations with Tel Aviv until January 1992, the early positive signals towards normalization have generally been neglected. Nehru actually made statements which demonstrated his initial openness to normalization following recognition. In January 1951, Nehru met the Israeli ambassador in London, Eliahu Epstein, and told him that some procedures would have to be followed prior to establishing full diplomatic relations (Gerberg 2008: 79). The Government of India proved more flexible on the issue of opening a consular office in Bombay. In September 1951, F. W. Pollack, the representative of the Jewish Agency in Bombay, was officially appointed Honorary Consular Agent of Israel to India in Bombay.[56] This was the first official Israeli diplomatic office to open in independent India.

In March 1952, Walter Eytan, director general of the Israeli MFA, visited New Delhi. Eytan was sent by Israeli Prime Minister David Ben-Gurion to explore the possibilities of strengthening bilateral relations. This demonstrated that India was a priority for Israeli diplomats. Eytan was apparently given firm assurances by Nehru on 4 March that the establishment of diplomatic relations would happen after the results of the first elections which were to be announced a few weeks after their meeting (Eytan 1958: 120; Gopal 1979: 170). There was also a working draft budget for the diplomatic mission that was being prepared and Nehru was just awaiting ratification from his Cabinet (Eytan 1958: 120). During this conversation, Eytan was seemingly told by Nehru that the major stumbling block to normalization was Nehru's consideration for India's Muslims who had suffered a great shock with Partition. But Nehru also assured Eytan that this factor was evolving and that India's position would be reconsidered. Eytan further noticed how Nehru no longer seemed 'affected by Arab opposition to Israel' (Eytan 1958: : 169). During his visit, Eytan met other Indian diplomats and public figures, such as the MEA Secretary General G. S. Bajpai, Foreign Secretary K. P. S. Menon, and India's ambassador in Washington, Vijaya Lakshmi Pandit. Following these meetings, Eytan left with the impression that the Indian bureaucracy supported the normalization of diplomatic ties. Later in 1952, Eban, the permanent representative of Israel to the UN, met his counterpart, Mrs Pandit, in New York. Pandit reportedly referred to budgetary constraints to explain the delay in the exchange of diplomats (Gerberg 2008: 220). In December 1952, K. P. S. Menon, who was now India's ambassador to Moscow, assured Eytan that the exchange of missions between the two countries would happen 'without further delay' (Gerberg 2008: 156).

In public, most Indian political personalities and diplomats invoked budgetary problems rather than political reasons to justify the absence of diplomatic relations. According to the MEA 1948–9 report, there were very few Indian embassies in West Asia (Cairo, Istanbul, and Tehran) (Ministry of External Affairs [MEA], *Annual Report*, 1948–1949: 1–2). In 1950, the opening of many consular and embassy missions was on hold (MEA, *Annual Report*, 1949–1950: 2). The ambassador in Cairo was, for instance, accredited to different countries, including Jordan, Lebanon, and Syria (MEA, *Annual Report*, 1950–1951: 4). The lack of diplomatic relations was therefore not solely confined to Israel.[57] In parliamentary debates in December 1952, Nehru officially recognized the 'financial reasons' explaining the delay in setting up diplomatic exchanges with Israel as his government was 'anxious to avoid additional commitments abroad at present' (India, *Provisional Parliament Debates*, 11 December 1950, 793). A later MEA report argued that 'financial stringency' explained the absence of an embassy in Israel (as well as in Saudi Arabia) (MEA, *Annual Report*, 1951–1952: 10). In a later interview, an Indian diplomat and close adviser to Nehru, Krishna Menon, also discussed the financial argument and confirmed that India did not have that many ambassadors in the early 1950s (Brecher 1968: 79). This had reportedly led Israeli diplomat Yacoov Shimoni to suggest in December 1951 a concurrent accreditation to Israel of India's ambassador to Turkey (Kumaraswamy 2010: 124). These different statements tend to demonstrate that India had seriously intended to establish a mission in Tel Aviv.

A new important step towards normalization was taken in January 1953 when Israel was allowed to update its consular agency to a consulate in Bombay and Pollack was named honorary consul (Roland 1989: 244). In June 1953, Pollack was replaced by Gabriel Doron who was the first official career diplomat to be nominated as regular consul in Bombay (Kumaraswamy 2010: 129). However, the consular mission quickly raised problems over different interpretations of its role and of its territorial jurisdiction in Tel Aviv and Delhi.[58] The official opening of the Consulate in 1953 raised high expectations from Israeli diplomats over the possibility of normalizing relations with India. When asked about the recognition of Israel during a visit to Egypt in June 1953, Nehru said at a press conference that India would not withdraw its recognition of Israel as the new state was now an undeniable fact in the region (Nehru 1954: 33). By 1953, Indo-Israeli relations were not consolidated but were not unfriendly either. India had recognized Israel and refused to go back on this pledge despite strong Arab objections. Instead, the Government of India had allowed the establishment of a Consulate in Bombay, a limited two-way trade had begun to develop (mostly diamond), and the emigration of Indian Jews to Israel was facilitated by Indian authorities.[59] On the Israeli side, there were many actors endorsing a rapprochement with India. For instance, the Mapai party, which was a socialist movement, led the government coalition and and one of its leaders held the portfolio of the MFA. Prime Minister Ben-Gurion had a general interest in India which he described as a gateway to Asia in his essay 'Israel among the Nations' in 1952 (Brecher 1972: 163, 264, 383). In the early 1950s, the Mapai party had internal debates about its foreign policy orientation and its international priorities in general and in Asia in particular (Shlaim 2004). At the Mapai's Central Committee in April 1952, Sharett, for instance, discussed Israel's 'return' to Asia and considered links with India as important as Israel's relations with the US (Bialer 1981). Israel considered itself an Asian state, at least in terms of its geographic location, but its early quest for Asian acceptance ran into difficulties. Israel's conflict with most contiguous Arab states led to its isolation in its immediate neighbourhood. As a result, Israel concentrated on the West as a source of military equipment, economic aid, and international recognition. In order to break with diplomatic isolation in West Asia, Ben-Gurion and the Minister of Foreign Affairs Sharett sought to actively engage other Asian countries, and especially the Government of India which was considered to be an emerging leader in the Afro-Asian community. Israel therefore hoped Indian recognition would open the doors for political and economic activities in Asia (Eytan 1958: 8). Israeli leaders even expected that relations with India would help Israel win over the friendship of a number of Muslim Asian states (such as Malaysia, Indonesia, and Afghanistan). The Mapai party also considered Nehru to be a highly respected leader among the Arab states and hoped he could prove to be a bridging figure between Israel and its neighbours (Brecher 1963: 129). Eytan argued, for instance, that good relations with India would provide Israel with an entry in the society of Asian nations and a new legitimacy in Asia (Eytan 1958: 170).

The original invitation to the ARC had raised high hopes among Mapai party leaders on Israel's possible integration in the family of Asian nations which could be facilitated by India. Delegates from both countries were also present at the Asian Socialist Conference (ASC) held in Burma in 1952.[60] The influential socialist leader Jay Prakash Narayan was also a staunch advocate of closer relations with Israel, which he visited several times (Jansen 1971: 309–10). As a consequence of these early ideological connections, many Indians, mostly from trade unions and the Socialist Party (the Praja Socialist Party), travelled to Israel to undergo professional training in 1953. In the same year, sponsored by UN fellowships, Indian participants took part in agricultural courses in Israel, while Israeli agricultural experts were sent to various Indian states to share their experience. There were also student exchanges and an India mission came to Israel to study the organization of trade unions and Kibbutz cooperative movements in Israel (Gerberg 2008: 224–7). The contact between the socialist parties in both countries led to the organization of the Afro-Asian meeting in Delhi in 1955 which was attended by an Israeli delegation (Jansen 1971: 226–7).

It was the MFA, and in particular the Asian experts in the ministry, that directly interacted with Indian officials and carried off lobbying efforts for the establishment of diplomatic relations. The new state of Israel aspired for membership in the nascent group of non-aligned nations of which India was one of the main leaders. In 1951, an Asian Department was set up in the MFA.[61] In October 1951, the new head of the Asian Department submitted a tentative plan to establish diplomatic ties between Israel and Asian countries, including the opening of an Israeli chancellery in New Delhi (Gerberg 2008: 215). However, Moshe Sharett was against such a unilateral diplomatic move and preferred to wait for a positive sign from the Government of India on opening an embassy in Israel. Consequently, both the Israeli politicians in power and the bureaucrats had placed India as a top diplomatic priority.[62]

Remaining Obstacles

By the mid-1950s, Israeli hopes of a rapprochement with India were dampened by the lack of actual progress in negotiations and the existence of remaining obstacles both in India and in the West Asian region. Eytan himself was disappointed when he met Nehru in Bremen in 1953; just a year after the Indian prime minister had made a firm pledge to move towards normalization. The government had now been formed after the election results, but normalization was not planned and Eytan was not given any official explanation for the prolonged delay (Eytan 1958:

169). Although no official justification was ever publicly given to the Israeli government (other than budgetary constraints), India's refusal to establish full diplomatic relations with Israel can be attributed to different factors, and most notably to the opposition of the old orthodoxy which still promoted a pro-Arab policy.[63]

According to some observers, India's sudden change of mind in 1952 can be almost solely attributed to Maulana Azad's 'forceful intervention'.[64] Azad was at the time the minister of education in Nehru's government, a close personal friend, but most particularly an expert in 'Arab affairs' and a 'respected leader of India's 40 million Muslims' in Nehru's mind.[65] Nehru had mostly a secular and nationalist interpretation of the Palestine issue but the sentiments of the domestic Muslim population were mainly conveyed to him through Azad.[66] Nehru was convinced by Azad that the time for normalization was not opportune because it would lead to negative diplomatic fallout with the Arab states (Agwani 1973b; Brecher 1963: 130; Gopal 1979: 170; Heptullah 1991: 166; Kozicki 1958). Azad notably warned against the probable loss of Arab support on the Kashmir issue if India openly engaged Israel. Azad was also concerned that an opening of diplomatic relations with Israel would be used by Pakistan to disseminate anti-India propaganda in West Asia (Brecher 1963: 130). In addition, Azad was concerned about the possible impact that a diplomatic overture to Israel could have on India's large and insecure Muslim minority. To summarize, Azad argued that the immediate benefits linked to normalization of relations with Israel would not overcome the more direct and visible diplomatic costs and the risks for internal cohesion. Nehru had hoped to get the unanimous endorsement of his Cabinet (as he did in 1950 for the recognition of Israel) but he met the strong opposition of Maulana Azad and he was not ready to overrule him and other ministers on this particular issue.[67] While it is difficult to find prima facie evidence to support these strong claims, there seems to be a consensus that Azad was regularly consulted by Nehru over West Asian affairs, and that his position was an important factor in determining Nehru's decisions on the Israel question.[68]

Internal opposition to normalization was an important factor but it was certainly not the only or even the most decisive one. The pressure of Arab countries was still present in the 1950s. While Israel had no representative in Delhi, the Palestinian cause was directly defended in the Indian capital by the office of the Representative of the Arab League to India and Southeast Asia (Kozicki 1958). On some specific regional issues, India also continued to side with the Arab states. New Delhi voted for the internationalization of Jerusalem through the UNGA Resolution 303 of December 1949 (UNGA, A/RES/303 (IV), 9 December 1949). In 1950, India supported Syria's complaint at the UNSC against Israel which was accused of diverting water from the river Jordan for irrigation purposes (Singh 1979). India also abstained on Resolution 95 of the UNSC adopted in September 1951, which referred to freedom of navigation in the Suez Canal and which called on Egypt to stop all discriminatory practices against Israeli shipping in the Canal.[69]

India's ongoing political and territorial disagreements with Pakistan also had consequences for its West Asia policy. The Kashmir dispute was now at a standstill. In the 1950s, Pakistan pursued its efforts to gain Pan-Islamic solidarity among West Asian countries on the Kashmir issue with little success. This led Islamabad to look for support elsewhere and to agree to enter an Anglo-American alliance initiative, which was officially conceived to contain Soviet expansion in West Asia (McGarr 2013: 16–25). This alliance was institutionalized in 1955 as the Baghdad Pact. Nehru was concerned that the Anglo-American assistance to Pakistan under the auspice of the Baghdad Pact would push Pakistan to seek a military solution on the Kashmir issue, and would encourage an arms race in the region. In order to counter this new military alliance project, and the intrusion of Cold War politics in West Asia in general, Nehru reinforced his links with various Arab states, including Egypt.

Nehru strongly criticized the pact which divided West Asian countries in two blocs. Nehru was concerned this would disrupt Arab unity and weaken the Arab League which had been created for the purpose of facilitating cooperation among Arab states (Nehru 1961: 94). Opposition to the Baghdad Pact brought Nehru and the Egyptian President Gamal Abdul Nasser closer. In February 1955, Nehru emphasized their 'similarity of outlook' on international affairs, notably in reaction to the 'Turko-Iraq Pact' (Parthasarathy, Vol. 4, 1954–57, 135). Nehru strongly supported the emergence of secular Arab nationalism in West Asia and perceived Egypt to be taking the lead in this regional trend, 'under the wise leadership of President Nasser' (Nehru 1961: 282–3). Relations with Egypt were guided not only by ideological affinities but also by a pragmatic need to defend India's national and diplomatic interests. Egypt was instrumental in limiting efforts from Pakistan to isolate India either through Pan-Islamic solidarity or through the Baghdad Pact. In 1955, Egypt played a pivotal role in West Asian politics, and was able to mobilize different countries in support of India. An isolated Israel could not fulfil this role. Both countries signed a Treaty of Friendship and Cooperation in April 1955. According to some observers, this period also marked the beginning of India's long-term Cairo-centric approach of West Asian affairs (Gordon 1975; Rao 1972: 45; Ward 1992: 27–8).

At that time, Nehru was very reluctant to change his Israel policy. India countered Pakistan's diplomatic efforts by emphasizing its shared outlook with Arab nations on most West Asian events. This strategy was initially very successful as Anglo-American efforts to form a large military alliance in the Arab world were quickly stifled. Furthermore, beyond Egypt, other Arab states lauded India for its opposition to the Baghdad Pact and criticized Pakistan's membership. Saudi Arabia's King Saud, two years after he had supported Pakistan on the Kashmir issue, expressed his disappointment that the 'Islamic State of Pakistan should accede to those who have joined hands with the Zionist Jews' by joining a Western Military Pact'.[70] The rapprochement between India and key Arab states helped to check Pakistan's diplomatic attempts to convince Muslim Arab states that India was mistreating its own domestic Muslim population and that the Government of India was pro-Zionist following the recognition of Israel.

In the 1950s, there was an unstated but bitter rivalry with Pakistan for Arab support on the Kashmir dispute. India's policy on that issue was under severe attack in the UN. In exchange for its pro-Arab policy, New Delhi hoped to receive a reciprocal support on Kashmir, or to at least neutralize Arab support for Pakistan. In the early 1950s, there were thirteen Arab votes at the UN against one Israeli vote. National interests therefore dictated a pro-Arab position. Israeli diplomats were reportedly notified by their Indian counterparts that a normalization of relations with Israel could have been misinterpreted by Arab states at the time.[71] In his autobiography written in 1958, Eytan lamented that Nehru had been 'prepared to appease Arab susceptibilities by keeping away from Israel' (Eytan 1958: 170–1). The Arab factor was crucial for another neglected reason. Just like British India before 1947, independent India's vital sea and air communication lanes with the West ran across Arab lands. Consequently, India needed to preserve good relations with Arab states and especially with Egypt, which controlled traffic in the Suez Canal, to ensure access to resources and markets in West Asia and Europe.

In the first half of the 1950s, the establishment of diplomatic relations with Israel was yet to be achieved but did not seem like an improbable possibility either. There is strong evidence to suggest that Nehru was open to the idea of normalization. There were also indications that there was a strong internal obstacle with Azad. Nehru was also concerned by the Arab factor which led him to be very cautious in his dealings with Israel. The Kashmir dispute, the rivalry with Pakistan, and the emerging partnership with Egypt made Indo-Arab relations a landmark of early Indian diplomacy in the region. At the same time, India did not withdraw its recognition of the Jewish state despite direct Arab pressure to do so.[72] In September 1953, the Israeli ambassador to Britain, Eliahu Epstein, reported to Eytan about his meeting with the Indian High Commissioner Panikkar. Epstein was reportedly told that an exchange of diplomatic missions was not a viable proposition at the time. As long as Nehru thought he needed the support of the Arabs, or to the minimum their neutrality, on the issue of Kashmir, he could do no more than to maintain the status quo (recognition without relations) (Gerberg 2008: 232).

A lack of clear understanding of Indian diplomatic concerns also led Israel to demand full diplomatic reciprocity and to lose an important opportunity. In the 1950s, there were some indications that Nehru would have accepted an Israeli embassy in New Delhi, without the obligation of immediate reciprocity and the establishment of an Indian mission in Israel. This argument seemed logical since India had recognized Israel but delayed the option of sending an Indian delegation for budgetary reasons. However, Sharett insisted on full reciprocity as a matter of principle (Brecher 1972: 560; Medzini 1972: 28; Ward 1992: 103). This created a deadlock as India was not ready, for both financial and other reasons discussed earlier, to open an embassy in Tel Aviv. Some have therefore argued that Sharrett and Israel made a crucial diplomatic mistake in 1953 by insisting on reciprocity and not unilaterally opening an Israeli embassy in New Delhi. This refusal to compromise on Israel's part made it easier for Nehru's opponents to pressure the government to reject all offers which would lead to full normalization. The threshold for change was now placed at a higher level: the need for reciprocity made any incremental and intermediary changes, such as the unilateral opening of an Israeli mission in Delhi, difficult to achieve.

Afro-Asian Conference in Bandung: A Lost Opportunity

In 1954–5, the Afro-Asian movement was rapidly expanding with the independence of colonized states. Asian states like India, Burma, Indonesia, Pakistan, and Sri Lanka started discussing the possible institutionalization of a larger Afro-Asian movement to promote economic and cultural cooperation between them (Tan and Acharya 2008). The newly independent Asian countries began to prepare for the first large-scale Afro-Asian conference (which would be later known as the Bandung Conference) in 1955. Since Israel wanted to be integrated into the Afro-Asian movement, it hoped to be part of the conference There was a first preliminary meeting in Colombo (Sri Lanka) in April–May 1954 to discuss mutual problems.[73] At the meeting, Pakistani Prime Minister Muhammad Ali introduced a draft resolution condemning the creation of Israel as a violation of international law and Israel's aggressive policies towards Arab states, as well as expressing concern over the plight of Palestinian refugees (Jansen 1971: 250–1). Nehru, who had recognized Israel, opposed the resolution along with Burmese Prime Minister U Nu.[74] As Burma and Sri Lanka had also recognized Israel by 1954, Pakistan was in a minority. Eventually, the final statement was very different from the original Pakistani proposal. While it still expressed concern for the sufferings of Arab refugees in Palestine and called for their rehabilitation in their original homes, it no longer contained any direct condemnation of Israel. This is further evidence that Nehru did not have a fixed and hostile position on Israel. Nehru's mediating pressure led to a compromise resolution and communiqué.

The Israel question came up again at the second preparatory meeting between the five heads of government in December 1954 in Bogor (Indonesia). The objective was now to work out an agenda and to determine the list of Afro-Asian countries to be invited to the conference in Bandung. Two invitations were originally controversial: the PRC and Israel. Originally, Nehru supported the participation of both countries. He argued that both states were independent and geographically part of Asia (Jansen 1971: 252–3; Kochan 1976). He was joined by U Nu who also supported extending an invitation to Israel.[75] However, Nehru was conscious that a compromise was possible with the Arab and Muslim states on China but not on Israel. The PRC was finally invited on the condition that the acceptance of an invitation by one country had no implications for its diplomatic recognition of that country.[76] By contrast, the invitation to Israel was dropped in the preliminary discussions.

The Arab League Council had sent an official note to the five Asian leaders indicating that the Arab states had agreed at a meeting in Cairo a few days before to not participate in any regional conference where Israel was represented (Kochan 1976: 251). Through this notification, the Arab countries essentially threatened to boycott the Bandung Conference if Israel was invited. This ultimatum meant that Nehru and U Nu would have to choose between the participation of Israel and of the Arab states. The two Asian leaders finally bowed to the pressure of the Arab states. Nehru believed that the absence of the Arab states and of many Muslim states (including Pakistan and Indonesia) would have deprived the Conference of much of its substance and legitimacy. If Nehru had stuck to an ideological position that all independent Asian states had a right to participate, he would have invited both Israel and the Arab states, in spite of the possible diplomatic consequences. Instead, Nehru reluctantly took a pragmatic decision to not invite Israel and to ensure that there would be a broader (if not complete) representation at the Conference.[77]

In January 1955, David Hacohen, who was Israeli ambassador to Burma, met Nehru and Krishna Menon in Rangoon and complained that India had supported the exclusion of Israel from the Bandung Conference. They explained to Hacohen that, although they were bothered that Israel would be left out, they were compelled to take this decision because the only other alternative would have been to call off the conference (Brecher 1968: 79; Eytan 1958: 172–5). Israel's Minister of Foreign Affairs Sharett also criticized the Bogor resolution which did not recognize Israel's status and 'rightful place at the conference' (*Jerusalem Post*, 17 March, 1955). In all practical matters, Nehru had indirectly given the Arab states a veto power over India's Israel policy.

Despite Israel's absence at the Bandung Conference, it took three days for the Afro-Asian states to agree on a resolution on West Asia. Even though it was not an independent state, Palestine was indirectly present at the Conference as some of its representatives were part of various Arab delegations. For instance, Hajj Amin al-Hussayni, the former grand Mufti of Jerusalem, was present as a member of the Yemeni delegation and openly made the case for Palestine against Israel (Goldstein 2004). There was, however, an important debate between Nehru and the Arab delegations over the Palestine issue.[78] Nehru made a speech which expressed sympathy for the Arab refugees from Palestine and which called the establishment of Israel under UN auspices an 'immoral violation of human principles' (New York Times, 19 April 1955; Ward 1992: 103). But he also urged the Arabs not to rule out negotiations with Israel as a means of settling the Palestine issue.[79]

The Arab delegates said they were open to negotiations but only on the basis of the UN resolutions on the problem of refugees, the territorial question, and the status of Jerusalem (Jansen 1971: 257). They argued that Israel had refused to negotiate on these grounds. As a result, the Arab states and Pakistan were originally determined to ignore Nehru's advice. Pakistan made a first unsuccessful bid to condemn the creation of Israel in a draft resolution (Kochan 1976: 252). Pakistan and the Arab states then realized the Conference had a voting procedure which required a unanimous agreement. As a result, under Nehru's indirect pressure, they agreed on a compromise resolution. The final joint statement of the Conference shied away from a direct condemnation of Israel, and only referred to a support for the 'rights of the Arab people of Palestine', and called for the implementation of the UN resolution on Palestine (UN Resolution 194/III from December 1948) and the 'achievement of a peaceful settlement of the Palestine question.'[80]

Nevertheless, in spite of Nehru's conciliatory role, the Bandung precedent signified the long-term institutionalization of Israel's exclusion from the Afro-Asian community. Israel's Foreign Minister Sharett sent a telegram of protest to the Indonesian government expressing Israel's surprise that the Conference discussed and passed a resolution on the Arab–Israeli problem in its absence (Haaretz, 23 April 1955). Eytan also admitted in his memoirs that the Afro-Asian Conference was a blow to Israel's standing in Asia. In fact, he argued the Afro-Asian Conference had been a severe diplomatic setback for Israel which was further isolated in the region (Eytan 1958: 175).

The absence of any headway towards the normalization of relations with India, and the more general lack of success in engaging Asian states, reduced the influence of actors within the MFA and the Israeli political scene who had supported Israel's integration in Asia. By contrast, the Bandung setback consolidated pro-Europe actors in foreign-policy making in Israel. Some also argued that the Bandung Conference was a turning point in India–Israel relations because it made it more difficult for Indian policymakers to push for full diplomatic relations (Kochan

1976). However, Nehru still hoped for a negotiated settlement in West Asia and did not explicitly oppose the prospect of normalization. There were still cultural exchanges between the two countries such as the visit of Professor L. A. Meir from the Hebrew University to the All-India Universities Conference in Calcutta in January 1956 (Gerberg 2008: 236). I will argue in the next section that the 1956 Suez crisis decisively cemented India's no-relationship policy.

1956: Suez as a Turning Point

In the mid-1950s, relations between India and Egypt had grown stronger as the two countries shared similar concerns. Both countries did not want to see great powers intervene in their immediate neighbourhoods and had an interest in pursuing a non-aligned foreign policy. Nehru also developed close personal relations with Egypt's President Nasser (Agwani 1973a; Heptullah 1991: 180–3; Kozicki 1958). Nehru and Nasser met eight times between 1953 and 1955 as Nehru made Cairo a regular stopover on his trips to Europe (Heikal 1973: 280). In April 1955, Nasser stopped in Delhi on his way to the Bandung Conference and even addressed the Indian Parliament. It is during this visit that both countries signed a Treaty of Friendship and Cooperation. However, in spite of the Indo-Egyptian rapprochement, India's West Asia policy stayed neutral in nature as most of Nehru's criticism was directed at the Western powers' influence and the Baghdad Pact rather than directly against Israel. The nationalization of the Suez Canal and subsequent events would modify Nehru's position by bringing together the Western powers and Israel.

In July 1956, Nasser decided to nationalize the Suez Canal. The move was the culmination of a protracted political dispute developed over a proposal between Egypt, the US, and the UK for the funding for the construction of the Aswan High Dam.[81] As the Suez Canal was a strategic trade link which had remained under British control after Egyptian independence, Nasser's bold gesture was considered as move defying European powers. The same day as the nationalization, Egypt closed the access to the Canal and to the Straits of Tiran to Israeli shipping. Nehru officially agreed with the nationalization move in a statement made in the Lok Sabha on 8 August 1956. He stated that the Egyptian nationalization decision complied with the terms of sovereign Egypt's laws. However, Nehru also referred to the 'international character' of the Suez waterway according to the Anglo-Egyptian Agreement of 1954. Nehru also regretted the 'suddenness' of the decision and of its implementation, which had led to the violent European reactions.[82] Nehru deplored the lack of consultation between the UK and Egypt on this matter.[83] He finally warned against any war-like gestures and encouraged the holding of an international conference to resolve the crisis.

India's position during the Suez crisis was also dictated by practical considerations and national self-interest. Nehru was in fact preoccupied by the closing of the Canal to international circulation as India was not a 'disinterested party' but a 'principal user of this waterway' whose 'economic life and development' was directly affected by the disputes (India, Lok Sabha Debates, Vol. 7, Pt 2, 8 August 1956, pp. 2536–44). The nationalization had come as a bad surprise for the Indian Prime Minister. Nehru had not been warned beforehand by Nasser in spite of having met him just a few days before at a summit in Brioni and in Cairo. Given his good relations with the Egyptian President and India's stake in the Suez Canal, Nehru had visibly been disappointed by Nasser's unilateral move (Agwani 1973b). Despite his reservations about when and how nationalization had occurred, Nehru supported Nasser and counselled moderation to resolve the dispute. The legitimacy of the nationalization itself was not an issue for India, but Nehru wanted Egyptian guarantees that the Canal would remain available to all users without discrimination (Gopal 1989). Consequently, India called on all the involved countries to abandon threats, violence, and unilateral acts in order to avert a conflict in the region (India, Lok Sabha Debates, Vol. 7, Pt 2, 8 August 1956, 2536–44). Nehru also supported the principle of a conference reuniting the parties to the Convention of 1888 in London on 16 August 1956.[84]

India was invited to the conference as a concerned party. The Indian delegation was led by Krishna Menon. The objective of the Indian delegation was to update the 1888 Convention (which had been negotiated by the British) to ensure freedom of navigation and security for the users of the Canal. It is interesting to observe how independent India shared in this context the same geo-economic priorities as the British Raj, such as the preservation of free access to this decisive international waterway. Menon addressed the conference on 20 August and emphasized India's dependence on the Canal: in 1956, about 76 per cent of India's imports and 70 per cent of its exports passed through Suez (India 1956: 41–56). Menon then criticized the composition of the conference and the absence of Egypt. He was concerned that a solution should not be decided without the consent of the Egyptian government (Eayrs 1964: 141–2). India attempted to keep open a line of communication between the UK, France, and Egypt to find a mutually satisfactory solution.[85] Nasser had initially asked India to boycott the conference but Nehru had felt it wiser to keep the dialogue open and to directly present Egypt's grievances to the conference (Heikal 1973: 282). At the conference, Menon suggested a five-point proposal (as an alternative to the US plan) which demanded that the 1888 Convention be recognized; that efforts should be made to update this Convention; that Egyptian ownership should be confirmed; that a consulting association of users of the Canal be created on a geographical basis; and finally that Egypt transmit an annual Report of the Egyptian Corporation for the Suez Canal to the UN (India 1959: 249–50). The US plan was supported by 18 nations and submitted to Nasser who rejected it. Instead, Nasser suggested another proposal, which India supported and which called on all user nations to meet and create a consultative body to review the 1888 Convention (Ward 1992: 54).

There was a second London Conference which was held in September 1956. The 18 users met again and rejected the Egyptian offer. Nehru was concerned by the refusal of European countries to further negotiate and by the risk of escalation of the crisis. Because the functioning of the Suez Canal was of 'vital importance' to India, Nehru was still pushing for a 'peaceful negotiated settlement' (India, *Lok Sabha Debates*, Vol. 8, Pt 2, 13 September 1956, 6963–8). In the Lok Sabha, Nehru suggested this time the establishment of a User's Association and sent Krishna Menon to the UN to consult other countries. These efforts led to a new Indian proposal which intended to satisfy all parties to the dispute and to prevent military action. India suggested an agreement which recognized the Suez Canal as an integral part of Egypt and as a waterway of 'international importance'; which called for free and uninterrupted navigation in accordance with the 1888 Convention; and which required toll charges and cooperation between the Canal Authority and the Canal users (India 1959: 247–59).

The new revised proposal attempted to accommodate all interests but had one serious flaw: it did not consider the interests of Israel nor its integration in the User's Association. Even though the Government of India was calling for free and uninterrupted navigation for all nations, it failed to address the charge that the Egyptian government had regularly denied Israeli shipping access to the Canal for the past five years, in strict violation of the UNSC resolution of 1951 and the 1888 Convention. On this question, Krishna Menon even supported Nasser and opposed the UNSC resolution of 1951.[86] As a result, India failed to explicitly reassure Israeli grievances and indirectly pushed Israel to side with the Western powers.[87]

On 13 October 1956, the UNSC adopted Resolution 118 (sponsored by the UK, France, and Egypt), very similar to the Indian plan with respect to Egyptian sovereignty and open transit through the Canal.[88] India and other countries like the US were optimistic about a peaceful settlement until Israel launched a sudden military attack on Egypt on 29 October 1956. Two days later, British and French troops took control of the Suez Canal. India reacted in very harsh terms to the Anglo-French-Israeli operation. An official statement issued by the MEA on 31 October 1956 denounced the Israeli invasion and the Anglo-French ultimatum on the cession of the Suez Canal as a 'flagrant violation of the UN Charter' (MEA, *Foreign Affairs Record*, 2:10, 10 October 1956). In a letter sent to the US secretary of state, Nehru called the Israeli military operation as a 'clear, naked aggression.'[89] Nehru expressed similar criticism and condemned the reversion to past colonial 'predatory methods' in a letter sent to Anthony Eden, the UK's foreign minister, in November 1956.[90] India was disappointed by the attack which followed weeks of negotiations and by the fact that Israel had decided to side with two former colonial powers.

India's priority was to put an end to a conflict which closed the access to the Suez Canal. India supported the UNGA's efforts in a Special Emergency Session to obtain an immediate ceasefire by all parties and the withdrawal of troops behind the armistice line. Additionally, on 4 November, India sponsored a new resolution, indicating that all parties had not complied with UN Resolution 118 and urging the UNGA to take effective measures to ensure the implementation of the resolution. On the same day, India supported a Canadian-sponsored resolution requesting the UN secretary-general to demand the creation of a UN Emergency Force (UNEF) to supervise the ceasefire in the region.[91] The ceasefire was accepted the next day but India co-sponsored two other resolutions in November which pressed for the withdrawal of foreign troops from Egypt (Rao 1972: 55). India also agreed to contribute to the UNEF on the condition that Egypt would agree to have such forces based on the 1949 demarcation line separating Egypt from Israel.[92]

Nehru again condemned Israel for launching a premeditated attack on Egypt, in a speech to Parliament on 16 November 1956. He criticized

Israel's persistent refusal to evacuate Gaza, which was a violation of the UN resolutions (Nehru 1961: 536, 538). He also lamented Israel's 'foolish gamble' of joining up with two European powers which had reverted to past colonial methods to attempt to coerce Egypt by force (India, *Lok Sabha Debates*, Vol. 9: 5, 20 November 1956, col. 595). Nehru's reference to colonialism was intentional: the Suez conflict was framed as a de-colonization and self-determination problem. The Suez Crisis directly linked Israel with Western imperialism. As Menon explained in a later interview, Israel had 'lost by joining the French and British' and the invasion of the Suez Canal had placed them 'in the role of allied and abettors of imperialism'. Menon further argued that the rivalry with Pakistan and India's traditional anti-imperialist stance made any 'normal' relations with Israel impossible in the short term (Brecher 1968: 78, 80–1). Similarly to the 1930s, when the Jewish national movement was directly linked to British imperialism, Israel was again perceived as an associate of British imperialist ventures in the region. Israel's Suez military operation weakened the legitimacy of the new orthodoxy which favoured normalization of relations with Israel. Groups which usually promoted the development of relations with Israel supported the Government of India's position on Suez.[93]

The Suez Canal military operations had surprised the former Minister of Foreign Affairs of Israel, Moshe Sharett, who was travelling to Delhi in an unofficial position at the time of the events. Sharett, who was now out of the government, was heading the Maipai party's delegation at the Second Asian Socialist Conference which was held in Bombay in November 1956.[94] Coincidentally, Sharett met with Nehru on 30 October 1956 (just one day after the operations had started) and Nehru expressed his direct criticism of the military actions in the Sinai. Nehru emphasized that sentiments in India towards Israel were not negative and that the two countries should increase their cooperation in the field of technology and science. Nehru, for instance, praised the agricultural assistance provided by Israeli experts in the Rajasthan desert. However, in spite of this expression of interest for further cooperation, Nehru added there would be a strong Arab reaction to the establishment of diplomatic relations following the Suez attack. Sharett did not support the Sinai campaign because he had anticipated the negative diplomatic repercussions in Asia, but he still attempted to justify the Israeli objectives. He pointed out that the military operation had been an attempt to eliminate an

Egyptian military threat against the state of Israel and to open the Gulf of Aqaba for Israeli shipping (Caplan 2002; Rafael 1981: 87–8). On 20 November 1956, Nehru informed the Lok Sabha that any exchange of diplomatic personnel with Israel was difficult 'in light of the existing passions' (India, *Lok Sabha Debates*, Vol. 9:45, 20 November 1956, 595). In March 1959, Menon also told the US press that any establishment of diplomatic relations with Israel would 'probably add' to the complications in West Asia.[95] This was a formal acknowledgement that the window of opportunity for full policy change vis-à-vis Israel had closed.[96]

As the crisis progressively de-escalated, Anglo-French troops completed their withdrawal by 22 December 1956. Krishna Menon, who was leading the Indian delegation at the UNGA, strongly criticized in February 1957 the invading Israeli forces which had not yet withdrawn from Egyptian territory.[97] In reaction to this delay, India co-sponsored two other resolutions on 19 January and 2 February 1957, deploring Israel's non-compliance with the withdrawal resolutions (Ward 1992: 56–7). Israel finally fulfilled its armistice obligation by withdrawing its troops in March 1957. On 25 March, Nehru welcomed the departure of Israeli troops from Egyptian territory. He hoped this act would ease tensions and lead to a 'satisfactory resolution' with regards to the working and functioning of the Suez Canal (India, *Lok Sabha Debates*, Vol. 2, 25 March 1957, 2801). This confirms that the highest priority for the Government of India was the reopening of the Canal to international (and Indian) traffic. However, Nehru equally added that such a settlement would not solve other ongoing disputes in West Asia, notably Gaza and the Gulf of Aqaba. The withdrawal also did not keep Krishna Menon from again condemning the military operation in a speech to the Lok Sabha on 26 March 1957. He termed the invasion as contrary not only to the UN Charter but also to 'any kind of civilized law' and described it as 'wantonly brutal' (India, *Lok Sabha Debates*, Vol. 1, No. 8, 26 March 1957, 800–3). He reiterated India's position that states cannot establish legal rights through military invasion.

On the other hand, Menon also stated that there was no hostility with Israel and that India recognized its existence as a sovereign state, thereby confirming the irrevocability of the September 1950 decision.[98] At the UNGA, Menon also differentiated India's position from the Arab countries which did not recognize its right to exist.[99] In the Rajya Sabha debates, there was also a suggestion that the issue of freedom of passage of Israeli ships should be submitted to the jurisdiction of international courts, a position in contrast to the Arab stand (India, *Rajya Sabha Debates*, Vol. 16:8, 27 March 1957, 850). The Government of India preferred to refer to the dispute between Egypt and Israel on the access to the Gulf of Aqaba in neutral legal terms (Brecher 1968: 67–8, 77). Nehru finally added in August 1958 that the 'invasion of Egypt by Israel' was still fresh in their minds, and that while 'recognizing' Israel as a political entity, India needed not to exchange diplomatic personnel with Israel at this stage (India, *Lok Sabha Debates*, Vol. 18:4, 14 August 1958, 869–70). This view was reiterated before the Rajya Sabha in December 1960 when Nehru explained that the position of diplomatic exchange was entangled in 'important and rather dangerous international issues' (Srivastava 1967).

Nehru's change of position on Israel following the Suez military operations was determined by various factors. First, the rivalry with Pakistan for Arab support on the Kashmir problem seemed to have shaped India's position during the crisis. While it is true that Pakistan's attempts to portray India as an anti-Islamic country failed, Nehru still perceived it was in India's interest to engage and cultivate its relations with progressive Muslim countries and secular Arab states in order to obtain their diplomatic support on Kashmir and other international issues. The early benefits of this policy were visible during the Goa crisis when most Arab states like Egypt supported India's decision to terminate Portuguese colonial rule in the enclave of Goa.[100] Despite not being informed in advance of Nasser's objectives, the Suez crisis cemented Indo-Egyptian ties. Nehru opted to uncritically back Nasser despite the consequent aggravation of India's diplomatic relations with Britain. Nehru still supported Egypt and Arab states with the ambition of receiving reciprocal support on future disputes. Second, Israel's joint military venture with France, and especially with Britain, in Egypt strengthened the sentiment that Israel was an outpost of Western interests. Israel's actions in 1956–7 seemed to confirm pre-independence statements that had linked Zionism and British imperialism. The events reinforced the old orthodoxy's case which supported a continuation of India's pre-independence policy in favour of the Arabs and which was sceptic towards any opening of relations with Israel.

Third, the economic and trade considerations in India's policy-making vis-à-vis West Asia became salient with the Suez crisis. West Asian sea-lanes and air space were of vital economic and strategic importance to India's early economic development and to the progress of its initial five-year plans.[101] Historically, most of India's imports came by sea, through old trade routes with West Asia and Eastern Africa. These old links were reinforced by the consolidation of British sea power in the subcontinent in the nineteenth century and by the construction of the Suez Canal. Interestingly, India's dependence on these routes and the Canal drove it to follow similar policies (mostly in the goals, less in the means) as British India. As a result, India's economic interests and trade routes were dependent on friendship with Arab countries, as well as on stability in the region.

The Indian and West Asian economic trajectories were actually very much interlinked since the British Raj. From the beginning to the middle of the twentieth century, the Indian rupee was extensively used as currency in the countries of the Gulf and Arabian Peninsula. Even after independence, the rupee issued by the Government of India and the Reserve Bank of India was used for trade purposes in the region. However, a decade after independence, a separate currency was created in order to reduce the strain put on India's foreign reserves cause by the external use of the rupee. The Gulf rupee was introduced by the Indian government in 1959 as a substitute for the Indian rupee, for circulation exclusively outside the country and in the Gulf states.[102] The existence of the Gulf rupee until 1966 considerably facilitated trade with some of the Gulf states.[103] Some Arab nations also became important trade partners, such as Egypt, which exported cotton to India, as well as other Gulf states which were India's nearest sources of energy. At that period, as indicated by Krishna Menon, approximately 70 per cent of India's exports and 76 per cent of its imports passed through the Suez Canal. In the year before the Suez crisis, India carried through the Canal about 650,000 tons of merchandise (India, *Lok Sabha Debates*, Vol. 1, No. 8, 26 March 1957, 800–3).

The Indian government emphasized the need for a quick solution to the Suez crisis and to avoid any military actions which would affect the long-term flow of shipping through the Canal. Menon was very explicit in a speech to Parliament that India's West Asia policy was a 'practical approach' dictated by 'self-interest' including the imperative to maintain open the Suez Canal—referred to as India's 'life-line' (India, *Lok Sabha Debates*, Vol. 1, No. 8, 26 March 1957, 800–3). While Nehru recognized India's emotional and political interests in the Suez crisis, he also considered the issue as a dispute which directly affected India's economy.[104] The Government of India was satisfied with the resolution of the crisis only when the Suez Canal finally reopened to traffic in May 1957.[105]

The Policy Compromise of 1956

Contrary to popular belief, moral considerations have never played a decisive factor in the initial formulation of India's Israel policy. The policy of limited recognition with deferment of diplomatic relations and the decision to normalize relations in the 1990s were indicative of careful pragmatism and diplomatic prudence on India's part. To understand the strategic thinking linked to the September 1950 decision to maintain a limited relationship with Israel, it is necessary to go back to the origins of India's West Asia policy. After independence, the policy consensus which had progressively emerged before 1947 within the INC was confronted with new realities. In a first period, the new Government of India tried to maintain the pre-independence policy despite changes in domestic and international conditions. There were, for instance, important diplomatic costs to ignore the creation of Israel as the USSR, the US, and the UN had recognized the Jewish state by 1949. The perception of a costly policy was highlighted by a group of new actors who supported a policy alternative. These were mainly diplomats who directly interacted with Israeli officials in multilateral institutions as well as domestic actors who were criticizing India's incoherent recognition policy. After two years of intense debate, Prime Minister Nehru decided to change India's position to come to terms with the state of Israel as an international political reality in September 1950.

However, the 1950 decision was not a complete foreign policy change. The defenders of the previous policy managed to influence the debate and narrowed Nehru's options. Representing this old orthodoxy, Maulana Azad was concerned that a radical policy change vis-à-vis Israel would upset Indian Muslims as well as Arab states at a time when their diplomatic support was considered decisive. The result was a cryptic recognition which acknowledged the existence of the state of Israel but remained vague on the subsequent establishment of diplomatic relations. The new policy compromise was one of consistent support of the Arab line, but which also managed to maintain a certain measure of judicious restraint towards Israel. Nehru himself appreciated Israel's achievements in science and agriculture and shared ideological links with the Israeli socialist leadership. However, Nehru's emotional sympathy went first to Arab nationalist leaders in West Asia, most of whom he had been in contact with during the independence struggle. It was originally possible for India to maintain a vague pro-Palestine support as there was no functioning or legitimate Palestinian leadership in the 1950s.

The advantage of this policy compromise was that it left the option of normalization open in the early 1950s to satisfy the diplomatic elites who had given assurances to their Israeli and Western counterparts. In Nehru's mindset, the limited recognition policy instituted in the early 1950s was a good middle-ground which permitted India to have good relations with both Arab and Western states. Nehru had indeed said that India's attitude towards Israel 'was adopted after a *careful consideration of the balance of factors. It is not a matter of high principle* but it is based on how we could best serve and be helpful in that area ... After careful thought, we felt that *while recognizing Israel as an entity, we need not at this stage exchange diplomatic personnel.*'[106] In an interview a decade later, Krishna Menon also justified this obligation to maintain an ambiguous policy because India was not a big power like the US or the USSR and could not afford to make too many 'enemies'.[107]

As a result, the recognition and no-relationship policy was a strategically weighted decision which took into account India's security (territorial integrity with the Kashmir issue, boundary disputes with Pakistan) and the continuation of its independent foreign policy (open-ended policy to further relations with both Arab states and Israel and its international partners like the US). This policy helped India meet the challenges of the time and to satisfy what were perceived to be its national interests. For example, by refusing to directly engage Israel, India successfully managed to counter Pakistan's attempts to exploit Pan-Islamism in the Kashmir dispute. Nehru was very careful when he justified India's attitude towards Israel because of political developments in West Asia. Nehru had always aimed to maintain, in form if not in substance, a semblance of balance in India's West Asia policy. Both Nehru and his close adviser Krishna Menon wanted to keep diplomatic options open with both Arab states and Israel in the context of evolving strategic circumstances.

However, the 1950 compromise proved to be irreversible by the mid-1950s when events in West Asia gradually isolated Israel. New international developments reinforced the influence and legitimacy of the old orthodoxy. Pakistan's prolonged efforts to create a united Islamic front, and then a Western military alliance in West Asia, as well as the internationalization of the Kashmir dispute, persuaded India to seek sound relations with Arab-Muslim states. Furthermore, the growing importance of the Arab world in the international arena, and especially in the UN and in the nascent Non-Aligned Movement (NAM), made support of the Arab countries a key factor from the Indian point of view. The Arab states' numerical asymmetry with Israel in terms of voting power at the UNGA seemed to have been a decisive factor in India's calculations. Consequently, India consistently took a pro-Arab position on different international issues like the nationalization of the Suez Canal. India's stance was not ideological but the result of a realistic assessment of how to effectively defend what Delhi believed to be its national interests in the 1950s. Nehru confessed in an interview in 1961 that India's Israel policy was 'not logical but it was practical' (*The Times* [London], 18 March 1961). While the 1950 recognition decision should have led to the development of diplomatic relations, this step was indefinitely delayed to preserve India's national and regional interests.

The 1956 Suez crisis marked a clear departure from Nehru's earlier position which had always left open the possibility of diplomatic exchanges. After 1956, the diplomatic option was explicitly discarded as it would have deteriorated India's relations with Arab states and complicated India's potential role as a mediator in the region. There was no new hostility against the Israelis but Tel Aviv had committed a clear act of aggression against its Arab neighbours in October 1956 and India stayed firm in condemning this precedent. At the Conference of the Non-Aligned Movement in Belgrade in 1961, Nehru declared that he had been 'terribly frustrated' by the Suez crisis and that it had become 'utterly difficult' to recognize Israel after these events (*Jerusalem Post*, 5 September 1961).

Following the Suez crisis, Nehru consistently supported Egypt's position in most disputes with Israel. For instance, in February 1958, Egypt and Syria formed the United Arab Republic (UAR). In a speech in Parliament, Nehru referred to the UAR as the legitimate will of two Arab nations, and lamented Israeli criticism against this union (*Asian Recorder*, 7–13 July 1958). In his reply in the Knesset on 21 May 1958, Ben-Gurion expressed the wish that India would soon establish diplomatic relations with Israel and regretted Nehru's statement regarding possible Israeli reaction to the Syrian–Egyptian merger (Avimor 1991: 335). In August 1958, Nehru referred to Nasser as the 'prominent symbol of Arab nationalism' in West Asia, thereby confirming India's perception that Egypt had taken the lead of Arab nationalism in the region (Nehru 1961: 281). Another consequence of this pro-Cairo tilt was the deference to Egypt's judgement on the Palestinian question after 1956. Until the mid-1950s India had financially supported Palestinian refugees and refused to recognize the Palestinian authority, which it considered as a political instrument of the Arab League and which was believed to be devoid of any national legitimacy. However, in the final communiqué of the Bandung Conference in 1955, India supported Cairo's position which asked for self-determination of Arabs in Palestine (*Asian Recorder*, 23–29 April, 1955: 191–2; MEA 1981: 5). On 10 April 1960, Nasser visited India and published a joint statement with Nehru reiterating their shared view that the 'question of Palestine should be solved in conformity with the provision of the UN charter, the resolutions of the UN and the principles unanimously adopted at the Bandung Conference' (*Middle East Records* 1960, Vol. 1: 182–3). At the Non-Aligned meeting in September 1961 in Belgrade, Israel was again excluded, and Nehru supported Nasser in his criticism of Israel's imperialist behaviour in West Asia (Gerberg 2008: 86). As Egypt was one of the organizing nations of the Belgrade Conference, the West Asian conflict was included in the agenda despite India's explicit recommendation that local and bilateral conflicts ('local quarrels') be excluded from the Conference programme (Jansen 1971: 261). Nehru also supported Tito and U Nu's efforts to change the final Conference draft which originally condemned the creation of the state of Israel. In the end, a milder Burmese–Yugoslav draft pressing Israel to implement the UN resolutions regarding the Arab refugees was passed (Kochan 1976; MEA 1981: 5).

The 1956 compromise was important because it became a policy template for most Indian leaders until 1992 when dealing with Palestine and West Asia. Successive administrations and MEA bureaucrats build on a perception of national consensus towards the Palestine issue, derived from what they defined as Nehruvian principles. What some defined as a policy consensus was an interpretation of Nehru's initial statements and policy decisions on Palestine in the early 1950s. This interpretation evolved to become a rigid policy model to follow when dealing with the

Arab–Israeli dispute. But this policy compromise was the result of a specific configuration of international determinants and domestic actors' perceptions and preferences. The policy towards Palestine and Israel evolved between 1947 and 1950 and was still in flux until 1956 when it was consolidated into a new policy compromise. But how did the Nehruvian ideational legacy on Palestine endure despite changes in leadership and international and domestic circumstances? What can explain this path-dependence which apparently prolonged the 1950 policy compromise until 1992?

One lasting effect of the 1950s' debate was the formation of a new advocacy coalition defending the 1956 policy compromise, composed of both the MEA and the INC. These two actors were not directly cooperating or coordinating to maintain the status quo but both had their own political and organizational interests in preserving it. The MEA's role in consolidating and maintaining the existing policy consensus was essential after 1956. After the mid-1950s, the MEA's approach to West Asian affairs became consistently pro-Arab (while not overtly anti-Israel). Paradoxically, Indian diplomats based in Western embassies (and especially in the US and the UK) had initially supported a diplomatic rapprochement with Israel. Before the creation of an Indian Foreign Service, Indian diplomats had been appointed under the British administration or were personalities close to Congress and Nehru. In the late 1940s and early 1950s, these diplomats had regular interactions with their Israeli counterparts and were acquainted with Israel's security concerns. This group was also conscious of the potential diplomatic costs that India's hostile policy towards Israel could create with some of Israel's most important sponsors like the US and the UK.

The change happened in the mid-1950s when the Government of India committed itself to the building of Afro-Asian institutions and when the MEA opened many legations in West Asia.[108] The new MEA bureaucrats received their training and international experience within the context of Bandung, and they developed their regional expertise in these new embassies. Israel was progressively banned from the Asian community and had no regular channel of communication to present its official position on regional events to Indian diplomats. Unlike their predecessors who had regular (albeit informal) links with Israeli diplomats in the 1950s and who had developed a sophisticated understanding of Israeli concerns and interests, the new MEA bureaucracy mostly interacted with Arab and other Asian diplomats within the Afro-Asian or Non-Alignment conferences. This formative influence had a lasting effect on the international and regional perceptions of this new generation of diplomats. Paradoxically, the gradual professionalization of the MEA led to a more conservative approach to the Israel issue. Indirectly, officials of the MEA defended and enforced in a rigid manner the 1956 compromise. Israeli bureaucrats themselves regarded the MEA as a highly professional but conservative governmental organization with difficulties to adjust to international changes. This explains why the MFA was initially sceptic about changing India's official policy and why there were relatively few diplomatic efforts directed at transforming India's position towards Israel (Eytan 1958; Tsur 1957). In 1959, the director of the Asian and African division of the MFA gave specific instructions to the Israeli Consul in Bombay to not pursue controversy in India by constantly trying to raise the issue of diplomatic relations between the two countries. The director also requested that the issue of the transfer of the Israeli Consulate from Bombay to New Delhi should no longer be raised (Gerberg 2008: 238–9).

However, it is important to clarify that the MEA is and remains the maker and implementer of policy towards Israel on the basis of directions given by the political leadership. The party in power during this period, the INC, was a strong supporter of the 1956 policy compromise. In the 1950s, Azad was the main spokesperson in the Indian government for India's Muslim minority, whose sentiments he personally believed were in line with their fellow Muslims in West Asia. Nehru respected Azad's opinion as a 'respected leader of India's 40 million Muslims' and never put into doubt this claim.[109] After Azad's death in 1958, the INC continued to support Indian Muslim interests for two reasons. First, to defend its secular credentials, the INC was ready to accommodate the minority's interests. Second, the INC was also trying to convince the Muslim electorate which was increasingly pivotal in certain local elections. For the next three decades, the existing assumption that Indian Muslims homogeneously opposed normalization was rarely questioned in the INC. After Nehru, very few leaders had the same foreign policy experience, domestic popularity and legitimacy, and personal connections with Arab leaders. As a result, we will see in the next chapter that successive INC leaders like Lal Bahadur Shastri and Indira Gandhi preferred to loyally pursue Nehru's original West Asia policy or to the least what they perceived to be his policy, without taking into account the contextual determinants which had dictated this particular position. The INC became increasingly risk-adverse and cautious when it came to West Asia. For decades, these perceived costs linked to change outweighed the prospective advantages related to a diplomatic overture to Israel.

Notes

1. Quoted in Parthasarathy (Vol. 1: 1947–1949, p. 275).

2. However, he was assisted by the nascent ministry of external affairs. See Bandyopadhyaya (1970: 286); Kapur (2009: 180); Cohen (2001: 38–9).

3. Interestingly, Sir Feroz Khan was considered to be Jinnah's special diplomatic envoy and would become a Pakistani politician after Partition. He, therefore, was not representative of the INC's position. See Gerberg (2008: 192).

4. The Central Jewish Board of Mumbai is an inclusive organization, with which all synagogues and other Jewish institutions in India are affiliated. It serves as a spokesman for Indian Jewry as a whole. It has had institutional links with the Jewish Agency which has provided direct financial aid to the organization.

5. Pollack encouraged the Agency to send a 'capable personality' of the Israeli Labor Movement to be based permanently in Bombay and which would be assisted by pro-Zionist British and American politicians to persuade members of the INC. See Gerberg (2008: 192).

6. US Congressman Celler, who was the chairman of the Judiciary Committee House, was well-known and popular in India because of his support of the Indian struggle for independence in the American Congress. In the 1940s, Celler was also an advocate of more flexible US immigration laws to help Jewish refugees fleeing the Holocaust. He also encouraged Britain to relax its immigration laws for Jews who wanted to establish themselves in Palestine following the war.

7. Quoted in Gerberg (2008: 202).

8. The delegation also met with Acharya Kripalani, the president of the INC; Sarojini Naidu; the writer and journalist Shinta Shiva Rao and her mother Rama Rao (a leader of the all-India Women's Association). Gerberg (2008: 201–2).

9. Dr S. K. M. Panikkar served as a foreign representative of the Indian princely states of Bikaner and Patiala in London in the 1930s and the 1940s, where he met important Zionists such as Chaim Weizmann in 1926 and David Ben-Gurion in 1937. See Kumaraswamy (1995b).

According to some observers, Panikkar was sympathetic to the Zionist cause. He apparently even offered advice to the Israeli delegation at the ARC on how to persuade Indian leaders and Indian opinion. See Kumaraswamy (1995b; 2010: 34–5, 82–4, 186); Gerberg (2008: 73).

However, in his autobiography in 1955, Panikkar gave a more nuanced perspective. He explained that he had sympathized with the 'claims of the Jews for a National Home' but he strongly criticized the 'religious exclusivism' which had been the base for the creation of Israel, which had been both unjust to Palestinian Arabs and which had created the conditions for the revival of 'Islamic fanaticism'. See Panikkar (1955: 12).

10. According to Gerberg, Nehru appeased the Jewish delegation by allowing David Hacohen to chair the economic committee. He also invited the delegation to a private dinner with his sister Vijaya Lakshmi Pandit and his daughter Indira Gandhi. See also Appadorai (1948: 281–2); Jansen (1971: 192); Gopal and Sharma (2007: 13); Gerberg (2008: 201).

11. The unit stayed open until 1955, when the ARO disappeared with the Bandung Conference. See Gerberg (2008: 203); Kumaraswamy (2010: 187).

12. UN document, A/AC. 1/P.V. 74 and Asaf Ali's statement in UN: Official Record of the First Special Session of the General Assembly, Vol. III, Main Committee 28 April–13 May UN document, A/C. 1/136.

13. Ministry of External Affairs telegram to Asaf Ali of 24 April 1947, quoted in Kumaraswamy (2010: 87).

14. Both the US and the USSR supported partition, a proposal that India rejected. UN document A/AC. 1/P.V. 79; UNGA, First Special Session, A/C.1/P.V.51, 8 May 1947, 57–62; Heptullah (1991: 156).

15. Arab states were also not included because of their partiality in this matter.

16. It was judged to be incompatible with the situation on the ground and the previous British proposals. UNGA, First Special Session, A/BUR/P.V./30, 30 April 1947, 12.

17. Asaf Ali argued that not inviting the Jewish representatives to testify before the UNSCOP would be like 'playing Hamlet without the Prince of Denmark'. UNGA, First Special Session, A/BUR/P.V.30, 30 April 1947, 2–10, and A/C.1/P.V.48, 7 May 1948.

18. Nehru was concerned about British reactions because his provisional government was still in negotiations with London over independence and political transition logistics. See Gopal, Sarvepalli, ed., Nehru, Selected Works, Series II, 2: 497.

19. The UNSCOP was initially composed of Canada, Czechoslovakia, Guatemala, Iran, the Netherlands, Peru, Sweden, Uruguay, and Yugoslavia.

20. It was decided that there would be a vote for the other two slots after the US had nominated the original seven members and Chile the other two. Australia won the other vote to represent the South Pacific.

21. There have been questions over Rahman's nomination and its impact on India's Palestine policy. Kumaraswamy (2010: 93) argued that the nomination of an eminent Muslim judge was an indicator of India's Islamic bias when shaping its Palestine policy. This emphasis on the singular role of individualities is misleading. It might be argued that Rahman was influenced by the partition of India, and

more especially by the fate of his home region of Punjab. The UNSCOP was indeed meeting as events unfolded in India. However, Rahman was not the sole decision-maker when it came to the UNSCOP. He received strict orders from Nehru and was ordered to push for the federal plan. Kumaraswamy (2010: 94) even himself conceded that Rahman was just a messenger with little agency.

22. After Partition, Rahman opted to migrate to Pakistan to become a judge of the Pakistani Punjab High Court.

23. Quoted in Gopal and Sharma (2007: 122–3). Surprisingly, Rahman also warned against religion being a political foundation for separatism and irredentism. Rahman judged that the partition of Palestine would be a bad precedent in the region. In his personal note, he disputed the validity of the Balfour Declaration and was also concerned about the issue of double loyalty of the Jews. See UN (UNSCOP) (1947, Vol. 1, 59, and Vol. II, 45).

24. UNGA, *Official Records of the Second Session of the General Assembly*, A/364/Add.2 PV.16, 4 July 1947, and A/364/Add.2 PV.19, 7 July 1947.

25. Quoted in Gerberg (2008: 193–4).

26. UNGA, *Second Session, Ad Hoc Committee on the Palestinian Question, 25 September–25 November 1947, Summary Records of Meetings*, 62.

27. See Pandit's letter to U. S. Bajpai, the MEA's general secretary, quoted in Kumaraswamy (2010: 104).

28. Gerberg (2008: 194–5); Jansen, Mudiam, and Upendra Mishra also discussed the divisions in the delegation and Pandit's suggestion of an abstention. See Jansen (1971: 210); Mudiam (1994: 144–7); Mishra (1982). Before the final voting in the General Assembly on the partition plan, Sharett and Weizmann again appealed to the Indian delegation and the Indian government to not vote for the federal plan. But Pandit had specific voting instructions from Delhi. See Gerberg (2008: 207–8).

29. There were also 10 abstentions. UNGA, *Second Session*, Vol. II, 110–128th meetings, 1424.

30. The Arab–Israeli dispute was then the most discussed foreign policy issue in the Constituent Assembly debates. K. P. Misra and Kumaraswamy have both noted how the issue of the recognition of Israel was brought up in the debates of the Constituent Assembly five times. See Misra (1966: 52–3); Kumaraswamy (2010: 158).

31. Pandit warned Delhi after 29 November 1947 that the federal plan could be re-introduced given an increasing support from the Arab states which opposed partition. Nehru referred to this last-minute Arab support for India's plan in India, *Constituent Assembly Debates* (Vol. 1, session II, 4 December 1947, 1261).

32. The US recognized the state of Israel within hours of its proclamation on 14 May 1948, while the USSR recognized Israel three days later on 17 May. However, there were debates in other countries as well. For example, France, and especially

the UK, debated and delayed their recognition of Israel. It was also a debate in the Truman administration in the US. See Wilson (1979); Devine (2009).

33. For instance, on 1 February 1948, Ben-Gurion sent a cable of condolence to Prime Minister Nehru after the assassination of Mahatma Gandhi, on behalf of the Jewish Agency. Ben-Gurion highlighted the example of the Mahatma's 'life and teaching'. Quoted in Gerberg (2008: 195).

34. There is a debate on the exact date when Nehru received Sharett's letter. Nehru originally told the Constituent Assembly in August 1948 that he had received the Sharett letter in June 1948. But in a letter to the chief ministers of India that was sent on 20 May 1948, Nehru acknowledged he had received the Israeli request for recognition. See India, *Constituent Assembly Debates* (20 August 1938, Vol. 6, Session 1, 380–1); Parthasarthy, *Letters to Chief Ministers*, Vol. 1, 1947–49, pp. 127–8. For more on the request imbroglio, see Misra (1966: 52).

35. Nehru also strongly condemned the US role on the Palestine question, describing is as 'ineptitude and opportunism'. See Parthasarthy, *Letters to Chief Ministers*, Vol 1, 1947–49: 126–8.

36. The Central Provinces was a province of British India. When the Constitution of India went into effect in 1950, an important part of the Central Provinces became the new Indian state of Madhya Pradesh.

37. The Palestinian movement had nothing close to an independent political organization like the Jewish community which had even before independence its executive (Jewish Agency), legislature (Vaad Leumi), trade union system (Histadrut), and military wing (Haganah). The Jewish organization had also already decided on who would govern the future state.

38. Quoted in Kumaraswamy (2010: 112).

39. Nehru is quoted in Parthasarathy, *Letters to Chief Ministers*, Vol 1, 1947-49 : 275.

40. In the end, Israel was accepted as a UN member by a vote of 37 in favour to 12 against and 9 abstentions.

41. Cited in Rao (1972: 68).

42. For more on the Kashmir conflict, see Ganguly (1997).

43. Interestingly, the Nizam of Hyderabad who refused integration had been a constant financial supporter of the Palestinian Arab cause. See Srivastava (1967).

44. The Arab states that were present at the UNGA at the time were Egypt, Iraq, Lebanon, Saudi Arabia, Syria, and Yemen.

45. This was in a note sent to Indian embassies, quoted in Kumaraswamy (2010: 110–1).

46. Quoted in Kumaraswamy (2010: 112).

47. In fact, the historic leader of the Hindu Mahasabha, Vinayak Damodar Savarkar, supported the Zionist aspirations and the creation of a Jewish state.

Ideologically, Savarkar also believed in the concept of a nation-state based on religion. See *Indian Annual Register* 2 (1943): 10. Paradoxically, Savarkar backed the creation of a religious state in Palestine while also endorsing the persecution of Jews in Germany which he justified for reasons of national and cultural purity. See Janmohamed (2003). Savarkar publicly supported the creation of an independent Jewish state in Palestine on 19 December 1947. He criticized the Indian delegation at the UN for voting against the creation of Israel and for trying to secure the goodwill of the Muslim states and of India's Muslim minority. He argued that the development of a strong Jewish state would help to check the 'aggressive tendencies of Moslem fanaticism'. See Vinayak Savarkar, 'Glad to Note that Independent Jewish State is Established'. For more on the Mahasabha's position, see Abhyankar (2012).

48. Tara Singh congratulated, for instance, the creation of the Israeli state in *India and Israel* (Bombay), 1:2, August 1948. See also Gopal and Sharma (2007: 84).

49. There are two types of basic international recognition in international law and diplomacy: de jure and de facto. De jure recognition implies the complete diplomatic acceptance of a new state or government while de facto recognition normally refers to the provisional recognition of a particular government which has some minimal attributes of sovereignty, usually the control of a territory. See Fabry (2010).

50. Yugoslavia had also originally supported the federal plan and had recognized Israel in 1949.

51. Mohammed Yunus, who was chargé d'affaires at the Indian Embassy in Iraq, had, for instance, explained India's changing position to the Iraqi foreign minister in August 1950, a few days before recognition. See Yunus (1980: 102).

52. *The Hindu*, 18 September 1950. India had been defending the rights of Palestinian Arab refugees through the UNRWA and by endorsing the UNGA Resolution 194 (111) on 11 December 1948. This resolution supported the right to return for refugees and compensation for those not wishing to return. For the full text of the resolution, see Hadawi (1967: 39–43).

53. In August 1948, Hyderabad informed the UNSC of its dispute with India and asked for help to settle it in accordance with international law and justice. The Hyderabad question was presented but never discussed at different UNSC meetings until May 1949. See U.N. Doc. S/986, Security Council, *Official Records*, 3rd Year, Supp., September 1948, 5. See also Eagleton (1950). Apparently, Nehru had mentioned that he would take steps to demonstrate to the Arab states that India's support was not unconditional in May 1949. See Gopal (1979: 169).

54. Quoted in Schechtman (1966).

55. Speech by the Indian Ambassador to Israel, Shiv Shankar Menon (1997).

56. Before the creation of the state of Israel, the Jewish Agency had had official representatives in Bombay. First, there was an office to facilitate the immigration of an important number of Jewish refugees from Europe who were temporarily based in India before moving to Israel. The Jewish Agency then decided to name a trade commissioner for South East Asia and India (Pollack) in May 1950 in Bombay but there were misunderstandings with the Indian administration over the official role of this commissioner. See Avimor (1991: 382); Kumaraswamy (2010: 126–9).

57. Israel was hardly an exception in Asia. For instance, India did not have full diplomatic relations with South Korea until 1973.

58. This opacity would lead to operational problems, especially as the opening of an Israeli embassy in Delhi seemed nowhere in sight. This would lead Louis Rukeyser of the *Baltimore Sun* bureau in New Delhi to assert that the Consulate was asked to be based in the 'diplomatic Siberia of Bombay'. See Schechtman (1966). According to the *New York Times* correspondent to India Bernard Winraub, Bombay was labelled 'the loneliest post in the world' in Israeli diplomatic circles. See Winraub (1974). In a practical sense, the Consulate in Bombay was mainly engaged in information and public relations efforts in the Bombay presidency and then in Maharashtra after the division of the state.

59. The early 1950s witnessed the emigration of a substantial number of the approximately 25,000 Indian Jews to Israel. See Gordon (1975).

60. Socialist ideological connections proved essential for Israel to establish diplomatic relations with other Asian states like Burma, Philippines, and Nepal. Brecher (1961); Jansen (1971: 222–4, 227–30).

61. Until then, the British Commonwealth Department in the ministry handled relations with India, Pakistan, and Sri Lanka.

62. One needs to put into perspective Israel's initial diplomatic efforts to engage India. Israel's priority in the early 1950s was first and foremost the preservation of its territorial integrity and of its national identity. During the immediate post-independence years, the purchase of weapons was an important component of the Israeli defence policy and for all practical reasons, it was obvious that independent India could not and would not supply weapons to Israel. Prime Minister Ben-Gurion confirmed this reality in a statement before the Knesset: 'We must not forget, even for a moment, that we cannot obtain the equipment for the Israeli defense forces from Asia and Africa.' See Brecher (1963: 52).

63. Eytan discussed the scarcity of personnel and a lack of urgent priority for India, but did not rule out a 'political explanation' for the delay in normalization. See Eytan (1958: 170).

64. Brecher's interviews with various Indian decision-makers, including cabinet ministers, in the late 1950s have led him to argue that Azad was the main,

if not the single, factor to explain the absence of normal diplomatic relations with Israel. See Brecher (1959: 571–2; 1963: 129–30).

65. Although Azad never held an official position linked to foreign affairs, various observers have defined him as an influent personality on Nehru on West Asian affairs. See Brecher (1957: 14; 1959: 610; 1963: 130); Kumaraswamy (2010: 18, 145–50). Azad's grand-niece, Heptullah, also considered that Azad had been a 'guide' to Nehru on 'matters concerning West Asia'. See Heptullah (1991: xi, 3). The other influence on Nehru had been René Grousset whose writings on West Asia had a bearing on Nehru's discussion of the region in his book *Glimpses of World History*. See Heptullah (1991: 8–9).

66. Brecher has argued that Azad was 'naturally' biased in favour of the Arabs because he was Muslim (and had Arab origins). But Heptullah disagreed with this observation. She argued instead that her great-uncle was not decisively 'influenced by the Muslim sentiments in India'. See Brecher (1963: 130); Heptullah (1991: 152).

67. According to Brecher (1963: 10).

68. For instance, Nehru's biographer Gopal also emphasized Azad's influence on India's Israel policy, but he quoted Brecher to support this position. See Gopal (1979: 170).

69. The Egyptians claimed that they were still at war with Israel and therefore were free to embargo goods destined for Israel and routed through the Suez Canal. The UNSC found that this practice was in contradiction to the armistice agreements. See Gordon (1975).

70. Cited in Ghosh (2009: 305).

71. For instance, in March 1953, an Israeli diplomat reportedly told Eytan that normalization was still a prospect and that the main obstacle was no longer the domestic Muslim factor but the Kashmir dispute. This report came following a discussion between the Indian and Israeli delegations in New York in 1953. See Eytan (1958: 170–1); Schechtman (1966).

72. Nehru made this point very clear in a press conference in Cairo in 1953. See Nehru (1954: 33).

73. The five participants were Burma, India, Indonesia, Pakistan, and Sri Lanka.

74. Sri Lanka and Indonesia expressed no opinion.

75. Sri Lanka also supported inviting Israel. Krishna Menon in a later interview with Brecher argued that even Indonesia could have been persuaded at the time. See Brecher (1968: 79).

76. Out of the 29 countries that were invited to attend the Bandung Conference, 18 had not yet recognized the PRC. See MEA *Annual Report*, 1954–1955: 55–8.

77. According to Gerberg, Nehru met Nahum Goldman, the president of the Jewish World Congress, on 27 June 1957 and told him that he had tried with

U Nu to get Israel invited but had had to face the threat of Arab boycott. See Gerberg (2008: 82). Nehru also explained his position to Brecher (1963: 210–11). The decisive nature of the Arab boycott threat was confirmed by Krishna Menon in Brecher (1968: 52).

78. In fact, Zhou Enlai, the PRC's foreign minister, noticed and exploited the disagreements between India and the Arab states. The Bandung Conference marked the beginning of a rivalry between the two Asian powers on who would champion the Palestinian cause within the Afro-Asian community. Gopal (1979: 242–4).

79. Nehru notably criticized the Palestinian delegate Ahmed Shukairy's statement regarding the impossibility of a negotiated settlement in the Arab–Israeli conflict. Because there was no official Palestinian delegation, Shukairy had come to the Bandung Conference as a member of the Syrian delegation. See Jansen (1971: 257–8); Kochan (1976).

80. Quoted in MEA (1968: 71–2).

81. For more on the background politics of the nationalization, see Kyle (2011).

82. The Canal Corporation was an Egyptian company subject to Egyptian law and the nationalization was considered to be within the competence of Egyptian law. See India, Lok Sabha Debates, Vol. 7, Pt 2, 8 August 1956, 2536–44.

83. This was confirmed by Krishna Menon, India's Minister of Defence and Indian representative at the London Conference, who judged that Egypt was competent to nationalize the Suez Canal but should have done so in 'the normal way of international expropriation'. See a copy of Menon's statement at the Conference in United States, Department of State (1956: 159–78).

84. The Constantinople Convention of 1888 was signed by nine parties. The main provision was that the Suez Canal should remain open to all merchants and naval vessels in times of war and peace.

85. According to Ambassador Arthur Lall who was at the London Conference with Menon, the Indian delegation was in regular touch with Egypt during the entire negotiations. One of Nasser's personal advisors, Ali Sabri, was even a member of the Indian delegation. See Interview with Arthur Lall (1990).

86. He understood Arab intransigence against Israeli ships travelling through their country because they were still at war with Israel, but also offered options like having Israeli goods carried through the Canal by non-Israeli ships. See Brecher (1968): 67–8, 77).

87. Until the nationalization, there had been Israeli statements hinting at Israel's intention to integrate the Asian concert of nations. Israel's new Minister of Foreign Affairs, Golda Meir, had, for instance, stated that it was natural for Israelis to view themselves as an integral part of the Asian continent. See Medzini (1972). By October 1956, however, Israel's collaboration with Britain and France against

Egypt in 1956 was deemed compulsory. Egypt had just signed an important arms deal with Czechoslovakia 1955 and had imposed a blockade of the Eilat harbour and the Gulf of Aqaba.

88. UNGA, *Official Records: Twelfth Session, Supplement 2 (A/3648). Report of the Security Council to the General Assembly Covering the Period July 16, 1956 to July 15, 1957.*

89. Quoted in Rajan (1964: 151).

90. Letter to Eden in Gopal (1979: 286).

91. India, *Lok Sabha Debates*, Vol. 7, Pt 2, 8 August 1956, 2536–44; interview with Arthur Lall (1990).

92. Nehru told the Indian Parliament about this condition on 19 November 1956. In another speech in December 1956, he further detailed the size of the Indian contingent and its specific mission. Krishna Menon also later explained that the deployment of the UNEF was dependent on the consent of the territorial sovereign power (Egypt) and on the approval of the UN command structure. The unresolved question of Egypt's necessary approval of the UNEF presence would become a major factor in the escalation of the 1967 crisis. Nehru, *Selected Speeches*, Vol. 3: 323–4; India, *Lok Sabha Debates*, Vol. 7, Pt 2, 8 August 1956, 2536–44; India, *Lok Sabha Debates*, Vol. 9, Pt 1, 13 December 1956, 1426–8. For Menon's statement, see UN Document, A/PV/651.

93. The Bharatiya Jana Sangh (BJS) did not support the Government of India on ideological principles but because of the economic importance of the Canal for India. For the BJS, the Government of India needed to ensure that there was a guarantee of free navigation for ships of all countries at all times through the Canal, without any exception. In another resolution, the BJS condemned actions by France and England but nevertheless recognized the provocations of Nasser and criticized the unilateral violation of an international agreement by the government of Egypt. See 'Text of the Resolution on the Suez Crisis adopted by the Central Committee of the BJS', Pune, 5 October 1956, in Bharatiya Jana Sangh, *Party Documents* (Vol. 3, 1957–72: 44–5, 314–15); 'Text of the Resolution on the Suez Crisis adopted by the Fifth All India Session of the BJS', Delhi, 30 December, 1956, in Bharatiya Jana Sangh, *Party Documents* (Vol. 3, 1957–72: 45).

94. The Israeli delegation disagreed with the final draft of the Conference session which criticized the Suez operation. However, some Indian socialist leaders exculpated Israel for Suez. See Jansen (1971: 224–5, 239–40).

95. Menon did, however, recognize that normalization could have brought India an 'advantage'. *The Hindu*, 25 October 1959.

96. Although Nehru still met with Israeli diplomats such as Aban Eban in Washington in December 1956 and Nahum Goldmann, the president of the Jewish World Congress, on 27 June 1957 in London. In a meeting organized by

the American diplomat Chester Bowles, Goldmann did not succeed in convincing Nehru of the necessity of having diplomatic relations with Israel. He reportedly judged Nehru's attitude towards Israel to be 'ambivalent'. See Srivastava (1967); Goldmann (1969: 310).

97. Statement by Krishna Menon, UNGA, 11th Session, 2 February 1957, UN Document, A/PV/651.

98. While India refused to go back on its 1950 decision, Turkey used the Suez crisis as an opportunity to downgrade the Turkish legation to the level of chargé d'affaires in Israel.

99. GAOR (General Assembly Official Records), 11th session, Plenary Meetings, 329.

100. By 1955, India and Portugal had cut off diplomatic relations because of Portugal's refusal to surrender its enclaves of Goa, Daman, and Diu on the Indian west coast. In 1958, Egypt accepted to perform all consular activities for Indian interests in territories under the jurisdiction of Portugal in India. See MEA, *Foreign Affairs Record*, 4:7, July 1958; Heptullah (1991: 5).

101. Menon in India, *Lok Sabha Debates* (Vol. 1, No. 8, 26 March 1957, 800–83); Nehru's speech to the Lok Sabha, 2 September 1957, in India, *Lok Sabha Debates* (Vol. 6, No. 37, 2 September 1957, 11318–29).

102. I would like to thank Manjeet S. Pardesi for alerting me to the existence of this regional monetary union. See Legrenzi and Momani (2011: 24).

103. The Gulf rupee was used by the Persian Gulf states of Kuwait, Bahrain, Qatar, Oman, the Trucial States, and in parts of Muscat.

104. Nehru in *Lok Sabha Debates* (Vol. 6, No. 37, 2 September 1957, 11318–29).

105. The Indian President Rajendra Prasad welcomed this development in a joint session of the Lok Sabha and Rajya Sabha; India, *Lok Sabha Debates* (Vol 1, No 3, 13 May 1957, 57–8).

106. Jawaharlal Nehru, statement at press conference, New Delhi, 7 August 1958, quoted in Nehru (1961: 414–15; emphasis added).

107. However, Menon also believed that the partial recognition might have been an error of judgement as India failed to establish normal diplomatic relations when the time seemed ripe in the early 1950s. He believed that an exchange of ambassadors would have been feasible before the 1956 crisis. Brecher (1968: 79–80).

108. By the mid-1960s, India had 12 embassies in Arab countries and no representation in Israel. See statement of the Minister of External Affairs Swaran Singh to the Lok Sabha (India, *Lok Sabha Debates*, Vol. 47, No. 10, 17 November 1965, 2419–22).

109. See Brecher (1957: 14); Heptullah (1991: 3).

3   Crises and Debates

Contestation and Revision of India's Israel policy (1956–1974)

The Near East is far more important to India than India is to the Near East.

—Werner Levi (1952: 60)

In the Middle-East, India is so firmly committed to the Arabs that she will go to almost any pain to humiliate Israel...critics of India's Middle-East policy argue that India has had little support in return from the Arabs. They contend that a few signs of friendliness toward Israel would be a healthy reminder to the Arabs that Indian support should not be taken for granted.

—Anthony Lukas (*New York Times*, 14 May 1966)

UNTIL THE EARLY 1960s, India had adopted a voluntarily ambiguous no-relationship policy with Israel. India generally sympathized with broad Arab nationalist causes but left options open vis-à-vis the Jewish state. Israel had a working consulate in Bombay and there were exchanges (albeit limited) in the agricultural and cultural fields. Initially, this policy had successfully prevented Pakistan from weaning Arab states away from India. After Nehru died in 1964, the successive governments of Lal Bahadur Shastri and Indira Gandhi took a more rigid approach to Israel. Under Nehru, there had been some semblance of balance, both in rhetoric and in practice. Nehru consistently supported Arab refugees, condemned Israeli actions in 1956, and demanded that Tel Aviv respect the United Nations (UN) resolutions on Palestine. However, he also actively encouraged his Arab counterparts to accept the existence of Israel and to initiate a dialogue to find a regional settlement. The situation changed when his successors began to directly engage the Palestine Liberation Organization (PLO) and to unconditionally support the Arab states in their disputes with Israel.

In the 1960s and 1970s, the Government of India had more difficulties convincing critics at home that the existing policy compromise was the best option to promote India's interests in West Asia. Some of the earlier considerations behind the original policy compromise had become less salient. Partition was now part of the past and the national allegiance of Indian Muslims was no longer an issue. Additionally, the different wars in South Asia and the West Asian crises of 1967 and 1973 revealed a one-sided relationship between India and the Arab states. While India unreservedly supported its Arab allies, and particularly Egypt, Delhi did not receive the expected reciprocal diplomatic backing in its territorial disputes with China and Pakistan. Why did these apparent policy failures not lead to a reassessment of India's position vis-à-vis Israel? For instance, some Asian countries like Thailand and Japan, which regularly voted at the UN against Israeli interests, managed to simultaneously maintain good relations with Tel Aviv. Why could India not differentiate its multilateral rhetoric from its bilateral relations with Israel?

In this chapter, I look at the various events in West Asia which seriously weakened the bases of the 1956 policy compromise. The 1956–74 time period can be understood as a 'most likely' case study when there were important conditions for a possible reassessment of India's Israel policy.[1] Despite the diplomatic failure in getting support from Arab states in India's disputes with Pakistan (and China), domestic pressure against the government's West Asia policy, and an urgent need for new military suppliers during the Indo-Pakistani conflict of 1971, the Indira Gandhi government refused to normalize relations with Tel Aviv. Concentrating on this case helps determine which factors played against change and why certain domestic actors had an interest in resisting change.

The fact that India's Israel policy was in flux in the late 1960s and early 1970s contradicts the existing narrative that India pursued a single and continuous policy towards the Palestine question for four decades. The Government of India's responses to the West Asian crises in 1967 and 1973 were neither spontaneous nor consensual as Nehru's strong opposition to the tripartite aggression against Egypt in 1956 had been. There was no longer a unanimous backing from the population, media, and political parties for India's West Asia policy. In the 1950s, India's policy seemed open-ended and flexible. After 1957, there was an impression that the Government of India had lost the initiative and was simply reacting to events in the region. Much of India's reactive policies of the period were later rationalized as consistent with India's pro-Arab approach. However, the inarticulateness of the government's responses led to a debate on the rationale and legitimacy of India's West Asia policy initiated by the opposition in Parliament.

This chapter also explains why there was no complete policy change vis-à-vis Israel despite the propitious conditions in 1956–74. The old orthodoxy held up against new challenges to the policy with three strategies. First, the old guard reframed the existing policy objectives by identifying new interests that were effectively secured by India's pro-Arab position. By the early 1970s, the old orthodoxy argued, for example, that the existing policy was crucial to preserve India's energy and especially oil needs.[2] While this was a priority substitution with oil and energy interests now taking precedence in decision-making vis-à-vis West Asia, it was adroitly framed as policy continuity by the old orthodoxy. Second, the old orthodoxy made some minor policy concessions to actors promoting change in India's approach to West Asia. One of the main criticisms by the emerging new orthodoxy was that India's policy was too Cairo-centred. To counter this reproach, the pro–status quo actors rebalanced India's regional policy by engaging other local actors like the Gulf states, Iraq, and Iran. Third, India recognized the PLO as an official interlocutor for the Palestinian people. This was quite a drastic change in India's Israel/Palestine policy. Between 1950 and 1973, India had given recognition only to the government of Israel and had refused to make a similar gesture towards the All Palestine Government (APG), which was considered as illegitimate and unrepresentative at the time. Because of domestic and international pressures, the Government of India started actively engaging the PLO in the 1970s.

The First Signs of Discontent: India's Policy towards Israel between 1956 and 1967

This section looks at the evolution of India's Israel policy following the Suez crisis up to the West Asian crisis of 1967. The section specifically analyzes West Asian reactions to India's border conflicts with Pakistan and China in 1962 and 1965. It also highlights how the lack of explicit Arab support in favor of India's position was increasingly criticized by various domestic Indian actors. However, the section concludes that the emergence of a vocal minority in favor of a policy change was not a sufficient conditions to observe a complete policy change vis-à-vis Israel

The Post-1956 Situation

Paradoxically, Israel's military operation in 1956 actually increased its prestige among Asian and African countries (Brecher 1961; Kohn 1959). As a result of the attack, Israel managed to obtain the end of the maritime blockade over the Tiran Straits and the Gulf of Aqaba.[3] The year 1956 also marked a turning point for Israeli diplomacy. As Sharett was pushed to the sidelines, India and Asia were no longer priorities for the Ministry of Foreign Affairs (MFA). Disappointed by years of unsuccessful diplomatic efforts to convince Asian nations of its goodwill, Israel opted in 1956 to turn to Western nations to defend its economic and security interests (Shlaim 2004). Ben-Gurion confirmed this new policy direction by arguing that the 'friendship' of France was worth more than the opinion Asians had of Israel at that time (Ministry of External Affairs [MEA] 1968: 31). Ben-Gurion was particularly disappointed with Nehru's attitude towards Israel. In 1959, Ben-Gurion referred to the unfulfilled promises Nehru had made to Eytan in 1952 about the establishment of normal diplomatic relations between the two countries (Brecher 1976: 223). Ben-Gurion and the Israeli Minister of Foreign Affairs Golda Meir also criticized India's 'less than neutral' attitude towards Israel (*Middle East Records* 1960, Vol. 1: 304).

The Israeli government also tried to invite Nehru to Israel. In July 1960, Ben-Gurion sent an invitation through Rajkumari Amrit Kaur, who was the former Indian minister of health and the head of the Indian Red Cross Organization, and who had visited Israel that same year (Gerberg 2008; Gopal and Sharma 2007: 93). Nehru rejected the invitation, and in his reply explained that it would not be advisable to undertake a visit at that time as it might have negative effects on the peace process. Kaur also responded to Ben-Gurion to explain that Nehru did not have any 'animosity' towards the Government of Israel but that at that time any diplomatic overture could have complicated matters with the Arab world (Gerberg 2008; Kumaraswamy 2010: 126). On 15 February

1961, Gideon Rafael, the director general of the MFA, participated in the annual conference of the World Health Organization (WHO) in Delhi. During his visit, he met with Nehru who again reportedly acknowledged that India should have established diplomatic relations with Israel back in 1950. Nehru reportedly said that he had probed Arab leaders about the possibility of a settlement with Israel, with little success. Consequently, Nehru feared a strong Arab reaction to the establishment of diplomatic relations between Delhi and Tel Aviv (Rafael 1981: 87–9). After Egypt, Syria, and Iraq decided to form an Arab federation in July 1963, Ben-Gurion sent a personal note to Nehru to express his security concerns. The Israeli prime minister pressed on Nehru to dissuade Nasser from escalating tensions and to encourage the Egyptian president to start peace negotiations with Israel. Ben-Gurion did not receive any official answer from Nehru.[4]

In spite of the absence of diplomatic relations, there were still some contacts between India and Israel. In October 1958, the Israeli Minister of Finance, Levi Eshkol, visited India to assist two conventions of the World Bank and the International Monetary Fund (IMF) and met with his Indian counterpart, Morarji Desai (Gerberg 2008: 237–8). In February 1959, Yigal Allon, a member of the Knesset (and representative of the Achdut Haavoda Party), travelled to Delhi and met with Nehru and Krishna Menon on the recommendations of Aneurin Bevan, a British Labour party leader.[5] Allon was reportedly told by Nehru that Israel was now a political fact not to be ignored, and that India should have established ties with Israel in the early 1950s, but that at the time there were unfavourable circumstances. Nehru still agreed to send a governmental delegation to Israel to study agrarian and cooperative methods (India, *Lok Sabha Debates*, Series II, Vol. 43, 21 April 1960; Allon 1981: 139; quoted in Gerberg 2008: 221). Despite the lack of progress in establishing diplomatic relations in the 1950s, there had been informal discussions about agricultural cooperation, visits of Israeli scientists to India and of Indian scientists to Israel, including Homi Bhabha, the chairman of the Indian Atomic Energy Commission (Gopal and Sharma 2007: 92–3; Kumaraswamy 2010: 134–5). Between December 1959 and January 1960, there would be various governmental missions sent to Israel.[6] In April–May 1960, the Israel question and, most especially, the trade motivations for normalization were debated in the Indian Parliament but the consensus at the time was that the Israeli market was not attractive for

Indian exports. Nehru also attended in December 1960 the premiere of the Israeli Philharmonic Orchestra which was visiting New Delhi (*Middle East Records* 1960, Vol. 1: 304). However, in September 1963, during a parliamentary debate, the Government of India explained that there was not enough 'consular work' to justify the creation of an Indian mission in Israel (India, *Lok Sabha Debates*, Series III, Vol. 20, 9 September 1963, p. 5019).

In the last month of Nehru's tenure, there was an important diplomatic incident which brought to light the ambiguities and limits of the existing policy compromise. The Israeli Consul Peretz Gordon, who was based in Bombay, decided to organize a reception to commemorate Israel's independence day in a hotel in New Delhi. Since these celebrations were usually held in Bombay the preceding years, the holding of the event planned for 15 April was not authorized by the central government. The Consul was also criticized by the Government of India for making political statements against Egypt (Schechtman 1966). The issue was debated in Parliament in April–May 1964 when members of the opposition such as R. Masani, the leader of the conservative Swatantra Party, demanded that the government formally apologize for 'gross discourtesy' in ordering the cancellation of the Israel independence day reception (*Jewish Telegraphic Agency*, 19 April 1964). The socialist Member of Parliament (MP) Kamath also questioned the government on the exact territorial jurisdiction of the Israeli consulate (India, *Lok Sabha Debates*, Series III, Vol. 31, 4 May 1964, p. 14014). In a reply in the Rajya Sabha,[7] the Deputy Minister of External Affairs Dinesh Singh argued that a function such as the independence day celebration should never have been permitted in the capital (India, *Rajya Sabha Debates*, Vol. 47, 5 May 1964, p. 1777). He, however, gave no clarification on the territorial accreditation or of the exact prerogatives of the Israeli consulate.[8]

The incident, however, led to a public outcry and to the formation of an 'Indian Friends of Israel Society' which was composed of 100 members, including eminent personalities such as the writers Kushwant Singh, Nirad C. Chaudhuri, and Ruth Prawer Jhabvala; the historian Romila Thapar; and the influential editor of the *Indian Express* Frank Moraes. In May 1965, in defiance of the government's policy, the Indian Friends of Israel Society organized a farewell reception for Consul Peretz Gordon in New Delhi. The Government of India could not intervene because it was a private event which was not sponsored by the Consulate. Ultimately, however, the Consul could not attend the reception (Schechtman 1966: 49). The establishment of the Society upset the Arabs and led to another diplomatic incident in Delhi. In October 1964, Romila Thapar, who was a member of the Indian Friends of Israel Society, was invited to an official Ministry of External Affairs (MEA) dinner in honour of a Lebanese newspaper editor. The invitation and presence of Thapar led to a walkout of the ambassadors of Lebanon, Iraq, Morocco, and of the Arab League representative (*Times of India*, 17 January 1965).

Following Nehru's death on 27 May 1964, his successor, Prime Minister Lal Bahadur Shastri, mostly continued the previous policy. Until 1964, India's foreign policy, and India's Israel policy in particular, were the products of Nehru who enjoyed an overwhelming support from the Indian public and within the Indian National Congress (INC). By contrast, Shastri, whose political career had mostly centred on domestic politics, hardly had any grounding in India's foreign affairs and most of his statements were just a repetition of Nehru's position. Unlike Nehru, Shastri named a full-time minister of external affairs (Swaran Singh).[9] Under Shastri's tenure, there was a greater control by the MEA of India's West Asia policy. The MEA had a conservative approach on the Israel–Palestine question and did not envisage any change. Soon after taking office, Shastri's first foreign trip was to the Second Non-Aligned Movement (NAM) summit in October 1964 in Cairo. In a joint communiqué with President Nasser, Shastri supported the 'just' claims of the Arabs to Jordan waters and the rights of Palestinian refugees. Unlike Nehru in previous Afro-Asian gatherings, Shastri did not oppose the Conference's strong condemnation of Israel's 'imperialistic policy' in West Asia, nor did he diverge from the mention of support for self-determination of the Arab people of Palestine in their 'struggle for liberation from Colonialism and racism' (MEA 1981: 21). Shastri's passive diplomatic behaviour at the NAM summit marked a clear departure from Nehru's moderating posture in previous Afro-Asian meetings.

As a result, there were some criticisms of Shastri's performance in Cairo which broke with Nehru's more prudent approach to the Arab–Israel question. Shastri moved closer to the Arab position when the Government of India organized in November 1964 an official reception to greet a delegation of the newly created PLO.[10] Until then, India had prudently declined to recognize any Palestinian political authority and stuck to a broad and open-ended support to the rights of the Arab refugees of Palestine. The PLO, a paramilitary movement initiated by the Arab League, was no more a legitimately elected or territorially sovereign political authority than the previous APG. Furthermore, at the time, the PLO openly advocated the destruction of Israel. The hosting of the PLO in 1964 constituted a radical change from India's prudent approach to Palestinian nationalism. India also subsequently decided to grant full diplomatic status to the chief representative of the Arab League in July 1965 (Schechtman 1966). Until then, no other country had recognized the League as a diplomatic entity.

While there were signs of a more explicit pro-Arab approach during Shastri's short tenure as prime minister, there were also contacts between India and Israel. In an interview with an Israeli newspaper which took place in 1965, but was published after his death, Shastri reportedly spoke highly about Israel's achievements and did not rule out the possibility of technical cooperation in agricultural development (*Jerusalem Post*, 14 January 1966). Exchanges in the agricultural domain continued as an Israeli delegation participated in the international trade fair of the state of Gujarat in 1964 (Gerberg 2008: 241). However, the Indian government apparently blocked a few agricultural cooperation initiatives which were taken by Indian states.[11] After the death of Shastri in January 1966, the Government of Israel sent a condolence message and welcomed Indira Gandhi's nomination to the office of prime minister. Israel's Minister of Foreign Affairs, Abba Eban, said at a press conference that the formation of a new Government of India seemed like a 'suitable opportunity' to renew discussions for a closer relationship (*The Israel Digest* 9, 1966: 2–3.). There were other signs that India's policy could evolve. The evolution of India's Israel policy in the 1960s must also be evaluated in light of the various international crises of the 1960s.

The Sino-Indian Conflict of 1962: Reactions from West Asia

In October–November 1962, India and China went to war along the disputed Himalayan border.[12] Following the outbreak of the conflict, Nehru sent written communications to a large number of leaders, including Israeli Prime Minister Ben-Gurion, and the leaders of the Arab states, explaining the Indian position and asking for support.[13] While the Government of India did not expect material assistance, it hoped for reciprocity after giving its unequivocal support to Egypt during the 1956 crisis. There were varying diplomatic responses from West Asia to the crisis and to Nehru's letter. Some states such as Iran, Jordan, Kuwait, Saudi Arabia, Turkey, and Yemen supported, either officially or unofficially, India's position that China was an aggressor.[14] Turkey offered military aid to India.[15] Iraq and Syria preferred to remain neutral.[16] Egypt wished to remain neutral but also wanted to play an active mediating role in resolving the dispute (Heikal 1973: 294; Singh 1963).

Egypt offered an initial proposal which seemed to favour India because it demanded an immediate withdrawal of Chinese forces to the position held prior to 8 September 1962 as a prerequisite for negotiations. However, the Foreign Minister of the People's Republic of China (PRC) Zhou Enlai refused the proposal and argued that the September reference was not a workable basis for a peaceful settlement. In his response to Enlai and Nehru on 31 October, Nasser exhorted both governments to conciliate. This time, Nasser suggested that China and India should revert to their 20 October positions as a basis for negotiations.[17] Egypt's new proposal again favoured India because China would not be allowed to retain some of the territories gained through its offensive. However, at a conference convened in Colombo in December 1962, Egypt modified its position to a more neutral stand.[18] India did not manage to get any majority support for its proposal demanding a Chinese withdrawal of 20 km from the customary lines (Retzlaff 1963). As a result of the 1962 conflict, India found itself in a rivalry not only with Pakistan for allegiances in West Asia, but also with China.

Ben-Gurion's reply to the Nehru letter was polite but non-committal. In his response, Ben-Gurion expressed the hope that the fighting between India and China would be ended quickly by direct negotiations, and he reminded the Indian prime minister of Israel's equal commitment to a peaceful resolution of tensions in West Asia (Ben-Gurion 1972: 667). Nonetheless, the lack of explicit political support from Israel did not stop India from seeking military help from Israel (Heikal 1973: 297; *India Today*, 6 April 1998; Kumaraswamy 2010: 199; Maxwell 1970: 385). Based on Ben-Gurion's recommendation, the Israeli Minister of Foreign Affairs Golda Meir approved the selling of heavy mortars and mortar ammunition to India.[19] However, the collaboration was never explicitly recognized by the Government of India. Reportedly, Nehru also ended these exchanges when Nasser raised his objection to the deal (Gopal 1979, 3: 224; Heikal 1973: 297–8; Heptullah 1991: 191). Nehru never showed any signs of gratitude towards Israel and did not change his position on

Israel despite the apparent military support. Interestingly, an MEA report officially recognized the 'understanding attitude' of the Arab states during the conflict, but did not refer to the Israeli assistance given to India (MEA *Annual Report*, 1963–1964: 45–8).

In fact, Nehru created a precedent in obtaining military assistance from Israel without requiring any diplomatic exchange, or even publicly acknowledging the existence of such security assistance.[20] Israel also used India's conflict with China to put into place back-channel diplomacy. This was a new and unexplored dimension in Indo-Israeli relations as most bilateral cooperation until then had been on agricultural projects. Three months after the Indian defeat in the Sino-Indian war, in January 1963, Israel responded favourably to an Indian request for military and intelligence cooperation. The chief of the military intelligence of the Israeli army as well as the head of the operations branch in the Israel Defence Forces (IDF) visited Delhi and met with India's top military brass, including the chief of army staff (*Hindustan Times*, 15 May 1980; Gerberg 2008: 107–8, 241). However, these discussions were leaked to the Indian press and then denied by the Government of India. While these initial military-to-military exchanges proved to be only a short passing episode, it was the first contact established between the two armies.

The India–Pakistan Conflict of 1965: The Limits of India's Pro-Arab Policy

In the early 1960s, India–Pakistan relations were at a new low point. While the Kashmir territorial conflict was still the predominant issue dividing the two nations, there were other pressing border disputes, most notably over the Rann of Kutch, a region in the border-state of Gujarat.[21] When the conflict erupted in April 1965, Pakistan was able to mobilize an overwhelming majority of Arab and Muslim states on its side. Barring Egypt, no Arab country in West Asia was prepared to support India's position. During the conflict, Jordan and Saudi Arabia gave direct monetary assistance to Pakistan,[22] while Iran and Turkey sent military aid in the form of ammunitions, guns, and jet fuel.[23] Iran also provided the Pakistani air force with access to bases in Zahedan and Mehrabad for refuelling and protection from Indian bombers (Burke 1974: 190; Hoodboy 2012). Nasser stayed neutral during the crisis, but he was instrumental in toning down a pro-Pakistani resolution that Arab states wanted to adopt at the Arab Summit of September 1965 in Casablanca.[24] Nasser's mediating role during the summit was appreciated in Delhi, and particularly in the Indian Parliament (India, *Rajya Sabha Debates*, Vol. 54, 22 November 1965, p. 2127). Once more, there was no reciprocity in diplomatic support between India and the Arab states. For instance, India decided to grant diplomatic status to the chief representative of the Arab League in July 1965, during the first skirmishes with Pakistan, but did not get any immediate diplomatic gains from this symbolical gesture throughout the conflict (*New York Times*, 14 July 1965).

In the course of the Indo-Pakistani conflict, India again approached Israel to acquire heavy mortar and ammunition.[25] Publically, Israel was non-committal. Its Minister of Foreign Affairs, Golda Meir, praised at the United Nations General Assembly (UNGA) the efforts of the UN to reach a ceasefire in South Asia, and criticized the recourse to 'local wars' to settle territorial disputes.[26] Golda Meir was reportedly opposed to shipping the ammunition to India, but she was overruled by Prime Minister Levi Eshkol who approved the Indian request (Gerberg 2008: 219). However, the provision of military aid and the frustration with the Arab reactions did not convince Shastri to modify India's West Asia policy.[27] The structural changes (both at the domestic level with leadership change, and at the international level with the two conflicts) and the negative policy feedback (the absence of clear reciprocal Arab support) were necessary but not sufficient conditions for the policy to change. An additional and necessary factor is the presence of policy entrepreneurs who can emphasize the failures of the existing approach and who can offer clear policy alternatives.

Opposition to the Policy Compromise: Emergence of a New Orthodoxy?

There had already been debates within the Constituent Assembly and in Parliament over the opportunity of developing relations with the Jewish state. Between 1948 and the mid-1960s, some leading intellectuals had unfailingly supported the establishment of diplomatic relations with Israel, such as the poet and nationalist Sarojni Naidu, the journalists and writers Kushwant Singh, Frank Moraes, and Nirad Chaudhuri, as well as the historians and academics Romila Thapar and Manohar Lal Sondhi.[28] Many of these personalities joined the Indian Friends of

Israel Society. Although the support of these Indian intellectuals was appreciated in Israel, they only had a limited influence in the debates shaping India's foreign policy. The Indian media had generally supported Nehru's approach to West Asian affairs. There were some exceptions: in 1960, the participation of a hundred Indians in courses organized by Israel's international cooperation programme encouraged some Indian newspapers to openly call for the exchange of diplomatic envoys with Israel (*Indian Express*, 9 April 1960; *Times of India*, 10 May 1960). However, there was no regular group or lobby in a formal sense that pushed for the normalization of relations with Israel. The strength and visibility of actors demanding a policy revision grew only in the 1960s.

Following the two crises, a group of political actors started openly criticizing India's West Asia policy. Parties in the opposition in the Lok Sabha condemned the Arab responses to the 1965 crisis. In response to this new criticism, the Minister of External Affairs Swaran Singh discussed for the first time the reactions of the Arab states in front of the Lok Sabha in November 1965. Swaran Singh downplayed the disappointment linked to the attitudes of individual states like Jordan and Saudi Arabia. He argued that most Arab countries had demonstrated an understanding of the Indian position and had not taken a communal view of the conflict. To defend his point, Swaran Singh mentioned Nasser's mediating efforts at the Casablanca summit. In a first explicit public reference to the domestic Muslim factor, Swaran Singh also denied allegations that these considerations had had an important influence (India, *Lok Sabha Debates*, Vol. 47, No. 10, 17 November 1965, pp. 2419–22). He added in another statement to the Lok Sabha that there had been disagreements in the Arab world over the explicitly pro-Pakistani position that Jordan had taken at the United Nations Security Council (UNSC).[29]

The Bharatiya Jana Sangh (BJS), the Swatantra Party, and the Praja Socialist Party (PSP) were traditional supporters of the establishment of diplomatic relations with Israel, but these parties lacked the political access and leverage to press the INC-dominated government to implement change. The BJS was a right-wing Hindu party which argued that most Arab states did not deserve India's unconditional support at the expense of better relations with Israel.[30] Balraj Madhok, one of the co-founders of the BJS and the president of the Indian Friends of Israel Society from 1967 to 1973, lamented that the Arab countries had generally taken a pro-Pakistan line and perceived 'India's support for granted' (Madhok 1967:

5). The BJS questioned India's decision to maintain diplomatic relations with states with which it had been in direct conflict, such as China and Pakistan, but not Israel. The BJS also accused the INC of adopting double-standards as it accepted the divisions of British India, Korea, and Germany but refused to recognize Palestine's partition (Bharatiya Jana Sangh [BJS], *Party Documents 1951–1972*, Vol. 3: 34–5). As a result, the BJS promised in its party manifesto that it would 'establish full-fledged diplomatic relations with Israel if it came to power' (BJS 1967: 5).

The PSP also criticized the Government of India's Israel policy but for different reasons.[31] The PSP had a long history of dialogue with the Mapai party (which would become the Labour Party) in Israel. The PSP admired Israel's network of cooperatives and Kibbutz. The Jewish state had an early supporter in the person of the socialist H. V. Kamath who had already discussed the question of the recognition of Israel in the Constituent Assembly debates. In March 1950, the Indian United Socialist Organization (USO) passed a resolution which deplored the fact that the Government of India had not yet recognized Israel which was branded as a 'secular state based on progressive socialist principles' (Gerberg 2008: 148). Representatives of the PSP and the Mapai party also regularly met through international summits. The PSP developed good relations with the Israeli delegation present at the first Asian Socialist Conference in Rangoon in January 1953 (Srivastava 1967). Important PSP leaders visited Israel such as the Secretary General of the PSP Ashok Mehta in April 1953 and the party President Jaya Prakash Narayan in September 1958. Moshe Sharett was invited by the PSP to participate in the Second Congress of Asian socialists in Bombay in 1956. Although it condemned the Israeli participation in the Suez operation in 1956, the PSP sent delegates in April 1960 to participate in the Socialist International Conference in Haifa (Aynor *et al.* 1989: 42–3; *Janata* 11: 40–41, 11 November 1956, 11; *Middle East Records*, p. 183). In June 1960, a PSP delegation participated in training courses at the Afro-Asia Institute for Trade Unions and Cooperation Activities in Israel (Aynor and Avimor 1990: 308–9; Gerberg 2008: 148–9). As a result, the PSP openly advocated normalization of relations with Israel in its October 1966 manifesto (*Janata* 21:39, 16 October 1966: 11).

The right-wing and liberal Swatantra Party also pushed for the establishment of diplomatic relations and economic links with Israel. The Swatantra Party felt a close affinity with Israel because of its pro-Western and especially pro-American policies. It was also sceptic of any rapprochement with the Arab states which were gradually relying on Soviet military support. Its leaders such as C. Rajagopalachari, M. R. Masani, N. G. Ranga, and K. M. Munshi had been long-time advocates of normalization. One of the party leaders, the economist Rajah Hutheesing visited Israel in 1960 to study trade prospects (*Middle East Records*, p. 183). He notably told the Israeli press to distinguish India's official unreceptive policy, which it had to adopt because of domestic and international constraints, from India's genuine sympathy towards Israel (*Haaretz*, 17 April 1960). In its 1967 manifesto, the Swatantra Party qualified the absence of diplomatic links with Israel as an 'utterly indefensible' position (Swatantra Party 1967: 6). However, the party's political influence was limited as it had very few seats in the Lok Sabha in 1965 (18 seats).[32]

By 1966–7, the opposition to India's Israel policy existed but was strongly divided. Three of the major political parties in the parliamentary opposition criticized the existing policy compromise and supported normalization with Israel. All three parties also highlighted the absence of results of the present pro-Arab policy. On the other hand, the BJS, the PSP, and the Swatantra Party opposed the government's position for varying political reasons. The BJS emphasized the lack of reciprocal support from Arab states while the PSP and Swatantra Party stressed the potential gains from engaging Israel. Consequently, there was little coordination and cooperation between these different actors. Until 1967, it was complicated to see a new and united orthodoxy strong enough to challenge and to substitute the existing policy compromise. Furthermore, the INC held a clear majority of the seats in the Lok Sabha. Also, the Indian Parliament has had traditionally limited input in the conduct of Indian foreign policy, and the prime minister, who was also the leader of the majority party, had an important freedom of action in foreign policy-making. Parliamentary support on foreign policy issues was generally assured.

It took a succession of other crises from 1967 to 1974 to further weaken the policy compromise of 1956 and to prompt the various opposing groups to cooperate, albeit in a haphazard and limited fashion. During the 1967 war, for instance, all opposition parties (with the exception of the communist parties) criticized the official Indian position.[33] Looking at the policy ideas of these advocates of change after 1967 is necessary to understand why the policy was not reversed despite propitious conditions at the international level. Furthermore, concentrating on the forces at play in a renewed debate also helps explain why India modified its West Asia policy but stopped short of establishing relations with Israel. The reasons impeding a rapprochement with Israel were very different in 1974 than they were in 1956. The circumstances and debates behind the formation of a new policy compromise in 1974 are crucial to understand the obstacles to policy change vis-à-vis Israel for the next two decades.

India's Israel Policy under Fire: Regional Crises, Misunderstandings, and Space for Change (1967–73)

Contrary to Shastri, Indira Gandhi was more involved in foreign affairs, and especially in the formation of India's West Asia policy. Indira Gandhi curtailed political dissent within the party and there was consequently no open dissent as far as her West Asia policy was concerned. According to many observers, Indira Gandhi pursued a hostile anti-Israel foreign policy and was a staunch supporter of the Arab countries (Jansen 1971: 269–70). At the beginning of her tenure, during a visit to Cairo, Indira Gandhi made a statement that confirmed India's traditional support to the Arab states but also seemed to put into question the recognition of Israel. She stated that India's support to the Arab countries was due to India's commitment to the 'principle that states should not be carved out or created on the basis of religion' (Jansen 1971: 302). This statement was in consonance with India's pre-1950 statements but indirectly contradicted India's acknowledgement in September 1950 that Israel was now an accepted political fact.

The steady deterioration of relations was also confirmed by the fact India now refused to issue visas to Israeli delegations to attend international conferences and sport events in India (Gerberg 2008: 108). An exception to that new rule led to an important diplomatic incident. In March 1966, Israel requested a 24-hour stopover for the President of the state of Israel, Zalman Shazar, on his way to a state visit to Nepal. The short stopover was cleared by Delhi, but the Government of India refused to have the president land in Delhi and only authorized the Israeli delegation to land in Calcutta. Upon his landing, Shazar was ignored both by the central government and the government of West Bengal which did not send any official delegation. Instead, pro-Arab demonstrators mobilized in front of the hotel where the Israeli president was staying.

As a result, the Israeli Knesset passed a resolution expressing regrets over the treatment of the Israeli president (*Jerusalem Post*, 4 March 1966). Ten Indian members of Parliament (MPs) also submitted a memorandum criticizing the government's diplomatic 'discourtesy' towards the Israeli president. India's Deputy Minister of External Affairs Dinesh Singh replied in the Rajya Sabha that the MEA had indeed not greeted the Israeli official but added that the arrangements had been explained in advance to Israel (India, *Rajya Sabha Debates*, Vol. 55, 25 March 1966, pp. 4546–7). In another answer to the Rajya Sabha, Dinesh Singh explained that India had not extended 'hospitality' but its 'courtesies' to the Israeli president (*Rajya Sabha Debates*, Vol. 56, 3 May 1966, p. 23). Singh's reply led to further criticism, including from members of Congress like the former Deputy Minister of Finance Tarkeshwari Sinha who denounced the 'cavalier way' in which Dinesh Singh had answered the questions.[34] In May 1966, India also refused an Israeli aid offer during the drought.[35] The rejection was officially admitted by the Food and Agriculture Minister Chidambaram Subramanian in a reply to a question from the socialist MP Kamath about the Israeli government's offer of food grains. Subramanian explained that India could not accept an Israeli offer of fertilizers at that time because of 'political considerations' and he explained that India needed to consider 'other reactions'.[36] In parallel, the Government of India pursued its support for the plight of Palestinian refugees through regular communiqués.[37]

India's Initial Reaction to the 1967 Crisis

In 1966–7, there was a series of skirmishes on the Syria–Israel border, as well as Palestinian raids against Israel from bases in Jordan. India did not officially condemn the Syria-based terrorist movements but also did not react after Israel's reprisals against Syria in April 1967.[38] Because of the deterioration of the situation, UN Secretary General U-Thant appealed to both countries to reconvene in a Mixed Armistice Commission for the first time since 1960. There was another major military clash on 7 April 1967 that pushed both countries to write to the Security Council to accuse each other of violating the armistice agreement. The situation further escalated as Nasser formally asked the United Nations Emergency Force (UNEF) on 18 May 1967 to vacate Egyptian-controlled areas near the demarcation line. This move started a debate at the UN over the right of Egypt to unilaterally ask for such a withdrawal.[39]

India was directly involved in the West Asian crisis of 1967 for various reasons. First, India was the largest contributor of troops to the UNEF contingent and was directly concerned by the Egyptian demand for withdrawal. Second, as a non-permanent member of the UNSC at the time of the events, India could not remain a neutral observer and was asked to take explicit positions and to vote on the West Asian disputes.[40] Consequently, India argued that Egypt had a sovereign right to request the withdrawal of the UNEF, and supported the UN Secretary General U-Thant's decision to comply with the Egyptian demand on 18 May. India had an understanding that the UNEF was merely allowed to station on Egyptian soil, and that the removal of Egypt's consent automatically meant the departure of the UN troops.[41] Already in 1957, in a speech to the Lok Sabha, Krishna Menon had explained that India had agreed to contribute to the UNEF troops on the condition that UN forces would not 'be asked to violate the sovereignty' of Egypt and that they would not take 'the functions of invading forces' or become 'armies of occupation'.[42]

Indira Gandhi also argued that since Israel had refused to allow UNEF troops to station on its side of the border, sovereign Egypt could demand for the UNEF to be pulled out (*The Hindu*, 22 May 1967). The Minister of External Affairs, M. C. Chagla, and the Indian ambassador to the UN, G. Parthasarathy, both confirmed in May 1967 that the consent of Egypt was necessary for the UNEF to station in Egypt and that Indian troops would not remain in the UNEF if there was no Egyptian approval.[43] Chagla also quoted U-Thant who had said that since Egyptian consent had been withdrawn, it was incumbent on the Secretary General and the UN to remove the force (India, *Lok Sabha Debates*, Vol. 3, No. 3, 25 May 1967, pp. 871–6). Additionally, Parthasarathy expressed India's understanding of Egypt's decision to move troops in the Sinai as 'defensive' and 'precautionary' measures.[44]

As Egypt closed the access to the Gulf of Aqaba and the Strait of Tiran to Israeli ships on 22 May, India also supported Egypt's sovereign rights over these waters. Both Chagla and Parthasarathy reiterated the position taken by India and Krishna Menon at the UNGA in March 1957 that the Gulf of Aqaba was an 'inland sea', and that Cairo was entitled to close it to Israeli shipping, especially since it remained formally at war with Israel.[45] The government also supported Egypt's argument that the blockade was necessary to prevent strategic weapons from reaching Israel through the Gulf of Aqaba (India, *Lok Sabha Debates*, Series 4, Vol. 3, session 2 of

1967, cols 875, 891). Nevertheless, Parthasarathy also added that Egypt should try to find a 'modus vivendi' with other nations to ensure the free access to these waters.[46] There was some opposition to this unconditional support to Egypt. Arthur Lall, who was also in the Indian delegation, had argued that U-Thant's decision was illegal as the UNEF had been created by the UNGA. Lall therefore judged that questions related to UNEF's functioning could only be addressed by a special emergency session of the UNGA.[47] Parthasarathy also discussed a phased withdrawal of the UNEF, as it had played a crucial security role in Gaza and the Sinai for the past decade (Rikhye 1980: 131).

The Six-Day War between Israel on the one hand and Egypt, Syria, and Jordan, on the other, erupted on 5 June 1967. Within a few days, Israel had won a decisive land war and had taken control of the Gaza Strip and the Sinai Peninsula from Egypt; the West Bank and East Jerusalem from Jordan; and the Golan Heights from Syria. During the brief conflict, Indira Gandhi gave an unequivocal support to Egypt and the Arab states. One day after the first Israeli raids, Indira Gandhi accused Israel of escalating the situation into a full-scale armed conflict.[48] Parthasarathy also regretted that what he considered to be a 'largely juridical dispute on shipping rights' had spiralled into a 'tragic conflagration'. Parthasarathy placed the full responsibility of the 'grave situation' on Israel.[49] The Government of India asked for an immediate ceasefire and for the withdrawal of Israeli troops to positions held before 4 June 1967.[50] India also argued that Israel should not be able to enjoy the territorial benefits of its aggression.[51]

India's support of the Arab position was again confirmed by Chagla's speech to the UNGA on 21 June 1967, wherein he condemned Israel's violation of the general armistice agreements signed with Egypt, as well as Israel's intention to expand its territory and to expel Arabs from their lands and homes. Chagla argued that Israel had violated the UN Charter and attempted to impose a new territorial 'fait accompli' in the region. Citing Nehru's statement from November 1956, Chagla reiterated India's support for Egypt's sovereign right to demand the withdrawal of the UNEF. Chagla further indicated that India had registered an official complaint to the Israeli government over the attack on UNEF soldiers. However, Chagla also added India had 'no quarrel with the people of Israel', and that India had always followed an 'objective attitude' towards the state of Israel.[52]

The Government of India's strong condemnation of Israel in 1967 resulted from the fact that Indian troops from the UNEF had apparently suffered casualties during the initial Israeli artillery and air strikes against Egyptian forces in Gaza. India still had an important contingent on Egyptian soil which had not yet been evacuated from the border zone.[53] The UNEF found itself on the path of the advancing IDF and had all its vehicles wrecked, its communications knocked out, and some Indian soldiers were killed.[54] Indira Gandhi described the Israeli raids, leading to the deaths and injuries among the Indian personnel in the UNEF, as 'wanton', 'deliberate and without provocation' and called upon the Indian Parliament to 'unreservedly condemn this cowardly attack on our men' (India, *Lok Sabha Debates*, Vol. 4, No. 11, 6 June 1967, pp. 3292–5). Gandhi asked for the UN to ensure the safety and evacuation of the Indian troops by sea. When the news of the attacks on the UNEF reached New York, the Indian delegation at the UN also criticized the 'irresponsible and brutal action by the ruling circles of Israel' (*Times of India*, 6 June 1967). The Indian ambassador to the UN also regretted the deaths of UNEF soldiers following 'unprovoked', 'deliberate', and 'cowardly' attacks.[55]

While the parliamentary opposition in general condemned the Israeli attack, the pro-Israel BJS leader and president of the Indian Friends of Israel Society, Balraj Madhok, criticized the UN for not evacuating the troops by air. He also accused the Government of India for failing to repatriate the Indian soldiers in Gaza and Sinai (India, *Lok Sabha Debates*, Series IV, Vol. 3, Session 2, p. 3302). There were legitimate bases for this criticism: General Rikhye, who led the UNEF mission in Gaza, explained that India had promptly supported Egypt's demand for removal of UNEF, but had not provided the necessary air transport for its troops based in Gaza.[56] Rikhye's more nuanced account of the events in June 1967 revealed a shared responsibility vis-à-vis the killings of UNEF soldiers. While some Indian soldiers were killed or injured under Israeli artillery, others, including an Indian officer, died because their cars rode over Arab mines (Rikhye 1980: 154). Furthermore, according to Rikhye's first-hand description of the situation, the geographical proximity of the UNEF to Egyptian and Palestinian forces in Gaza made it initially difficult for the IDF to separate them. By early June, when the development of the events was still vague, the Government of India had therefore mostly relied on rumours of Indian casualties to justify its pro-Arab rhetoric.

In reaction to the difficulties of reaching a working ceasefire agreement, Parthasarathy first suggested in June 1967 a new four-point programme to restore peace in the region (although not in the form of a resolution).[57] The Indian government took a strong position against Israel on the issue of the Gulf of Aqaba and the Strait of Tiran. Parthasarathy condemned Israel's intention to change the status quo through a preemptive attack and to have the UNSC accept the new fait accompli. India recognized Israel's claims of passage but, according to the Indian ambassador, the dispute should have been peacefully resolved at the UN with the recognition of Egypt's sovereignty over these waters. India stood by its traditional position that the assailant should not benefit from the fruits of its aggression.[58] This proposal was severely criticized by Israeli Foreign Minister Abba Eban because Israel had not been consulted and because a return to the pre-war positions would have prejudiced Israel's negotiating position in the advent of talks.[59]

The Aftermath of the 1967 Crisis: Widespread Opposition to the Government's Position

For the first time, all the Indian opposition parties (with the exception of the communists and the Muslim League), most newspapers, and even some members of the Congress party openly called for a new approach to the Arab–Israel dispute. While this was not the first time that India's Israel policy had come under criticism, there were new conditions in May–June 1967. First, the death of Nehru had removed the permissive consensus which existed regarding India's West Asia policy. Second, the poor showing of Congress in the February 1967 parliamentary elections had eroded the party's popularity and partially restricted its leverage in foreign policy debates.[60] Third, as detailed in the previous section, there was a growing perception that India's West Asia policy had been unsuccessful in light of the limited Arab support received on some vital political issues.

Consequently, the INC's West Asia policy was further scrutinized and debated than ever before in Parliament. This new opposition led to repeated clashes with government personalities during the different phases of the 1967 conflict. The first turbulent session took place on 25 May. Chagla's unconditional endorsement of Egypt's demand for the withdrawal of the UNEF and for the interdiction of Israeli shipping in the Gulf of Aqaba was perceived by the parliamentary opposition as too partisan (India, *Lok Sabha Debates*, Series 4, Vol. 4, 6 June 1967, p. 3296). The opposition had become disillusioned with Arab neutrality during the 1965 conflict when countries like Jordan and Saudi Arabia had directly supported Pakistan. Support of Arab states was absent in other international issues. Most Arab countries voted against India's election to the UNSC in 1966 because Syria was a competing candidate.[61] Groups like the BJS and the PSP argued that the diplomatic behaviour of Arab states did not justify India's policy of constant support against Israel (Madhok 1967).

India was receiving little tangible political gains from its existing approach, and it only played a limited role as an active peace-broker in the region. The PSP leader, Nath Pai, called the Chagla statement a 'wretched document' which did not help reduce the tensions in the region (*Janata* 12: 9, 28 May 1967, 4). However, most of the parliamentary criticism came against Chagla's statement that the creation of Israel had generated tensions between Israel and Arab countries. The BJS asked if Chagla's statement meant that the disappearance of Israel would remove tensions and demanded that the government rectify that it did not demand the destruction of Israel (India, *Lok Sabha Debates*, Series 4, Vol. 3, No. 3, 25 May 1967, p. 892). Balraj Madhok later cited Chagla's mention of 'peaceful coexistence' in the region and questioned how this was compatible with Nasser's call for the extinction of Israel (India, *Lok Sabha Debates* Series 4, Vol. 6:4, 15 July 1967, pp. 12150, 12160–2). The PSP and the Swatantra party made similar demands of clarification following Chagla's ambiguous statement (India, *Lok Sabha Debates* , Series 4, Vol. 3, No. 3, 25 May 1967, p. 918). As a result, the main opposition parties believed that India's systematic alignment with the Arab states was neither beneficial in a pragmatic sense nor legitimate and consistent as it directly contradicted with India's 1950 decision to recognize Israel.

There was another direct disagreement between the Government of India and some parties in the opposition over the responsibility of who precipitated the crisis. While the Indian government condemned Israel's raid from 6 June, the opposition argued that there was no pre-planned design and that the Israeli preventive strike had been forced by the Egyptian actions and statements.[62] The BJS questioned, for instance, the wisdom of blaming Israel when the UN had not explicitly done so (India, *Lok Sabha Debates*, Series 4, Vol. 3:40, Session 2 of 1967, p. 3302). Likewise, PSP leader Kripalani considered it was 'foolish diplomacy' to prematurely call Israel an aggressor before peace was restored and a commission of inquiry had been set up (India, *Lok Sabha Debates*, Series 4, Vol. 4:7, Session 2 of 1967, pp. 12383–93). Chagla had indeed blamed Israel's belligerent statements as the main cause of the rising tensions, thereby disregarding the responsibility of Syria-based terror movements and Egypt's decision to move troops to the border in the escalation of violence (India, *Lok Sabha Debates*, Series 4, Vol. 3:3, 25 May 1967, 871–6).

In contrast, the BJS discussed the role of the Palestinian commandos coming from Syria and Jordan prior to the Israel attack, and judged that the government should have assessed the situation before giving its all-out support to Egypt (India, *Lok Sabha Debates*, Series 4, Vol. 3:3, 25 May 1967, pp. 892–3; *Organiser* 20:41, 28 May 1967, p. 3). This perception of one-sided alignment on the Arab arguments led the M. L. Sondhi (BJS MP) to accuse the government of behaving like the '14th Arab state' (India, *Lok Sabha Debates*, Series 4, Vol. 4, p. 3937). The PSP also considered that Egypt's demand for the removal of the UNEF was too hasty and partly responsible for the rising tensions.[63] The Swatantra Party further argued that India was not justified in endorsing Egypt's aggressive action of rearming the Sinai because Cairo had not directly been involved in the Syria–Israel tensions (India, *Lok Sabha Debates* Series 4, Vol. 3, No. 3, 25 May 1967, p. 885). The BJS judged that the withdrawal of the UNEF had generated an 'explosive situation' (*Organiser* 20:41, 28 May 1967, p. 3).

Similarly, Kripalani of the PSP, interpreted the closure of the Gulf of Aqaba as the sign of an undeclared war by Egypt on Israel (India, *Lok Sabha Debates*, Series 4, Vol. 6:7, 17 July 1967, pp. 12389–93). M. R. Masani of the Swatantra Party also described the closure as an 'act of aggression' (ibid., Series 4, Vol. 6:40, 15 July 1967, pp. 12132–8). Swatantra Party leader Rajagopalachari argued that the Strait of Tiran was not exclusively on the Egyptian side, and that therefore the Egyptian decision to build military installations on the islands of Tiran and Sonafer to restrict navigation was illegal (*Swarajya* 11:50, 17 June 1967, pp. 1–2). He added that aggression in West Asia was caused not only by 'gun-fire' but also by 'military strangulation' (*Swarajya* 12:1, 1 July 1967, p. 25). The BJS also condemned Nasser's closure of the Gulf and his threat to bombard Elath, which was Israel's only viable link with Asia and Africa (*Organiser* 20:41, 28 May 1967, p. 3). The BJS had traditionally argued that the Suez Canal and the Gulf of Aqaba were international waterways and it was contrary to international legal opinion for Egypt to have closed the Gulf to Israeli ships.[64] India's early support for U-Thant's decision to withdraw the UNEF was therefore considered to be 'unnecessary and precipitate' (*Swarajya* 11:51, 17 June 1967, pp. 1–2). Commenting on the subsequent efforts by Chagla and the Indian delegation at the UN to give back control of the Gulf of Aqaba to Egypt, Rajagopalachari deplored that 'not a gulf but a whole ocean' divided the government from its public opinion on the Israeli question (*Swarajya* 12:1, 1 July 1967, p. 25).

As events unfolded, the opposition parties were convinced that the evacuation of the UNEF, the blockade, and the mobilization of the Egyptian and Syrian armies were direct provocations from the Arab side, which had left few alternatives for Israel. Despite the evidence of shared responsibilities over the escalation of the crisis and the multiple warnings of caution from the opposition, the Government of India maintained its strong anti-Israel position in the initial stages of the conflict. This pushed the leaders of the Swatantra Party, the BJS, and the PSP to cooperate for the first time. As the hostilities broke out on 5 June, the three party leaders appealed through a joint letter to Indira Gandhi to abstain from apportioning blame at that early stage to one disputant (Israel) and to adopt a more objective attitude towards the conflict.[65] By adopting a more neutral attitude, the three parties judged the government would have the 'support of the country' and would be in a better position to play an 'honourable part' in helping to resolve the dispute (India, *Lok Sabha Debates*, Vol. 6, No. 40, 15 July 1967, pp. 12132–8). The heated clashes over India's policy even forced Parliament to adjourn on 9 June (Jansen 1971: 303).

Given the adverse repercussions of the closure of the Suez Canal on the Indian economy, the opposition parties felt that the priority was to bring about an immediate suspension of the hostilities. Blaming Israel and asking for unilateral concessions was not considered as the adequate strategy to reach these goals. PSP leader Rammanohar Lohia argued, for instance, that the question of identifying the aggressor was irrelevant, and judged that subsequent diplomatic efforts should concentrate on restoring peace in the region (India, *Lok Sabha Debates*, Series 4, Vol. 4:11, 6 June 1967, pp. 3305–8). The opposition also noted the legal and practical contradictions of the Indian position. The Government of India was signatory to the UN resolution of 1957 on the freedom of navigation and argued that the Suez Canal needed to be open to all countries, on one hand, but took a different position when it came to the Gulf of Aqaba where it officially supported the establishment of an Egyptian blockade (India, *Lok Sabha Debates*, Series 4, Vol. 3, Session 2 of 1967, pp. 911– 12). Some even argued that the Egyptian blockade was a problematic precedent for India's own interests (*Indian Express*, 5 June 1967). The urgent need to resume Indian shipping through the Canal explained the gradual evolution of India's anti-Israeli rhetoric at the UN. By late 1967, the Government of India no longer defended exclusive Egyptian control over the disputed waterways.

The contradictions of the Indian policy and the mounting resistance in Parliament raised concerns within the Congress party itself. Some Congress members in the Rajya Sabha criticized the government for supporting Egypt too hastily (Jansen 1971: 303). Some members of the parliamentary executive of the party also regretted Chagla's ambiguous statement over the existence of Israel. They recommended a more neutral position. Even within the cabinet's foreign affairs committee, there were serious doubts expressed by senior ministers over the wisdom of India's position. Nevertheless, they finally agreed to support the policy statement made by Indira Gandhi in Parliament on 6 June (*The Statesman*, 9 June 1967). The resolution adopted by the All India Congress Committee (AICC) on 23 June also revealed internal divisions within the governing party. Parting with the government's official position, the party's resolution did not directly condemn Israel and did not refer to the UNEF soldiers who were killed (Kumaraswamy 2010: 206). In his autobiography, Chagla himself discussed internal criticism of the official Indian position during the crisis (Chagla 1973: 426). Some of the Congress members were reportedly concerned with the implications of India's anti-Israel policy for the continuing support of the US (Jansen 1971: 303).

Beyond the parliamentary reaction, the Indian national press was also very critical of the government's official policy. The strongest backlash came from the most influential English-language dailies (Kozicki 1967; Srivastava 1968). The *Hindustan Times* editorial condemned the Israeli raid and the killing of Indian troops but also criticized Indira Gandhi's one-sided attack on Israel and blamed the Arab states, and especially Egypt, for the escalation of the crisis (*Hindustan Times*, 8 June 1967). According to the newspaper, the Indian opinion was 'divided' on this issue. In the *Statesman*, the famous editorialist Inder Malhotra supported the pro-Arab policy but discussed the growing disappointment with the Egyptian ally that had not proved to be a 'dependable asset'. Malhotra thought the government should have discouraged Nasser from demanding the UNEF removal and from 'hostile' actions such as the closing of the Gulf of Aqaba. Finally, Malhotra also criticized India for supporting an impractical ceasefire resolution and asking for the return to the 4 June positions, a proposal that did not take into account 'Israel's need for security against a ring of encircling neighbours' that were still at war against Tel Aviv (*The Statesman*, 12 June and 13 June 1967). Similarly, another *Hindustan Times* editorial disapproved the demand for Israel's unconditional withdrawal and instead asked for a negotiated settlement between Israel and the Arab states (*Hindustan Times*, 15 June 1967). The press considered that India's position in 1967 was no longer open-ended and non-aligned. A survey conducted at the time by the Indian Institute of Public Opinion in important Indian cities demonstrated a general support for the Arab cause, but also the demand for a 'more objective and impartial stand on the Arab–Israeli issue' (*Monthly Public Opinion Surveys* 1967: 3–19). Within the MEA, there were also reservations about the unconditional support given to Egypt. Foreign Secretary C. S. Jha regretted that India had not warned Nasser of the potentially negative consequences of his actions (Jha 1983: 308–9). Another group of actors began to look at the region differently: the officers of India's armed forces. Looking at the conflict from a strictly strategic standpoint, Indian officers expressed admiration for the IDF's military achievements.[66]

Why the 1967 Crisis did not Lead to a Policy Change

By July 1967, the situation on the ground in West Asia was deadlocked, the Suez Canal was still closed, the parliamentary opposition was for the first time united against India's West Asia policy, and there were reports of heated exchanges in Indira Gandhi's own government over the direction to take. There were favourable conditions for a complete policy change. According to some observers, the opposition was sufficiently widespread to threaten the political survival of the government. Various sources reported at that time that Indira Gandhi had told members of her cabinet that she was even willing to call for anticipated elections, and to seek a new mandate on her West Asia policy (*Hindustan Times*, 20 July 1967; *The Statesman* 20 July 1967; *Times of India*, 9 June 1967). Why did this important domestic political crisis in the May–July 1967 period not lead to a policy change?

There were various reasons that can account for the lack of policy reversal by 1967. The shock of the 1967 crisis, which highlighted a failure of the existing policy, enabled the rise of partisans of an alternative course of action, a 'new orthodoxy', to offer innovative foreign policy prescriptions. By contrast, the old orthodoxy, represented by the Indira Gandhi government, was weakened in 1967. Nevertheless, I argue that there needs to be a second step for foreign policy change to be complete. In accordance with Legro's model, I argue that change will ultimately depend on the distribution of replacement ideas and on how united the 'new orthodoxy' remains (Legro 2005: 14–15, 28–29). My model therefore argues that complete foreign policy change will happen if there is a prominent, unified, and sustained alternative to the existing policy.

The emerging 'new orthodoxy' in May 1967 was particularly critical of Nasser's imprudent behaviour and demanded a more balanced and genuinely neutral approach towards West Asia. The opposition considered India's policy to be too Cairo-centric. For instance, the socialist Nath Pai judged that the government, by unconditionally supporting Nasser, had seriously compromised its position when it could have otherwise played a 'useful part' in the crisis (India, *Lok Sabha Debates*, Series 4, Vol. 4:7, 18 July 1967, pp. 12640–2). The case supporting Egypt was not as solid as in 1956. The government had not taken into account the evolution of the regional situation and how it affected its own national interests. For instance, the Egyptian military gamble of 1967 went against India's economic interests because of the consequent closing of the Suez Canal.

Instead of advising caution to Nasser over the potential diplomatic drawbacks of his policy, India effectively gave 'carte blanche' to Cairo (Jha 1983: 308–9). Chagla's statement of support for Nasser further revealed how India interpreted the Arab world as one homogeneous diplomatic block and perceived Nasser's Egypt to be its sole spokesperson (India, *Lok Sabha Debates*, Series 4, Vol. 7, 18 July 1967, pp. 12703–4). Indian policy ignored the growing political disagreements between Egypt, Kuwait, and Yemen (which had always supported India); Iraq and Lebanon (traditionally neutral during the South Asian crises); and Saudi Arabia, Jordan, and Syria (which had provided strong political and material support to Pakistan in 1965). By contrast with the 1950s, India's policy left little room for diplomatic manoeuvre. In fact, the uncritical pro-Nasser policy led to the alienation of other Arab leaders like King

Hussein of Jordan and King Saud of Saudi Arabia who did not agree with the Egyptian president.

However, many of the actors of the apparent 'new orthodoxy' were not supportive of Israel's actions. The rising opposition to the policy status quo was hardly uniform. While there was a general consensus in favour of a reassessment of India's regional policy, there was no agreement on the direction this new policy would take. The BJS had consistently been supportive of normalization of relations with Israel in its different manifestoes. It promoted a build-up of relations with Israel as a necessary counterbalance in a predominantly Muslim region, extending from Morocco to Pakistan (Madhok 1967). By contrast, the secular Swatantra Party also supported a rapprochement with Israel but it did not share the anti-Muslim bias that led the BJS to privilege relations with Tel Aviv over the Arab states. The PSP also advocated the establishment of diplomatic relations, but stated that 'friendly relations with Arab countries' were compatible with 'similar relations with Israel' (*Janata* 21:39, 16 October 1967, p. 11). In spite of the initial contacts with the Mapai party, the secular PSP had grown disillusioned with the theocratic nature of Israel and the segregation of the non-Jews. The PSP therefore qualified its support for Israel by emphasizing the need for Israel to come to peaceful terms with its immediate neighbours (*Janata* 12:26, 17 July 1967, p. 2).

As a result, all these parties only agreed when they were criticizing the government for fully committing itself behind the Arab viewpoint. However, even that semblance of unified opposition was ephemeral. The opposition remained cohesive during the limited duration of the Six-Day War and its immediate aftermath. There were various explanations for the subsequent dismemberment of the new orthodoxy. First, as the situation in West Asia shifted to the question of peace settlement, the divergences between the three parties became salient. The BJS supported Israel for not withdrawing until it had obtained explicit security guarantees from the Arab states (India, *Lok Sabha Debates*, Series 4, Vol. 4, Session 2 of 1967, p. 3298; Series 4, Vol. 6, Session 2 of 1967, p. 12140). By contrast, the PSP supported the Indian resolution at the UN calling for a return to the positions held before the outbreak of hostilities on 5 June (India, *Lok Sabha Debates*, Series 4, Vol. 3, Session 2 of 1967, p. 3311). The press and the opposition parties (with the exception of the BJS) gradually moved away from their initial position as it became clear that Israel would not withdraw from the Arab territories it had taken. The long-term occupation of East Jerusalem, West Bank, Gaza Strip, Sinai, and the Golan Heights damaged the little sympathy Israel had obtained in April–June 1967 in the Indian public opinion.

Second, the Government of India—which represented the old orthodoxy—made some strategic concessions to the emerging opposition. I argue that the intention was both to co-opt some elements of the opposition and to divide the emerging new orthodoxy. Under pressure, the government progressively retreated from its original anti-Israel rhetoric and began to reframe the rationale behind its West Asia policy. In a parliamentary debate in July 1967, Chagla justified India's pro-Arab policy because it protected India's interests in the region. India needed 'friendly' relations with the West Asian states because the area was important for India's trade and for its regular supply of oil. India also needed to guarantee the security of Indian residents in the Gulf and to safeguard access to the strategic Suez Canal (India, *Lok Sabha Debates*, Vol. 7, No. 41, 18 July 1967, pp. 12678–712). Breaking with the previous ideological statements in support or the Arab cause, the government henceforth evoked pragmatic economic and energy rationalizations. With this new reasoning, the government wanted to appease the concerns of some of the opposing parties like the Swatantra Party and the PSP. Chagla also attempted to rectify what he had meant in his earlier statement when he had put into doubt India's continuing recognition of Israel.[67] Defining it as a 'factual statement' that was merely meant to describe the state of tensions in the region since the creation of Israel, Chagla did not suggest that India had withdrawn its recognition of Israel. Chagla also clarified that India was not opposed to a discussion between the Arab states and Israel on issues such as the recognition of Israel, the navigation in the Suez Canal and the Gulf of Aqaba, and the question of refugees (India, *Lok Sabha Debates*, Vol. 7, No. 41, 18 July 1967, pp. 12678–712). Quoting the corroborating statements of various international actors like US Secretary of State Foster Dulles, British Foreign Secretary George Brown, and French President Charles De Gaulle, Chagla also attempted to dilute the impression shared by parliamentary opponents that India was isolated in its pro-Arab position (India, *Lok Sabha Debates*, Vol. 7, No. 41, 18 July 1967, pp. 12678–712).

In the following months, India also altered its position on the status of the disputed waterways. In his June statement at the UN, Chagla conceded that the legal status of the Gulf of Aqaba was open to controversy.[68] As the discussion on the crisis moved to the UNGA in July, India supported a 14-nation resolution requiring the UNSC to seek political, legal, and humanitarian ways to resolve all problems.[69] In October 1967, Indian Defence Minister Swaran Singh outlined another Indian plan for peace in West Asia, which mostly restated ambassador Parthasarathy's initial four points.[70] The one difference was that Singh encouraged all states to respect the territorial integrity and political independence of the other, thereby recognizing the right for Israel to exist independently.[71] In November, Parthasarathy introduced a draft resolution that prolonged India's support for the Arab nations. The resolution called for the withdrawal of all Israeli troops from the occupied territories and for the just settlement of the Palestinian refugee problem. However, in the November 1967 resolution, India equally called for a 'guarantee of freedom of navigation through all international waterways in accordance with international law' (MEA, *Foreign Affairs Record* 13, November 1967, p. 183).

As a result, India had moved away from its pro-Egyptian position on the disputed waterways. Following the crisis, India supported a resolution which left the status of the Gulf ambiguous. Taking in account Israel's claim for passage, the Government of India hereafter left it for international courts to settle the status of the Gulf of Aqaba and the Strait of Tiran. In the end, the resolution never came before the Security Council for a vote, and a slightly different British resolution was accepted unanimously as UNSC Resolution 242 (UNSCR 242) (Lall 1967: 309–10). The change in India's position was due to the lack of international support for its initial proposal to resolve the situation at the UNSC but it was also the consequence of strong domestic opposition over the status of these waters.

In spite of these partial concessions to the emerging new orthodoxy, Indira Gandhi maintained her strong condemnation of Israeli actions. The Indian prime minister reiterated her unconditional support to Nasser during her visit to Cairo in October 1967. In a joint communiqué, the two sides reaffirmed their adherence to the UN principle that the use of force to achieve territorial gains was impermissible (Gerberg 2008: 89). In a speech at the UN in October 1968, Gandhi again stated that it was not acceptable to redraw borders by force, and that a peaceful settlement would only be possible with the withdrawal of foreign forces from all occupied Arab territories.[72] In addition, India regularly discussed the consequences of the June 1967 conflict on the refugee situation at the

UN.[73] As one of the main contributors to the UN High Commission for Refugees (UNHCR), India believed that a lasting and just solution to the West Asian crisis depended on the rehabilitation of the Arab refugees.

Despite the new orthodoxy's criticism with regard to the lack of Arab reciprocity, the Government of India maintained its pro-Arab position in multilateral institutions. The legitimacy of the government's position was facilitated by Israel's behaviour, which refused to evacuate the conquered territories. Tel Aviv's refusal to comply with UNSCR 242 was progressively condemned by those at home who had initially challenged Indira Gandhi's policy (*Times of India*, 23 March 1968). Ambassador Parthsarathi again demanded in March–April 1968 that the UNSC resolution of 1967 be implemented to ensure peace and security in the area. Parthasarathy explained that it was not only a position of principle but a 'practical' one.[74] As a result, UNSCR 242 and its effective implementation became the new benchmark for Indian diplomacy for any possible progress in Indo-Israeli relations.

In May 1969, Minister of External Affairs Dinesh Singh reaffirmed India's continuation of its pro-Arab policy and explained that India had not yet established diplomatic relations with Israel because Israel had followed 'wrong' policies against the Arabs, and particularly against the Palestinians. Given the lack of Israeli compliance with UN resolutions, Dinesh Singh argued it was difficult for India to revise its policy. He added that India's policy was justified in regards to its 'national interests' (MEA, *Foreign Affairs Record* 15:5, May 1969: 110). Following the conflict of 1967 and the rise of alternative viewpoints on India's Israel policy, the Government of India reframed its defence of the no-relationship policy in pragmatic and legal terms. The 1950 compromise was slightly modified in order to appease rising demands for policy change. The old orthodoxy—mostly represented by the Government of India and the MEA—was partly successful in dividing and containing the rise of the new orthodoxy.

The Indira Gandhi government nevertheless began to develop covert contacts with Israel. Soon after the inception of the Research and Analysis Wing (RAW, India's main external intelligence agency) in 1968, Indira Gandhi reportedly allowed its director R. N. Kao to open a line of communication with its Israeli counterpart, the Mossad (Raman 2008: 127). In the 1960s and 1970s, at a time when Israel was diplomatically isolated, the Mossad under the supervision of Meir Amit acted as an alternative diplomatic service and maintained relations with the intelligence agencies of various countries, including India, which had no public diplomatic ties with Tel Aviv (Klieman 1988: 47). The Mossad offered a convenient and secret way to circumvent the economic and political boycotts and offered military, medical, and agricultural advice through these informal channels. The contact was established through RAW officers posted in Western Europe, and particularly in Geneva, Switzerland.[75] The Mossad also posted a permanent officer in New Delhi under the cover of a South American businessman.[76] Intelligence cooperation reportedly concentrated on Pakistan which was in a territorial dispute with India and which gave military assistance to the Arab countries (Raviv and Melman 1990: 157). India also wanted to benefit from Mossad's knowledge of West Asian affairs and from its experience in counter-terrorism (Raman 2008: 127). This low-level cooperation was successfully established in spite of Indira Gandhi's strong condemnation of Israel in June 1967.

The Diplomatic and Domestic Repercussions of the 1969 Rabat Conference

For 20 years, Pakistan had attempted to form a Pan-Islamic organization, notably by sponsoring and organizing international summits. The intention of the Pakistani leadership was to court the Islamic world's support in its disputes with India. Between 1949 and 1952, three Karachi-based organizations, the Muslim World Conference, the International Islamic Economic Conference, and the Muslim People's Organization, were created (Burke 1973: 135). Although Pakistan was careful to emphasize the non-official nature of these organizations, the government of Prime Minister Liaquat Ali Khan played an active role in convening the conferences. The second Muslim World Conference held in Karachi in 1951 was attended by 120 delegates from 36 Muslim countries and chaired by the Jerusalem Mufti, Amin al-Hussayni.[77] The Conference declared that an aggression against any Muslim state would be viewed as an aggression against all, and directly deplored the plight of Muslims in Kashmir and Palestine. In his address to the Congress, Liaquat Ali Khan suggested the creation of a 'commonwealth of Muslim nations' (Hasmi 2009: 189). However, these initial efforts failed to institutionalize this nascent transnational movement into a long-term functioning inter-state organization. The failure to create a Pan-Islamic organization can be explained by various factors. Pakistan's decision to join the Baghdad Pact alienated it from Arab states like Saudi Arabia and Egypt. In the early 1950s, most West Asian states were secular regimes and reluctant to join a religious movement. Furthermore, other Muslim countries had different interpretations of what form Islamic cooperation should take in international affairs (Hasmi 2009: 187–8). Nevertheless, at the Jerusalem Congress of 1962, 20 Muslim countries declared their support for Pakistan's case in Kashmir (Ward 1992: 86–7). However, this resolution was not binding. In December 1964, the Sixth World Muslim Conference was organized in Somalia and rejected the attendance of an Indian delegation.[78]

In December 1965, a few months after the Indo-Pakistan war, Iran and Saudi Arabia called for the convening of an Islamic summit (Manchanda 1966: 140). The idea of the summit was a reaction to the increasing polarization between traditional monarchical states (such as Iran, Jordan, and Saudi Arabia) and other progressive secular Arab states like Egypt. Nasser called the possibility of a pact 'reactionary', and condemned the exploitation of religion to criticize secular regimes in West Asia (Ward 1992: 87). The Indira Gandhi government was equally suspicious of any religious pact or organization which would favour Pakistan. The divisions in the Muslim world kept the summit from actually becoming a reality until the late 1960s. The defeat of the Arab states during the 1967 war changed the regional geopolitical situation at the detriment of secular-nationalist forces like Nasser's Egypt, and in favour of more conservative regimes like Saudi Arabia. Finally, in August 1969, the Al Aqsa Mosque incident was the immediate catalyst for the organization of an Islamic summit that would lead to the creation of the Organisation of Islamic Cooperation (OIC). The Al Aqsa Mosque, third holiest site in Islam, located in Jerusalem, was damaged by a fire. While the incident was caused by an Australian Christian, the Arab states blamed Israel's occupation (and lack of protection of such sites) as the main cause (*Time Magazine* 1969). Following the uproar in the Muslim world over the Al Aqsa fire, some states agreed on the convening of an Islamic summit at Rabat (Morocco) in September 1969.

India's response to the events of August 1969 was ambiguous. Traditionally reluctant to intervene on religious matters, it was forced to officially react because of its large Muslim population and its rivalry with Pakistan. India could not leave an open space for Pakistan to gain the sympathy of Muslim states in West Asia. There were indeed large protest rallies of Indian Muslims in various cities to condemn the arson.[79] Dinesh Singh quickly condemned the act of desecration and held Israel directly accountable for this outrage because of its continued occupation of Jerusalem in defiance of UN resolutions (India, *Lok Sabha Debates*, 32:26, 26 August 1969, pp. 251–68). Indira Gandhi equally denounced the incident as a 'deplorable' act and as a sacrilege of the holy shrine (*The Hindu*, 10 September 1969). From the onset, the Government of India refused to see the incident as an Islamic issue but as a direct consequence of the broader problem of Palestinian territorial rights on Jerusalem, of the preservation of all sacred places in the region, and of the strict respect and implementation of the adequate UN resolutions (India, *Rajya Sabha Debates*, Vol. 69, 28 August 1969, p. 5919). India's ambassador to the UN Samar Sen confirmed this position when he described the incident as a spiritual injury not just to followers of Islam but also to people 'belonging to all religions'.[80] Peace would only be possible with a withdrawal of Israeli troops from the occupied territories in accordance to UNSCR 242 and the reform of the juridical status of Jerusalem.

Most Arab leaders interpreted the incident as a religious affront. King Faisal of Saudi Arabia and King Hassan of Morocco suggested gathering all Muslim states in one conference in Rabat in September.[81] At a preliminary meeting which included Iran, Malaysia, Niger, and Somalia, two basic criteria for participation were decided: countries should have a Muslim-majority population and/or a Muslim head of state (Singh 2006: 105). The holding of the Rabat Conference put the Government of India in front of a dilemma. In a 1955 directive, Nehru had explicitly rejected India's participation in any religious grouping (Nanda 1976: 77). There was, however, a loophole as Nehru had left open the possibility for non-official delegations to participate in Islamic conferences. Building on this ambiguity, the Government of India contemplated the possibility of participating in the Rabat Conference. New Delhi did not want to leave an open platform for Pakistan to criticize India. Although India did not fit the necessary conditions for participation, the government argued it deserved an invitation because it had the third largest Muslim population (60 million). The Government of India publicly expressed its desire to take part in the conference on 12 September. As no invite was forthcoming, protest letters were sent to ambassadors representing the countries organizing the Conference (Noorani 1969). The Government of India officially protested against the 'serious discrimination against the people of India and its Muslim population' (Dhamji 1969: 11–12; *The Hindu*, 26 September 1969). On 22 September, due to lobbying from states close to India such as Egypt and Malaysia, King Faisal reconsidered the issue and allowed an official Indian delegation to represent the Muslim minority of India (Dhamji 1969: 11; Soz 1998: 125). A quasi-unanimous support for the new proposal to extend the invitation to India made it difficult for Pakistani president Yahya Khan to object (Bagchi 2008).

This invitation came at the last minute and India had no delegation present in Rabat. For the first day sessions, it was therefore decided that India's ambassador to Morocco, Gurbachan Singh, would assume the responsibility of representing Indian interests until the delegation led by the Minister for Industrial Development Fakhruddin Ali Ahmad arrived the next day.[82] Yahya Khan, who had reluctantly agreed to King Faisal's request to allow an Indian delegation, questioned the legitimacy of Gurbachan Singh, who was not Muslim but Sikh, to represent the Muslim minority in India at the Conference (Bagchi 2008; Soz 1998: 125). The Pakistani president also complained that there were also four non-Muslim members in the Indian delegation that would reach Rabat the next day.[83] Khan ironically argued that if a criterion for participation was to have a large Muslim population, then the Conference should have equally invited the USSR, China, Albania, and even Israel. Khan added that India's treatment of its Muslim minorities was no different than Israel's behaviour vis-a-vis the Arabs (*Asian Recorder* 16, January, 1970).

While the Conference resumed its deliberations on 23 September, Khan ultimately decided to boycott the summit and to paralyse the Conference proceedings on 24 September.[84] While Algeria, Egypt, Sudan, and Libya supported the Indian participation, Iran, Jordan, and Turkey backed Pakistan's position. Morocco and Saudi Arabia tried to convince Khan to come back to the Conference sessions. Two mediating missions suggested that the Indian delegation voluntarily refrain from taking part in the final Conference meeting or accept an observer status.[85] In response, the head of the Indian delegation argued that India should be considered a full member of the Conference (after having been unanimously invited) and rejected a change in its status (Singh 2006: 110–13). To avert the imminent collapse of the Conference, the consensus among most participants progressively shifted to the decision to exclude India from the concluding session.[86] The Pakistani president only accepted to come to the final session after he was assured that the Indian delegation would not attend. A final joint statement was issued in the name of all the participants, including Indian Muslims (and not the state of India), but the Indian delegation did not sign the document (Singh 2006: 114–15, 117). The statement called notably for the withdrawal of Israeli forces from occupied territories and for the strengthening of links among Islamic states.

The Rabat diplomatic fiasco was perceived as yet another example of the failure of India's pro-Arab policy. The Indian media questioned the reasoning behind the decision for secular India to actively lobby to participate in an Islamic conference. Criticism also focused on Arab states such as Jordan which supported Pakistan's decision to expel India from the Conference (Ward 1992: 90). There was also a strong parliamentary reaction. The Swatantra Party expressed shock at India's treatment, calling the government's attempt to join the Conference a 'blunder' (*The Hindu*, 26 September 1969). The leader of the BJS, Balraj Madhok, called for a complete revaluation of India's West Asia policy. The opposition even moved a censure motion over the Rabat issue that was defeated (India, *Lok Sabha Debates*, 4:33, 17 November 1969, p. 430). Following the Rabat incident, even traditional supporters of the existing policy in the Communist Party and in Congress were critical of the government. A Congress MP, R. T. Parthasarathy, demanded the resignation of the External Affairs Minister Dinesh Singh (Ward 1992: 90). Upon his return from Rabat, Fakhruddin Ali Ahmad made a statement about the 'discourtesy' shown by the organizers of the Conference in not honouring its invitation and argued that India's position needed to be revised.[87] Responding to the mounting criticism, the Indian government took measures to publicly express its disappointment over the outcome of the Conference and the disrespect demonstrated to its official delegation. As an immediate response, the Government of India recalled the Indian ambassadors from Morocco and Saudi Arabia and the chargé d'affaires from Jordan.

The public embarrassment caused to India's reputation and the subsequent domestic criticism did not push India to modify its traditional pro-Arab policy. The Indian MEA tried instead to reframe the issue as a principled refusal to compromise its values, and as a vindication of its secular and non-religious approach to international problems. The Government of India also defended the pragmatic decision to initially attend the Rabat conference as necessary to counter Pakistan's anti-

Indian propaganda, especially in the context of the Hindu–Muslim riots in Gujarat (India, *Rajya Sabha Debates*, Vol. 70, 21 November 1969, p. 810). The riots in Ahmedabad made the presence of a delegation even more imperative to allay the concerns of Muslim nations. Dinesh Singh criticized Pakistan's 'consistent policy to drive a wedge between India and Islamic countries by creation anti-Indian feeling in these countries'.[88] Pakistan attempted to draw the Conference's attention to the Gujarat riots, by highlighting the fact India had refused to let an official of the Pakistani high commission in New Delhi visit the riot-stricken areas (Ward 1992: 91). In a later statement, Dinesh Singh again supported India's 'deep relations' with the Arab countries but also warned against the rise of Pan-Islamism as a 'danger' for West Asia and condemned the idea of further institutionalizing this movement in a 'secretariat'.[89] India never again tried to seek membership to the organization.[90]

The Rabat event served to further highlight the one-sided relationship that existed between India and the Arab countries. While Arab states expected full support on all issues of concern to them, especially on Palestine, they neglected India's concerns. Indira Gandhi's government was ultimately able to stay in power with the support of the left parties after the opposition's motion was introduced in Parliament to censure the government. While the vote was a decisive victory for Congress (306 votes), the motion censure was supported by most opposition parties (140 votes) that had again joined up in disapproval of India's West Asia policy.[91] This was the second time in two years that the survival of the government had been contested in Parliament because of a foreign policy issue—the Israel–Arab dispute. In spite of these pressures for change, Indian diplomacy continued to unconditionally support pro-Arab resolutions from 1969 to 1972. On the other hand, contacts with Israel were still happening as Dinesh Singh met Abba Eban a month after the Rabat Conference, during the UNGA in New York (Gerberg 2008: 110). Similarly, in an October 1970 interview, Indira Gandhi said that Israel had every right to exist in peace and understanding with its neighbours (Kumar 1982; Singh 1979). In spite of these statements, India still resisted any policy change vis-à-vis Israel.

The 1971 East Pakistan Crisis: Further Disillusions

India's West Asia policy was again criticized during the 1971 war with Pakistan which led to the creation of Bangladesh.[92] Most Arab countries stayed indifferent towards India during the conflict. There was again a clear contrast with the explicit support India had provided to the Arab states against Israel in 1956 and 1967. On 11 December, just as the conflict in South Asia was escalating, the Indian delegate at the UNGA condemned Israel for its refusal to commit to a withdrawal from the occupied territories, and criticized the US for supporting the Israeli position.[93] By contrast, most Arab countries remained mostly silent on the Bengali struggle for self-determination.[94] Some states even backed Pakistan. Before the conflict broke out, the government of Saudi Arabia deplored India's interference in the domestic affairs of Pakistan.[95] During the war, Syria, along with Saudi Arabia and Tunisia, supported the Pakistani position that the Bengali struggle was an internal Pakistani matter. Accusing India to be the aggressor, these states pleaded for non-interference and asked for the immediate withdrawal of Indian forces.[96] Syria was a member of the UNSC and voted in favour of three of the draft resolutions condemning India. Syria also introduced a draft UNSC resolution on 15 December 1971 which urged for a ceasefire and a withdrawal of Indian armed forces. This resolution was unacceptable to India because it meant that it would have to remove its troops without any guarantee that Pakistan would not resume its repression of the Bengali population. Most draft resolutions incriminating India were eventually vetoed by the USSR.[97]

There was also a debate at the UNGA on 7 December that resulted in the adoption of Resolution 2793 which called for the immediate cessation of hostilities, the withdrawal of military forces to the respective sides of the borders, and for assistance to help the refugees.[98] All West Asian states (except for Oman which abstained) voted in favour of the resolution. The resolution was criticized by India because it demanded for only Indian troops to withdraw. There was a consensus among Arab delegates that India was to be blamed for the war, and that the Bengali issue was a domestic concern of Pakistan.[99] Saudi Arabia was more critical as it warned India on 7 December that the present conflict could 'fan the flames of religious intolerance'.[100] Kuwait even called for a holy war in support of Pakistan (Ward 1992: 83). The Saudi ambassador at the UN also argued that the conflict could have grave implications for the allegiance of India's 60 million Muslims.[101] In another statement, just as the Pakistani troops were surrendering in Dhaka, Saudi Arabia criticized India for intervening in a domestic conflict and expressed its doubts on the political feasibility and survival of an independent East Pakistan. The Saudi ambassador asked again for the respect of territorial integrity and supported a united and reconciled Pakistan.[102]

Beyond the moral and political support at the UN, Pakistan also received monetary support (about $200 million) from Abu Dhabi, Kuwait, and Saudi Arabia.[103] Pakistan also obtained weapon transfers from Jordan and Iran. In fact, US President Richard Nixon approved a covert supply of US fighter airplanes via Jordan, Turkey, and Iran.[104] Saudi Arabia and Jordan offered the Pakistani air force to use their air bases which would be safe from Indian attacks (Saliba 1972; Singh 1975: 158–9, 183; Wriggins 1976: 790). Egypt and Iraq voted in favour of Resolution 2793 at the UNGA. According to the Indian ambassador in Cairo, Egypt maintained a 'studied indifference', was not sympathetic to India's refugee problem, and wanted to prevent Pakistan's partition.[105] However, unlike the conflict of 1965, Turkey and Iran did not allow Pakistani fighter jets to use their bases.[106] Before the crisis escalated, Iran had also offered to be a mediator in the Indo-Pakistani dispute and to organize a meeting between Indira Gandhi and Pakistani president Yahya Khan, which the Indian prime minister rejected as a suggestion which was 'divorced from any sense of reality'.[107]

The Government of India was disappointed by the lack of support from the Muslim world. Indira Gandhi's principal secretary P. N. Haksar expected that India's resolute support to the Arab states against Israel would ensure their support or at least neutrality in its dispute with Pakistan.[108] Following the conflict, the annual report of the MEA emphasized the 'inadequate appreciation' of West Asian states for India's refugee crisis (MEA, *Annual Report*, 1971–1972: 42–3). There was no outcry in the Arab world over the Pakistani army's oppression of the Bengalis and the consequent influx of millions of Bengali refugees into India. India also criticized the medical assistance provided by the Arab states to Pakistan (MEA, *Annual Report*, 1971–1972: 45–50). India was particularly disappointed by the position of its closest partner in the region, Egypt, which had taken Pakistan's side at the UNGA. In a statement at the Lok Sabha a year after the conflict, the Minister of External Affairs Swaran Singh formally expressed India's disappointment at the Arab attitude and its misunderstanding of the Bangladesh crisis. Recalling India's relentless support on the Arab–Israeli issue, Swaran Singh encouraged the Arab states to recognize Bangladesh as a political reality.[109]

By contrast, India was offered political, medical, and even military assistance from Israel. Israel demonstrated its intention to help with the problem of Bengali refugees by sending medical aid and personnel to help the displaced populations (India, *Rajya Sabha Debates*, Vol. 75, 31 March 1971, p. 123–4). The Israeli Knesset passed a resolution on 23 June to express its sympathy for the Bangladesh struggle (India, *Rajya Sabha Debates*, Vol. 77, 28 July 1971, col. 8; India, *Rajya Sabha Debates*, Vol. 77, 4 August 1971, p. 68; *News From Israel*, 1 August 1971; *Times of India*, 10 August 1971). When the war broke out, the Israeli deputy prime minister openly defended India's position (*Times of India*, 4 December 1971). Israel was also one of the first countries to recognize the new Bangladesh government on 4 February 1972 (*News From Israel*, 15 February 1972). Just like in 1962 and in 1965, India was provided military assistance after asking Israel for help. Despite the fact that India had no diplomatic relations with Israel, Indira Gandhi asked Israel for artillery weapons (160 mm mortars and ammunition) manufactured by Israel (Bass 2013: 140; Gerberg 2008: 89, 218–9; Raghavan 2013: 182–3). Golda Meir secretly arranged for an Israeli weapons manufacturer to airlift artillery equipment to India, along with instructors.[110] Israel also reportedly sent aid directly to the Bengali national movement, the Mukti Bahini (Prasad 2008: Vol. 9, pp. 862–9).

In times of strategic need and of international embargoes, the Israeli provision of mortars and ammunition was decisive. Golda Meir hoped that Indira Gandhi would 'know how to appreciate [Israel's] help at a time when they were in difficulties in the past'.[111] However, the Government of India cautiously avoided recognizing the aid provided by Israel and did not reconsider the question of establishing diplomatic relations. India only officially acknowledged Israel's offer to provide medical assistance to help the refugees (India, *Rajya Sabha Debates*, Vol. 75, 31 March 1971, pp. 123–4; India, *Rajya Sabha Debates*, Vol. 77, 28 July 1971, col. 8; India, *Rajya Sabha Debates*, Vol. 77, 4 August 1971, p. 68).

Given the lack of reciprocity in Arab support and Israel's eagerness to help India in times of duress, various critics called for a reassessment of Delhi's pro-Arab policy. Some opposition leaders and newspapers again pointed out the lack of Arab support on India–Pakistan disputes.[112] However, in spite of the clear negative feedback on the existing policy, the opposition to the Government of India was not as strong as in 1967. In March 1971, Indira Gandhi had led the Congress to a landslide victory, winning 352 seats—an improvement from the party's poor showing in the 1967 elections. Additionally, most of the opposition parties that had previously criticized India's West Asia policy, and had promoted the normalization of relations with Israel, lost the majority of their seats.[113] The important electoral mandate and the lightning military success consolidated Indira Gandhi's control of the foreign policy agenda. The absence of explicit Arab support was considered a negligible factor as India had ensured the backing of the USSR and achieved a major military and diplomatic victory.

As a consequence, India pursued its pro-Arab policy over the following years. The delays in coordinating the peace summit to discuss the outcome of the 1971 conflict offered a chance for both India and Pakistan to try to explain their respective positions to West Asian states. India wanted to counter Pakistan's new efforts at developing Pan-Islamic solidarity. Bhutto, who became president of Pakistan, toured the West Asian capitals to further develop religious ties in January and May 1972 (Ward 1992: 83–4). As a response, India sent high-ranking cabinet members and official delegations to explain India's position.[114] In April 1972, Swaran Singh argued that the 'disappointment' over the 1971 war should not damage the 'close relations' with the Arab countries (India, *Lok Sabha Debates*, Vol. 14, No. 32, 26 April 1972, pp. 227–8). India also continued to lend its support to the Arab states against Israel at the UN. At every possible occasion, Swaran Singh and ambassador Samar Sen criticized Israel for its refusal to withdraw from the Arab territories and for not respecting Resolution 242.[115] Ambassador Sen also denounced terrorism against Israel, including the Munich tragedy in September 1972, but he qualified these acts as resulting from the absence of any political settlement in West Asia.[116] In these statements, the Indian representatives also reminded the need to respect the sovereignty and territorial integrity of all the actors, as well as Israelis' right to a homeland (within the confines of the UN-mandated territories of 1947).

The 1973 West Asian Conflict: The Window of Opportunity for Change Closes

On 6 October 1973, a coalition of Arab states led by Egypt and Syria launched a surprise attack on Israel on the Jewish Yom Kippur holiday. Within three days, Israel had remobilized its forces and halted the joint assault, as well as started a counter-offensive in Syria and Egypt. On 25 October, a ceasefire was imposed by UNSC Resolution 340 which effectively ended the war.[117] In continuation of its traditional policy, India expressed its support for Egypt and Syria, despite the fact that these two countries had launched a coordinated military attack against Israel. On the day the war began, India asserted that Israel was to blame for the escalation because of its persistent refusal to vacate the territories occupied after the 1967 war.[118]

India also reiterated its sympathy to the Arabs because their demands were based on the implementation of Resolution 242.[119] According to Indian diplomacy, Egypt and Syria were only trying to uphold the provisions of the UN resolution, and their decision to desist from respecting Israel's territorial integrity was caused by accumulated frustration linked to the lack of progress in international mediation.[120] Indira Gandhi presented two reasons to justify India's position. She first mentioned the old and solid relations with the Arabs, and then criticized Israel's refusal to evacuate the conquered territories (*Indian and Foreign Review*, 1 November 1973). The Indian ambassador to the UN also accused Israel of expanding the area of conflict and of bombing cities like Damascus.[121] The Government of India supported the two UN resolutions which demanded a ceasefire, the immediate withdrawal of the Israeli troops from the Arab territories, and the introduction of UN military observers and the formation of a UN emergency force.[122]

In 1973, there was limited parliamentary and media backlash against India's pro-Arab policy. Although the BJS supported the implementation of Resolution 242 and welcomed the ceasefire, it also judged India had taken sides in a too blatant manner with the Arabs, and lamented the fact that India did not play an effective mediatory role. The BJS condemned the Congress party's obsession with communal (Muslim) votes when deciding its West Asian policy and reiterated its demand for a policy overhaul and a normalization of relations with Israel.[123] Some Indian newspapers denounced Israel's use of force but agreed that Israel had little alternative but to fight back the Arab offensive.[124]

Responding to these concerns in a speech to the Rajya Sabha, Swaran Singh acknowledged that India had also offered some material support to the Arab countries and that medicines and doctors had been sent to both Egypt and Syria. He argued that Israel's 'intransigence' and 'arrogance', which were encouraged by the active support of Israel's 'mighty friends'

(US), had led to the outbreak of hostilities of October 1973. According to Singh, India's position was not only moral but justified by international law. In further support to the Indian policy, Swaran Singh described the increasing isolation of Israel and cited other condemning statements from the European Community, Japan, and some African countries (India, *Rajya Sabha Debates*, Vol. 86, 6 December 1973, pp. 256–7). In a later speech, Swaran Singh mentioned a consensus in the lower house in support of the Arab cause. Answering directly to the BJS criticism, Singh argued justice was clearly on the Arab side and an unconditional support to countries with which India had fraternal ties was the only attitude possible (India, *Lok Sabha Debates*, Vol. 34, No. 19, 21 December 1973, pp. 249–73).

India's West Asia Policy after 1974

The time period between 1967 and 1974 seemed like a most likely case for change in India's Israel policy. If we follow the existing theoretical frameworks in the study of foreign policy change, a lot of the propitious conditions are present. There was a series of exogenous shocks (crisis-inducing events) in 1967, 1969, 1971, and 1973, which provided a window of opportunity for a renewed debate over the benefits and costs of the existing approach. There were clear policy failures, notably the lack of Arab diplomatic reciprocity, which were publicly admitted by the government in 1969 and 1971. Some actors argued that the status quo was no longer sustainable as it incurred painful costs. Finally, there were also alternative courses of actions and powerful domestic interests favouring change and the recognition of Israel. Both in 1967 and 1969, there was a strong and united domestic opposition to the government's pro-Arab policy that resulted in a joint appeal for a policy change and even in a censure motion in Parliament over the existing policy direction. Why was there no policy U-turn at that time?

This chapter has demonstrated how some negotiated changes had been made to the 1956 policy compromise. First, the perceived need for Arab diplomatic support still motivated India's West Asia policy but was altered. India's growing energy and oil needs also now shaped its approach to the region. These new economic considerations, the isolation of Egypt in Arab politics, and the domestic opposition to India's Cairo-centric policy encouraged engagement with other regional actors (albeit not Israel). Moving away from its special relationship with Egypt, India opened to the Gulf states, Iran, and the PLO. The Government of India also made concessions to the new orthodoxy. The government built on the international legitimacy provided by the adoption of Resolution 242 in November 1967. The emphasis on international legal obligations, which Israel failed to respect, divided the rising pro-change orthodoxy. While there was still a strong opposition to India's unconditional pro-Arab position, there was no consensus that the establishment of diplomatic relations with Israel was a viable policy alternative. These negotiated changes became the basis of the new policy compromise of 1974. The consolidation of this new policy compromise limited the scope for change. As a result, this section will show how the leadership change of 1977 did not bring about a policy change despite the political willingness to do so.

Policy Concessions: Finding Diplomatic Alternatives to Cairo

The emergence of the OIC in 1969 revealed a new development in West Asian politics that Indian diplomats had failed to anticipate. For almost two decades, Indian leaders had indeed perceived Nasser's Egypt to be in a leadership position in the Arab world and believed Cairo to be speaking for Arab interests (India, *Lok Sabha Debates*, Series 4, Vol. 7, 18 July 1967, pp. 12703–04). The 1967 military defeat accelerated the decline of Egypt's prominent position in Pan-Arab politics in favour of traditional monarchical regimes (Louis and Shlaim 2012). The Rabat Conference in 1969 confirmed this geopolitical realignment. Following the ideological rifts that had marked the late Nasser years, the Arab–Israeli war of 1973 created a new impression of unity among Arabs. However, the new Arab unity which emerged in the early 1970s was different in two ways. First, after the failure of Egypt and Syria to shape a Pan-Arabic group, new efforts to build inter-state ties were of a more religious nature. Second, Saudi Arabia, Iraq, and Iran emerged as new major regional players. The 1973 oil crisis demonstrated the new international leverage of the Organization of Arab Petroleum Exporting Countries (OAPEC). Arab oil producers had decided to punish US and Western support for Israel during the 1973 conflict by proclaiming an oil embargo. To end the embargo, the US administration negotiated a partial Israeli pull-back from the Sinai and the Golan Heights, after the Arabs also withdrew from Israeli territory. The embargo was finally lifted in January 1974.[125]

By 1973, Indian diplomacy had adapted to these regional developments. It was not a major foreign policy change but rather a subtle turning point. India remodelled its West Asia policy for two reasons. First, India's Cairo-centric policy had gradually been contested by domestic actors who questioned the gains of sticking by the traditional Egyptian partner. Indian diplomacy had not effectively monitored the mounting resentment amongst Arab states against Nasser's leadership and in opposition to its unilateral and imprudent actions taken against Israel. The most illustrative example was the progressive Indo-Saudi estrangement since the mid-1950s. Saudi Arabia was concerned with Nasser's defence of Pan-Arabism and Egypt's active involvement in the civil war in Yemen (Safran 1988: 120–1). Under these circumstances, Saudi Arabia did not see positively New Delhi's consistent and unequivocal endorsement of Nasser's Egypt. Riyadh's support to Pan-Islamic institutions was a counter-strategy against Egyptian-backed Pan-Arabism. As a consequence, the Indian leadership misinterpreted the several different reactions of the Arab world to the crises in South Asia. The major criticism was that India no longer had any flexibility in its West Asia policy.

Second, India needed to find more effective ways to counterbalance Pakistan's efforts to win over the military and diplomatic support of West Asian states. Because India had good relations with Egypt and received a nominal support from Cairo in various crises, the Indian government did not originally believe a policy change was in order. The 1969 Rabat Conference and the 1971 Bangladesh crisis demonstrated how a majority of the Arab states consistently chose to support Muslim Pakistan over India. Since 1962, India was also in competition with China for the loyalty of Arab states. In order to court Arabs, China had adopted an openly anti-Israel policy, notably by offering financial assistance to the PLO and by pressing for many anti-Israel resolutions at the UN. At the outbreak of the June 1967 war, Zhou Enlai had sent a message to the PLO to express Beijing's support for the Palestinian people in their struggle against Israel. In March 1970, Yasser Arafat was invited to visit China. An embassy of the PLO was also opened in Beijing during the summer of 1974 (Cooley 1972; Mehrish 1975).

From 1967 to 1974, there was a shift away from an overreliance on Indo-Egyptian relations as the foundation of India's West Asian policy to a broader engagement with various West Asian actors. The oil embargo of 1973 further cemented relations with Persian Gulf countries like Iraq and Iran. New Delhi looked for a guarantee of access to oil at a reasonable price of payment. India had to let go of its initial inhibitions about Iran and Iraq being members of the pro-Western Baghdad Pact, and the fact Iran had been a traditional supporter of Pakistan during the South Asian crises. By 1968, India and Iran had begun negotiating the construction of a chemical and industrial complex in Gujarat (Ward 1992: 66). The Shah of Iran also visited India in January 1969 and the two governments announced the establishment of a joint commission on economic, trade, and technological cooperation. The Shah even offered India two transit routes to Europe as alternatives to the closed Suez Canal (Ward 1992: 33). The 1971 Indo-Pakistani war slowed down the rapprochement. Like other Muslim states, Iran had argued that the East Pakistani crisis was an internal matter for Pakistan and advised against any external intervention. However, Iran never stopped supplying oil to India. Contrary to 1965, Iran did not give Pakistan direct material assistance nor did it give the Pakistani air force access to its airbases during the conflict. The resolution of the conflict through the tripartite agreement between India, Pakistan, and Bangladesh in 1974 opened the way for improved Indo-Iranian relations. Indira Gandhi visited Tehran in April 1974 and both countries agreed in a communiqué on the importance of guaranteeing stability and peace in the Persian Gulf. The Shah of Iran paid a reciprocal visit to India in October 1974 (Mudiam 1994: 82–3).

Parallel to developing ties with Iran, India started engaging Iraq. Just like Iran, Iraq had joined the Baghdad Pact and originally supported the Pakistani case over Kashmir. But the Baathist coup in 1958 was a blow to the nascent military alliance and a welcome development for India.[126] Iraq, for instance, supported India during the 1962 conflict.[127] However, Iraq's rivalry with Egypt for Arab leadership initially limited any substantial rapprochement. Relations began to change in the late 1960s. In 1966, Iraq decided to publicly abandon its pro-Pakistan stance on the Kashmir issue (*Asian Recorder*, 26 March–1 April 1966: 7002). The Iraqi foreign minister visited India in 1967 and rejected the creation of regional groupings of an Islamic nature. The two countries developed defence relations in 1968 and India offered to train Iraq's air force (Mudiam 1994: 63). In February 1970, the two countries signed an agreement on technical and scientific cooperation (MEA, *Foreign Affairs Record* 1, January 1970:

15–16). India then supported Iraq's nationalization of the Iraqi Petroleum Company in 1972, a move which was contested by both the US and the UK (MEA, *Foreign Affairs Record* 6, June 1972: 170). In August 1972, Iraq became the first Arab country to recognize Bangladesh. Starting in April 1973, Iraq supplied India with 30 million tons of crude over a 10-year period for the Mathura refinery. Iraq also agreed to extend a credit of $50 million in the form of supplies of crude oil (Mudiam 1994: 63–4). Iraqi Vice-President Saddam Hussein visited India in March 1974 and the discussions resulted in new agreements on crude oil supplies (MEA, *Foreign Affairs Record* 3, March 1974: 104–7). The deepening of relations with Iraq helped dilute India's image of having an exclusively pro-Cairo approach and also provided India with a stable supply of oil.

In addition, India stopped deferring to Egypt, Jordan, and the Arab League on the Palestine question. The rise of an armed Palestinian resistance movement, and of Yasser Arafat's al-Fatah faction within the PLO, was another important development during this period. Until the late 1960s, India had treated the Palestinian question mostly as a refugee problem and had played an active role within the UN Commission on Human Rights (UNCHR). India had been particularly cautious vis-à-vis the existing Palestinian movements which had no apparent popular legitimacy, and which were perceived as being subordinated to countries like Jordan. In parallel, the PLO progressively consolidated its position as the sole spokesman of the Palestinian people and won membership in the Arab Fund for Economic and Social Development. In July 1969, the PLO was also present at the Non-Aligned Movement Consultative meeting which endorsed the 'full restoration of the rights of the Arab people of Palestine' (MEA 1981: 32–4). The UNGA also moved away from talking about Palestinians as a refugee problem and started asserting the 'inalienable rights of the Palestinian people'.[128] A delegation of al-Fatah was then invited by the Communist Party of India (CPI) to the Indian Association for Asian Solidarity the same year. Following this visit, the CPI regularly demanded a discussion in Parliament over the diplomatic recognition of al-Fatah (India, *Lok Sabha Debates*, Series 4, Vol. 33, 19 November 1969, pp. 36–7; India, *Rajya Sabha Debates*, Vol. 73, 26 August 1970, p. 123).

By 1970, the Indian government was still prudent about the opportunity of establishing relations with the PLO. The MEA admitted the growing political importance of al-Fatah within the PLO as a 'viable' and 'effective' organization (MEA, *Annual Report* 1969–1970: 56). The Government of India also declared in March 1970 that al-Fatah was a secular organization fighting for the liberation of Palestine (India, *Rajya Sabha Debates*, Vol. 71, 26 March 1970, col. 28). At the NAM Summit in Darussalam in April 1970, Minister of External Affairs Dinesh Singh acknowledged the presence of PLO but also added that there was 'no question' of recognition at the time (India, *Lok Sabha Debates*, Series 4, Vol. 40, 22 April 1970, p. 230). Following the 1972 Munich massacre, India promptly and strongly condemned the terrorist attacks but never explicitly blamed al-Fatah (*Times of India*, 7 September 1972). Just a few weeks after the Yom Kippur war, at the Arab Summit in Algiers in 1973, the PLO was formally declared the sole representative of the 'Palestinian Nation' (in spite of Jordanian opposition).[129] The NAM summit in 1974 acknowledged the role played by the Palestinians in the October 1973 conflict and demanded a restoration of the Palestine people's national rights.[130] In October 1974, the seventh Arab summit conference held in Rabat again designated the PLO as the sole legitimate representative of the Palestinian people and reaffirmed the right of Palestinians to establish an independent state (Madfai 1993: 21). The new Arab consensus in support of the PLO encouraged the UNGA to grant the Palestinian organization the 'observer' status on 13 November 1974. The fact that the PLO was now an internationally recognized organization, relatively independent from the influences of other Arab states, was perceived as a permissive condition for the Indian government to engage the new Palestinian nationalist movement.

There were also domestic pressures for India to react to this new political reality. The Bihar state council of the Indo-Arab Friendship Society and the Indo-Arab Society in Allahabad urged the government to recognize the PLO (Mehrish 1975). In December 1974, 30 MPs demanded that India grant diplomatic status to the PLO (*Hindustan Times*, 23 December 1974). At the governmental level, there was a first sign of change in the speech of Minister of External Affairs Swaran Singh, who mentioned the 'recognition of the inalienable rights of the Palestinians' along with the need to implement Resolution 242 at the UNGA in October 1973.[131] In October 1974, India's permanent UN representative urged the UN to invite the PLO to the UNGA deliberations because it represented the people of Palestine. While the PLO had not been elected by the Palestinian people, the ambassador insisted on the fact that the PLO had been recognized by all Arab states as representing the Palestinian people.[132] As a result, India co-sponsored the draft resolution that supported the PLO's bid for observer status at the UN in November 1974.[133] Following the PLO chairman's speech at the UNGA, Indian Foreign Secretary Kewal Singh expressed India's solidarity with the Palestinian cause and recognized the PLO as the sole representative of the Palestine people in the context of the West Asian peace process.[134]

Finally, in January 1975, India officially recognized the PLO.[135] On 10 January 1975, India's ambassador to Lebanon, S. K Singh, and PLO Chairman Yasser Arafat signed the necessary documents granting certain privileges and diplomatic immunities to Palestinian representatives. India immediately permitted the PLO to open a diplomatic mission in New Delhi.[136] In its official statement, the Government of India noted that two important conditions had been fulfilled. First, the PLO was now considered as the legitimate representative of the Palestinian people. Second, it had achieved 'wide' recognition at the international level (*Hindustan Times*, 11 January 1975). Until 1975, India had only recognized Israel as a sovereign political entity in the Israel–Palestine dispute. However, India had not yet exchanged diplomats with Israel. By contrast, the PLO was simultaneously granted diplomatic recognition and the right to open a diplomatic office. This recognition was a radical change in India's position as only one party to the dispute would have a diplomatic representation based in New Delhi.

India's improved relationship with the PLO was a reaction to international and regional changes, as well as a response to domestic criticism. As the PLO was widely supported amongst Arab states, the Indian government perceived it was in its interest to establish relations with the Palestinian organization. It was another way to offset Pakistani and Chinese attempts to garner diplomatic support from Arab states. The PLO missions in Karachi (and later Islamabad) also received diplomatic recognition in 1975 (Kumaraswamy 2000: 34). Similarly, while China had established diplomatic relations with the PLO in 1965, a PLO embassy was opened in 1974. This diplomatic strategy which aimed at gaining the support (or to the least the neutrality) of Muslim states in West Asia also led India to co-sponsor the UNGA Resolution 3379 in November 1975 that equated Zionism with racism and that sought sanctions against Israel. To justify its position, the Government of India argued that Zionism was a 'form of racial discrimination' because of the negative impact 'Zionist occupation' had had on people in West Asia (MEA, *Annual Report*, 1975–1976: 76). Pursuing this strong criticism of Israel at the UN in December 1975, India condemned the 'unacceptable' occupation by Israel of vast areas of Arab territories. India called again for the withdrawal of Israeli troops. Nevertheless, it also condemned Arab calls to destroy Israel, as the Jewish state had 'asserted its right to exist in no uncertain manner'.[137] While India refused to establish diplomatic relations with Tel Aviv, it maintained its recognition of Israel.

It is therefore misleading to argue that India's West Asia and Palestine policies did not evolve in the 1960s and 1970s. There were some drastic changes which were prompted by international crises and domestic criticism. The major change was a de-emphasis on relations with Egypt and a new policy of multi-engagement with Iran, Iraq, and the PLO. These three regional actors had decisively emerged during this period of policy flux from 1967 to 1974. Indian policymakers realized that they did not have to make either/or choices between regional actors who shared core interests. India equally managed to play on the emerging rivalry between Iraq and Iran to obtain economic and political support from both. By the early 1970s, the two regional rivals competed to cultivate India, an emerging regional power, on favourable terms. India's success in engaging both regional rivals demonstrated the benefits of this new policy compromise. While the Government of India altered its existing policy to engage different actors, it did not open to Israel. There were in fact other policy alternatives to India's Cairo-centered policy which presented more direct and explicit gains in the early 1970s. There was therefore a new policy compromise (engagement with multiple regional Arab actors) but not a major policy reversal (normalization of diplomatic relations with Israel).

Change and Continuity in India's West Asia Policy: Old and New Economic Interests

India's overture to new actors in West Asia was not only a response to geopolitical realignments in the region but also an economic necessity. During the 1956 crisis, economic considerations, such as the free access to the Suez Canal, had been a major factor explaining India's reaction to the events and its overall pro-Egypt policy. This initial crisis had demonstrated the importance of a stable West Asia for India's economic well-being. Trade routes were still an important factor in the late 1960s.[138]

In 1967, 70 per cent of Indian exports and 80 per cent of its imports went through the Canal (Rangaswami 1969). The second and long-term closing of the Suez Canal during the events of 1967 was very costly for India. As the canal remained closed until 1975, the costs of India's exports to the West considerably increased. Immediately after the closure, shipping companies levied a surcharge on freight because a longer distance had to be covered around the Cape. India had to pay an additional 15–35 per cent on the price of imports from Europe, US, and USSR (Jansen 1971: 292). More than any other country, India had a vast economic stake in ensuring stability and free commerce in West Asia, and therefore in the re-opening of the Canal. India considered this economic burden to be a result of the presence of Israeli troops and consequently demanded their withdrawal from Egyptian territories. Israel was therefore perceived as an economically disruptive force.

The late 1960s and early 1970s also coincided with an increased dependence of India on foreign energy sources. Oil was of vital necessity to the growing Indian industry in the late 1960s. By 1969, India's crude oil needs reached 30 million tons per year, while its assured domestic reserves provided only 10 million tons per year (*The Hindu*, 14 June 1969). Since independence, India's major suppliers had been Iraq and Saudi Arabia, but India had tried to develop relations with other Gulf states to guarantee a steady supply of oil needs for its internal development. The oil crisis in 1973 pushed India to harmonize its pro-Arab policies with its oil and trade policies. At that time, the OAPEC decided to increase oil prices and to cut on export quotas. In spite of being directly affected by these measures, India supported the Arab position on Israel and on the price hike. The fourfold increase of oil prices in 1973 was, for instance, described by Prime Minister Indira Gandhi as a 'just' measure (Dietl 2000: 209–24).

In fact, the Minister of Petroleum and Chemicals D. K. Barooah informed Parliament in 1974 that it was India's continued pro-Arab policy that had assured a stable oil supply from the Arab states. For instance, Saudi Arabia, which had signed a deal to supply India with crude oil until 1976, originally informed Oil India Ltd that it would impose a 10 per cent cutback. The minister of external affairs officially complained to the Saudi government and obtained with the mediation of the Arab League that the quotas would remain at the same levels (Ward 1992: 34). Since the OAPEC refused to adopt a dual pricing system, India could not expect a favourable price treatment. However, India managed, through bilateral agreements with Iraq, the United Arab Emirates, Qatar, and Kuwait, to have guaranteed stable prices over a fixed time period and to ensure a steady supply of oil (Mansingh 1984: 372). India negotiated similar arrangements with Iran and Iraq.

Beyond the oil needs, the Arab market was also attractive for a developing Indian industry. Before 1973, India had mostly exported textile and Egypt was India's most important trade partner.[139] However, it was in the early 1970s that India's export of engineering goods and services considerably increased. From $155 million in 1970–1, these exports grew to close to a billion dollars by 1980–1.[140] India started important industrial projects such as the 42-megawatt diesel power station in Jizan, Saudi Arabia, and a 400-km railway line in Iraq (Thomas 1982: xi). West Asian countries were interested by India's technological expertise but also by its skilled workers. The oil-rich Gulf states embarked on ambitious economic development programmes, which led to a consequent demand for labour. India with its surplus labour and its geographic proximity became a major source of supply.[141] An increasing number of semi-skilled and unskilled workers from south India went to work in the Gulf countries on temporary migration schemes in the oil industry and in services and construction.[142] Since these overseas Indians had families back in south India and sent back important remittances, New Delhi has always demonstrated an interest in their welfare.[143]

By contrast, there were very limited trade prospects with Israel. Israel was considered to be a small and negligible market as far as India was concerned. In fact, it was even argued that India's trade with Israel would be competitive and not complementary.[144] Furthermore, Indian companies or ships risked being boycotted by Arab and Muslim states if they engaged with Israel or stopped by Israeli ports. The Arab League had indeed put into place since 1948 a systematic effort to economically isolate Israel. Officially, the boycott covered products and services originating in Israel, businesses in non-Arab countries that did business with Israel, and businesses shipped or flown to Israeli ports.[145] Indian companies were particularly affected by the two latter categories. Despite Indian reassurances that there were no direct commercial dealings with Israel or Israeli companies, 128 Indian firms were blacklisted by the Arab League in 1976.[146] A 1975 report by the Federation of Indian Chambers of Commerce and Industry (FICCI) relayed the concerns of many Indian companies over the boycott's negative impact for commerce in the region, and encouraged diplomatic efforts by the government to take Indian companies off the blacklist.[147]

India took into account the long-term closing of the Suez Canal, the need to guarantee oil supply at reasonable prices, and the new economic leverage of the Arab League through the boycott when it expressed its position on the Arab–Israel dispute. However, after 1973 India's new economic partnerships in the region were with actors it had previously neglected in the Persian Gulf. While India still supported Egypt in its struggle with Israel, it was no longer the special and exclusive partnership that had been established in the 1950s. In spite of an impression of policy continuity, India's West Asia policy had evolved into a new policy compromise based on new economic interests. From an economic standpoint, Israel was not an attractive partner and the government saw no pressing incentive to establish diplomatic relations. By justifying its pro-Arab policy on economic terms, the Government of India also received an important support at the domestic level. Much of the internal criticism from opposition parties in 1967 had revolved around the defence of India's national economic interests. Indian diplomacy took into account India's internal economic problems when modifying its policy in the early 1970s. There was therefore a more disparate group of actors supporting the new policy compromise and who saw no pressing need to engage Israel. The old orthodoxy managed to enlist new supports and build a new and consolidated policy compromise after 1974.

The Dog That Did Not Bark in 1977: The Janata Government and Normalization

A major domestic political change happened in 1977 as the ruling Congress lost control of the government for the first time since India's independence in 1947. The election came after two years of Emergency rule imposed by Prime Minister Indira Gandhi.[148] The Emergency suspended democracy and elections, and severely restricted the actions of the opposition and of the media.[149] As a result, a coalition of opposing parties, the Janata Alliance, which had called for the restoration of democracy, handily won in March 1977 the Sixth Lok Sabha elections with 345 seats (against 189 seats for the INC and its allies).[150] This unprecedented electoral outcome opened the possibility for change in India's Israel policy for four reasons.

First, the political parties that had previously criticized the INC's pro-Arab policy and that had supported the establishment of diplomatic relations with Israel, such as the BJS and the PSP, were present in the new ruling coalition. The new prime minister, Moraji Desai, a former member of the Congress party, had himself been critical of Indira Gandhi's position (Desai 1974–1979: 2: 257). Similarly, Atal Bihari Vajpayee, a BJS leader who had been a vocal and long-time supporter of Israel, became the minister of external affairs.

Second, the first political transition in independent India also meant that the new Janata government did not share the same political, ideological, and historical constraints that had kept the INC from modifying its West Asia policy. We have seen in the previous chapters how the INC had established historical links with Arab nationalist movements and states, as well as a deep-seated attachment to non-alignment, two factors which initially limited any rapprochement with Israel. Third, the Janata coalition had also openly expressed its willingness to change India's foreign policy orientation (Vajpayee 1979). For instance, the Janata government took the initiative to establish a new dialogue with China, and expressed the need for a balanced and open policy towards the US. Fourth, the new Janata government had won a convincing majority in the lower house, which made the implementation of major foreign policy change feasible.

In spite of these auspicious conditions, the government quickly indicated it would not make drastic changes to India's foreign policy. In his inaugural speech to the Conference of Foreign Ministers of the Coordinating Bureau of Non-Aligned Countries in April 1977, Desai announced that foreign policy was 'an area of consensus, not one of controversy' (MEA, *Foreign Affairs Record*, April 1977: 35). Similarly, when questioned about his past criticism of India's West Asia policy, Vajpayee explained that he was in a new government which had to reassure its friends. Shortly after the elections, Vajpayee reiterated the demand that Israel 'vacate all occupied Arab territories' and that the 'legitimate rights of the Palestinian people' be restored. As for relations with Israel, Vajpayee said there would be no change in India's position.[151] To further allay the emerging concerns of Arab leaders, Vajpayee declared to Parliament that the new government would not only continue to seek to maintain 'old links' with the entire Arab world, but would also work to strengthen India's economic cooperation with it. He added that India would continue to lend support for a settlement of the West Asia problem based on UN resolutions that required the vacation of occupied territories and that recognized the 'inalienable rights of the Palestinian people'.[152]

In his address to the UNGA in October 1977, Vajpayee suggested a peaceful resolution of international disputes by negotiations but criticized the denial of the 'right of their homeland' to the Palestinians.[153] Vajpayee reiterated this position in January 1978 at the meeting of the Indo-Arab League in Hyderabad where he called Israel an aggressor and explained that any lasting peace agreement would need to involve the PLO (*The Hindu*, 3 January 1978). Vajpayee explained that the Janata Government's continuation of India's traditional policy resulted from the fact that Israel's aggressive acquisitions and claims, inferred from biblical history, were 'untenable' (Vajpayee 1979: 64). Vajpayee made the same claim at the Conference of Foreign Ministers of Non-Aligned countries in Belgrade in July 1978.

In spite of these initial statements signalling policy continuity vis-à-vis West Asia, there were in fact discrete attempts to establish some channels of communication with Israel. These limited openings demonstrated a new willingness by some actors in the government to actively engage Tel Aviv. Some changes in Israeli domestic politics created favourable conditions for a change. In May 1977, there was also an important political transition in Tel Aviv as the Likud Party won the elections for the first time. Israel's new Minister of Foreign Affairs, Moshe Dayan, showed an interest to engage various estranged international actors such as India.[154] There is no consensus on the details of Dayan's visit to India in August 1977.[155] Dayan explained that the first contacts had been established between a business acquaintance of his and another Indian businessman in Europe.[156] The Indian businessman, who had good relations with Desai, helped transmit an invitation to Dayan from the Indian prime minister (Dayan 1978: 27–8). Other accounts say that the Dayan visit had been engineered by RAW which had maintained covert links with Mossad since the late 1960s.[157] After Dayan accepted to visit India, the Prime Minister's Office (PMO) and the Indian intelligence agencies carefully organized the visit and circumvented the MEA.[158]

The objectives of the incognito visit were to clarify both the respective positions on the peace process in West Asia and to explore the option of establishing diplomatic relations.[159] Desai described his efforts to convince the Arab leaders, including Egyptian President Anwar Sadat, that Israel was now an 'established fact'. He nevertheless told Dayan that diplomatic relations would not be established until Israel had withdrawn its forces from the territories captured in the Six-Day War. He also mentioned adverse reactions from the Indian Muslims and from the Arab states if he normalized relations with Tel Aviv. It was clear that the Indian policy had not changed. Dayan replied that he could not comply with India's demand of withdrawal at the moment (Dayan 1978: 28–32). He also asked for India to allow Israel to either move the Bombay consulate to Delhi or to open a second consulate in the capital. Dayan highlighted the fact that India did not have equal relations with both parties of the Arab–Israel dispute since India had no diplomatic relations with Israel. Desai explained that it was not possible to open a diplomatic office in Delhi at that point because of Muslim sensitivities. According to Dayan, Desai also emphasized the political risks he had taken and that he could lose his premiership if the news of his visit was to become public. Despite the disagreements, this was a historical visit which happened 12 years after the last visit of an Israeli minister (Yigal Allon). Both Desai and Dayan agreed on the need to maintain a dialogue through meetings between their foreign ministers in Europe and in the US.[160]

Despite the meeting between Desai and Dayan, there was no sustained progress in Indo-Israeli relations. In the following months, the Israeli government increased the number of permanent settlements in the West Bank. On 27 August, the MEA criticized the Israeli actions which complicated the implementation of Resolution 242 and the possibility of a permanent settlement of the Arab–Israeli dispute (MEA, *Foreign Affairs Record* 23:8, January 1977: 138). Furthermore, the news of Dayan's visit became a matter of public knowledge through media leaks. In an electoral strategy aimed at winning back the support of the Muslim vote, the talks were criticized by Indira Gandhi who questioned the government's support of the Palestinian cause. In 1980, Indira Gandhi and Congress leader Narasimha Rao even claimed that Dayan had visited India more than once.[161] Vajpayee denied the meeting ever took place. In fact, the Janata government acknowledged this visit only in May 1980.[162] This demonstrated that the question of Israel was still considered to be a sensitive issue in domestic politics.

For the rest of its tenure, the Janata government maintained a pro-Arab position and reiterated the bases of the existing policy compromise of 1974. For instance, the Janata government confirmed its tilt towards Iran. The Shah visited Delhi in February 1978 (Mudiam 1994: 83). The Janata government also continued to move away from Cairo. The Indian position towards Sadat's diplomatic overtures to Israel in 1977–9 was cautious. In a speech before the Lok Sabha, Vajpayee said that India's official policy was to 'not take sides in inter-Arab disputes'.[163] In a later speech in January 1978, Desai supported the Egyptian–Israel peace initiative (Gangal 1979: 70). Desai was also regularly informed by US President Jimmy Carter about the developments of the negotiations (*Times of India*, 21 September 1978). Following the signing of the Camp David Accords in September 1978 between Israel and Egypt, India's position changed.[164] In October 1978, Vajpayee moved from a cautious observation of the talks to a more critical assessment of the Accords. Joining the general sceptic Arab mood, Vajpayee specifically criticized three shortcomings of the Accords: there was no mention of the rights of Palestinians and of the creation of a Palestinian state; there had been no discussion on the status of Jerusalem; and the PLO was not recognized as the legitimate representative of the Palestinian people (*Hindustan Times*, 11 October 1978; *Times of India*, 1 October 1978). These were some of the minimal requirements that the Indian leadership had flagged as necessary to start discussions with Israel. Desai himself commended the efforts to bring about a peaceful settlement to the West Asian crisis but nonetheless expressed his disappointment over the limits of the Accords.

India also had its doubts about the success of the Camp David Accords as Egypt was increasingly isolated in the Arab world. Iraq, Syria, and the PLO were opposed to Egypt's initiative which conflicted with the Arab League's Khartoum resolution of 1967 and the UNSC Resolutions on Palestine.[165] Egypt's membership was also suspended from the Arab League at the Arab Conference in Tripoli in December 1978. India, which had progressively distanced itself from Cairo, preferred to side with the rest of the Arab states, and more specifically with the oil-producing states. In April 1979, Vajpayee reiterated the basic requisites for peace in the region and argued that at present the treaty fell short of a comprehensive solution of the West Asia problem (Kumar 1982). India again sided with the Arab states to condemn the Camp David Accords at the NAM summit in September 1979 at the Havana.[166] Additionally, there were important divisions within the Janata Party on the policy to follow vis-à-vis the Accords. The parliamentary party leader Jagjivan Ram and its General Secretary Madhu Limaye publicly criticized the Accords (Gandhi 1983: 235–6; *Janata* 16, 5 November 1978: 19). Ram also met with Arab ambassadors in New Delhi to reassure them of the party's opposition to the Camp David Accords (*Tribune*, 10 November 1979).

By 1977, the window of opportunity for policy change vis-à-vis Israel had closed. There were various domestic and foreign constraints which precluded any real change in India's Israel policy under the Janata tenure. Internal political battles left the prime minister with hardly any scope for any new foreign policy initiative. Following the Dayan visit, Desai's assumption was that an improvement in relations with Israel needed greater political consensus. To hold its coalition together and to respond to criticisms coming from Indira Gandhi in the opposition, the Janata government concentrated on domestic issues and was less interested in foreign affairs. In fact, most of the foreign policy issues were deferred to the MEA which traditionally held a pro-Arab attitude. Just like the INC, the Janata leadership believed there would be an opposition from Indian Muslims to an overture to Israel. Following the Emergency, the Janata Party had benefitted from a large Muslim vote in 1977 (Ward 1992: 102). There were also international factors which limited the Janata government's options. New energy considerations that had emerged in the early 1970s made the uninterrupted flow of oil from West Asia an imperative to support the growing industrial sector. As a result, the Janata government ultimately resumed the policy compromise of 1974.

The Policy Compromise of 1974

The 1967–74 time period is critical because it was a most-likely case for change in India's Israel policy. During that period, there were a series of shocks which put into serious doubt the performance of the existing policy. The asymmetry in Indo-Arab relations following the different South Asia and West Asia crises was flagrant and created a policy dilemma for the Indian government. The Indira Gandhi government was clearly confronted with a difficult choice between its loss-inducing, long-term policy commitments in the region and the choice for policy change that also incurred potential losses (Arab diplomatic support, domestic Muslim electoral support for the INC).

In the 1960s, there was the emergence of a 'new orthodoxy', which included opposition parties (BJS, PSP, and Swatantra Party), academics, and the media, and which began to criticize the existing West Asian policy. Until 1967, this new orthodoxy was divided and politically insignificant. The electoral results of February 1967 and the government's mismanagement of the 1967 crisis encouraged these disparate actors to coordinate their opposition. The crisis of 1967 clearly demonstrated that the policy compromise that Nehru had built on West Asia was no longer operative. India's reaction to the 1967 crisis also showed that it was no longer in phase with the different Arab positions and that Cairo's policies were not always in conjunction with India's national interests. As a consequence, advocates of change jointly asked for a policy reevaluation in light of the absence of reciprocity with the Arab states. This criticism intensified from 1967 to 1971 and then mollified and dispersed by 1973.

Gradually, the Government of India also adapted its policy to take into account new international developments. New Delhi gradually distanced itself from Egypt's position on the Arab–Israeli dispute. Instead, India developed direct relations with the PLO which had emerged as a legitimate political force. However, this new type of multi-engagement with various regional actors did not translate into a rapprochement with Israel. On the contrary, India supported and even sponsored various anti-Israel resolutions, including the UNGA Resolution 3379 which equated Zionism with racism. India no longer limited itself to a no-relationship policy but also agreed with the imposition of sanctions against Israel.

The pro-Arab position was deemed necessary in order to preserve Arab support or to the least to cancel out anti-India propaganda efforts from both Pakistan and China. The overture to new Arab actors was equally crucial because of economic and especially oil interests. India secured diverse sources of oil by engaging Iraq, Kuwait, Iran, Saudi Arabia, and the United Arab Emirates. In the 1967–74 period, the Cold War rivalry affected both South Asia and West Asia adversely. Following the 1967 conflict, Israel was progressively associated with the US while India signed the Indo-Soviet Treaty of Peace, Friendship and Cooperation with the USSR in 1971. India increasingly criticized the US intervention in West Asian politics and its bias towards Israel. As a consequence, India was critical of the US-sponsored Camp David Accords.

India also defended its West Asia policy and no-relationship with Israel on the basis of the UNSC Resolution 242. For instance, the Government of India consistently argued that Israel should withdraw to its pre–June 1967 borders and evacuate the Sinai, Gaza, and the Golan Heights. There were different implications behind this new position. First, until there was no effective implementation of the resolution by Israel,

India's sympathy would integrally go to the Palestinians and Arabs, even if it meant supporting the Arab offensive of 1973. Second, India's West Asia policy was considered to not be hostile to Israel as the resolution recognized the sovereignty, territorial integrity, and political independence of Israel. Finally, the reference to a UN resolution was also a way for the Government of India to frame its pro-Arab policy on legal (and not just moral) standards. The old orthodoxy was able to counter any criticisms by referring to Israel's pursued violation of the resolution. The new orthodoxy which seemed to emerge in 1967 was indeed divided on the issue of Israel's occupation of Arab territories. The change of heart of the socialist Jay Prakash Narayan is a good example of the gradual disillusion of the new orthodoxy. Narayan was a committed advocate of closer relations with Israel which he had visited several times. However, by mid-1968, Israel's refusal to withdraw from the occupied territories led him to become a critic of Tel Aviv's actions (*Hindustan Times*, 11 May 1968).

A combination of propitious conditions was not sufficient to induce foreign policy change. The choices and strategies of the two orthodoxies were also critical. According to the existing literature, there was continuity in India's pro-Arab policy between the 1950s and 1992, which was carried out by the INC and by a foreign policy bureaucracy that had traditionally supported the Arab positions. By 1967, however, India moved away from its exclusively pro-Cairo policy to a greater sensitivity to different Arab perspectives and to an unprecedented support to Palestinian nationalism. In this chapter, I argued that there was an uncertain period of policy flux because of a combination of shocks, adverse policy feedback, and the rise of alternative policy ideas. However, despite a window of opportunity for a change in India's Israel policy, India did not establish diplomatic relations with Israel. This does not, however, mean that India's West Asia and Palestine policy did not considerably evolve in the early 1970s. The policy change in 1967–74 was subtle rather than abrupt and radical. In fact, the Government of India adapted effectively to the new regional developments, and to quell mounting internal criticism. The identification of this new policy compromise is necessary and essential to understand the new rigidity in India's Israel policy after 1974.

The new policy compromise centred on the following points:

- For any change to happen in India–Israel relations, all Israeli forces should be completely withdrawn from the Arab lands seized during the 1967 war, in accord with UNSC Resolution 242.

- India continued to recognize Israel's territorial integrity (in its pre-1967 limits) and its political independence. This was both a confirmation of the 1950 decision to recognize the state of Israel and a principle of UNSC Resolution 242.
- India wanted Israel to recognize the rights of the Palestinian people, their right to self-determination, and the creation of a Palestinian state. Contrary to the previous policy compromise, India now recognized and discussed with a Palestinian political authority. For any change to happen in India–Israel relations, Israel needed to negotiate a settlement with the PLO.
- India no longer exclusively deferred to Cairo's judgement on regional affairs. India now engaged with various regional actors who shared strategic and economic interests like Iran and Iraq.
- India's West Asia policy concentrated on preserving important national strategic and economic interests like access to oil and trade routes.

The consolidation of a new policy compromise based on the aforementioned principles and interests helped explain the absence of policy change during the Janata government's tenure. During the Nehru tenure, the policy was more open-handed and flexible. India took a pro-Arab position but was not explicitly hostile to Israel. Nehru and his ministers also kept meeting with Israeli ministers through their trips to Europe and the US. By contrast, Indira Gandhi refused to meet any Israeli representative, and not one Israeli minister came to India between Yigal Allon's visit in 1965 and Moshe Dayan's brief stopover in 1977. The new policy compromise, which required the implementation of UNSC Resolution 242, placed a higher threshold for change to happen. In spite of the political willingness to normalize relations with Tel Aviv, the Janata Party had limited policy leverage when it was in power from 1977 to 1980.

Notes

1. In a most-likely case study, the variables posited by a theory are at such a value that it intuitively suggests a certain extreme outcome. For an extended discussion on methods of case-selection and the usefulness of identifying 'most likely' cases, see George and Bennett (2005).

2. Ward, for instance, argued that India's trade relations with West Asia can be divided in two distinct periods with the early 1970s as a decisive critical

juncture. In the immediate post-independence years, India tried to export to West Asian markets like Egypt to reduce its trade deficits. After 1972, India began to import oil from Iran and the Gulf states. See Ward (1992: 26–33).

3. Even the Indian diplomat Arthur Lall recognized that Israel benefitted from an increased freedom of passage guaranteed by the UN troops based in the Sinai. See *Interview with Arthur Lall* (1990).

4. This lack of response led Ben-Gurion to apparently believe that Nehru was the main obstacle to normalization. See interview with Pearlman in Pearlman (1965: 178).

5. Achdut Haavoda (Unity of Labour) Party was an Israeli leftist party which supported the NAM. In April 1955, an Achdut Haavoda delegation participated in the Conference of the Communist Parties (COMIFORM), which took place in New Delhi. Together with the Mapai party, they became the Israeli Labor party in 1968.

6. Between December 1959 and January 1960, an official delegation from India visited the Afro-Asian Institute for Labor Studies and Cooperation in Israel in order to learn about the Israeli development experience. A special three-month seminar was organized for leaders of the Budhan Movement of India and the Praja Socialist Party. See *Middle East Records* (1960: Vol. 1, p. 304). In fact, from the opening of the Afro-Asian institute in 1958 up to 1961, more than 500 participants from India studied at the Afro-Asian Institute in Tel Aviv. See Laufer(1967: 277).

7. The Rajya Sabha is the upper chamber of the Indian Parliament.

8. There would be no clarification for two decades. The Government of India de facto authorized consular activities limited to Bombay and Maharashtra but never explicitly defined the territorial jurisdiction of the Consulate's powers. This would change only in 1987 when the Consulate's jurisdiction was officially expanded to Kerala.

9. Until then, Nehru had been both prime minister and minister of external affairs.

10. Since India was competing with Beijing for Arab diplomatic support and that the delegation was travelling to China, the Government of India decided to also meet with the delegation to demonstrate its support for the Palestinian cause. Indian concerns proved accurate as China officially recognized the PLO three months later. See Schechtman (1966); Ward (1992: 103).

11. According to Gerberg, in 1963–4, the governments of the states of Gujarat, Rajasthan, and Mysore applied for the services of Israeli technical experts for help in agriculture, irrigation projects, and water supply but the Government of India refused to issue official requests to the Israeli government. See Gerberg (2008: 226).

12. For a discussion of the causes and the developments of the Sino-Indian war of 1962, see Garver (2001); Hoffman (1990); Maxwell (1970) .

13. The letter to Ben-Gurion was discussed in the *Jerusalem Post*, 29 October 1962.

14. Lebanon was officially neutral but seemed to favour India's cause. See Agwani (1963a); Singh (1963).

15. This Turkish position notably created problems within the Baghdad Pact. See Ward (1992: 92).

16. Iraq had close ties with the PRC and Syria was disappointed by India's delay in recognizing the new political regime which had taken over after the 1961 coup d'état. See the statement by Abdul Karim Dassim, Prime Minister of Iraq, Baghdad, 20 November 1962, *Iraq Times*, 21 November 1962; Ward (1992: 92).

17. Statement of the United Arab Republic Presidential Council, 31 October 1962, *Al Ahram*, 9 November 1962.

18. The other five states present at the Conference were Burma, Cambodia, Sri Lanka, Ghana, and Indonesia. See Singh (1963); Ward (1992: 92–3).

19. See Maxwell (1970: 385); Gerberg (2008: 218–19).

20. Both prime ministers Shastri and Indira Gandhi also asked for Israeli military help without establishing diplomatic ties or publicly acknowledging the contacts in 1965 and 1971, respectively.

21. To read more on the causes and developments of the Indo-Pakistani war of 1965, see Ganguly (2002: 31–50).

22. Interestingly, Jordan was one of the most ardent supporters of India against China in 1962. In 1965, however, Jordan directly defended Pakistan's interests at the UNSC and strongly condemned India. See the Speech of Rifa I of Jordan at the UNSC, 17 September 1965, UN Document, S/PV/1239; 'A Note on Jordan's Support', *India and Foreign Review* 3:1, 1 November 1965; Minister of External Affairs Swaran Singh's statement to Lok Sabha (India, *Lok Sabha Debates*, Vol. 47, No. 10, 17 November 1965, pp. 2419–22).

23. Iran's open support to Pakistan came despite India's attempts to develop relations with the Shah of Iran in the 1950s. Being part of the Baghdad Pact, Iran and Turkey had an obligation to support their Pakistani partner.

24. India was in fact a direct victim of emerging intra-Arab disputes during the meeting. Most of the Arab states were not voting against India but in defiance of the position promoted by Egypt. See Agwani (1966).

25. According to an interview with the Israeli Consul-General at the time, Yaakov Morris, in *The Statesman*, 17–23 December 1970. See also Singh (1979); Kumaraswamy (2010: 202).

26. GAOR, 20 Sess, 1352 Plen Mtg, 8.

27. However, Shastri kept the dialogue open in certain areas of cooperation. The Israeli Minister of Labour, Yigal Allon was for instance authorized to visit India in 1965. *Hindustan Times*, 15 May 1980.

28. By contrast, while initially supportive, the historian Sarvepalli Gopal had grown sceptical of Israel's political actions in the late 1960s and early 1970s, as he explained in an essay he wrote after his visit to Israel in 1973, in *Imperialists, Nationalists, Democrats: The Collected Essays*, ed. Srinath Raghavan (New Delhi: Orient Blackswan, 2013), Chapter 30.

29. Swaran Singh said there had been mostly neutral statements from Arab states like Iraq, Kuwait, Lebanon, and Algeria at the UNGA. See India, *Lok Sabha Debates*, Vol. 54, No. 15, 24 November 1965, pp. 2569–70.

30. The BJS, also called the Jana Sangh, existed from 1951 to 1980 when some of its former members created the Bharatiya Janata Party (BJP). The BJS's initial policy positions on Israel are important to study because they shaped the opinions of future BJP leaders like Atal Bihari Vajpayee and L. K. Advani.

31. In March 1948, the socialists who formed a wing within the INC, called the Congress Socialist Party, parted ways. In 1952, together with the Praja Party and the Janata Front, the former Congress socialists formed a new party: the Praja Socialist Party.

32. The Swatantra Party eventually disappeared soon after C. Rajagopalachari's death in 1974.

33. The Government of India has been able to count on the regular support from the Communist Party of India (CPI) for its Israel policy. The CPI criticized Zionism and linked it to US imperialism. See the Communist Party of India resolution on the West Asian crisis adopted at the eighth congress held at Patna, 7–15 February 1968 (*Documents of the 8th Congress of the CPI* 1968: 236–7).

34. Quoted in Schechtman (1966).

35. Following the 1966 famine, India had asked the UN and the Food and Agricultural Organization to make a global appeal for aid.

36. The minister also said that Israel did not offer grains but fertilizers. *Jewish Telegraphic Agency*, 12 May 1966.

37. The Minister of External Affairs M. C. Chagla reiterated India's support for the 'legitimate rights' of the Palestinians during a visit to Kuwait in April 1967. See Kozicki (1967).

38. By contrast, India had condemned the Israeli raids into Jordan in November 1966. See Srivastava (1968).

39. U Thant, 'The United Nations as Scapegoat', address delivered on 3 December 1970, quoted in Moore (1974: 713–36).

40. See Chagla's speech in the Lok Sabha on 18 July 1967: 'As a member of the Security Council, [India] has got to review and pass judgment on world events', (*Lok Sabha Debates*, Vol. 7, No. 41, 18 July 1967, pp. 12678–712).

41. India was prudent vis-à-vis any precedent over the involvement of UN peace-keeping forces as Pakistan had also been requesting since 1957 to have UN troops stationed in Kashmir to supervise a plebiscite.

42. India (*Lok Sabha Debates*, Vol. 1, No. 8, 26 March 1957, pp. 800–83).
Earlier, on 6 November 1956, India's Deputy Permanent Representative to the
UN Arthur Lall had sent a letter to the Secretary General explaining that if the
UNEF had to be based in Egypt, Egyptian consent for its establishment was
necessary. See Eayrs (1964: 360).

43. Statement of M. C. Chagla to both houses of Parliament on 25 May 1967
(India, *Lok Sabha Debates*, Vol. 3, No. 3, 25 May 1967, pp. 871–6); G. Parthasarti's
statement in the UNSC, 29 May 1967, UN Document, S/PV/1343.

44. UN Document, S/PV/1343.

45. India (*Lok Sabha Debates*, Vol. 3, No. 3, 25 May 1967, pp. 871–6); UN
Document, S/PV/1343; Brecher (1968: 67–8).

46. UN Document, S/PV/1343.

47. Ambassador Lall had previously been the deputy permanent representative
of India to the UN. Although in 1967 he held a teaching position at the Columbia
University in New York, he was also a member of the Indian delegation at the
UN. See Lall (1967:14); *Interview with Arthur Lall* (1990).

48. Prime Minister Indira Gandhi's statement in Lok Sabha (India, *Lok
Sabha Debates*, Vol. 4, No. 11, 6 June 1967, pp. 3292–5).

49. G. Parthsarathi's Speech to the UNSC, 6 June 1967, UN Document S/
PV1348.

50. India rejected the US's draft resolution at the UNSC which asked for a
simple ceasefire with no withdrawal obligation. See India (*Lok Sabha Debates*,
Vol. 4, No. 11, 6 June 1967, pp. 3292–5).

51. India notably referred to its withdrawal from occupied territories in
Pakistan in 1965.

52. Minister of External Affairs of India M. C. Chagla's speech to the Fifth
Emergency Special Session of the General Assembly on 21 June 1967, UNGAOR
session 22, plen metg, 1530.

53. Rikhye (1980: Chapter 12). Indar Jit Rikhye was a major general in the
Indian Army. As an adviser to Secretary General U Thant at the UN in 1967, he
was in charge of overseeing the withdrawal of the UNEF from Gaza and the Sinai
in June 1967. Much less discussed is the fact that the Indian hospice in the Old
City of Jerusalem was also bombarded and severely damaged during the War of
1967; see Menon (1997).

54. The exact number of Indian casualties has never been clear. See Rikhye
(1980: 110). Initially, the Government of India reacted to unconfirmed media
reports of UNEF deaths. On 6 June, Indira Gandhi mentioned that eight soldiers
were killed. See India (*Lok Sabha Debates*, Vol. 4, No. 11, 6 June 1967, pp. 3292–
5). On 9 June, at the UNSC, Ambassador Parthasarathy reported nine deaths.
In a later statement on 18 July 1967, Chagla gave another figure of 14 dead. In
a report to the Permanent Mission of India to the UN, Rikhye announced nine

deaths. See Rikhye (1980: 125–6). In his book, Kumaraswamy (2010: 207) mentioned five deaths.

55. UN Document S/PV1348.

56. By contrast, the Canadian contingent had been evacuated before the hostilities started. Rikhye (1980: 154).

57. Parthasarathy's Speech at UNSC, UN Document, S/PV/1361.

58. S/PV/1348, 1354, 1361.

59. UNSCOR, yr 22, mtg 1375, 16–28.

60. Following the fourth Lok Sabha elections, the INC still had a comfortable majority with 283 seats (in a Lok Sabha of 520 seats) but the party had never had less than 60 per cent of the seats in the lower house. It had also lost 60 seats compared to the last elections. The BJS (35 seats), the PSP (13 seats), the Swatantra Party (44 seats), and the Samyukta Socialist Party (23 seats) had 115 seats together. See 'General Election of India 1967, 4th Lok Sabha', *Election Commission of India*, 5.

61. By contrast, Israel supported India's candidature. See India (*Lok Sabha Debates*, Vol. 49, pp. 5667–8); Srivastava (1968).

62. Interestingly, an independent MP, sympathetic to the Israeli position, compared the strategies of Israel in 1967 and of India in 1965. He argued that India had also undertaken pre-emptive military action at that time. See *Hindustan Times*, 8 June 1967.

63. Statement of H.V. Kamath at Bangalore on 24 May 1967 (*Janata* 12:19, 28 May 1967, p. 2). The PSP and its leader in the Lok Sabha, Nath Pai, still considered the demand was 'right' as Egypt was free and sovereign but it was judged unnecessary in the present circumstances. India (*Lok Sabha Debates*, Series 4, Vol. 4:2, session of 1967, p. 3943).

64. *Organiser* 20: 41, 28 May 1967, p. 3; Press statement of Balraj Madhok in the *Indian Express*, 5 June 1967.

65. The letter was quoted by M. R. Masani from the BJS in a statement to Parliament. See (*Lok Sabha Debates*, Vol. 6, No. 40, 15 July 1967, pp. 12132–8).

66. The Indian Army was so impressed by Israel's military efficiency that the operational details of some of the military operations of 1967 became an integral part of the promotional exam for Indian officers. Interviews with senior Indian military officers in Delhi, fall 2011 and summer 2012.

67. Although in a later book Chagla defended his 25 May statement, claiming that it had been approved by the MEA and the Indira Gandhi cabinet. See Chagla (1973: 425).

68. Chagla's speech to the Fifth Emergency Special Session of the UNGA, 21 June 1967, UN Document, A/PV/1530.

69. The resolution received a majority but not the necessary two-thirds for its implementation. See *UN Monthly Chronicle* 4 (1967): 32–4.

70. In another 24 October 1967 statement, Parthasarathy had also repeated the need for a ceasefire and a withdrawal of Israeli troops. See UN, S/PV/1369.

71. MEA, *Foreign Affairs Record* 13, October 1967, p. 159. Similarly, on 22 January 1968, the Indian President Zakir Hussain, in a speech at a banquet in honour the Yugoslavian President Tito's visit, said that India adhered to the principle that 'every state has the right to live in peace and security with its neighbors' in West Asia. See President Zakir Hussain's Speech in MEA (*Foreign Affairs Record* 14:1, January 1968).

72. Prime Minister Indira Gandhi's Address to the UNGA, 14 October 1968, UN A/PV/1693.

73. Statement by Minister for Education and Planning D. P. Dhar in the United Nations Special Political Committee (UNSPC), 15 December 1967 (MEA, *Foreign Affairs Record* 13:12, December 1967); India's Representative M. N. Naghnoor's statement at the UNSPC, 29 November 1968, UN A/SPC/SR.624; 'Rehabilitation of Palestine Refugees', *India and Foreign Review*, 15 January 1969.

74. UN S/PV/1402 and 1411.

75. B. Raman, a former RAW officer, had notably worked at the Geneva office. Raman (2008: 180–1).

76. Since Israel had no diplomatic agent in New Delhi, this undercover agent was the only diplomatic contact between the two counties. Raman (2008: 181).

77. In spite of its important Muslim population, India was not invited.

78. See Statement from the Deputy Minister of External Affairs Dinesh Singh in India (*Lok Sabha Debates*, 3:38, 22 February 1965, p. 651).

79. There was a massive demonstration in Gujarat, for instance. See Shani (2007: 161–4). In reaction, Balraj Madhok said that the public agitation was proof that Indian Muslims were invested in foreign concerns that were irrelevant to India. See Valiani (2011: 167).

80. Samar Sen's Statement to the UNSC, 10 September 1969, UN S/PV/1508.

81. The two monarchs were successful in discarding the initial proposal from Nasser to organize an Arab summit. See Singh (2006: 105).

82. Gurbachan Singh suggested as an alternative the participation of Dr Abudl Alim, the vice-chancellor of the Aligarh Muslim University, who was coincidentally present in Morocco for another event. The suggestion was immediately rejected by the Moroccan foreign minister as he was not an official representative. Dr Alim was finally present at the Conference to accompany Ambassador Singh. See Singh (2006: 108).

83. There was, however, no specification that only Muslims could form the delegation. For instance, there was one Christian in the Lebanese delegation.

84. Some authors have directly linked India's exclusion to the decision to name a Sikh ambassador to represent India at a Pan-Islamic meeting. The diplomat J. N. Dixit qualified it as an 'impractical exercise in assertive secularism' and as 'ineptitude' on the Indian part. See Dixit (1996: 300–1). Other scholars have also emphasized the decision to send Gurbachan Singh to the early sessions as a diplomatic faux-pas. See Agwani (1995: 240); Kumaraswamy (2010: 213); Mansingh (1984: 212); Ward (1992: 89).

Others mentioned the development of the Ahmedabad anti-Muslim riots as another possible explanation for Yahya Khan's sudden change of mind. See Ward (1992: 91). Gurbachan Singh argued, however, that Pakistan's volte-face was due to domestic political criticism in Pakistan linked to India's belated invitation to the Conference. See Singh (2006: 113). According to a presidential aide of Khan who was present at the Conference, the rising domestic uproar was conveyed through Pakistani journalists who had visited Khan on the evening of 23 September. See Bagchi (2008).

85. The first mediation was attempted by the Moroccan delegation. In a last mediation effort, members of the Afghan, Malaysian, Niger, and Egyptian delegations tried to convince India to change its position.

86. It had been argued by the Moroccan delegation that most of the drafting of the final resolution had already been done and that the closing session was simply a formality. See Singh (2006: 111).

87. Quoted in Gopal and Sharma (2007: 19).

88. Quoted in Ward (1992: 89–90).

89. Dinesh Singh defined the rise of Pan-Islamism in West Asia as a counter-move against Israel which was also mixing politics with religion. See India (*Lok Sabha Debates*, Vol. 39, No. 33, 8 April 1970, pp. 227–8).

90. India also neglected the OIC because Pakistan failed to use the Islamic gathering as an effective platform against India on the Kashmir dispute. The 1971 military defeat of Pakistan and the subsequent Simla Agreement of 1972 limited any discussion of the Kashmir issue within the context of the OIC. The insurgency in Kashmir in the late 1980s gave Pakistan a renewed opportunity to bring up the issue of Kashmir at the OIC.

91. For the censure motion debate, see India (*Lok Sabha Debates*, 17 November 1969, pp. 251–2, 308–24, 430).

92. For more details on the conflict, see Bass (2013); Ganguly (2002: 51–78); Raghavan (2013); Sisson and Rose (1991).

93. Statement by Indian delegate I. J. Bahadur Singh at the UNGA, 11 December 1971, UN A/PV/2013.

94. The only exception was Yemen that recognized the refugee problem as a 'burden' for India in October 1971. See Speech of the People's Democratic Republic of Yemen at the UNGA, 11 October 1971, UN A/PV/1961.

95. Speech by Saudi Arabia at the UNGA, 11 October 1971, UN A/PV/1961.

96. These states criticized India at the UNSC. Syria was a non-permanent voting member, while Saudi Arabia and Tunisia had been invited by the UNSC to participate in the debates. *UN Monthly Chronicle* 9 (1972): 3–26.

97. India and USSR had signed the Indo-Soviet Treaty of Friendship and Cooperation in August 1971. This treaty ensured Soviet support to India during the Bangladesh war.

98. Text of the Draft Resolution proposed by Sudan and Tunisia in the UNGA, 7 December 1971, UN A/L/647.

99. See Statement by the Syrian Arab Republic at the UNGA, 4 December 1971, UN S/PV/1606; Speech by Lebanon at the UNGA, 7 December 1971, UN A/PV/2003; Speech by Jordan at the UNGA, 7 December 1971, UN A/PV/2003. By 1971, Jordan had developed a special military relationship with Pakistan. In 1970, the future Pakistani President Zia ul-Haq was present in Amman as King Hussein's military adviser. The military unit he headed reportedly participated in the Jordanian civil war and fought against the Palestine Liberation Organization (PLO). See *Times of India*, 13 February 1970; Kumaraswamy 2010: 305); Ward (1992: 82–3).

100. Speech from Saudi Arabia at the UNGA, 7 December 1971, UN A/PV/2003.

101. 7 December 1971, UN A/PV/2003.

102. Speech from Saudi Arabia at the UNSC, 16 December 1971, UN S/PV/1616.

103. A few years before the conflict, the minister of External Affairs Chagla had expressed India's concern to the Saudi ambassador about newspaper reports detailing the transfer of Saudi arms to Pakistan. See Mudiam (1994: 89).

104. However, Iran refused to directly send aircrafts and pilots to Pakistan. Instead, Tehran offered to send the planes to Jordan. Bass (2013: 140, 217, 293–302, 341–2); Raghavan (2013: 246).

105. Quoted in Bass (2013: 140).

106. The Shah of Iran reportedly refused to respect a secret military pact by which it would have directly taken responsibility of the air defence of Karachi. Iran argued that the 1971 war was not just a bilateral dispute. See Yunus (2011: 36).

107. Quoted in Raghavan (2013: 178).

108. Quoted in Bass (2013: 139). Although appointed by Indira Gandhi to lead the secretariat during her term in office, Haksar was described as the de facto minister of external affairs. See Kapur, *India's Foreign Policy*, 185–7.

109. The reconciliation with Bangladesh would finally happen at the OIC meeting in Pakistan in 1974. Statement from Swaran Singh, India (*Lok Sabha Debates*, Vol. 14, No. 32, 26 April 1972, pp. 227–8).

110. The managing director of the firm, Establissements Salgad, Shlomo Zabludowicz was a personal acquaintance of Haksar from his stint in London. Establissements Salgad had also secretly procured weapons to India in 1962 and 1965. See Raghavan (2013: 182–3).

111. Letter from Golda Meir to Shlomo Zabludowicz (in Hebrew), cited in Raghavan (2013: 183).

112. In his statement to Parliament, Minister of External Affairs Swaran Singh acknowledged the dissatisfaction of some MPs with the country's Arab partners. See India (*Lok Sabha Debates*, Vol. 14, No. 32, 26 April 1972, pp. 227–8).

113. The BJS lost 13 seats (22 seats), the PSP lost 11 seats (2 seats), and the Swatantra Party lost 36 seats (8 seats). See 'General Election of India 1971, 5th Lok Sabha', *Election Commission of India*, 6.

114. These diplomatic efforts were rewarded in 1974 when Pakistan and other West Asian countries recognized Bangladesh.

115. Ambassador Samar Sen's Statement at the UNSC, 27 February 1972, UN, S/PV/1644; Ambassador Samar Sen's speech at the UNSC, 24 June 1972, UN S/PV/1649; Speech of Minister of External Affairs Swaran Singh at the UNGA, 3 October 1972, UN A/PV/2051; Ambassador Samar Sen's speech in the UNGA, 7 December 1972, UN A/PV/2103; Ambassador Samar Sen's statement at the UNSC, 14 June 1973, UN S/PV/1726; Ambassador Samar Sen's speech in the UNSC, 25 July 1973, UN S/PV/1734; Ambassador Samar Sen's explanation of India's vote on UN Draft Resolution on West Asia, 26 July 1973, UN S/PV/1735; Minister of External Affairs Swaran Singh's Statement in the UNGA, 2 October 1973, UN A/PV/2136.

116. Samar Sen's statement at the UNSC, 10 September 1972, UN S/PV/1661; Samar Sen's statement at UNSC, 18 April 1973, UN, S/PV/1709.

117. For more on the war of 1973, see Bregman (2002); Heikal (1975); Herzog (2003 [1975]).

118. Statement by the Minister of External Affairs Swaran Singh, 7 October 1973, *Indian and Foreign Review*, 15 October 1973; India (*Rajya Sabha Debates*, Vol. 86, 30 November 1973, 92; MEA, *Annual Report 1973–1974*: 45).

119. Ambassador Samar Sen's statement in the UNSC, 9 October 1973, UN S/PV/1744.

120. Ambassador Samar Sen's statement in the UNSC, 9 October 1973, UN S/PV/1744; Ambassador Sen's statement in the UNSC on the Draft Resolution, 21 October 1973, UN S/PV/1747.

121. Sen also reported that the Indian ambassador and his family had been either killed or injured during the bombing. Ambassador Samar Sen's statement in the UNSC, 9 October 1973, UN S/PV/1744.

122. Statement by the MEA expressing satisfaction over the acceptance of the UNSC Resolution, 22 October 1973, *Indian and Foreign Review*, 1 November 1973;

Ambassador Sen's statement at the UNSC, 25 October 1973, UN S/PV/1750; Ambassador Sen's statement in the UNSC, 2 November 1973, UN S/PV/1754.

123. 'Resolution adopted by All India Working Committee of the BJS, Rajkot, 3–4 November 1973', *Annual Register of Indian Political Parties*, Vol. 2, 1973–1974, pp. 441–3.

124. *Hindustan Times*, 23 October 1973; *Hindustan Times*, 27 October 1973; *Indian Express*, 23 October 1973; *The Statesman*, 23 October 1973; *The Hindu*, 27 October 1973; *Times of India*, 23 October 1973.

125. For more details on the 1973 oil crisis, see Venn (2002).

126. Nehru had welcomed Iraq's departure from the Baghdad Pact in a speech to the Rajya Sabha; see Nehru (1961: 95).

127. 'Statement by Abdul Karim Dassim, Prime Minister of Iraq, Baghdad, 20 November 1962', *Iraq Times*, 21 November 1962.

128. UNGA Resolution 2535 (24), 10 December 1969.

129. 'Declaration of the Arab Summit Conference at Algiers, 28 November 1973', in Rabinovich and Reinharz (2008: 334).

130. MEA (1981: 123). In a later interview with the All India Radio, Arafat explained that Indira Gandhi had promised that India would recognize the PLO during the conference. Nielsen (1977: 372).

131. The UNSCR 242 made no mention of the Palestinian rights. This was a voluntary addition from Swaran Singh. MEA, *Foreign Affairs Record*, October 1973, p. 347.

132. India's Permanent Representative R. Jaipal's Statement at the UNGA, 14 October 1974, UN A/PV/2268.

133. Draft Resolution Sponsored by India at the UNGA, 21 November 1974, UN A/L. 741, Add.1.

134. Indian Foreign Secretary Kewal Singh's Statement at the UNGA, 19 November 1974, UN A/PV/2290.

135. India was the second non-Arab state to recognize the PLO, after China in 1965. See the official statement in *Hindustan Times*, 11 January 1975.

136. Until then, the Arab League office in New Delhi had been representing the interests of the Palestinians. *Asian Recorder* 21, 5–11 March 1975, 12475.

137. India's Permanent Representative R. Jaipal's Statement at the UNGA, 4 December 1975, UN A/PV/2426.

138. There were not only sea-lanes of communication in West Asia but also important stops like Cairo and Beirut for India's West-bound air services. See Agwani (1995: 216).

139. Egypt notably exported cotton to India.

140. The new trade perspectives more than compensated the losses due to the end of the Gulf rupee system in the late 1960s, following the 1966 devaluation of the rupee in India. Hasan (1982).

141. India already had a relatively important expatriate community living in West Asia, totalling approximately 35,000. Most of these Indians were traders who had lived for years in the Gulf states and in Aden. See *Times of India*, 15 July 1967.

142. Most of these emigrants came from the south Indian states of Tamil Nadu, Kerala, and Andhra Pradesh. These states had a historic and cultural connection with the Gulf countries, had relatively large Muslim populations, and were experiencing high unemployment rates when migration picked up in the 1970s. For more on the Indian diaspora in West Asia, see Jain (2007).

143. Indian citizens had not been directly threatened by the West Asian conflicts, with the exception of the UNEF soldiers in June 1967. This would be the case until the Gulf War of 1991.

144. See Srivastava (1967).

145. For more on the boycott, see Feiler (1998); Turck (1977).

146. Some important Indian companies were included in the list such as Mahindra & Mahindra and Birla. See Sarna (1986: 185).

147. FICCI, 'Report of the Indian Delegation to West Asian Countries', quoted in Kumaraswamy (2010: 175).

148. During the Emergency, there were concerns in Muslim and Arab states that the new domestic political situation was creating hardships for India's Muslim minority. To reassure Arab leaders, India sent various delegations led by President Fakhruddin Ali Ahmad, Minister of External Affairs Y. B. Chavan, and Indira Gandhi's special envoy Mohammed Yunus. Most states expressed their understanding of the measures taken by the Congress government. Ward (1992: 100).

149. For more details on the Emergency and the 1977 elections, read Guha (2008: 491–518).

150. 'General Election of India 1977, 6th Lok Sabha', *Election Commission of India*, 6.

151. *Foreign Broadcast Information Service* (FBIS), South Asia, 31 March 1977, 1.

152. Vajpayee (1979: 85). India's delegation at the UN reiterated Vajpayee's position various times in November 1977 and added that the PLO should be party to any negotiations involving a peaceful settlement of the West Asian crisis. See *Indian and Foreign Review* 15(1977): 7; Statement by A. C. George, member of the Indian delegation to the UNGA, 30 November 1977, UN A/32/PV/86.

153. Minister of External Affairs A. B. Vajpayee's Address to the UNGA, 4 October 1977, UN A/32/PV/18.

154. Dayan had defected from the Labour Party and joined the first Likud government. In his new capacity as minister of foreign affairs, he played a major role in the peace process with Egypt and a decisive role in improving Israel's position in the international arena. See Dayan (1978: Chapter 3).

155. There was no consensus on the date of Dayan's visit either. Dayan said he visited New Delhi on 14 August 1977 in Dayan (1978: 27). By contrast, Desai dates it early 1978 (Desai's press conference in Bombay on 16 May 1980, quoted in *Indian Express*, 17 May 1980). Different accounts, however, seem to confirm the August 1977 date; see Gerberg (2008: 75, 92, 160, 222); Kumaraswamy (2010: 219); Raman (2008: 127–8).

156. Dayan only mentioned the name of the Israeli businessman: Azriel Eynav. Some other reports mentioned the mediation of another Israeli businessman, Shoul Isenberg. See *Hindustan Times*, 9 June 1980.

157. Raman (2008: 127–8). Dayan himself explained that he had been escorted from Bombay to Delhi by 'secret servicemen' (1978: 28).

158. Dayan was not greeted in Bombay by any diplomat but by intelligence servicemen and he was flown from Bombay to New Delhi in the prime minister's personal plane. See Dayan (1978: 27). According to the journalist Inder Malhotra, who talked to Vajpayee soon after the visit, the foreign minister was informed of Dayan's visit only after he had arrived at Desai's house. Interview with Inder Malhotra, New Delhi, 19 July 2012.

159. There was no official record of this meeting. The only account was in Dayan's autobiography.

160. Dayan (1978: 29). These planned meetings between the foreign ministers never occurred but Prime Minister Desai reportedly met the Israeli Defence Minister Ezer Weizmann in London in June 1978. See Gopal and Sharma (2007: 233); Kumaraswamy (2010: 221); Swamy (1982). Interview with Subramaniam Swamy, 21 October 2011, New Delhi.

161. Indira Gandhi, quoted in *Times of India*, 22 May 1980, and Rao's statement in India (*Lok Sabha Debates*, 7:4, 12 June 1980, p. 12).

162. Desai's press conference in Bombay on 16 May 1980, quoted in *Indian Express*, 17 May 1980.

163. Quoted in Gangal (1979: 70).

164. For more details on the Accords, read Stein (1999). The Khartoum resolution required all Arab League members to not recognize and negotiate with Israel. 'Essential Documents: Khartoum Resolution', *Council on Foreign Relations*. Retrieved from http://www.cfr.org/world/khartoum-resolution/p14841

165. Last accessed on 9 February 2013.

166. However, India refused to support the Arab demand to expel Egypt from the NAM. Egyptian Vice-President Hosni Mubarak visited New Delhi in May 1979 to clarify the Egyptian position. He stipulated that this was the first phase of a more comprehensive regional peace process. In response, Desai assured Mubarak that India would not support an Egyptian expulsion from the NAM. See Kumaraswamy (2010: 219); Ward (1992: 107–8).

4 Setting the Stage for Change

*From Estrangement to Engagement
with Israel (1984–1992)*

A s the indian national congress (INC) returned to power in
January 1980 with Indira Gandhi as Prime Minister, it resumed
its steadfast support for the Arab position.[1] The government's pro-Arab
credentials were tested very quickly: just a few days before, the USSR had
invaded Afghanistan.[2] The Arab states unanimously condemned the Soviet
invasion and asked for the immediate withdrawal of foreign troops. Given
India's close relationship with Moscow, Indira Gandhi did not explicitly
condemn the operation (Ghosh and Panda 1983). India attempted to
anticipate any possible ostracism in the Arab world by becoming the
first country in the world to grant full diplomatic status to the Palestine
Liberation Organization (PLO) mission in New Delhi. The PLO office
in New Delhi was upgraded to the level of a full-fledged embassy. In his
speech to Parliament, the Minister of External Affairs Narasimha Rao
confirmed that no settlement of the West Asian problem was possible
without the involvement of the PLO as 'an equal partner in negotiation'.[3]
Yasser Arafat was also invited to New Delhi in March 1980 for the first
time.[4] In addition, India pursued its support of Palestinian nationalism in
international fora. In July 1980 at the United Nations General Assembly
(UNGA), Rao noted 'Israel's continued intransigence, expansions and
aggression' and called again for an evacuation of the occupied territories.
In December, India supported three UNGA resolutions which called for
trade sanctions against Israel (Ward 1992: 110–11). In April 1981, an

Indian delegation attended the fifteenth session of the Palestine National Council (PNC) in Damascus.[5]

India also continued to defend Arab states against Israeli actions. On 7 June 1981, Prime Minister Gandhi condemned the Israeli air force attack on the nearly completed Osiraq nuclear reactor near Baghdad in Iraq.[6] India criticized the Israeli invasion of Lebanon in June 1982. India also decided to expel the Israeli consul in Bombay, Yossef Hassin, after he had openly criticized the government's position towards Israel.[7] In an interview, Hassin had implied that India's West Asia policy was dictated by the Arab states. He equally argued that the government's fear of the Muslim lobby and its concerns regarding its economic (and especially oil) interests in the region explained India's negative attitude towards Israel (*Sunday Observer*, 27 June 1982). However, it was merely a semi-symbolical sanction as the consulate remained open and continued working without any official consul. The Bharatiya Janata Party (BJP; formerly Bharatiya Jana Sangh [BJS]) and the Janata Party criticized the expulsion (*Hindustan Times*, 10 July 1982; Swamy 1982).

By the mid-1980s, Indo-Israeli relations were at their lowest point. By expelling the Israeli consul from Bombay, Indira Gandhi had effectively removed the only diplomatic link which existed between the two countries since 1953. Nevertheless, less than a decade after Yossef Hassin was asked to leave India, the two countries normalized their diplomatic relations. What happened over the spate of 10 years which led to this abrupt volte-face? There had already been favourable circumstances which could have led to a revision of India's approach. In the previous chapter, I demonstrated how the combination of certain variables in 1967–74 had been necessary to start an active policy debate but not sufficient to lead to a complete policy change. What specific conjunction of propitious conditions and of strategies led to the unprecedented diplomatic move of January 1992?

Rajiv Gandhi came to power after his mother's assassination in October 1984.[8] In similarity with the Janata government, Rajiv Gandhi wanted to carry out an important foreign policy reorientation. He managed to initiate some contacts with Israeli leaders, including with his Israeli counterpart, Prime Minister Shimon Peres, in 1985. However, despite a strong political willingness to change India's Israel policy, Rajiv Gandhi fell short of normalization. Just like the Janata coalition before him, he was confronted with multiple institutional and ideational obstacles which limited his actual policy leverage.

Nevertheless, the incremental approach initiated by Rajiv Gandhi helped pave the way for the normalization of relations by his successors in January 1992. The Gandhi tenure notably helped to reveal the existence of advocates of a new policy within the INC, the Prime Minister's Office (PMO), the ministry of external affairs (MEA), and within the security community. The rise of these new actors and the signalling of their preferences were crucial when India's Israel policy was again debated in the early 1990s. When Narasimha Rao came to power in June 1991, there were new international, regional, and domestic conditions which encouraged India to change its West Asia policy (Blarel 2009). The existence of clearly expressed policy preferences in favour of a rapprochement with Israel at this conjuncture facilitated complete foreign policy change and the establishment of diplomatic relations between the two countries in January 1992. Normalization had become possible because of the combination of structural and of more immediate factors, as well as by the nature of the debate between the old and new orthodoxies.

Attempts at Establishing a Dialogue (1984–91)

Rajiv Gandhi came to power in October 1984 at a time when Indo-Israeli relations were at their lowest point in history. Indira Gandhi had taken an explicitly pro-Palestinian position by granting full diplomatic status to the PLO mission in New Delhi in 1980, and had broken all remaining diplomatic contacts with Israel after expelling the Israeli consul from Bombay in 1982. Nevertheless, there was a renewed willingness to establish relations with Tel Aviv during Rajiv Gandhi's tenure as prime minister (1984–9). Rajiv Gandhi had stayed out of politics, and of the internal dynamics of the INC, until 1980 and the accidental death of his brother, who was the heir apparent to Indira Gandhi. As a consequence, Rajiv Gandhi was not as inhibited as most Congress politicians by the historical pro-Arab position of the party, and he did not feel tied to past policy positions (Dixit 1998b: 187–286). Breaking with the old guard of the party and of the MEA, he quickly demonstrated he was ready to talk to estranged actors like the US, China, and Israel. Rajiv Gandhi encouraged contacts and interactions with Israeli leaders as well as with pro-Israeli elements in the US. For instance, the Indian prime minister held a much publicized meeting with his Israeli counterpart Shimon Peres at a UN session in New York in 1985. This was the first meeting between the prime ministers of the two countries, and the first high-level dialogue since Moshe Dayan's visit eight years earlier.

However, despite these initial intentions, Rajiv Gandhi was unable to bring about a complete reversal of India's foreign policy towards Israel. There were multiple obstacles by the late 1980s which constrained his policy leverage. Domestic political constraints, including pressure from the old orthodoxy within his own party, and regional developments, like the Palestinian Intifada of 1987, restricted any further rapprochement with Israel.[9] At the end of Rajiv Gandhi's tenure, the same policy compromise of 1974 was still in place. India even became one of the first countries to recognize the state of Palestine, which had been proclaimed by the PNC in Algiers in November 1988. But Rajiv Gandhi's attempts at a rapprochement towards Israel revealed the existence of advocates of normalization in the INC and the MEA who were waiting for more propitious conditions to push their agendas. These structural changes at the international, regional, and domestic levels would only happen in 1991–2.

Rajiv Gandhi Signals a New Approach to Israel

As prime minister, Rajiv Gandhi left his mark on Indian foreign policy. Gandhi mostly made personal decisions and was assisted by the Indian intelligence service, his own secretariat, and close personal political advisers (Dixit 2004: 187–286, 2005: 195–203; Kapur 2009: 215–42). Rajiv Gandhi had little confidence in the MEA, which he perceived as a conservative institution which resisted new foreign policy initiatives (Cohen 2001: 89; Kapur 1994: 193). For instance, during his five-year tenure, he had six different ministers of external affairs. He also hired and changed foreign secretaries in a rather cavalier manner to assert his authority and direction in foreign affairs over the standard operating procedures.[10] The prime minister also preferred to deal with foreign policy issues directly with individual members of the Foreign Service (such as joint secretaries and ambassadors), thereby transcending the traditional hierarchical framework.[11] Substantive foreign policy issues were now directly managed by the PMO and no longer by the MEA. The December 1984 elections also gave Congress a landslide victory that provided Rajiv Gandhi with an unprecedented parliamentary support to implement reforms.[12] As a result, he was able to shape an innovative foreign policy which was less burdened by historical and ideological considerations.

Conscious of India's heavy reliance on the USSR for political and military support, Rajiv Gandhi wanted to diversify India's contacts to gain more diplomatic flexibility. Consequently, he attempted to normalize relations with China and to improve Indo-US ties.

On West Asian issues, Rajiv Gandhi stood rhetorically to the official line. In November 1984, he sent S. L. Yadav, the deputy chairman of the Rajya Sabha, to attend the seventeenth session of the PNC in Amman which was to decide on the fate of Arafat's leadership at the PLO (Mudiam 1994: 196). On his visit to Egypt in June 1985, he reiterated that a peaceful solution to the West Asian problem would only be possible with an active participation from the PLO in the discussions (Ward 1992: 122). In another interview, Prime Minister Rajiv Gandhi called the Israelis 'too bellicose' and said that India would not establish diplomatic ties with the Jewish state until it had changed its attitude on a 'number of issues'.[13] In an interview in the US, he explained that India was not trying to be a party in the West Asian process and that he preferred to watch how things evolved. In contrast with his mother, Rajiv Gandhi was less concerned about playing an active role in West Asian politics (Ward 1992: 122–3). He preferred a more cautious approach which could adapt to the developments on the ground. For instance, he also tried to not explicitly take sides during the Iran–Iraq conflict.

The Rajiv Gandhi government was also trying to find diplomatic strategies to improve India's relations with the US, and especially economic ties. Bilateral relations had considerably cooled down since the Soviet invasion of Afghanistan and the subsequent US military aid given to Pakistan. Another negative element was the increasing criticism of India's 'discriminatory' treatment of Israel coming from the Jewish community in the US, and particularly from the powerful Anti-Defamation League (ADL) (ADL 1987). The Indian government became conscious that efforts should be made to prevent pro-Israel American organizations from being obstacles to renewed diplomatic efforts to engage the US. Therefore, US criticism related to India's Israel policy would have to be taken into account. One of the immediate consequences was that unlike his immediate predecessors, Rajiv Gandhi openly met with Israeli officials and pro-Israel political leaders from the American Congress and from US Jewish organizations.[14] Henceforth, the issue of normalization of relations with Israel figured prominently in discussions with American officials.

Furthermore, one of the main stumbling blocks to a change in India's Israel policy was the concern of adverse reactions from Arab states. The regional situation in the mid-1980s was more permissive for an overture. For the first time in decades, the most pressing security concern was not the Arab–Israeli dispute but the Iran–Iraq war. This other conflict, along with the war in Afghanistan, concentrated the attention of most Arab states. Despite having normalized its relations with Israel, Egypt restored relations with most Arab states and was eventually reinserted into the Arab League in 1989. After Israel's invasion of Lebanon, the PLO moved to Tunis, Tunisia. During this period, the PLO in exile was distant from the Palestinians and their everyday struggle. The PLO was increasingly challenged from within and by movements based in Beirut and Gaza (Sayigh 1989). As a result of these internal struggles, the PNC decided to adopt a more moderate position and to vote to accept the United Nations Security Council (UNSC) Resolutions 242 and 338, thereby indirectly acknowledging Israel's existence. In parallel, some long-time critics of Israel, like the USSR and China, began moves to normalize their relations with Tel Aviv. There were also reports of Sino-Israeli discussions over military transfers (Kumaraswamy 1994; Shichor 1998). Consequently, there were multiple signals encouraging India to rethink its approach towards Israel.

Certain steps were taken by Rajiv Gandhi's government to amend ties with Israel. In June 1985, the Indian President Zail Singh attended the centenary celebrations of the Knesset Eliyahoo Synagogue in Bombay.[15] The President said that the Jewish community would continue to receive the government's support and added that India had always acknowledged and respected the rich contribution made by Jews to India's heritage.[16] A few days before the 1985 UNGA annual session, Israel bombarded the PLO headquarters in Tunis. Rajiv Gandhi condemned the attack and expressed his concern for the safety of Yasser Arafat (MEA, *Annual Report*, 1985–1986: 20). At the UN, India's Minister of External Affairs Bali Ram Bhagat also criticized Israel's 'aggressive and expansionist policies' and called the air raid a 'threat to peace and security' (*The Times of India*, 3 October 1985). At first glance, this position seemed in line with India's traditional support of the Arabs and Palestinians against Israel. However, the response in October 1985 was different. In reaction to the raid, 18 Arab states sponsored a UNGA resolution calling for the expulsion of Israel from the UN. Breaking with its traditional support for Arab-backed resolutions, India decided to abstain (Ward 1992: 124). In fact, despite the Israeli attack and the consequent criticisms, Rajiv Gandhi openly met with Israel's Prime Minister Shimon Peres during the fortieth UNGA session. This was the first public meeting between two active prime ministers of the two countries. Rajiv Gandhi also met with Congressman Stephen Solarz and members of the ADL during his stay in New York.[17] Soon after these discussions, India allowed an Israeli diplomat to be stationed in Bombay as vice-consul.[18] This was an important diplomatic move: since the expulsion of the Israeli consul in Bombay by Indira Gandhi, India had regularly refused requests to replace the position.[19] India therefore reestablished the consular-level relations that had existed until 1982.

In May 1987, the ADL published a report condemning India's discriminatory behaviour vis-à-vis Israel. The report highlighted the fact that India had refused to grant visas to Israeli citizens since the mid-1960s and quoted numerous statements hostile to Israel. The report suggested the imposition of US sanctions on India (ADL 1987). This led the Government of India to consider a new approach to Israel. As a first indication of change, the Rajiv Gandhi government allowed an Israeli tennis team to play against the Indian team in New Delhi for the Davis Cup Tournament in July 1987 (Kumaraswamy 2002: 29–40). Since the mid-1960s, India had refused to issue visas to Israeli delegations to attend sport events. This symbolic move led to speculation that India was going to upgrade its relations with Israel and that it could damage its relations with Arab states. However, Arafat announced in New Delhi in August that the Davis Cup match would have no negative influence on India's relations with the PLO (*Indian and Foreign Affairs* 1987, 24: 23). Even some important Congress figures like C. Subramaniam, who had been a cabinet minister under Indira Gandhi, became supporters of normalization after the event.[20] In reaction to the ADL report, India also decided to relax the visa restrictions for Israeli citizens.[21] However, the 'Davis Cup diplomacy' did not have long-term effects. The Indian government refused to allow its David Cup team to play a game in Tel Aviv in April 1988. By then, the Intifada had started and Rajiv Gandhi was not ready to take any radical decisions before two planned trips to Arab countries (Ward 1992: 128).

Rajiv Gandhi's visit to the US in June 1988 confirmed the new (albeit still limited) overture towards Israel. On 8 June 1988, the Indian prime minister had a high-profile meeting with US-based pro-Israeli groups in New York, upon the request of Congressman Solarz (Kumaraswamy 2002; Triparthi 1988). At the meeting in Rajiv Gandhi's hotel suite were present Solarz, the chairman of the Conference of Presidents of Major Jewish Organizations (and former president of the American Jewish Committee [AJC]) Morris Abram, the Conference's Executive Vice Chairman Malcolm Hoenlein, the president of the American Jewish Congress Robert Lifton, the executive director of the ADL Abe Foxman, and the executive director of the American Jewish Committee Ira Silverman (Lifton 2012: 255–6). Gandhi reportedly stated that he wanted to improve economic and political ties with the US. In response, the Jewish organizations criticized India's prejudiced conduct towards Israel and its citizens, notably on the question of visa restrictions (*Los Angeles Times*, 10 June 1988). They also asked India to pressure the Palestinians to renounce their call for the destruction of Israel and to follow the Egyptian example (Lifton 2012: 256). Some Israeli media later suggested that Prime Minister Rajiv Gandhi had pledged during the meeting to upgrade official ties with Israel (*Los Angeles Times*, 10 June 1988). The upgrade eventually happened in the following weeks but not in the form of normalization. The position of vice-consul of Israel in Bombay was upgraded back to the level of consul in August 1988 (Thakur 1994: 290). Since the expulsion of Yossef Hassin in 1982, the consulate had been headed by a deputy consul. In August 1988, that position was held by Amos Radian who was elevated to consul and succeeded by Giora Becher in 1989.[22]

There were other indicators of change in December 1988 and January 1989. First, during a special session of the UNGA, India's Minister of State of External Affairs K. K. Tiwari refrained from denouncing Israel, and instead referred to Israel's right to live in peace and security within internationally recognized borders, along with a Palestinian state and the other neighbouring Arab countries (*The Hindu*, 6 January 1989). India officially maintained a neutral position in spite of the ongoing Palestinian Intifada, and the fact that the US had refused to grant an entry visa to the PLO Chairman, Yasser Arafat. The same month, the deputy director general for Asia in the Israeli foreign affairs ministry, Joseph Hadass, was invited to visit India (*Foreign Affairs Record* 35: 1, 12 January 1989; Naaz 1999). In order to avoid domestic criticism, however, Hadass came to New Delhi in his individual capacity and not as official representative of Israel (*The Statesman*, 28 December 1988). During his visit, Hadass met with the Minister of External Affairs, Narasimha Rao. A three-member delegation of the ADL and Congressman Solarz then visited New Delhi in January 1989. Two of the members of this delegation had been signatories of the very critical 1987 ADL report. The delegation met Narasimha Rao, Foreign Secretary Alfred Gonsalves, and the MEA's Joint Secretary to the Prime Minister P. K. Singh (*The Hindu*, 6 January 1988). There is no clear consensus on what was exactly discussed during this meeting. One report said that the delegation of the ADL lobbied in favour of improved Indo-Israeli relations but was notified that change would not be imminent (Ward 1992: 128–9). Following the meeting, there was another diplomatic gesture towards Israel with the formal extension of the Israeli consulate jurisdiction by the Government of India to the southern state of Kerala which had a historical and relatively significant Jewish population. There was also a gradual liberalization of visa procedures for tourist groups and individuals (Gerberg 2008: 113–14).

In spite of American pressures and a number of significant steps in the direction of change, the Rajiv Gandhi government was unable to bring about a complete reversal of India's foreign policy towards Israel. Instead, in November 1988, India became one of the first non-Arab countries to recognize the newly proclaimed state of Palestine. Despite the nascent dialogue with Israeli authorities, what factors ultimately prevented Rajiv Gandhi from normalizing relations?

Rajiv Gandhi's Failure to Reverse the Trend

The Rajiv Gandhi government originally had unprecedented policy leeway to initiate changes due to favourable conditions at home (large parliamentary majority) and at the international level (inter-Arab divisions caused by the Iran–Iraq war). Furthermore, the increasing costs induced by the no-relationship policy with Israel on Indo-US relations gave Gandhi an impetus to revise the position towards Israel. By the late 1980s, however, the legitimacy and power of the INC government had considerably eroded. The threshold for policy change imposed by the previous 1974 policy compromise had been too high and imposed an incremental approach. While Rajiv Gandhi instigated a cautious rapprochement with Israel, he also had to regularly criticize Israel's aggressive behaviour. When greeting Arafat in New Delhi in August 1987, Rajiv Gandhi stated, for example, that 'any failure to understand and accommodate the legitimate Palestinian aspirations through the process of negotiations at an international conference' would only result in the 'intensification of armed struggle to assert and secure Palestinian rights' (*Asian Recorder*, 27 August–2 September 1987, p. 19627). In December 1988, India supported a UN resolution that called for a West Asian peace conference organized by the UN and which would include all the involved parties, including the PLO (Ward 1992: 126). From 1986 to 1989, the Indian prime minister maintained India's strong support to the Palestinian people and to their cause. This position was driven by domestic political constraints, including pressures from within Gandhi's own party, but also because of the need to accommodate Arab partners.

When considering its Israel policy, India also had to take in account its continued reliance on energy imports, and especially of oil, from West Asian states. The 1979 revolution in Iran, which was India's major supplier of crude oil in the 1970s, led to a severe oil shortage. India's oil imports from Iran fell from 4.5 million metric tons in 1978 to about 1 million metric tons in 1979. The Iran–Iraq war further disrupted India's supply line. Both Iran and Iraq provided about 40 per cent of India's yearly requirements (Ward 1992: 36). Since it could no longer rely on stable oil supply from its two traditional Gulf partners, India was vulnerable to oil embargoes and rapid oil price increases throughout most of the 1980s. As a reaction, the Indian government attempted to diversify its oil imports (Mudiam 1994: 133–8). India's relations with Arab states were further strained by New Delhi's support for the Soviet-backed regime of Mohammed Najibullah in Afghanistan. Most West Asian states criticized the Soviet invasion and the communist government in Kabul. For instance, important disagreements with Saudi Arabia on the Afghan issue had become flagrant during Indira Gandhi's visit to Riyadh in April 1982 (Ward 1992: 95–6). Pakistan also attempted to capitalize on India's position on the Afghan issue to gain the support of the Arab states.[23] The Pakistan factor was still present in the 1980s in India's calculations. Given its energy needs and its position on the Afghan conflict, India had no leverage to embark on an ambitious foreign policy change.

Regional developments, like the Israeli raid on the PLO's headquarter in Tunis in October 1985 and the eruption of the Palestinian Intifada in December 1987, further constrained Rajiv Gandhi's liberty of action. While attention had concentrated on the Iran–Iraq war and the Afghanistan conflict, the Intifada brought the Palestinian issue back to the forefront of West Asian politics and temporarily remobilized the Arab states behind a common cause. By 1986, Rajiv Gandhi no longer had the moderate Shimon Peres as his counterpart in Israel. The Israelis had agreed on a rotation of the premiership which resulted in the second tenure of Yitzhak Shamir in 1986. Shamir was a right-wing politician from the Likud who supported building Jewish settlements in the West Bank and Gaza. Shamir was also in power when the Intifada broke out and he ordered a military solution to the uprising. During a visit to Amman, Rajiv Gandhi strongly criticized Israel's brutality in attempting to crush the Intifada (*Hindustan Times*, 12–13 July 1988). Finally, Shamir was an uncompromising opponent of Palestinian statehood, and was therefore opposed to India's decision to recognize the state of Palestine in November 1988. Both the Intifada and Shamir's hardline approach eroded any possible domestic support for a new policy vis-à-vis Israel.

Israel's involvement in the Sri Lankan ethnic conflict also generated suspicion and concern in India. Israel's support, notably in intelligence cooperation, to the Colombo regime ran contrary to India's own security interests and support of the Tamil population.[24] J. N. Dixit, who was India's ambassador to Sri Lanka at the time, invoked Israel's military and intelligence support to the government of Sri Lanka against the Tamil rebels as a reason for the direct Indian intervention in 1987 (Dixit 1998a: 327). As a result, in the July 1987 Indo-Sri Lankan Accord, which formalized the Indian military intervention as a peace-keeping force in Sri Lanka, there was a reference to the need of an 'understanding' between India and Sri Lanka on the 'employment of foreign military and intelligence personnel' on Sri Lankan soil.[25] India wanted to ensure that Sri Lanka would not directly cooperate with Israel without Indian knowledge. In addition, Sri Lanka's contacts with Israel demonstrated that there was no inevitable Arab diplomatic sanction as a reaction to military and intelligence cooperation with the Jewish state.[26]

After 1987, Rajiv Gandhi also had to deal with domestic political problems linked to the Bofors weapons scandal and the intervention in Sri Lanka.[27] The military operation in Sri Lanka proved to be a debacle. The political fallout in India, the Indian Peacekeeping Force's numerous casualties, and international criticism led the Indian forces to start withdrawing by 1989. The allegation of arms bribery and the failed operation in Sri Lanka limited Rajiv Gandhi's manoeuvrability in foreign policy until the 1989 elections. The Congress believed that any further move towards Israel could have a negative impact on the party's chances in the Lok Sabha elections of 1989. In fact, in the middle of the November elections, Rajiv Gandhi even announced that he would award Yasser Arafat with the Jawaharlal Nehru Award for International Understanding (Gerberg 2008: 113). In spite of this concession to its pro-Palestinian constituents, Rajiv Gandhi lost the November 1989 elections to the Janata Dal.

There was no foreign policy change despite an evident political willingness on the part of the Rajiv Gandhi government. The Janata government (1977–9) had equally demonstrated an inclination for change but did not have the political and popular support to implement it. For the first time, it was an actor from the Nehru–Gandhi family with a preeminent position within the INC who was an advocate of normalization of relations with Israel. Rajiv Gandhi also had the legitimacy and a strong control over the INC and MEA apparatuses to implement a policy change. However, Gandhi faced unfavourable conditions after 1987 which constrained his possibility to act. Events like the Intifada and the Bofors scandal quickly closed any window of opportunity for change. The costs to change the existing policy were perceived to be more important than the costs linked to its continuation.

Nevertheless, there were some long-term tendencies which would prove to be decisive in the coming years. Gandhi's efforts to change the existing policy were an opportunity for new ideas and actors to surface. Some members of the INC and the MEA— like Narasimha Rao and P. K. Singh—directly worked with the prime minister in the rapprochement with Israel and interacted directly with their Israeli counterparts. As the prime minister, Rao would normalize relations with Israel in 1992 and P. K. Singh would become the first Indian ambassador in Tel Aviv. They both understood at this time that normalization was a necessary condition for a rapprochement with the US. J. N. Dixit also directly saw the benefits of military and intelligence collaboration on counter-terrorism and counter-insurgency when he was based in Sri Lanka. As foreign secretary in 1992, he would become one of the most ardent supporters of normalization. The Rajiv Gandhi tenure therefore encouraged the emergence of a new orthodoxy.

Coalition Governments and Policy Stasis

Because of the corruption charges, internal divisions within Congress, and the foreign policy fiasco in Sri Lanka, Rajiv Gandhi's government was voted out of office in favour of a coalition government, the National Front, led by the Janata Dal leader, V. P. Singh, who became the new prime minister.[28] The National Front stayed in power from December 1989 to November 1990. Many members of the Janata Dal had been present in Jayaprakash Narayan's Praja Socialist Party (PSP) and had therefore political connections with the Israeli Labour party which was in power in Israel. But the new government did not attempt to resume the contacts made between India and Israel under Rajiv Gandhi. Political survival was the primary objective of this fragile government and V. P. Singh had no leverage to initiate an important foreign policy change. Furthermore, in the last elections, the Janata Dal had gained Muslim votes which traditionally favoured Congress. As a result, the MEA, traditionally conservative when it came to India's West Asia policy, took back the initiative after five years of personalized foreign policy-making under Rajiv Gandhi. The new minister of external affairs was I. K. Gujral, a former member of Congress, who resumed India's pro-Arab policy.

V. P. Singh and Gujral had to deal with the Gulf war which started in August 1990 when Iraq invaded Kuwait. Traditionally, India had been neutral in regards to inter-Arab crises. But the Gulf crisis of 1990–1 had three major implications for India. First, about 40 per cent of India's crude oil imports were directly affected by the war. India was buying a major portion of its crude oil needs from Iraq, either directly or through a trilateral arrangement with the USSR.[29] To cope with the loss of supplies coming from Iraq during the conflict, India had to arrange for immediate imports to come from other countries like Saudi Arabia, the United Arab Emirates (UAE), and Iran. India's average import bill for oil suddenly doubled in the spate of six months (Boquerat 2001). Second, the war directly disrupted the flow of remittances coming from the 180,000 Indian nationals based in Kuwait and Iraq.[30] To ensure the well-being and the repatriation of this expatriate community, Gujral was sent on a controversial trip to Baghdad on 20 August 1990 to meet the Iraqi President, Saddam Hussein.[31] Third, Iraq had also been one of the rare West Asian countries to consistently support India in its disputes with Pakistan. Iraq had also assured India of its veto at the Organisation of Islamic Cooperation (OIC) if the Kashmir issue was put up to a vote by Pakistan.[32]

Given these three considerations, the V. P. Singh government gave contradictory signals on its position vis-à-vis Iraq in August 1990. While

India was reluctant to directly condemn the invasion, it also supported UN resolutions which demanded that Iraq withdraw from Kuwait. At the same time, India also kept contacts with Baghdad to ensure the safety of its citizens present in Kuwait. V. P. Singh supported a negotiated settlement of the conflict and opposed the use of force to solve the problem (*The Hindu*, 17 August 1990). Gujral toured different countries in the region to initiate a peace process (Baral and Mohanty 1992). The Indian government also organized a massive airlift to evacuate 170,000 Indian nationals in September 1990 from an airfield at Amman, Jordan, over a period of 30 days (Burns 1990; Cowell 1990). There was a strong domestic opposition to India's ambiguous approach to the conflict at a time when the US, the USSR, and China had all taken a clear stand against Iraq (Malik 1991). Some analysts and diplomats were calling for a change in India's approach to West Asia. For instance, following the war, former foreign secretary Jagat S. Mehta called for 'erasing old mindsets originating from the wasted decades of the Cold War' and added that India should 're-examine seated, old premises of policies' (*The Hindustan Times*, 23 November 1991). There was an increasing perception of the costs for India's trade and diplomatic relations with some Gulf states like Saudi Arabia and with the US if India did not modify its regional policy.

Just 11 months after coming into power, the Janata Dal split and the V. P. Singh government lost a vote of confidence in Parliament on 7 November 1990. The new government was formed by Chandra Shekhar from the Janata Dal (S).[33] Prime Minister Shekhar ran a caretaker minority government which depended on INC support to survive from November 1990 to March 1991.[34] Like his predecessor, Shekhar was mostly concerned with domestic politics and political survival. The MEA again played an important role in deciding the foreign policy agenda. Consequently, Shekhar did not make any active changes in India's West Asia policy, with the exception of his more explicit condemnation of Iraq's invasion of Kuwait.

The Joint Declaration of the South Asian Association for Regional Cooperation (SAARC) issued in November 1990 explicitly called on Iraq to leave Kuwait and to comply with UNSC resolutions. A few days later, India supported UN Resolution 678 which authorized the use of force if Iraq did not withdraw from Kuwait by 15 January 1991. In response to international criticism, the Iraqi regime tried to link the crisis to the Arab–Palestine problem. The Iraqi position was that it would not consider withdrawing from Kuwait until the Palestinian issue was resolved (Freedman and Karsh 1993: 258). Unlike his predecessor, Shekhar explicitly rejected any connection between the Iraqi withdrawal from Kuwait and the solution of the Palestinian problem.[35] US pressure was apparently decisive in explaining this policy shift in New Delhi. In addition, India allowed US military aircrafts en route from the Philippines to the Gulf to use Indian refuelling facilities in January 1991. Shekhar had mostly continued the policy of rapprochement with the US initiated under Rajiv Gandhi's tenure in the 1980s, and was taking into account the immediate need for crude oil. Since India could not import from Iraq, it looked for alternative sources in Saudi Arabia, Kuwait, and the UAE, which all condemned Iraq's invasion. Saudi Arabia was also actively courted by Pakistan which had offered to join the multinational forces based in the Saud Kingdom (Malik 1991).

In spite of the short tenure of his government and the Gulf crisis, there were some diplomatic gestures that Prime Minister Shekhar made towards Israel. He first allowed the junior Israeli national tennis team to participate in a tennis tournament in India in April 1991, and the Israel–India match was broadcasted by the India national television. A year earlier, a similar request had been rejected by the Indian government (Gerberg 2008: 151). Shekhar also met with the Israeli Consul Giora Becher in July 1991. However, the meeting did not result in any consequent political development (Gerberg 2008: 99). The Minister of State in the ministries of commerce and law, Subramaniam Swamy, tried to convince Shekhar of the need to normalize relations with Israel, or to the least to transfer the Israeli consulate from Bombay to New Delhi. Since India had recognized Israel *de jure* in 1950, Swamy argued India should honour its commitment towards Israel made 40 years earlier.[36] Shekhar was, however, reluctant to make any change in India's Israel policy. On his own initiative and in spite of the MEA's objections, Swamy openly met with the Israeli Minister of Trade and Commerce Moshe Nissim during a World Trade Organization (WTO) conference in Brussels in December 1990.[37] The MEA later stated this had been an unofficial meeting which had not been approved by the government.

The two coalition governments from 1989 to 1991 had neither the political legitimacy nor the willingness to change India's Israel policy. Priority went to the political survival of their fragile coalitions in Parliament. Consequently, these governments were mostly risk-averse when it came to their foreign policy. Nevertheless, both Singh and Shekhar had to deal with one of the most important West Asian crises of the past decades. The Gulf crisis was a major regional shock which revealed important inter-Arab divisions, notably on the Palestine question. The conflict also demonstrated that the Israel–Arab conflict was no longer the main source of instability in the region. Finally, the Gulf operations confirmed the increasing US involvement in the affairs and the security of the region (and the consequent decline of USSR influence). The haphazard and ambiguous reaction from the Indian governments to these decisive developments was criticized at the international, regional, and domestic levels. Because of India's slow and reluctant condemnation of Iraq, there was an impression among policymakers that India needed to repair the damages done in its relations with Saudi Arabia and Kuwait. The other conclusion was that India had to change its policy vis-à-vis US intervention in the region. Traditionally, because of its attachment to non-alignment but also because of its good relations with the USSR, India had been sceptical of US interference in inter-Arab affairs. The shift in India's approach to the Iraq war in the last weeks of 1990 and the authorization of refuelling of US planes in 1991 signalled an intention by Indian leaders to modify their position. The new Gulf crisis therefore encouraged a policy reassessment which would happen under the Narasimha Rao government.

The Path to Normalization in 1991–2

There were again parliamentary elections in India in May 1991. A day after the first round of polling, former Prime Minister Rajiv Gandhi was assassinated by the Liberation Tigers of Tamil Eelam (LTTE) while he was campaigning in Tamil Nadu. The assassination was an act of reprisal against Gandhi's decision to send troops to Sri Lanka in 1987. The elections were temporally postponed until mid-June. After the polling resumed, the INC managed to improve its standing over the 1989 elections by winning 244 seats. No party had a clear parliamentary majority, but with the support of the Left parties and independents, the INC was in a position to form a government in July (Andersen 1991). After an important internal debate over who would take the prime minister's position after Rajiv Gandhi's death, the party finally settled on Narasimha Rao. Rao was a neutral figure palatable to the different factions of the INC that sought, in the short time accorded to form a government, to build a consensus. This was an unusual choice at the time because Rao had not been popularly elected and was no longer a member of either of the Houses of Parliament. Rao also had had a long service record as chief minister of Andhra Pradesh, and most importantly, as a former defence and external affairs minister in the previous Indira and Rajiv Gandhi governments in the 1980s. In fact, he had more experience in foreign policy affairs than anyone else in his government and in his own party. Rao had therefore already been involved in India's foreign policy decision-making process, and notably in diplomatic exchanges with Israel.

Because he was heading a seemingly weak minority government of transition, Rao did not feel constrained by the INC's long-established ideological positions and by traditional domestic voting constituencies such as the Muslim vote. As a consequence of this greater flexibility, he gradually pushed for a reformist foreign policy agenda in West Asia (Bajpai 1992). Regional and domestic developments in the early 1990s progressively permitted the new government to expand its diplomatic options. At the regional level, the Kuwait crisis of 1990–1 and its consequences modified Israel's status vis-à-vis Arab states. Internal opposition within the Arab world and widespread criticism regarding the PLO's support of Iraq during the war limited the negative implications of opening up to Israel. The weakened position of the PLO in 1991 also encouraged Yasser Arafat to start negotiations with Israel. These regional transformations created an unprecedented window of opportunity for India to develop a strategic partnership with Israel while also maintaining good relations with other West Asian countries.

These were mostly permissive conditions at the regional, international, and domestic level for a new policy debate. But these shocks were not directly interconnected. I will therefore insist in this section on the role of the new orthodoxy in linking these various changes to their policy alternative: the rapprochement with Israel. In spite of the attractive narrative that linked the multiple structural changes in the early 1990s to the 1992 decision to normalize relations with Israel, the causal mechanism was not evident. A close reading of the events in 1991–2 demonstrates that nothing was ineluctable about the January 1992 decision. In fact, it took almost another decade for political, economic, and strategic relations between the two countries to really expand. The nature of the ideas and of the strategy of advocates for a rapprochement with Israel is critical to understand why foreign policy change happened in 1992.

Shocks and Window of Opportunity

The 1990–2 time period was exceptional because it was marked by concurrent shocks at the international, regional, and domestic levels.[38] At the regional level, the Gulf war demonstrated strong inter-Arab divisions. Many Arab states criticized the PLO's support of Iraq during the war. Arafat and Hussein were indeed closely cooperating at the time to strengthen their respective positions. Iraq had provided financial and military support to Arafat and the PLO during the 1980s. In exchange, Hussein was seeking to establish himself as the pivotal leader in the Arab world with an unwavering support for the Palestinian cause (Hijaz 1990; Sneh 1990). At a summit in Cairo in August 1990, twenty Arab League countries drafted a final statement that condemned the Iraqi invasion of Kuwait and which supported the anti-Iraq UN resolutions. Twelve Arab states even supported the use of force against Iraq. The PLO was one of the two delegations (along with Libya) to support Iraq (Ibrahim 1990). Arafat also travelled to Baghdad in January 1991 to confirm the PLO's support in the case of a conflict with the US. As a result, the PLO backed the losing side and alienated some of its traditional sponsors. Saudi Arabia immediately terminated its financial assistance to the PLO. Kuwait considered the PLO's support to Iraq as treacherous ingratitude after years of support. The emirate had also been home to hundreds of thousands of Palestinians since the 1970s. In response, the Kuwaitis funded a media campaign denouncing Arafat as a traitor for supporting Saddam (Tessler 1994: 737–8). Given the isolation of the PLO in the Arab world, India no longer felt obliged to permanently support the Palestinian movement in order to accommodate its West Asian partners.

The Iraqi intrusion into Kuwait also diverted attention from Israel as the Saddam Hussein regime became the new source of security concern in the region. During the Gulf war, Iraq fired 42 Scud missiles at Israel over the course of the war, hitting notably Tel Aviv. Despite the damage done to its deterrence power, the Israel Defence Forces (IDF) chose not to escalate and to retaliate. Israel was conscious that Iraq was trying to introduce an Arab–Israeli dimension to the conflict (Freedman and Karsh 1993: 331–41). Both India and the Arab states respected Israel's unprecedented military restraint in spite of the Iraqi bombing. The invasion and occupation of an Arab state by another Arab state forever changed the geopolitical dynamics of the region and dealt severe blows to the concept of Arab unity. In fact, following the conflict, some West Asian countries—including Oman, Qatar, Jordan, and Syria—and the PLO even sought new ties with the Jewish state. The Gulf war was indeed a major political and economic defeat for the PLO which was left with no other option than to negotiate with Israel if it wanted to still be offered financial assistance from the US. The US was also now the major military and political actor in the region. The Arab states could no longer depend on their declining Soviet patron.[39] The PLO's weakness and the lack of Arab unity facilitated the George H. W. Bush administration decision to launch a new Arab-Israeli peace process in the immediate aftermath of the Gulf war (Quandt 2001).

Consequently, a series of West Asian peace initiatives created a new era in the region where coexistence and negotiations with Israel were possible. The decrease in oil prices following the Gulf war also reduced India's dependence on the Arab countries. These regional transformations created a unique window of opportunity for India to start discussing with Israel. Normalization even became a requirement if India wanted to play a diplomatic role in the new peace process. Tel Aviv made it clear that any state that wanted to participate in the West Asian peace talks, including the Madrid Peace Conference which was scheduled for October 1991, needed to have established diplomatic ties with all parties to the conflict.[40] The Israeli Minister of Foreign Affairs David Levy insisted that India would not be able to participate in the Madrid Conference before formal diplomatic relations had been established between the two countries. Levy also refused India's participation in the Moscow multilateral negotiations in January 1992 for the same reasons (Gerberg 2008: 223–4). Given this new condition imposed by the Israeli leadership, New Delhi risked being barred from the peace process and from having any weight or say in West Asian politics.

The international situation in 1991 also dramatically evolved. The end of the Cold War left Indian decision-makers facing a completely uncertain strategic situation where the parameters of a new emerging global order were still undefined. The radical changes in the international strategic balance presented India with new opportunities and new challenges. Traditionally, India's Israel policy had corresponded to the position of the NAM, and Israel's identification with the West had provided an ideological basis for India's pro-Arab orientation during the Cold War. As the NAM lost its relevance after 1991, it became possible for India to revise its position. There was also the collapse of the Soviet Union, India's veteran ally and arms supplier, which was a blow to India's defence capabilities. The USSR had been India's largest arms supplier since the early 1960s, and in 1991, 70 per cent of India's military equipment was of Soviet origin (Gupta 1995). Almost overnight, India had to deal with a military industry that was dispersed in 15 countries, and with less favourable financial conditions offered by the Russian Federation. As a consequence, India sought assistance from all countries that could help to improve its precarious regional and international security situation.

In addition, in the wake of the Madrid Peace Conference, countries which were traditionally hostile to Israel judged that recognizing and establishing full diplomatic ties with Israel at that time would not affect their relations with Arab and Muslim countries. Russia, for instance, decided to normalize relations with Israel just days before the inauguration of the Madrid Peace Conference.[41] Henceforth, Russia actively participated in the West Asian peace process. China also chose to normalize relations with Israel. Although Israel had been the first West Asian country to recognize the People's Republic of China (PRC) in January 1950, the PRC had refused to reciprocate that move (Han 1993). China had traditionally been hostile to Israel, as an expression of Afro-Asian solidarity following the Bandung Conference in 1955. As China moved closer to the Arab world in the 1960s, it consistently supported the Palestinian movement and used anti-Israeli rhetoric in international fora (Cooley 1972). However, from the 1970s up to 1991, there were unofficial military contacts between Israel and the PRC (Goldstein 2004). India closely monitored this relationship, as collaboration with Israel had the potential to enhance the defence capabilities of rival China (Pant 2004). Accordingly, India announced its decision to establish diplomatic relations just five days after China (Ford 1992; *The Economic Times*, 28 January 1992).

Since independence, India had regarded Israel as a state that had been set up with the support of imperialist powers, and especially from the US. Prime Minister Nehru had famously pointed out that the US government had handled the Palestine question ineptly in 1947 (Parthasarathy, *Letters to Chief Ministers*, p. 126). In the 1980s, there were renewed pressures from the US government and from pro-Israel groups in Washington for India to change its policy vis-à-vis Tel Aviv. The US influence on India's West Asia policy further increased during the Gulf war. India's shift of position regarding Iraq and its acceptance to let US military planes refuel at Indian airports proved that it had to come to terms with increased American presence in the region. The domestic economic crisis in India in 1991 and the disappearance of its Soviet partner also made New Delhi more vulnerable to US economic pressure. In June 1991, Prime Minister Rao inherited an important economic crisis from his predecessor.[42] The crisis was an opportunity for a traditionally self-reliant India to liberalize and to open its economy to the world. With his Finance Minister Manmohan Singh, Rao fundamentally changed India's economic policies. Rao notably sought investments and loans from international institutions such as the International Monetary Fund (IMF) and the World Bank, as well as from Western countries like the US.[43] The objective for Rao and Manmohan Singh was to neutralize all obstacles in Washington to the urgent loans India needed. Improving relations with Israel was progressively perceived as a necessary condition to obtain crucial US financial assistance for India's economic recovery.

Alongside these regional and international factors, there were also amenable conditions at home for a policy change. At the domestic level, the development of a local insurgency in Kashmir in the late 1980s initially complicated India's relations with its West Asian partners, and especially with the OIC. The Kashmir issue had rarely been raised by Pakistan in the early years of the OIC's existence because of the Simla Agreement of 1972.[44] However, from 1987 onwards, Islamabad exploited the ongoing unrest and the reports of human rights violations in the Kashmir valley to mobilize Arab–Muslim support for Pakistan's position. In August 1990, at the nineteenth session of the OIC, Pakistan managed to have a statement issued on Kashmir which referred to Indian and international press reports about the ill-treatment of Muslims in Kashmir, and which called for action to enforce the respect of fundamental rights of Muslim citizens.[45] This statement was included in the agenda despite the divisions within the organization due to the Iraqi invasion of Kuwait.[46]

In August 1991, at the twentieth session in Istanbul, the OIC suggested to set up a fact-finding mission to visit Jammu and Kashmir in order to report on the situation.[47] This proposal further granted international legitimacy to Pakistani claims of human rights abuses. India refused to recognize the legitimacy of the OIC on this internal matter. Following India's refusal to let the fact-finding mission enter the country, the OIC decided to condemn India for its violation of human rights in Kashmir in December 1991. Henceforth, the OIC consistently took Islamabad's side and never condemned cross-border insurgency coming from Pakistan. It became evident that an unconditional pro-Arab policy did not provide India with any strategic support for its policies in Kashmir. The OIC resolutions led to a strong diplomatic response from the Rao government which asserted that Kashmir was an integral part of India (Baba 2008).

Additionally, the Indian press also actively followed the abduction and killing of Israeli tourists by the Jammu and Kashmir Liberation Front (JKLF) in Srinagar in June–July 1991. The Government of India condemned the attack on the Israeli tourists in Srinagar and declared that it was an attack on India itself and on its tourist industry. In parallel, the Gulf war and the Iraqi missile attacks against Israel were extensively covered by the Indian media. As a result, the media attention was mostly sympathetic and contrasted with the negative coverage of the US invasion of Iraq (Gerberg 2008: 114). The Indian media had traditionally depicted Israel as the aggressor in regional crises. As a result, after the Gulf war and the kidnapping situation, the Indian media started viewing Israel in a different and more favourable light. Some media outlets even began calling upon the government to consider the establishment of diplomatic relations (*Times of India*, 5 July 1991).

During the aforementioned Israeli tourists' abduction, the recently appointed Rao government facilitated the visit of the Deputy Director General for Asia of the Ministry of Foreign Affairs (MFA), Moshe Yegar, to New Delhi to conduct negotiations and to coordinate the hostage liberation efforts.[48] While this was a rescue mission, Yegar was reportedly told by the MFA to also inquire about any possible diplomatic opening while in New Delhi. Prior to Yegar's arrival, the MEA had, however, published a press release which stipulated that India's behaviour in regards to the incident in Kashmir was guided solely by humanitarian considerations; that Yegar's visit was of a 'consular' nature; that it would include no diplomatic discussions; and finally that there would be no change in India's policy towards Israel. In New Delhi, Yegar was only allowed to meet with the director of the consular branch of the MEA (Brilliant 2003).

Nevertheless, Yegar was also able to meet with senior Indian officials through the assistance of the academic and politician M. L. Sondhi.[49] While negotiations were conducted simultaneously in New Delhi and Washington, as well as at the UN headquarters in New York and Geneva to free the Israeli hostages, Yegar met with Ram Nath Kao, the former head of Research and Analysis Wing (RAW) and special security adviser to the prime minister, and with Naresh Chandra, the cabinet secretary.[50] Yegar also reportedly met with Minister of State for External Affairs Eduardo Faleiro.[51] While he did not publicity meet with senior ministers, Yegar saw important bureaucrats who were close and key advisers to the prime minister. After his trip, Yegar judged that the conservative nature of the professional staff of the MEA was a significant impediment to better bilateral relations. According to Yegar, the government, which was monitoring the improvement of Israel's relations with various countries and particularly with China, was too weak politically at that time to impose its views on the MEA bureaucracy. He equally considered that there was still resistance against normalization within the Congress leadership (Yegar 2010a, 2010b).

Immediate Steps towards Normalization

The combination of pulls and pressures at the international, regional, and domestic levels led to a renewed debate over India's Israel policy. As the Rao government was progressively asserting itself in the shaping of the foreign policy agenda, there were new signals that India would revise its Israel policy. In September 1991, the Minister of External Affairs Madhavsinh Solanki acknowledged the possibility of establishing bilateral relations with Israel but he did not give any specific date for the exchange of diplomatic missions. The MEA then indicated in October 1991 that Indian foreign policy towards Israel would be contingent upon substantial progress in the settlement of the West Asian problem (Gerberg 2008: 158). Solanki made a similar pledge to Egyptian officials when he visited Cairo (Dasgupta 1992). In November 1991, there was an important debate which took place on the issue of normalization in the upper house of Parliament (Rajya Sabha). On this occasion, various opposition members, led by Pramod Mahajan and Ram Jethmalani from the BJP, Subramaniam Swamy from the Janata Party, and Yashwant Sinha from the Samajwadi Janata Party, called for the establishment of complete diplomatic relations between the two countries.[52] There seemed to be an emerging consensus between some members of the INC and of the opposition on the need to change India's Israel policy.

On 21 November 1991, Isi J. Leibler, the Australian co-chairman of the governing board of the World Jewish Congress (WJC), headed a mission to New Delhi to meet with Narasimha Rao. The discussion concentrated on the possibility of establishing diplomatic relations and Rao promised a change in India's foreign policy regarding Israel, but without any specific commitment (Leibler 1991). Leibler later judged that, compared to Indira and Rajiv Gandhi, Rao was 'refreshingly pragmatic and an unorthodox politician' (*Times of India*, 23 November 1991). A few days later, Solanki again publicly stated in a parliamentary consultative committee that 'full diplomatic ties' were 'conditional upon genuine progress' in the West Asian peace process (*The Hindu*, 28 November 1991). The change in New Delhi's position was substantiated on 16 December 1991 when the Indian delegation voted for the revocation of UNGA Resolution 3379 which equated Zionism with racism. This was a drastic shift because India had originally co-sponsored the resolution in 1975. This change of position was criticized by some media, parties from the left, and some members of the INC as a betrayal of India's traditional policy towards the Arabs. The government, however, stood firm on its decision. In a following statement, India's permanent representative to the UN explained that the Indian decision was taken in the hope that it would facilitate the progress of the West Asian peace talks, and that India's position 'in no way reflected a dilution of its support for the Palestinian Cause' (*The Statesman*, 30 December 1991). Initially kept out, India hoped to play a greater role in the peace process as it modified its position towards Israel in multilateral institutions. The foundations of the previous policy compromise of 1974 were progressively being diluted. While the condition of acknowledging the PLO as an equal partner in peace negotiations was now fulfilled, the requirement of vacating the territories occupied since 1967 was not. This did not keep the Indian government from taking gradual steps to adjust its policy in tune with the new realities in West Asia.

In December 1991, the Israeli Consul in Bombay, Giora Becher, was allowed for the first time to meet the head of the consular department of the MEA in Delhi. Two weeks later, Becher was informed he would now be authorized to directly interact with the head of the West Asian department of the MEA. In the second week of January 1992, the

Director General of the MFA, Joseph Hadass, who had previously travelled to Delhi and discussed with Narasimha Rao in 1988, met with the Deputy Chief of the Mission of the Indian Embassy, Lalit Mansingh, in Washington. Reportedly, Hadass made it clear to Mansingh that it was up for India to take the initiative of establishing diplomatic relations, especially if India wanted to play a constructive role in the West Asian peace process.[53] However, while these discussions were under way, the MEA made a declaration on 17 January that there was no change in India's policy towards Israel, and the MEA also reiterated India's support for the Palestinian cause (*Times of India*, 18 January 1992).

To prepare the ground for a policy change, Rao invited Yasser Arafat for an official visit to New Delhi (Dixit 1996: 309; Gupta 2013). The PLO's explicit support for Saddam Hussein's Iraq during the Gulf war had left the movement isolated and divided. Furthermore, the PLO was in open negotiations with the government of Israel after the Madrid Conference. Arafat's visit was an opportunity for the Indian leadership to gauge his reaction and to build a political and domestic consensus behind the decision to normalize relations. During the discussions, Rao and his government directly asked Arafat about the Madrid Conference and his confidential discussions with the Israelis, which had the backing of the US, the USSR, and various Arab countries. Arafat told Rao there was a likelihood of official relations being established between the PLO and Israel in a period of six to eight months. He also expressed his conviction that India's participation in the peace process was necessary (*Foreign Affair Record*, 38:1, 20 January 1992). Since the PLO was itself negotiating with Israel and was considering the establishment of diplomatic relations, Arafat could not oppose India's intention to normalize its own relations with Tel Aviv. Arafat implicitly endorsed the pending Indian decision when he publicly said in Delhi that the 'exchange of ambassadors and recognition are acts of sovereignty on which I cannot interfere' (*The Indian Express*, 20 January 1992). The Rao government could now use this approval from the PLO to begin the negotiations regarding normalization.

The exact developments of the following 10 days which led to the final decision to change India's Israel policy cannot be ascertained for sure. The Indian and Israeli perspectives on the following days differ slightly. A detailed description appears in the memoirs of Foreign Secretary J. N. Dixit, who was directly involved in the decision-making process in the Rao government (Dixit 1996: 309–12). On the Israeli side are the first-hand accounts of Moshe Yegar (who was in regular contact with Giora Becher, the Israeli consul) and of Itzhak Gerberg who would become the new consul in Bombay in July 1992 (Gerberg 2008; Yegar 2010a, 2010b). While Dixit argued that there was a strong consensus for change early on, the story coming from the Israeli diplomats is one of a divided and reluctant Indian government which wanted above all to be included in the ongoing West Asian peace process. According to the accounts of the Israeli diplomats, the Indian government originally tried to find an intermediate solution which fell just short of full normalization. Eventually India modified its position when it became clear that Israel would not accept any other type of diplomatic arrangement other than the establishment of full diplomatic relations.

On 22 January, Consul Giora Becher was invited to Delhi for a late night meeting with Indian Foreign Secretary J. N. Dixit. It was an unprecedented meeting during which Becher was directly told that it was India's intention to bring about an improvement of its relations with Israel in the near future (Yegar 2010a). At this stage, it had not yet been decided if Israel would be allowed to open a consulate general in New Delhi as a first step, or if full diplomatic relations would be directly established. In response, Becher maintained the official position that Israel was solely interested in full-fledged diplomatic relations and that only normalization would allow India to participate in the working groups at the West Asian peace conference to be held in Moscow.[54] Statements from Moshe Yegar and the Minister of Foreign Affairs David Levy respectively on 23 January and 26 January confirmed that Indian participation in the West Asian peace process was conditional on the establishment of relations with Israel.[55] Given the rigid Israeli stance and the imminent Moscow multilateral talks, the Indian government understood that a drastic policy change was necessary.

According to Dixit, the timing of the establishment of diplomatic relations was discussed between senior cabinet members on 23 January 1992. Dixit said that only one minister opposed the change. The Human Resources Minister and Deputy Prime Minister, Arjun Singh, was concerned that normalization would affect Muslim support for the INC and that it could be interpreted as a departure from the 'Nehruvian' framework of India's foreign policy (Dixit 1996: 311). The discussion also happened only one day after Arafat's visit to New Delhi and Prime Minister Rao concluded the discussion 'by advancing the clinching argument that Arafat himself was supportive of India's decisions to open up contacts with Israel' (Dixit 1996: 312). The implicit approval of the PLO seemed to have legitimized the government's aspiration to change the policy.

Key events in the next few days accelerated the decision to normalize. On 24 January, the PRC and Israel established diplomatic relations.[56] On 28–29 January, the third round of the West Asian peace talks started in Moscow without India. It seemed that the MEA did not like the idea of being kept out of the negotiations, especially when the PRC, Russia, the US, and West Asian states like Syria and Jordan were present. According to Yegar, India suggested a compromise solution. Dixit reportedly suggested to Consul Becher that Israel could allow India to join the peace process as a first immediate step. During the following three months, the Indian government would mollify the remaining opposition to normalization, which was still prevalent within the INC, and then establish full diplomatic relations with Tel Aviv. Yegar told Becher to reject the proposal and to uphold the official line that normalization was a prerequisite for any participation (Yegar 2010b).

The next day, on 29 January, Dixit called Becher to announce that India intended to elevate the level of relations between the two countries to that of embassies. Becher asked for a minor postponement of the announcement in order to inform the Minister of Foreign Affairs David Levy and the Director General of the ministry Hadass, who were both at the peace talks in Moscow (Hadass 2002). Consequently, the establishment of full diplomatic relations and of the opening of embassies between India and Israel was publicized simultaneously in New Delhi, Moscow, and Jerusalem (Yegar 2010b). The statement was made in New Delhi by Dixit at a special press conference just hours before Rao was to take off to New York for a UNSC meeting (Gargan 1992). Dixit reportedly took the decision to publicly and personally announce the normalization of relations without Rao's approval.[57] On 12 February 1992, Israel's MFA notified the MEA that its consul in Bombay, Becher, had temporarily been appointed to Israel's embassy in New Delhi. In March 1992, the provisional office of the Israeli embassy in New Delhi was opened at the Meridian Hotel. In July 1992, a new consul, Itzhak Gerberg, arrived in India. Finally, in November 1992, the first nominated Israeli ambassador, Ephraim Duek, presented his credentials to the president to India. Forty-two years after India had recognized Israel, both countries had established full diplomatic relations.

The Role of the New Orthodoxy: The Rao Government's Rationale for Normalization

The decision to establish diplomatic relations on 29 January 1992 was not just the result of a series of shocks and structural changes. The shocks created a window of opportunity for policy entrepreneurs to promote new ideas. In his memoirs, Foreign Secretary Dixit identified three important developments which pushed the Indian government's decision to reassess its Israel policy: the Gulf war of 1991, the general attitude of the Arab states towards the problem of Kashmir (notably at the OIC), and the conclusion of a peace agreement between the PLO and Israel (Dixit 1996: 309–12). To these cited shocks, I would add the effects of the end of the Cold War. However, the complete causal mechanism and process of change must also look at the debate between the partisans of an alternative course of action—the new orthodoxy—and the partisans of the status quo—the old orthodoxy—to offer foreign policy prescriptions. The events of 1990–2 triggered a new debate about the benefits/costs of the existing policy vis-à-vis Israel. In fact, Foreign Secretary Dixit explained that the change in relations with Israel was a calibrated move 'after a very careful assessment of our national interests'.[58] But why did the policy change take the direction of normalization in 1992? Why did normalization only happen in 1992 and not in 1967? It is important to identify the rationale and arguments advanced by the new orthodoxy to understand the nature and direction of policy change.

One of the arguments advanced by the new orthodoxy to promote an engagement of Israel was the possibility of improved economic relations with the US. The economic support of the US became imperative after the economic crisis of 1991. In fact, the success of the Rao government's economic strategy based on market reforms depended on the investment and technological assistance from Western countries, and especially the US (Bhagwati 1993). India's economic recovery was also conditional upon receiving massive aid from the IMF and the World Bank where the US vote and influence were decisive. Washington had been pressuring New Delhi to adjust its Israel policy since 1948 with little success (except for the decision to recognize Israel in 1950). US influence on India's Israel policy had gradually increased in the 1980s.

As the prime minister, Rajiv Gandhi first realized the influence of pro-Israel organizations and of specific personalities in Congress like

Stephen Solarz on US policy towards South Asia. This perception motivated Rajiv Gandhi's meeting with Solarz and with representatives of these various organizations in 1988. As minister of external affairs at the time, Rao had been directly involved in these discussions and became himself conscious that establishing relations with Israel was a precondition to the improvement of Indo-US relations. In his project to open up the Indian economy to foreign investors, the lack of relations with Israel precluded a better understanding with Western economies, and especially with the US. Framed under this new light, the maintenance of the no-relationship-with-Israel policy implied painful costs for the Indian economy. Consequently, India first joined the US-backed move to revoke the UNGA Resolution 3379 equating Zionism with racism in December 1991. Symbolically, the establishment of diplomatic relations with Israel was announced on the eve of a visit of Narasimha Rao to the UN in New York where he would meet with US President George H. W. Bush. Following the announcement, Congressman Stephen Solarz also issued a press release welcoming the new diplomatic development (Gerberg 2008: 336).

Furthermore, the Rao government argued that Israel was an interesting partner in the context of India's economic liberalization and its opening to investments from abroad. The PSP and the Swatantra Party had already emphasized Israel's comparative advantages in certain fields of interest to India such as agriculture, telecommunications, electronics, and medical equipment. But the Government of India officially prohibited the government sector in India from having direct trade relations with Israel. Prior to 1992, the business community and the private sector in India had not exerted any significant political pressure on the Indian government to change its foreign and trade policies towards Israel. The meeting between the Minister of Commerce and Law Subramaniam Swamy and his Israeli counterpart at a conference in Belgium in 1991 was not the result of pressure from the Indian private sector but the consequence of Swamy's personal support of Israel. As a result, before the establishment of diplomatic relations between the two countries, the monetary value of the trade between India and Israel was only of US$ 129 million (Feiler 2012). The trade mostly concentrated on the diamond and chemical industries. Businessmen like the Hinduja brothers had, for instance, maintained business relations with Israeli companies through third countries (Gerberg 1996). Prior to normalization, in October 1991, India allowed the Israeli trade attaché in Singapore, Samuel Offri, to visit India in his official capacity and with a working visa to discuss trade prospects between the two countries (Gerberg 2008: 169). Dixit directly recognized the importance of the economic factor in India's decision to establish diplomatic relations with Israel in 1992. He referred to the 'prospect of beneficial economic and technological equations' in motivating the diplomatic move (*The Indian Express*, 11 December 1997). He added that the Israelis had been interested in establishing economic relations and were willing to invest and to initiate scientific and technological collaboration with India. Dixit believed Israel's agricultural experience in dry farming, desert irrigation, agro-industries, and agricultural cooperatives would be valuable to India (Dixit 1996: 312). Consequently, the prospect of economic and agricultural cooperation played an important role in the Rao government's push for normalization.

Prime Minister Rao and Foreign Secretary Dixit also wanted to change India's policy vis-à-vis the Arab–Muslim countries after the recent OIC votes on the Kashmir issue. Just like in 1967, there was a realization that India's largely pro-Arab and especially pro-PLO stance had not been adequately reciprocated by the Arab countries. India had not received any worthwhile diplomatic backing in its own crises, especially on the Kashmir dispute. Until the early 1990s, India had made sure that Iraq and Iran would keep the Kashmir question off the OIC agenda. By 1990, however, the Arab and Muslim countries firmly stood by Pakistan. At the OIC, Arab countries expressed their concerns over the insurrection and the human rights violations in Kashmir. India reacted very strongly against what it considered to be a direct interference in its domestic affairs. Members of the Indian Parliament expressed concern over the resolutions supported by many Arab states that were traditionally considered to be supporters of India (Noorani 1994). By criticizing India's management of the Kashmir insurrection, the OIC gave an incentive for India to reassess its relations with Arab states and with Israel. However, this was not the first time that the lack of reciprocity in Indo-Arab relations had been criticized. What changed in 1992?

There was a growing perception within the Government of India that if Arab nations, such as Egypt and Jordan, had been able to maintain their traditional ties with the Palestinians intact, while building a new relationship with Israel, there was no reason for India not to take a similar route. The international and regional reputation of Israel had improved after the Gulf war and the start of the West Asian peace process. The divisions in the Arab world over Israel and the PLO's isolation were an opportunity for the Rao government to change its policy. The invitation to Arafat to come to New Delhi in January 1992 was not coincidental given the existing debate within the Rao cabinet over Israel. It was an indirect way to gauge Arafat's reaction to a possible decision on normalization. Dixit had also verified through embassies in the Gulf that Israel–PLO contacts had the endorsement of important Arab countries such as Saudi Arabia, the UAE, and Kuwait (Dixit 1996: 309–12).

In addition, contrary to the debate in 1967–74, there was this time a common ground between pre-eminent members of the government and the opposition. The main opposition parties kept a constant pressure on the government to establish diplomatic relations with Israel. Pramod Mahajan from the BJP pointed out that although both China and Pakistan had occupied large parts of Indian territory, India had maintained diplomatic links with them (*The Statesman*, 26 November 1991). He was supported in Parliament by Subramaniam Swamy from the Janata Party, and by Yashwant Sinha from the Samajwadi Janata Party who argued that India had not been able to get the support of Arab countries during critical times (*Financial Express*, 28 November 1991). The domestic Muslim factor also seemed to be less of an issue in the early 1990s. The Hindu–Muslim tensions in Indian domestic politics in the late 1980s concentrated all the attention. The INC was not too concerned with the loss of Muslim electoral support to the Hindu nationalist BJP. Rao was also at the head of a minority government which did not feel wedded to traditional voting blocs. Normalization was therefore a calculated political risk which paid off as there were no serious objections from the domestic Muslim community (Cohen 2001: 247–8).

By late 1991, the Indian government realized that diplomatic relations with Israel could generate new rules for its interactions with the Muslim world. For the Rao government, normalization served as a calibrated signal to the Arab–Muslim states that New Delhi's support could not be taken for granted. Dixit explained that 'close relations with Israel' served to 'counter moves by those Muslim countries, which were inclined to act against Indian interests if instigated by Pakistan' (Dixit 1996: 312). India's frustration with the Arab countries was also explicitly articulated by Dixit when he conducted a briefing for Arab ambassadors in New Delhi. Dixit explained that 'there was no change in India's politics on the Palestinian question', nor on the importance India attached to 'nurturing close friendship with Arab countries'. Nevertheless, Dixit added that India 'had not received any reciprocity on the Kashmir issue despite [its] long-standing support to several Islamic countries' (Dixit 1996: 312). Dixit also argued that 'Arab countries themselves had close relations with the US despite its closeness to Israel', and there was no logical reason for them to sanction India for getting closer to Israel (*The Indian Express*, 11 December 1997). Again, in an interview a week after normalization, Dixit criticized the continuous lack of Arab support, especially during the East Pakistan crisis of 1971.[59]

Another argument invoked by advocates of normalization was the potential military assistance that India could receive from Israel. The absence of diplomatic ties had not inhibited India from seeking Israeli assistance. There had already been contacts during military crises such as the Sino-Indian conflict in 1962 and the Indo-Pakistani wars in 1965 and 1971. On these occasions, India received limited military imports from Israel, such as mortar ammunition. The operational impact of these weapons was marginal during the conflicts but signalled possible complementary ties. Israel had also sent a delegation to India after the 1962 conflict to establish the first contacts between the two militaries. In addition, the Indian military had always looked with attention and admiration at the Israeli experience in military operations in its various conflicts with the Arab states.[60] Israel's military adventures and successes, such as the bombing of the Osiraq nuclear reactor near Baghdad in 1981 and the destruction of Syrian MiGs over Lebanon the following year, had been closely analysed by the Indian security establishment. As a result, even when the political leadership was adopting hostile policies towards Israel, a different opinion prevailed in the Indian military and security establishment. Both the military and RAW had a professional appreciation of Israel's military expertise and had therefore a stake in the improvement in bilateral relations. However, these actors had traditionally not been included in India's foreign policy decision-making.

Why did the input of the military/security establishment play a more significant role in 1991–2 than previously? In his memoirs, Dixit stated that the need for weapons was one of the motives for the change in India's Israel policy, especially since Israel had developed expertise in improving the weapons systems of Soviet origin which were still predominantly used by the Indian army (Dixit 1996: 310). There were two important lessons from the Gulf war for the Indian military and Indian politicians (Thakur 1994: 176). First, the conflict had demonstrated the superiority of American weapons over Soviet equipment. It had also raised concerns about India's military ability to face adversaries who had access to US weapons and technology, like Pakistan (Thomas 1993). Second, the USSR finally decided to side with the US-led coalition against Iraq.[61] One of the main advantages of the Soviet Union as a defence supplier was its reliability, especially during military crises. Following the Gulf war, there were new concerns that the USSR might no longer be dependable in case of a future conflict. Dixit also attached a great deal of importance to the Israeli experience in counter-terrorism since his stint as ambassador to Colombo in 1987. Dixit considered that 'Israel's knowledge and experience in countering terrorism would be of immediate relevance to India and dealing with secessionist movements in different parts of the country' (Dixit 1996: 310). The role of the Rao government and of Dixit in linking these security problems and the gains from potential cooperation with Israel was decisive. They argued that collaboration in the military–defence field was a key reason for the establishment of diplomatic relations with Israel.

Why Change Happened in 1992

Forty-two years after it recognized Israel, India finally exchanged diplomatic missions with the Jewish state on 29 January 1992. There had been other periods of policy flux when the establishment of diplomatic relations had been discussed. In the 1950s, there had been high-level and concrete negotiations between Nehru and Israeli diplomats to prepare the opening of embassies. Despite political willingness from both sides, these initial contacts did not survive the Suez crisis of 1956. There was another window of opportunity for change in 1967 when India's pro-Arab policy was severely criticized at home. At the time, the lack of diplomatic reciprocity led the Indian government to reassess its policy. However, there was no agreement on the need to engage Israel at that time.

Some of the arguments presented by the new orthodoxy in 1992 were not new. The perception of a lack of reciprocity in diplomatic support with the Arab states on the Kashmir dispute had been a constant issue. However, the new orthodoxy, which emerged under Rajiv Gandhi, was different for three reasons. First, the initiative for change materialized this time from within the traditionally conservative institutions which had resisted any amendment to the no-relationship policy: the INC and the MEA. In previous policy debates, the pressure from change had come from outside. In 1967, for instance, the pressure for change came from the parliamentary opposition. This time, Prime Minister Narasimha Rao, who had been involved in previous discussions with Israel, was convinced of the need to reform India's West Asia policy. Similarly, J. N. Dixit, who was foreign secretary, the most senior career diplomat position in the MEA, was equally in favour of policy change. There was also a growing consensus between the opposition parties and the ruling government on the new policy direction.

Second, advocates for change effectively accommodated concerns from the remaining old orthodoxy. The new orthodoxy, for instance, highlighted the existing negotiations between Arab states and Israel, and also worked on getting the blessings from Yasser Arafat and the PLO for the policy change. Furthermore, the Rao government also argued that it did not risk losing Arab–Muslim support since it had never been forthcoming when it was truly needed. Just like Nehru in September 1950 when he decided to recognize Israel, the Rao government wanted to signal its disappointment with the Arabs' pro-Pakistan bias in multilateral fora. Dixit also directly replied to Arjun Singh's concerns about a possible departure from the Nehruvian framework of traditional Indian foreign policy, by saying that 'there would be no departure from the Nehruvian framework, because Panditji himself had given formal recognition to Israel' in 1950.[62] There was under the Rao government a clear shift from a preoccupation with domestic repercussions to concerns with the external consequences of maintaining the non-recognition policy.

Third, the new orthodoxy also registered the support of new actors. For the first time, the new orthodoxy not only criticized the failures of the existing pro-Arab policy, but also explicitly emphasized the benefits of collaboration with Israel. The new orthodoxy offered clear policy alternatives which redefined the policy debate over Israel and which attracted previously uninvolved actors. The new orthodoxy had an incentive to enlarge the dimensions of the debate in order to mobilize a greater number of interests and supporters on the side of policy change. The introduction and presentation of replacement ideas with a larger receptive audience made the policy change possible. According to the government, India could gain on the military and economic fronts by engaging Israel. Consequently, there were economic interests which encouraged a rapprochement with Israel because it was presented as a precondition for better economic and trade relations with the US. Similarly, the military and security establishment, which was pressing for alternatives to Soviet military supplies, equally supported increased cooperation with Israel.

The decision to establish diplomatic relations with Israel in 1992 was a major foreign policy change. However, the 1992 decision did not pave the way for a smooth and substantial bilateral partnership at the onset. The decision was still strongly debated and contested at the domestic level. Normalization was seen by many officials within the MEA as premature and in conflict with the traditional pro-Arab foreign policy. There was still an opposition by some MEA officials despite the 1992 decision.[63] The literature has concentrated only on the sudden and abrupt changes and the decision to normalize in 1992 but has rarely analysed the immediate post-normalization years, when the Indian government was prudent about publicly discussing its new Israel policy. Trade and defence ties were also insignificant until the late 1990s. The next chapter will look at the often ignored consolidation phase of India's new Israel policy during the last decade and how different governments have managed the apparent contradictions between engaging Israel in important economic and defence deals while maintaining a pro-Palestine rhetoric in parallel.

Notes

1. During the electoral campaign, Gandhi disclosed the Moshe Dayan visit to question the Janata government's commitment to the Palestinian cause. Indira Gandhi used the Israel–Palestine issue to sway the Muslim vote and to expose the divisions within the Janata coalition over its Israel policy. She was successful as an important leader of the Janata Party, Jagjivan Ram, expressed his surprise about the visit and distanced himself from Moraji Desai.

2. For more details about the motivations behind and the developments of the USSR's invasion of Afghanistan in December 1979, see Feifer (2009).

3. Statement of Minister of External Affairs Narasimha Rao, India (*Lok Sabha Debates* 7:3, 26 March 1980, pp. 313–4).

4. *Hindustan Times*, 29 March 1980. Arafat was again invited to New Delhi in May 1982.

5. The PNC was the Palestinian parliament in exile. See Kumaraswamy (2010: 178–9).

6. Interestingly, there were some media reports that India had been offered by Israel the possibility of undertaking a similar Osiraq-style attack against the Pakistan nuclear reactor at Kahuta in 1981 and again in 1985. Israel said it had satellite imagery of the reactor and argued it could destroy the facility. See Kumaraswamy (2010: 229); Perkovich (1999: 240–1); Ward (1992: 127); Thakur (1994: 292); Interview with Air Commodore Jasjit Singh in New Delhi, 11 October 2011. The claim was officially denied by a government spokesman on 29 July 1981. See *Foreign Affairs Record* 27(1981): 203.

7. The consul had been interviewed by the Bombay-based newspaper *Sunday Observer*. See the interview in *Sunday Observer*, 27 June 1982.

8. The Indian National Security Guards (NSG), the elite commando unit responsible for protection of very important persons (VIPs), which had been created in 1984 following the assassination of Indira Gandhi, developed limited cooperation, mostly in the form of training courses, with the Israeli Security Service (SHABAK); see Kumaraswamy (1998: 6, 18).

9. For more details on the first Intifada, read Alimi (2007).

10. The abrupt dismissal of foreign secretary A. P. Venkateswaran was openly criticized by the Indian Foreign Service (IFS) in 1987. See Bandyopadhyaya (1970: 270–1).

11. Interview with Ronen Sen, New Delhi, 16 July 2012.

12. In December 1984, Congress won 80 per cent of the Lok Sabha seats and 49 per cent of the popular vote. Neither Nehru and nor Indira Gandhi ever reached such a large majority during their terms in office. See *Statistical Report on General Elections*, vol. 1, 1985.

13. Quotes from *Le Monde* in *Jewish Telegraphic Agency*, 'India's President Attends Ceremony for Centenary of Synagogue in Bombay', 6 June 1985.

14. His grandfather, Nehru, would also regularly meet with pro-Israel political leaders in the US.

15. The Knesset Eliyahoo Synagogue was built in 1884 by Jacob Sasson to commemorate the name of Elias David Sasson who fled to India from Iraq to escape persecution.

16. *Jewish Telegraphic Agency*, 'India's President Attends Ceremony for Centenary of Synagogue in Bombay', 6 June 1985.

17. Stephen J. Solarz was a US Congressional representative from New York. In the 1980s, he chaired the Asian and Pacific Affairs Subcommittee of the House Foreign Affairs Committee. In the House, Solarz represented a district that had one of the country's largest Jewish populations and he had been a long-time supporter of Israel. He also had an interest in India, and was instrumental in setting up the South Asia Bureau in the department of state. See Gerberg (2008: 246); 'Solarz, A Friend of India, Dies', *Times of India*, 1 December 2012.

18. However, the Israeli representation was not upgraded back to its pre-1982 position of consulate.

19. The MEA had apparently been one of the main obstacles to the replacement. See Kumaraswamy (2010: 227).

20. Subramaniam had notably been the minister of agriculture in 1966 when India refused an Israeli offer of fertilizers.

21. Although Israeli visitors had to come in their individual capacity and not as official representatives of Israel.

22. According to Kumaraswamy, the decision to restore the pre-1982 position of consul had already been made prior to the meeting in New York. See Kumaraswamy (2010: 228). This seems also to correspond with the Israeli Minister of Foreign Affairs Shimon Peres's statement in June 1988 that the upgrade was supposed to have happened before but had been delayed. See *Los Angeles Times*, 10 June 1988.

23. However, these efforts were not successful in the early 1980s as Pakistan had explicitly sided with Iran during the first Gulf war.

24. Somaratna (1989, 1993); Dixit (1998a: 327). For more details on the Sri Lankan conflict and on the Indian intervention, see Devotta (2004).

25. See 'Exchange of Letters between the Prime Minister of India and the President of Sri Lanka', 29 July 1987, in *Indo-Sri Lanka Agreement to Establish Peace and Normalcy in Sri Lanka*, available at http://www.satp.org/satporgtp/countries/shrilanka/document/papers/indo_srilanks_agreement.htm (accessed on 25 March 2013).

26. While in Colombo, Dixit himself witnessed the benefits of military and intelligence cooperation with Israel. The Sri Lankan experience probably influenced his future thinking about normalization as foreign secretary in 1991–2.

27. In March 1986, an arms deal was signed between the Government of India and the Swedish arms company Bofors for the supply of Howitzer field guns. In April 1987, media reports in Sweden alleged that Bofors had paid bribes to important INC politicians, including Rajiv Gandhi. See 'Chronology of the Bofors Scandal', *DNA*, 27 February 2007.

28. The Janata Dal was an Indian political party which was formed through the merger of Janata Party factions which had been in power in 1977. The new party was created by V. P. Singh on 11 October 1988.

29. An important part of the crude oil supplied by the USSR to India in exchange for Indian goods actually came from Iraq. Iraq was exporting the oil in exchange for military hardware. The deal was particularly advantageous for India because New Delhi paid the Soviets for Iraqi oil in rupees. See Boquerat (2001).

30. This was the figure mentioned by Prime Minister V. P. Singh to the Lok Sabha on 20 September 1990, in Singh (1993: 179).

31. 'Inder Kumar Gujral Dead, but His Doctrine Still Relevant', *The Economic Times*, 1 December 2012.

32. By contrast, just before the Iraqi invasion, the Kuwaiti government decided to support Pakistan on the Kashmir issue. See Ward (1992: 141).

33. This was the split faction from the Janata Dal.

34. The INC allowed the Shekhar government to hold charge while it prepared for the elections to be held in the summer of 1991.

35. Shekhar's statement was criticized by the INC as well as by Arab diplomats in New Delhi. See Kapur (1994: 201); Gerberg (2008: 99).

36. Swamy had already expressed his opinion on the need to establish diplomatic relations in an article in 1982, 'The Secret Friendship Between India and Israel' (Swamy 1982).

37. Interview with Subramaniam Swamy, 21 October 2011, New Delhi.

38. For a discussion of this transformative period for India's foreign policy, read Muni (1991); Mohan (2005); Raj Nayar and Paul (2003). For a more specific argument about the role of international and domestic factors in shaping India's new Israel policy, see Blarel (2009).

39. The decision of the USSR to ultimately vote alongside the US in the UNSC against the Iraqi invasion demonstrated that Moscow was no longer a diplomatic and political alternative to US intervention in the region.

40. Lalit Mansingh, who was deputy chief of mission at the Indian embassy in the US in 1991, confirmed he had discussed with Israeli diplomats in Washington about this pre-condition for an Indian participation in regional peace conferences. Interview with Ambassador Lalit Mansingh, 12 October 2011, New Delhi.

41. Political relations between the two countries had remained limited after the 1973 Arab–Israeli war as the Soviet Union had provided political and military support to Syria and Egypt.

42. For more on the economic crisis, read Panagariya (2010: 95–109).

43. 'Economic Crisis Forcing Once Self-Reliant India to Seek Aid', *New York Times*, 29 June 1991.

44. The Simla Agreement stipulated that the Kashmir dispute should be resolved through bilateral negotiations and not through any third-party interventions or within multilateral fora. See 'Simla Agreement, 2 July, 1972' in Bilateral/Multilateral Documents, Ministry of External Affairs, available at http://www.mea.gov.in/bilateral-documents.htm?dtl/5541/Simla+Agreement (accessed on 25 March 2013).

45. The report cited the firing on the funeral procession of the Mirwaiz Maulvi Farooq, *Foreign Affairs Record* 36, 13–19 August 1990, 21296.

46. In fact, only Iraq questioned the inclusion of the Kashmir issue in the agenda but was overruled by the rest of the Conference members. See Baba (2008).

47. Final communiqué of the twentieth Islamic Conference of Foreign Ministers (Istanbul), 4–8 August 1991, ICFM/20-91/FC/FINAL.

48. Allegedly, Yegar was also under constant surveillance. See Brilliant (2003); Yegar, quoted in Gerberg (2008: 115); Yegar (2010a, 2010b).

49. M. L. Sondhi was an academic at Jawaharlal Nehru University (JNU) and a former BJS member who had been a long-time supporter of normalization of relations with Israel, notably during the 1967 debate in Parliament. At the beginning of the 1960s, Professor Sondhi had visited Israel as a guest of the MFA. As a young and junior official in the Asian department of the ministry at that time, Yegar was assigned to accompany and to schedule meetings with him. Sondhi was also the convener of the Sanskrit Hebrew Society in Delhi. In 1991, Sondhi brought to Prime Minister Rao's attention the existence of the letter of Franz Baermann Steiner to Mahatma Gandhi in 1946. Allegedly, the Steiner letter played a role in the shift of Gandhi's position about the legitimacy of Zionist claims. See *The Statesman*, 19 September 1991. For a discussion on the role of M. L. Sondhi, see Brilliant (2003); Nanda (2008: xxxi); Yegar (2010a).

50. The cabinet secretary is the most senior civil servant in the Government of India and is a special adviser to the prime minister. Chandra also became Indian ambassador to the US in 1996. The meeting was reportedly held at midnight to not attract any attention; Brilliant (2003); Yegar (2010a, 2010b).

51. See Kumaraswamy (2010: 236).

52. In fact, the BJP convention of October 1991 had introduced a clause calling for full relations with Israel. See Gerberg (2008: 141).

53. Interview with Ambassador Lalit Mansingh, 12 October 2011, New Delhi.

54. This was the message that Joseph Hadass had passed on to Lalit Mansingh in Washington. Levy reportedly also refused India's participation in the Moscow multilateral negotiations in January 1992.

55. Moshe Yegar was visiting Beijing to attend the ceremony in celebration of the establishment of diplomatic relations with China. He was asked about an Indian participation in the peace process. David Levy was also asked if India would participate in the Moscow multilateral talks. Levy also said that Delhi 'must make up for lost time' in Indo-Israeli relations. *Times of India*, 25 January 1992; Yegar (2010) 'The Normalization of Relations Between India and Israel: II', *Indian Defence Review*.

56. However, J. N. Dixit later argued that the Chinese move did not have an immediate influence on India's ultimate decision. See *Hindustan Times*, 31 January 1992.

57. Kumaraswamy (2010: 238); Interview with Inder Malhotra, 19 July 2012, New Delhi.

58. Quoted in *The Statesman*, 30 December 1991.

59. Interview to *The Week*, 9 February 1992.

60. Interview with various Indian military officials in fall 2011 and summer 2012.

61. Before the Iraqi invasion of Kuwait, the USSR and Iraq had a strong strategic partnership. The USSR had also actively supported Iraq in its war with Iran. See Smolansky (1991).

62. Panditji was an honorific reference to Pandit Jawaharlal Nehru. See Dixit (1996: 310).

63. Interview with Mani Shankar Aiyar, 29 November 2011, New Delhi.

5   From Prudent Rapprochement to Strategic Partnership?

The Consolidation of India's New Israel Policy (1992–2012)

The sky is the limit for Indo-Israeli cooperation, but we have a lot of catching up to do and must eliminate all inhibitions of the past.
—Ephraim Duek (first Israeli ambassador-designate to India)[1]

The secret part of Indo-Israel defence ties will remain a secret.
—Mark Sofer (Israeli ambassador to India, 2008–11)
(Sirohi 2008a)

THE DECISION TAKEN ON 29 January 1992 to establish diplomatic relations was labelled as a 'paradigm shift' in Indo-Israeli relations (Aaron 2003; Berman 2002; Gerberg 2008; Inbar 2004; Inbar and Ningthoujam 2012; Kandel 2009; Kumaraswamy 2010; Naaz 2005; Nair 2004; Pant 2004). The normalization seemed to have paved the way for a significant increase in the volume of bilateral trade from $200 million in 1992 to $6 billion today.[2] Normalization also permitted the development of an unexploited and complementary military partnership. The limited weapons acquisitions during the crises of 1962, 1965, and 1971 had demonstrated a potential for further cooperation. Two decades later, Israel had become one of India's main arms suppliers (*The Economic Times* 2012). Some analysts have equally cited India's new engagement with Israel as an illustration of India's more pragmatic post–Cold War foreign policy (Cohen 2001; Mohan 2005; Raj Nayar and Paul 2003). Likewise, there has been an impression when looking at studies written over the last decade that the sudden change in India's Israel policy after January

1992 had been complete and unchallenged (Berman 2002; Inbar 2004; Kumaraswamy 2010). As a result, the common wisdom on India's Israel policy is that India suddenly moved from an ideological to a pragmatic approach to the issue. The problem is that this one-dimensional narrative undermines other changes in the relationship that happened after 1992 and overlooks the real difficulties in entrenching the new foreign policy orientation until the late 1990s.

It was discussed earlier that the decision to normalize ties with Israel was not the result of a pre-planned design. Although there were actors who had been exhorting for a policy change, their efforts only succeeded because of a combination of favourable conditions at the international, regional, and domestic levels. In spite of these propitious circumstances, the government also carefully worked to get the support of a majority of relevant players to accept the foreign policy change. The Rao government apparently attempted various other intermediary solutions before finally accepting to completely reverse the existing policy when it considered it had no other alternatives. This gradual and cautious approach was deemed necessary because normalization was contested. Most existing studies have also failed to account for the lack of real progress in bilateral relations until the late 1990s when trade figures and military exchanges drastically increased.[3] The literature has also not effectively explained how the Indian government has managed to develop its relations with Israel while also maintaining a strong pro-Palestinian stand in multilateral fora (Blarel 2011; Desai 2012; Rajiv 2011). As a result, the new Israel policy did not completely break with past positions. In this chapter, I demonstrate how the immediate post-1992 developments did not support the narrative of a sudden and uncontested improvement in Indo-Israeli relations.

If one expects most diplomatic activity to happen at the decision-maker's level, and to identify high-level political visits, highly publicized bilateral treaties, and joint statements between political leaders as the main indicators of the quality and stability of a partnership, the mostly secretive Indo-Israeli partnership would not be qualified as a substantial relationship (Tables 5.1 and 5.2). The day after the establishment of relations, Israel's Prime Minister Yitzhak Shamir invited Prime Minister Narasimha Rao to Israel to 'have an opportunity to discuss common matters for the first time in history' (*Asian Recorder*, 30 January 1992). Rao never reciprocated nor even officially acknowledged Shamir's offer to visit Israel. There were very few high-level visits. However, in 2000,

Table 5.1   Israeli Political Visits to India since 1992

Year	Nature of visit	Outcome
1993 (May)	Foreign Minister Shimon Peres	First visit by an Israeli foreign minister to India
		Met with external affairs, finance, agriculture, and commerce ministers
		Accompanied by chief executives from IAI, Elbit, and Elul Technologies
		Signed an economic MoU
		Discussions on terrorism and support for India's territorial integrity
1994 (April)	Deputy Foreign Minister Yossi Beilin	Met with Indian leaders and discussed the sale of UAVs
1996 (January)	Minister of Finance Avraham Shochat	Signed with Minister of Finance Manmohan Singh three agreements on avoidance of double taxation, customs cooperation, and bilateral investment protection
1996–7 (December–January)	President Ezer Weizmann leading a 24-member delegation	First head of the Jewish state to visit India
		Met with Indian President Shankar Dayal Sharma and Prime Minister H. D. Deve Gowda
		Offered Israel's expertise in fields of missiles technology and avionics to India, as well as assistance in upgrade of weapon systems
		Opened an agricultural demonstration farm in New Delhi
		During his visit, the two countries decided to exchange military attaches

(*Cont'd*)

Table 5.1 (*Cont'd*)

Year	Nature of visit	Outcome
2000 (August) and 2001 (January)	Minister for Regional Cooperation Shimon Peres	
2002 (January)	Deputy Prime Minister and Foreign Minister Shimon Peres	Met Defence Minister George Fernandes, External Affairs Minister Jaswant Singh, and Prime Minister Atal Behari Vajpayee
		Supported India in its dispute with Pakistan
2002 (February)	Minister for Environment Tzachi Haneqbi	Discussion of a MoU on environment
2003 (September)	Prime Minister Ariel Sharon with Deputy Prime Minister & Minister of Justice Joseph Lapid, Minister of Education Limor Livnat, and Minister of Agriculture Israel Katz	First visit by a ruling Israeli prime minister
		Joint statement of friendship and cooperation
		Signed six agreements covering the fields of environment; health; combating illicit trafficking of drugs; visa waivers for diplomatic, service, and official passport holders; education; and an exchange programme for cultural education
2003 (December)	Israel's Minister of Science & Technology Eliezer Sandberg	Signed a MoU with the Indian Space Research Organisation (ISRO) for the launch of the Israeli TAUVEX UV telescope on an Indian demonstrator Satellite GSAT-4
2004 (February)	Deputy Prime Minister and Foreign Minister Silvan Shalom	Accompanied by Israel's Supreme Court Chief Justice Aharon Barak
2004 (December)	Deputy Prime Minister and Minister of Industries, Trade, Employment, and Communications, Ehud Olmert	First high-level exchange since UPA government assumed power

(*Cont'd*)

Table 5.1 (Cont'd)

Year	Nature of visit	Outcome
	Accompanied by representatives from 50 Israeli companies	Met with External Affairs Minister Natwar Singh, Finance Minister Chidambaram, and five other ministers
		Objective to diversity relations beyond defence
		Two countries agreed to establish a joint study group (JSG) and signed an agreement with the ministry of finance to set up a mechanism guaranteeing Israeli investments
2006 (February)	National Security Advisor (NSA) Maj. Gen. (Retd) Giora Eiland	Held talks with his Indian counterpart M. K. Narayanan in context of framework of Indo-Israel National Security Council dialogue
2006 (December)	Deputy Prime Minister and Minister of Trade, Industry and Labour Eli Yishai	With a high-level business delegation
		Negotiated a preferential trade agreement eventually leading to a Comprehensive Economic Cooperation Agreement (CECA)
2007 (March)	Minister of Transport and Road Safety Shaul Mofaz	Explored the ways to enhance ties in areas such as civil aviation, railways, shipping, and road safety programmes
2007 (November)	Interior Minister Meir Sheetrit	Attended the second Asian Ministerial Conference on Disaster Risk Reduction
		Met Minister of External Affairs Pranab Mukherjee, Minister of Home Affairs Shivraj Patil, Panchayati Raj Minister Mani Shankar Aiyer

(Cont'd)

Table 5.1 (Cont'd)

Year	Nature of visit	Outcome
2008 (January)	Minister of Agriculture and Rural Development Shalom Simchon	Met with Union Agriculture Minister Sharad Pawar, Union Minister for Rural Development Dr Raghuvansh Prasad, Rajasthan Chief Minister Vasundhra Raje Scindia, Rajasthan Agriculture Minister Prabhu Lal Saini, Rajasthan Irrigation & Water Minister Prof. Sanwar Lal Jat
2010 (January)	Minister of Industry, Trade and Labour Binyamin Ben Eliezer	Joined by delegation of businesspeople from 25 companies
		Visit of the Chabad House in Mumbai
2011 (May)	Minister of Agriculture Orit Noked	Accompanied by a delegation of agro-business companies
		Met with her counterpart, Sharad Pawar
		Established a joint working team in order to finalize a bilateral agricultural action plan
2011 (September)	Minister of Tourism Stas Misezhnikov	Met with his counterpart Minister of Tourism Subodh Kant Sahai, and with Minister of Civil Aviation Vayalar Ravi
		Agreed on having follow-up discussions on aviation and establishing a steering committee on tourism
2011 (November)	Minister of Internal Security, Yitzhak Aharonovitz	Met with Minister for Home Affairs P. Chidambaram
2011 (December)	Minister of Finance Yuval Steinitz	Attended the Delhi Economic Conclave

(Cont'd)

Table 5.1 (Cont'd)

Year	Nature of visit	Outcome
		Met with Minister of Finance Pranab Mukherjee, Minister of Communication & IT Kapil Sibal. In addition, Deputy Chairman of Planning Commission Montek Singh Ahluwalia, and NSA Shivshankar Menon
		Offered to export natural gas to India
2012 (February)	Minister of Energy and Water Resources Uzi Landau	Discussed the prospect of Indian firms, including the state-run Oil and Natural Gas Corporation (ONGC), participating in the gas ventures
		Discussed the possibility of setting up a joint group in the energy sector
		Met with Minister for Petroleum S. Jaipal Reddy, Minister for Urban Development Kamal Nath, Minister for Rural Development Jairam Ramesh, Deputy Chairman of the Planning Commission Montek Singh Ahluwalia, Delhi Chief Minister Sheila Dikshit, and NSA Shiv Shankar Menon

Source: Information compiled from different sources, including the Indian embassy in Israel (http://www.indembassy.co.il), and various Indian and Israel newspapers.

India's Home Minister L. K. Advani and Minister of External Affairs Jaswant Singh visited Israel. In September 2003, Ariel Sharon became the first (and only) serving Israeli prime minister to visit India. According to some observers, this visit marked both a dramatic expansion in Indo-Israeli relations with the signing of multiple agreements, and the belated public recognition of what had until now been a discreet relationship

Table 5.2 Indian Political Visits (Cabinet-level and Minister of state) since 1992

Year	Nature of visit	Outcome
1993 (March)	Foreign Secretary J. N. Dixit	Discussed cooperation against terrorism
		Accompanied by Rakesh Sood, head of the disarmament division at the MEA
1994 (June)	Minister of Human Resource Development Arjun Singh	First bilateral agreement on periodic consultations
1996 (January)	Minister of Commerce P. Chidambaram	Discussed further areas of economic cooperation during the meeting of the Indo-Israel Joint Trade and Economic Committee
1998 (September)	Minister of Urban Affairs, Health and Welfare Ram Jethmalani	Met with housing minister of Israel and with directors of Disaster Management and Water Management of Israel
1998	NSA Brajesh Mishra	Made two trips to Israel (first as advisor at PMO than officially as NSA) to discuss expanded cooperation in the military and intelligence spheres
2000 (June)	Home Minister and Deputy Prime Minister L. K. Advani	First visit of a senior Indian minister since normalization
		Formalized intelligence-sharing and cooperation agreement in his meetings with MOSSAD chief and Israeli ministers
		Met with Israeli arms manufacturers
		Agreement to open Israeli intelligence offices in New Delhi
2000 (July)	External Affairs Minister Jaswant Singh	First visit by an Indian external affairs minister
		Set up joint commission at ministerial level for cooperation in combating terrorism in addition to Foreign Ministers Consultation Process

(Cont'd)

Table 5.2 (Cont'd)

Year	Nature of visit	Outcome
		Strategic discussions held every 6 months
		Purchase of Green Pine radar
2002 (January)	Minister for Communication & Parliamentary Affairs Pramod Mahajan	Created a JWG on information technology and electronics to promote bilateral trade in electronics and IT
2004 (January)	Minister of Commerce & Industry Arun Jaitly	Headed the Indian delegation to the Joint Economic Committee, which met in Israel
2005 (February)	Special Envoy of the Prime Minister to West Asia Chinmay Gharekhan	Met Vice-Prime Minister Shimon Peres and the Minister of Foreign Affairs Silvan Shalom, and also visited the PA
2005 (May)	Minister of State for Science and Technology and Minister of Earth Sciences Kapil Sibal	MoU on India–Israeli Research and Development Fund Initiative
2005 (September)	Minister for Housing and Urban Poverty Alleviation Kumari Selja	
2005 (November)	Minister of Agriculture Sharad Pawar	Represented India at the official memorial ceremony for late Prime Minister Yitzhak Rabin, marking the tenth anniversary of his assassination
		Exchanged ideas regarding the broadening and intensification of bilateral cooperation in agriculture, including in micro-irrigation and dairy farming
2005 (November)	Special Envoy of the Prime Minister to West Asia Chinmay Gharekhan	
2005 (November)	Minister of Commerce and Industry Kamal Nath	Established a joint study group (JSG) to boost bilateral trade from $2 billion to $5 billion by 2008

(Cont'd)

Table 5.2 (Cont'd)

Year	Nature of visit	Outcome
2006 (May)	Minister of Agriculture Sharad Pawar	Represented India at the Agritech 2006 exhibition
		Signed the Inter-Governmental three-year Work Plan on Agriculture Cooperation
2007 (August)	Minister of State for Industry Ashwani Kumar	Headed a high-level FICCI delegation
		Met with Israeli counterpart Eliyahu Yishai and Israeli President Shimon Peres
		Discussed a proposal for a free trade agreement (FTA) with India to boost burgeoning economic and bilateral ties
2007 (December)	Minister of State for Railways R. Velu	Came at the invitation of the Israeli government to cooperate for the installation of advanced simulators and radar systems for the rail network
2010 (February)	Minister of State for Commerce and Industry Jyotiradithya Scindia	Discussed an FTA with Israel's Minister for Trade, Industry and Labour Benjamin Ben-Eliezer
		Suggested the creation of a technology think tank with representation from both sides
2010 (March)	Minister of State for Science & Technology Prithviraj Chavan	Participated at the seventh round of India–Israel Joint Committee on Science and Technology
2011 (May–June)	Minister of State for Communications and IT Sachin Pilot	Met with Israeli Minister for Industry, Trade and Labour, and Minister for Communications
		Attended the Israeli High-Tech Industry's Annual Conference
2012	Minister of External Affairs S. M. Krishna	Met with President Peres, Prime Minister Netanyahu, and the ministers of foreign affairs and finance

(Cont'd)

Table 5.2 (Cont'd)

Year	Nature of visit	Outcome
		Signed an extradition treaty and an Agreement for Transfer of Sentenced Persons. He also announced the approval of the Government of India for the opening of a consulate general of Israel in Bengaluru.
2012 (February)	Minister of Urban Development Kamal Nath	Signed a declaration to create a JWG in the field of water technology
		Met with Minister of Industry, Trade and Labour Shalom Simhon, Minister for Energy and Water Resources Uzi Landau, and the Minister of Transportation and Road Safety Israel Katz
2012 (April)	Minister of Communications and IT Kapil Sibal	Met with President Shimon Peres, Minister of Communications Moshe Kahlon, Minister of Finance Yuval Steinitz, and Minister of Education Gideon Sa'ar
2012 (June)	Minister of Tourism Subodh Kant Sahai	Met with Minister of Tourism Stas Misezhnikov
		Participated in the first meeting of the JWG set up to promote tourism between the two countries
2013 (June)	Minister of Communications and IT Kapil Sibal	Promoted India's National Policy on Electronics of 2012
		Met with ministers of communications; finance and economy to discuss research, design, and manufacturing, in the electronics sector

(Cont'd)

Table 5.2   *(Cont'd)*

Year	Nature of visit	Outcome
		Announced that India would like to set up a joint fund with a contribution of $5 million from Government of India to create an eco-system to help navigate trade in hi-tech, especially electronics, given bilateral complementarities

Source: Information compiled from different sources, including the Indian embassy in Israel (http://www.indembassy.co.il), and various Indian and Israel newspapers.

(Luce 2003; Waldman 2003). This symbolically rich visit also confirmed the important political dialogue that had been engaged between the Bharatiya Janata Party (BJP) and Israel since 1999, and that had led the Indian National Security Adviser Brajesh Mishra to call for an 'alliance' between the two countries (and the US) in a May 2003 speech.[4]

As the much publicized rapprochement with Israel in the late 1990s coincided with the BJP-led government tenure, some observers have (over-)emphasized the role of ideology in the improvement of Indo-Israeli relations (Berman 2002; Jaffrelot 2003). The return to Congress and the limited bilateral visits after 2004 also seemed to confirm this impression of an ideology- or party-driven policy.[5] I argue in this chpater that while the BJP certainly played a role in the significant increase of defence and economic ties in the late 1990s, it was hardly the sole factor. It was in fact an Indian National Congress (INC) government which decided to normalize relations and which began discussions on the security field with Israel in 1992. It was again an INC government which resumed and even accelerated strategic ties after coming back to power in 2004. As a result, I also assess the influence of events like the nuclear test of 1998 and the Kargil war in 1999 in strengthening defence relations with Tel Aviv. I will argue that the new policy compromise on Israel consolidated during the time period from 1998 to 2004.

There were initial doubts about the endurance of this new privileged relationship with Israel as the United Progressive Alliance's (UPA's) electoral programme in 2004 had evoked a new beginning in relations with West Asia and a reaffirmation of India's support of the Palestinian cause.[6] However, despite the government's prudence in publicly discussing its policy vis-à-vis Israel, defence and economic relations have resumed and even increased dramatically since 2004 (see Table 5.3). Since public political exchanges do not seem to be the most accurate indicator of the status of this bilateral relationship, how can we account for the consolidation of India's new Israel policy in spite of limited political leadership involvement?[7]

Table 5.3 Indo-Israeli Military Trade since 1992 (in US$ million)

Years	Israel's export	India's export	Total bilateral trade
1992	127	75	202
1993	228	129	357
1994	363	151	514
1995	313	190	503
1996	311	251	562
1997	365	293	658
1998	332	343	675
1999	531	397	928
2000	551	453	1,004
2001	470	413	883
2002	648	608	1,256
2003	883	703	1,586
2004	1,123	1,021	2,146
2005	1,191	1,214	2,405
2006	1,270	1,433	2,703
2007	1,607	1,689	3,295
2008	2,361	1,649	4,012
2009	1,810	1,757	3,567
2010	2,890	1,969	4,859
2011	2,998	2,154	5,153

Source: Information compiled from data available from the Indian embassy in Israel (http://www.indembassy.co.il), the Israel Central Bureau of Statistics (http://www.cbs.gov.il), the Israeli ministry of industry, trade and labour official website (http://www.moital.gov.il), and the Government of India's ministry of commerce and industry website (http://commerce.nic.in/). This does not include defence deals (see Table 5.7).

In this chapter, I concentrate on the overlooked consolidation phase of India's new Israel policy and on how different governments have managed the apparent contradictions between engaging Israel in important economic and defence deals while maintaining a pro-Palestine rhetoric in parallel. The new theoretical framework on policy change will help demonstrate how policy-making vis-à-vis Israel in the 1990s was progressively opened to new types of actors in the military and economic sectors who have redefined Israel's policy. I first look at the immediate aftermath of normalization. The Indian government initially encouraged discussions with Israel while also accommodating the persisting concerns over its new policy. This period is important as it saw the emergence of new stakeholders in the stabilization and improvement of Indo-Israeli relations. In the second section of the chapter, I concentrate on the 1998–2004 period which was characterized by a series of political shocks at the national and international levels which modified the nature of India's Israel policy. Finally, in the last section, I look at how the INC government resumed and increased cooperation with Israel since 2004, albeit in a more discreet fashion. I finally evaluate the stability of the new Israel policy and attempt to anticipate its future directions.

First Timid Steps: India's Prudent Israel Policy (1992–8)

The decision taken by the Rao government to normalize relations with Israel was an important step but it did not translate immediately into a major policy shift. Most authors have preferred to look at the last 15 years of the relationship, and have consequently neglected this uncertain period in India's Israel policy.[8] Following the announcement of the establishment of diplomatic relations, the Rao government refrained from making public announcements related to the development of Indo-Israeli relations. Under Rao's tenure, only two cabinet ministers travelled to Israel (Table 5.2). There was no clear indication from the Government of India that it wanted to increase bilateral cooperation with Israel. Despite the government's cautious approach, there were some first low-level contacts between the two countries. These initial and unprecedented exchanges between bureaucracies, private actors, and between the Indian states and Israel proved decisive to identify future areas of cooperation.

Opposition at Home

The debates leading to the establishment of diplomatic relations revealed enduring domestic concerns about engaging Tel Aviv. The official statement Dixit made on 29 January 1992 clearly stated, for instance, that India would not change its policy of support for the Palestinian people's campaign to realize their legitimate national aspirations (Gargan 1992). This reference to the Palestinian cause was a concession to the old orthodoxy. Nevertheless, some members of the INC and elements in the opposition, like the Janata Dal and the Communist Party of India (CPI), openly expressed their dissatisfaction with the normalization of relations and its implications for India's West Asia policy. Critics felt that New Delhi should have waited until an independent Palestinian state was established. For them, the normalization of relations before a comprehensive settlement of the Arab–Israeli conflict was a betrayal of the Palestinian cause and of previous policy positions (Aiyar 1993; Dasgupta 1992). The old orthodoxy argued that there was no pressing need to change the policy. The CPI's National Council secretary described the decision as a step in haste. A member of Parliament (MP) from the Janata Dal argued that the decision at that time was neither morally nor politically justifiable (Gopal and Sharma 2007: 273). Former Prime Minister V. P. Singh also criticized normalization (Kumaraswamy 2010: 244). Some opponents even singled out Dixit's personal role in rushing the rapprochement with Israel (Shukla 1993). By contrast, the move was welcomed by the BJP through Vajpayee who judged that the move would help India play a more meaningful role in the West Asian peace process and would allow closer cooperation between the two countries (*Asian Recorder* 38:21, 20–26 May 1992, p. 22311).

Some members of the Congress party continued to believe that the establishment of diplomatic relations with Israel would prejudice the INC's electoral prospects at home by alienating the domestic Muslim population. According to J. N. Dixit, Arjun Singh had explicitly discussed the possible negative reactions from Indian Muslims at a cabinet meeting (Dixit 1996: 311). A day after the establishment of diplomatic ties, some Muslim leaders immediately condemned the decision, judging it 'ill-timed and hasty'.[9] India's ties with Israel were also affected by the events surrounding the Ayodhya episode of 6 December 1992.[10] Given the violent nature of the Hindu–Muslim riots that followed the destruction of the Babri Masjid in Ayodhya, the INC tried to keep its relations with

Israel limited to not further alienate its Muslim population and its Arab partners. Allegedly, a visit by Israel's Minister of Foreign Affairs, Shimon Peres, which was originally planned in January 1993, was postponed to May because of the widespread violence which followed the demolition of the mosque. Around the time of the Ayodhya events, the UAE also refused to welcome a scheduled visit by the Minister of State for External Affairs, R. L. Bhatia (*The Hindu*, 23 February 1993). Another sign that the old orthodoxy refused any deviation from its traditional support to the Palestinian cause was the refusal by the Government of India to let the Jerusalem Symphony Orchestra perform in Bombay and New Delhi in August 1993 if they did not drop Jerusalem from their name. Indian authorities still considered Jerusalem as a disputed city and refused any compromise. Consequently, the Jerusalem Symphony Orchestra decided to cancel the planned tour.[11]

The persistence of domestic opposition helped explain why the Indian government was originally very prudent in its discussions with Israel. Prime Minister Rao was conscious of the prevailing opposition and instructed that contacts with Israeli authorities should only be made at the low-key foreign secretarial level.[12] Because the government privileged these low-level contacts, Moshe Yegar visited India in March 1992 and then Dixit was the first representative of the Indian government to travel to Israel a year after normalization. In March 1993, Dixit was received by Israeli Prime Minister Yitzhak Rabin. The return of a Labour prime minister, who encouraged discussions with the Palestine Liberation Organization (PLO) and played a leading role in the signing of the Oslo Accords, facilitated the rapprochement. During the visit, Rabin stressed how Israel had always wanted to have full-fledged relations with India and was willing to cooperate with New Delhi in every sphere without any reservations. To Rabin, 'a democratic, stable, strong and secular India was a major factor in insuring stability and equilibrium in Asia' (Dixit 1996: 313). Dixit also learned during his visit that India had been invited by Israel to become a member of the five working groups engaged in the task of normalization of relations with the PLO. India's involvement was endorsed by the US, the Russian federation, and the other Arab participants.

While Israel was more than eager to collaborate with India in military production and anti-terrorism cooperation, the Indian government was initially reluctant to respond (Gupta 1992). For instance, Benjamin Netanyahu, who was deputy minister in Shamir's prime minister's office, discussed in an interview how both countries faced 'similar threats' such as 'terrorism and religious fundamentalism' (Gupta 1992). Prime Minister Rabin later said that Israel was ready to cooperate with India in the field of defence 'whenever and wherever it suits India' (*Strategic Digest*, 23:12, December 1993, p. 20114). The Indian Defence Minister Sharad Pawar also discussed the possibility of cooperating with Israel on counter-terrorism. His statement was, however, criticized by Muslim members of Parliament. Subsequently, the government informed Parliament that it would not confirm the authenticity of Pawar's statement (*The Indian Express*, 28 February 1992). Krishna Kumar, the minister of state for defence, had to reassure the Rajya Sabha that there had been no proposal, no initiative, and no offer for any kind of defence ties with Israel. He added that the issue of defence collaboration had not been 'formally discussed in the Defence Ministry' (*The Statesman*, 28 February 1992). The temporary Israeli ambassador, Giora Becher, equally clarified that discussions of defence cooperation were too premature at this early stage (*The Telegraph*, 10 April 1992). Politicians like the secretary of the Communist Party of India (Marxist) (CPI [M]) E. K. Naynar argued that behind the discussions of agricultural and commerce deals, the real interest of the government lay in defence deals with Israel (*The Hindu*, 1 June 1993). Henceforth, the Indian government avoided publicly talking about military cooperation.

Similarly, the economic rapprochement was initially restrained and discreet. After years of estrangement, there was still an impression that economic and trade relations between the two countries were competitive and not complementary. In May 1993, Shimon Peres visited India with a delegation of Israeli businessmen, including Danny Gillerman, president of the Israeli Federation of Chambers of Commerce. Peres became the first Israeli minister of foreign affairs to visit India since relations were upgraded in 1992 (and the first Israeli minister to travel to Delhi since Dayan in 1977). During the visit, Peres met with the ministers of external affairs, finance, agriculture, and commerce. Peres also signed an economic memorandum of understanding (MoU) with India's commerce minister.[13] While the Israeli delegation was keen on signing ten agreements covering various areas of cooperation, India only agreed to sign four. The government at that time was very selective in the areas it wanted to cooperate with Israel.

Following the visit, Gillerman was optimistic and estimated that the potential for economic cooperation between Israel and India—in commerce and joint projects—could reach $1 billion by 1995.[14] The next visit by Minister of Human Resource Development Arjun Singh to Israel in June 1994 was considered to be an important symbolic step given his earlier opposition to normalization.[15] The visit did not lead to any substantial developments with the exception of an agreement on the holding of periodic consultations. Another example of a subtle political change was that India no longer sponsored explicitly anti-Israeli resolutions at the United Nations (UN). It also abstained when the issue of nuclear proliferation in West Asia was discussed.[16] However, the Indian government maintained its unambivalent support for the Palestinian cause through resolutions at the UN General Assembly (UNGA).

Reactions from the Arab–Muslim World

In parallel with its diplomatic overture to Israel, India wanted to maintain its good relations with most Arab states. India's West Asia policy had traditionally been dictated by three important considerations. First, the Gulf states were amongst India's largest oil suppliers. Second, there were millions of Indian expatriates in West Asia who sent back remittances to India. The government had traditionally been concerned about their safety. Third, India had a stake in preserving the support, or at least the neutrality, of Arab–Muslim states with regards to its disputes with Pakistan.

Consequently, in the days leading to the decision to establish diplomatic relations, the Rao government took precautionary measures to reassure its Arab partners and to limit any diplomatic backlash. A priority was to confirm India's support of the Palestinian cause. Arafat was, for example, invited to Delhi a week before the normalization and gave his tacit approval to the exchange of diplomatic missions (*The Indian Express*, 20 January 1992). The PLO was itself negotiating with the Israeli government and wanted India to be able to participate in the West Asian peace process. Prime Minister Rao had also asked Dixit to brief the ambassadors of Arab–Muslim countries about the imminent decision to establish diplomatic relations with Israel. According to Dixit, some of the Arab ambassadors were 'aggressively resentful' and threatened India of 'uncertain consequences'. Dixit answered that 'India had not received any reciprocity on the Kashmir issue despite [India's] longstanding support to the Arab states in international fora'. Dixit apparently made it clear that

India would not accept 'extraneous limitations on its sovereign right of determining its policy decision within the framework of Indian interests' (Dixit 1996: 312–13). To further convince the Palestinians that the Shimon Peres visit to Delhi had not eroded India's support, the Indian Minister of State for External Affairs Bhatia was sent to Tunis in May 1993 to brief Arafat on the status of India's negotiations with Israel. Bhatia reassured the Palestinian statesman that India's 'commitment to a peaceful and fair settlement' of the Palestine problem had not evolved.[17]

The statements made by Dixit to the ambassadors marked a new Indian attitude towards the Arab world. India was less concerned about the sensitivities of Arab countries if it came at the cost of the direct and indirect benefits linked to closer relations with Israel. India still needed to cultivate relations with Arab states but from now on asked for genuine diplomatic reciprocity. Indian policymakers had become disillusioned with the increasing pro-Pakistan bias at the Organisation of Islamic Cooperation (OIC) in the months preceding the normalization. The condemnations of India's behaviour in Kashmir intensified in the following months and went beyond the routine accusations of violation of human rights. At the twenty-first session of the OIC in Karachi in 1993, there was a resolution equating the human rights violations to similar acts in Palestine, South Africa, and Bosnia. The resolution also asked of all member states to take the necessary steps to persuade India to allow the Kashmiris to exercise their inalienable right to self-determination (*Times of India*, 27 April 1993). This resolution was written in the context of the Babri Masjid demolition and the subsequent Hindu–Muslim riots that the OIC condemned. The OIC also decided to grant an observer status to the All Parties Hurriyat Conference, a political alliance of 26 political, social, and religious organizations in Kashmir, which demanded self-determination. The OIC's latest resolutions and the recognition of the Hurriyat were considered as a direct affront to India's national sovereignty and territorial integrity. The lack of support at the OIC was an incentive for India to reassess its relations with the Arab world and with Israel.

However, the OIC was hardly a monolithic block when it came to the issue of Kashmir. For instance, Pakistan withdrew its draft resolution on Kashmir at the UNGA in November 1993 because it was not sure of securing the backing of all of the 51 members of the OIC. Likewise, Pakistani resolutions on Kashmir at the UN human rights commission in

1994 failed to gather enough support from the Arab countries (Noorani 1994). Some of these countries did want to let the Kashmir (or even the Israel) issue become insurmountable obstacle to developing relations with an emerging power like India. In fact, states like Saudi Arabia have been actively seeking political and economic ties with India since the early 1990s.[18] Furthermore, in the context of the Oslo peace process, West Asian states could not rebuke India for normalizing relations when they were simultaneously developing political and economic relations with Israel. For instance, Turkey and Israel again raised their diplomatic relations to ambassadorial level in March 1992. Israel and Jordan signed a peace treaty on 26 October 1994 and a trade treaty in 1996. Qatar and Israel established trade relations in 1996. Instead of looking at West Asia as a zero-sum equation, India was now progressively engaging all actors in the region, including Israel.

The Slow and Cautious Development of Defence Ties

It quickly became evident that the Indian government had overestimated the possible negative response of the Indian Muslims regarding a change of India's Israel policy. The Muslim community was in fact more immediately concerned by the Babri Masjid episode and its direct consequences than in foreign policy realignments. The absence of adverse reactions at home and in the Arab world gradually led the Government of India to inquire into possible areas of cooperation with Israel. Following Israel's achievements on the battlefield at multiple occasions and in weapons production, the Indian military had developed a professional appreciation of Israel's military performance. Defence cooperation was one of the arguments given by governmental actors like Dixit to justify normalization (Dixit 1996: 310). Israel was an attractive partner for India's military and defence industry in the early 1990s for two reasons.

First, India's historical goal of self-reliance in its military industry has been one of the main factors determining its ambition to diversify its military supply lines after 1991 (Chari, 'India's Weapons Acquisition Decision-Making Process and Indo-Soviet Military Cooperation, 199; Gupta 1995; Hoyt 2006: 25–6.). In that context, Israel was an interesting partner as it had a very positive experience in developing a largely indigenous and self-sufficient military-industrial complex capable of competing with Western powers. The fact that Israel had a technology that was largely indigenous also facilitated technology transfers with no end-user problems (*Times of India*, 1 February 1992). Beyond the upgrade and the sale of spare parts, Israel was also willing, unlike the US or other alternative suppliers in Europe, to share technology and to set up joint ventures for defence manufacturing.[19]

Second, the dissolution of the USSR in December 1991, which had been India's largest arms supplier since the 1960s, created an urgent need to find procurement alternatives. Given its finite resources due to the economic crisis, India originally privileged the upgrade of its existing armament (mostly of Soviet origin) and the acquisition of force multipliers (Bedi 1993; *Times of India*, 1 February 1992). India, for instance, started talks with Yugoslavia which also possessed some Soviet equipment. Israel's industry was also an alternative as it had developed a specific expertise in upgrading Soviet-era equipment. This skill was the result of the capture of Arab military equipment (which had been bought from the USSR) during the 1967 and 1973 conflicts, as well as of the immigration of engineers and scientists from the former Soviet Union in the late 1980s and early 1990s. Consequently, Israel-based companies Elbit and Israel Aerospace Industries (IAI) competed to secure the contract to upgrade the ageing 200 MIG-21 Bis aircrafts used in the Indian Air Force (IAF) in 1993 (*The Economic Times*, 18 October 1993). The Israeli firms ultimately lost out to a Russian company but it demonstrated a future potential for cooperation between IAI and the IAF.

Less than a month after normalization, the Minister of Defence Sharad Pawar publicly stated that the formal establishment of full diplomatic ties with Israel was an opportunity to draw on Israel's successful experience to curb terrorism. Pawar said that India would try to build on Israel's experience in developing specific technology for anti-terrorist operations (*The Times of India*, 22 February 1992). His deputy, Krishna Kumar, also said that 'Israel had certain defence capabilities worth noting' (Hadass 2002: 27; *The Statesman*, 28 February 1992). In March 1992, Moshe Yegar, the deputy Director-general in the ministry of foreign affairs (MFA) visited India again to prepare for the opening of the Israeli embassy in New Delhi. He met members of the ministry of external affairs (MEA), including Dixit, but also India's Defence Secretary N. N. Vohra.[20] In May 1992, a six-member Israeli delegation, including manufacturers of military equipment, visited India at the invitation of the Indian ministry of defence.[21] The details of the discussion were, however, not disclosed.[22]

In August 1992, it was reported that a delegation from Malat, a division of IAI which specializes in the manufacture of unmanned aerial vehicles (UAVs), visited New Delhi. The Malat representatives reportedly offered the possibility of joint development of Searcher UAVs.[23] Another Malat delegation came to finalize the sale of Searcher and Ranger UAVs to the IAF in New Delhi in December 1992.[24] This was the first major defence deal signed by the two countries following normalization.

During his visit to Israel, Foreign Secretary Dixit was accompanied by Rakesh Sood, the head of the disarmament division at the MEA (*The Times of India*, 4 April 1993). Dixit discussed defence ties with Prime Minister Rabin and more specifically about the possibility of counter-terrorism collaboration (Dixit 1996: 313). In April 1993, a delegation of Israel's Manufacturers Association (IMA) came to India and included representatives from the defence industry (more specifically from the companies Elbit and Elul) (Sandler 1993). While he was no longer minister of defence, Sharad Pawar visited Israel in his new capacity as the chief minister of the state of Maharashtra. He led an Indian delegation to an agricultural exhibition in Tel Aviv in May 1993. While the visit was mainly publicized (notably to the domestic audience in India) as an opportunity to discuss agricultural cooperation, Pawar was also accompanied by a high-level military team, which visited Israeli military facilities including the Israeli Anti-Terror Unit (Naaz 2000). Both in 1993 and 1995, delegations from the National Defence College also reportedly visited Israel (Kumaraswamy 1998: 14).

The new Indian government signalled a new interest in Israel's military experience and capabilities, but this attention remained vague and unsubstantiated by major deals. Henceforth, the Israeli ministry of defence and Israeli defence companies began discreet but sustained efforts to establish local connections and to identify and initiate business opportunities in New Delhi. Brigadier General David Shoval of SIBAT, the Israeli ministry of defence's Foreign Defense Assistance and Defense Export Organization, visited New Delhi in November 1993 to discuss potential deals with representatives from the Indian army and IAF (*The Economic Times*, 12 November 1993). By the end of 1993, SIBAT had appointed over 50 local agents in New Delhi to sell various defence items to India (Kumaraswamy 1998: 16). In March 1994, there were reports that India would purchase 16 Hunter UAVs from Malat and that Israel would assist the indigenous UAV programme.[25] The Israeli Deputy

Minister of Foreign Affairs Yossi Beilin visited New Delhi the next month and further discussed the purchase of UAVs. In April 1994, both countries sealed a $50 million deal for the purchase of Harpy drones.[26] General Helz Bodinger from the Israeli air force visited India in April 1995 and reportedly offered a package deal to India, which included an airborne early warning and control systems, UAVs, and anti-detecting and anti-jamming technology (*Hindustan Times*, 8 April 1995). In return, the Israeli general asked about using IAF bases in Jodhpur and Bhuj as air-staging facilities (Kumaraswamy 1998: 17–18).

Progressively, Indian delegations too travelled to Israel to identify potential areas of cooperation. In January 1995, a delegation from the ministry of home affairs travelled to Israel to study the Israeli-developed barbwire system which was considered as an option to limit infiltration through the Indo-Pakistani Line of Control (LoC) in the Kashmir Valley as well as the borders of the states of Gujarat and Rajasthan (*Jerusalem Post*, 6 May 1995). In July 1995, an Indian delegation led by Defence Secretary K. A. Nambiar visited Israel. The delegation went to study the possibility of acquiring avionics and weapons systems for MIG-21 Bis, which were being upgraded for India under an Indo-Russian joint venture. There were also talks about the upgrade of the Russian-built T-72 tanks. Nambiar also discussed India's interest in Israeli UAVs (*The Hindustan Times*, 8 July 1995). In October 1995, the Director General of the Indian National Security Guards (NSG), Ashok Tandon, visited Israel in order to establish a first channel of cooperation, and to discuss the possible training of commandos and the purchase of specialized weaponry from Israel.[27] In November 1995, two Indian naval ships, INS Gomati and INS Subhadra, for the first time visited Israel as guests of the Israeli navy (Kumaraswamy 1998: 18).

This multiplication of these military-to-military contacts augured a new period of defence cooperation between the two countries. However, there were still problems and obstacles to a consolidation of military ties. First, there had been no diplomatic contacts between the two countries until 1992. The lack of knowledge of the structure of both defence industries meant that there would be an initial stage of discussion between the two security communities to identify potential areas of cooperation. Second, Arab and domestic pressure also led India to delay and even to decline some deals (Thakur 1994: 295). As detailed earlier, bilateral visits from defence delegations were not publicized, and little substance from the discussions was disclosed. The old orthodoxy was still present in New Delhi and ready to frame any defence deal as a deviation from India's traditional support to the Arab and Palestinian causes. Third, there were still international obstacles to technology transfer between the two countries. For instance, international arms control guidelines like the Missile Technology Control Regime (MTCR), of which India was not a member, originally prevented India from discussing with Israel the possibility of cooperation on ballistic missile technology. Some of the Israeli technology was also co-produced with the US, and Tel Aviv needed prior approval from Washington to enter in negotiations with third parties on technological collaboration. The US had previously criticized and even blocked the Israeli transfer of Lavi, patriot missile, and Phalcon technologies to China. These precedents served as cautionary tales for further joint ventures between India and Israel (Clarke 1995; Kumaraswamy 1996a; Shichor 1998; Dagoni 2004; Blarel 2006).

Fourth, since the 1970s, India had been committed to expanding the indigenous content of its defence equipment (Hoyt 2006: 39–61). The reluctance of Western countries to sell dual-use technology equipment and the disintegration of the USSR exacerbated the need to develop an indigenous industry. In 1995, the Indian government announced plans to increase self-reliance and domestic participation in defence procurement from 30 per cent to 70 per cent by 2005 (Singh 1998: 57). At that point, the possibility of learning from Israel's experience in developing an independent defence industry was an interesting prospect for some elements of the Indian military and the ministry of defence. However, the state-controlled Defence Research and Development Organisation (DRDO), which was in charge of most of India's national defence projects, had organizational interests in limiting purchases from and cooperation with the Israeli industry. The DRDO was directly in competition with Israeli companies like IAI and Rafael over projects like the upgrade of MIGs, the development of various missile systems, satellite technology, and even the production of UAVs (Hoyt 2006: 43–6). In 1994, the DRDO flatly denied all reports of cooperation with Israel on UAVs (*The Economic Times*, 5 May 1994).

Given India's difficulties in developing national programmes, some observers had discussed the possible benefits of cooperation between Israeli defence industries and the DRDO. However, the DRDO was not originally ready to let go of the control of its nationally funded programmes.

The national projects spearheaded by the DRDO enjoyed widespread and bipartisan domestic political support. All the political parties, from the CPI (M) all the way to the BJP, considered the DRDO-led projects as vital to India's national security. The lack of progress and achievements of the DRDO by the mid-1990s was not a sufficient condition to collaborate with Israel. Consequently, defence cooperation with Israel was not the Indian government's priority in the 1990s. For example, it took five years of lobbying from the military establishment to post a defence attaché at the Indian embassy in Tel Aviv in 1997. Nevertheless, there were many bilateral visits from the lower echelons of the defence ministry and many mil-to-mil visits following normalization. The first purchases of UAVs also seemed to indicate further cooperation in this particular field. These early contacts established and institutionalized a new channel of communication between the two security establishments.

Not All about Guns: The Identification of Shared Economic Interests

Unlike security ties, the economic cooperation between India and Israel was publicized and consensual. The lack of diplomatic relations had not inhibited Indian leaders like Nehru from formally approaching Israel for technical assistance, notably in the agricultural field as early as 1947. Israel had indeed evolved from a desert country to a net exporter of food. Some Indian socialist leaders, like Jaya Prakash Narayan, had an early and longstanding interest in Israel's agricultural methods and irrigation technology. Even at a time when relations had deteriorated, Indian citizens, mostly from trade unions and the Indian Socialist Party, travelled to Israel to undergo professional training (Gerberg 2008: 148–9). They participated in agricultural courses in Israel, while Israeli agricultural experts also came to India to share their experience in various Indian states. However, many companies in the agricultural sector were state-owned and were not authorized by the Indian government to develop relations with Israeli companies. As a result, the bilateral trade was limited to $200 million dollars, of which about 90 per cent consisted of polished diamonds.[28] In the context of India's economic liberalization of the early 1990s and of the normalization of diplomatic relations, Israel was gradually perceived as an interesting trading partner with an important scope for cooperation in agriculture, drip irrigation systems, and soil management methods. Following the economic reforms, the Indian government allowed both central and state public sector organizations to conduct direct trading negotiations with Israel.

Israeli industries in the early 1990s closely studied the Indian market and explored the possibilities of investing in joint ventures in order to take full advantage of the liberalized norms for foreign investment. At a seminar on India–Israel business opportunities organized by the Confederation of Indian Industry (CII) in 1993, Israeli ambassador Ephraim Duek said that bilateral trade would grow by 50 per cent over the next five years. The chairman of the Federation of Israeli Chambers of Commerce, Dan Gillerman, insisted that Indian companies had an interest in joint ventures with Israeli companies as they could use Israel as a base to gain free access to the trading blocks of the European Union (EU) and the US, both with which Israel had signed free trade agreements (FTAs) (*The Economic Times*, 16 April 1993).

In addition, business associations and chambers of commerce started signing MoUs and organizing bilateral visits to further cooperation. For example, there was a Joint Business Council Agreement signed between the Federation of Indian Chambers of Commerce and Industry (FICCI) and the Federation of Israeli Chambers of Commerce. Similarly, the Confederation of Indian Industries signed a MoU with the Israel Export Institute to promote trade and industrial cooperation (*The Economic Times*, 31 March 1992). A delegation of the Joint Business Council visited Israel in October 1993 to take part in the Jerusalem business conference to discuss bilateral trade. In 1994, a 15-member delegation sponsored by the Progress Harmony Development (PHD) Chamber of Commerce and Industry visited Israel to explore the possibility of joint ventures in the fields of water management, food processing, telecommunications, and dry-land farming (Khan 2000: 155). These non-state sponsored and direct contacts between the business communities of the two countries facilitated the emergence of mutual interests. The Israeli minister of agriculture also discussed the decision to set up three demonstration farms in Maharashtra, Gujarat, and Rajasthan, on the lines of those established in Egypt by Israeli firms. These farms would demonstrate the potential of drip irrigation, seed production, and low chemical fertilizer in India (Khan 2000: 155). These interactions on regular basis helped identify where the two economies were complementary and could collaborate: Israel could provide experience in high technology products while India had abundant and skilled human resources. On this basis, both business communities located areas of cooperation in agricultural equipment, electronics, chemicals, bio-technology, and pharmaceuticals.

There were also political initiatives to create a favourable atmosphere for trade and investment. An important example was the much publicized visit by the Israeli Minister of Foreign Affairs, Shimon Peres, in May 1993. During his trip, Peres met with Prime Minister Rao, President Shankar Dayal Sharma, Minister of Finance Manmohan Singh, Minister of External Affairs Dinesh Singh, and Minister of Agriculture Balram Jakhar. He also met members of the opposition like BJP leader L. K. Advani who had consistently advocated the normalization of relations with Israel.[29] The Israeli minister signed a MoU on economic cooperation with the commerce minister along with various agreements on scientific-technological and cultural exchanges, as well as an agreement on tourism (Hadass 2002; *India Today*, 15 June 1993). Unlike Arab states at the OIC, Peres publicly supported New Delhi's position on Kashmir in accordance with the Simla agreement (*India Today*, 15 June 1993; *The Hindu*, 19 May 1993). Accompanying Peres was a delegation of businessmen who held meetings, as well as an economic symposium, with leaders from major Indian firms. During Peres' visit, the two countries also set up a joint Indo-Israeli fund with each side contributing $1.5 million a year to coordinate efforts in research and development.[30]

As a result, by the mid-1990s, economic relations between the two countries had considerably increased. There were different levels of economic interaction that were established. First, there were direct joint ventures between Israeli and Indian companies. In the sole field of agricultural cooperation, there were more than 50 joint venture projects initiated in India from 1992 to 1997, including in irrigation and water management, fertilizers, greenhouses, tissue culture horticulture, use of solar energy, and dairy development.[31] For instance, Plastro Irrigation Systems (Israel) partnered with the Finolex group in Pune to market drip irrigation systems in India in December 1993 (*Israel-India Final Report of the Joint Study Group*, 10 November, 2005: 32). Equally in the irrigation field, Netafim, Israel's world leader in drip irrigation and water conservation technologies, and the Madras-based Pasumai Irrigation Company set up a plant next to Hyderabad to manufacture drip irrigation systems (Khan 2000: 162–3). Similarly, the Indian Telephone Industries,

India's largest telecom company at the time, signed an agreement with Israel's Tadiran Telecommunications. A textile company, Dalmia Brothers, set up an export-oriented plant in Israel to try to access the European market (Khan 2000: 165–6). These were a few of the prominent examples of early complementary cooperation between Indian and Israeli firms. There were also exchanges between state-controlled organizations in space-related technologies. In October 1994, Professor U. R. Rao, a member of the Indian Space Commission and former chairperson of the Indian Space Research Organisation (ISRO), visited Israel to meet with the heads of Israel's space agency and to discuss future cooperation in this field (Kumaraswamy 1998: 17).

Second, Israeli companies directly negotiated and signed agreements with Indian state governments. Following the liberalization reforms, Indian states had greater leverage when it came to dealing directly with external partners. Foreign policy remained an exclusive prerogative of the central government but state governments could take some foreign economic policy initiatives (Jenkins 2003). For instance, Tahal Consulting Engineers Ltd, which had played an important role in the development of Israel's water management and infrastructure, directly signed MoUs with the governments of Gujarat and Rajasthan in 1993 for the transfer of expertise and technology.[32] In fact, cooperation in agro-technology usually happened directly between the Indian states' governments and the Israeli government or the involved Israeli company. For instance, Sharad Pawar visited the Agritech in Tel Aviv in May 1993 as chief minister of Maharashtra. The agricultural conference was attended by 800 Indian farmers and resulted in various agro-commercial agreements with different Indian states such as Maharashtra, Andhra Pradesh, Karnataka, and Haryana. These states were the ones which would benefit most from Israeli agro-technologies like drip irrigation and fertilizers.[33] In September 1993, the Gujarat Chief Minister Chimanbhai Patel also went to Israel. His visit resulted in a MoU between Gujarat and the Israeli company Eisenberg Group to facilitate investments in communication, wasteland development, shipping, and agriculture (*The Economic Times*, 9 September 1993). Haryana also signed a MoU with the Eisenberg group in 1996, which planned to set up a thermal power plant on the Yamuna (Khan 2000: 163). Another example is the MoU signed between the Israel Dairy Board and the Punjab government in 1997, to establish the Modern Satellite Dairy Farm in Punjab.[34] The Government of Maharashtra also signed a MoU with the state of Israel during Chief Minister Manohar Joshi's visit to Israel in October 1996. The agreement set up a joint project between Maharashtra and AGRIDEV, Israel's Agricultural Development Company responsible for the transfer of agricultural technology abroad, on the production of cotton yields, notably with the assistance of drip irrigation.[35]

There were also cultural ties which were established during this time period. For instance, The Israel–India Cultural Association was created in 1992, and Zubin Mehta, the Bombay-born chief conductor of the Israeli Philharmonic Orchestra, was named as its honorary president. After 1992, Israeli publishers regularly participated in book fairs in India, and Israeli books were made available in English and 13 local Indian languages (Gerberg 2008: 383). There were also student exchanges set up between Israeli and Indian universities. A cultural agreement was signed by Israel and India in May 1993 during the visit of Shimon Peres, and within the framework of this agreement, two cultural exchange programmes were set up. In spite of the original problems linked to the cancelled visit of the Jerusalem Symphony Orchestra, the Israeli Philharmonic Orchestra finally visited India and several concerts were conducted by Zubin Mehta in Bombay and New Delhi in 1994 (Burns 1994).

By 1995–6, India and Israel had started exploring new avenues of economic cooperation. The volume of bilateral trade between 1992 and 1996 had steadily risen by an average of 50 per cent every year (Table 5.3). However, this gradual increase was still far from attaining the original high expectations of a $1 billion bilateral trade by 1995.[36] In addition, the trade was not very diversified and mainly limited to three major items: diamonds, chemicals, and cotton.[37] There were also institutional obstacles to an important trade increase. Both governments tried to solve these constraints by signing three agreements in January 1996 on avoidance of double taxation, customs cooperation, and bilateral investment protection. These agreements were signed in Delhi between the Indian Finance Minister, Manmohan Singh, and the visiting Israeli Minister of Finance Avraham Shochat (*Deccan Herald*, 30 January 1996). Under the agreements, investment from either country would be accorded most favoured nation status and national treatment. Manmohan Singh described the new agreements as the foundation for an increased flow of trade and investment in both directions. The same month, the Minister of Commerce P. Chidambaram visited Israel and discussed other areas of economic cooperation during the meeting of the Indo-Israel Joint Trade and Economic Committee (Gopal and Sharma 2007: 327–8). As a consequence, by 1996 there were economic and trade dialogues at many different levels but not a significant increase in bilateral trade.

The Return of the United Front: A Continuation of the Initial Dialogue

The concurring elections and changes of governments in May 1996 in Israel and in June 1996 in India could have had an adverse impact on Indo-Israeli relations. The change of government in Israel in 1996 marked the return of the right-wing Likud party with which Indian governments had had disagreements on the Palestinian issue. Dixit had explained how the 'rationale' for India's new Israel policy in 1992 had been 'validated' by the Labour's party desire to engage the Palestinians and to find a lasting West Asian peace settlement (*The Indian Express*, 11 December 1997). Naturally, as Prime Minister Benjamin Netanyahu and the Likud stalled the negotiations, the Indian rationale for engaging Israel was directly questioned at home. Likewise, the change of government in India following the June 1996 elections raised concerns in Tel Aviv. The winning United Front (UF) coalition had been led by the Janata Dal party which had objected in 1992 to the establishment of diplomatic relations.[38] However, the concern was less acute in the case of Prime Minister Deve Gowda (June 1996–April 1997), who had previously visited Israel as the chief minister of the state of Karnataka in February 1995 to look for technological assistance in the agricultural and horticultural sectors, than with his successor I. K. Gujral (April 1997–March 1998) who had promoted a pro-Arab policy as minister of external affairs in the V. P. Singh government.

In spite of explicit political disagreements at the governmental level, sub-national contacts by Indian states, Indian economic private actors, and Indian bureaucracies resumed with Israel. The military exchanges also continued and even increased during that period. The fragile political coalition in power mostly left the direction of military issues and procurement (to the least for the stage of dialogue and for minor defence contracts) to the ministry of defence and the military. For instance, a few days after the elections, the Chief Scientific Adviser to the Prime Minister and the Secretary of the DRDO, A. P. J. Abdul Kalam, visited Israel to discuss cooperation on various projects. While the substance of the deliberations was never publicized, it seemed that the DRDO was interested at the time by Israel's experience in anti-ballistic missile (ABM) systems and airborne warning and control systems (AWACS).[39] In July 1996, Air Chief Marshal S. K. Sareen went to Israel at the invitation of the Israeli air force commander to negotiate the purchase of the air combat manoeuvring instrumentation system for Indian MIGs.[40] In November 1996, Israeli naval chief Vice-Admiral Alex Tal visited India to meet with junior defence minister N. V. N. Somu (*The Hindu*, 7 November 1996). In December 1996, as the head of IAI Moshe Keret was visiting New Delhi, the Indian Navy awarded $10 million to a joint venture between the IAI's Ramta division and the state-owned Goa shipyard to build two Dvora MK-II patrol boats for maritime surveillance (*The Economic Times* 2012). In addition, the Israeli company Soltam announced it would supply artillery (155 mm self-propelled guns) to the Indian army (Gopal and Sharma 2007: 344). India's Defence Secretary T. K. Banerjee led a defence delegation to Israel in February 1997 to discuss the 'exchange of technology' (*The Hindu*, 5 February 1997; *The Jerusalem Post*, 16 February 1997). Finally, the nomination of Wing Commander Nak Browne as the first Indian military attaché to Israel in 1997 further institutionalized the links between the two militaries.[41]

An important symbolic step during the tenure of the UF government was the week-long visit of Israeli President Ezer Weizman to India in December 1996–January 1997.[42] Contrary to the Peres visit three years earlier that had witnessed pro-Palestinian demonstrations, there was a positive reception from the government, the media, and the public opinion.[43] There was now a growing public perception that the Oslo peace process was under way and that the Israelis and Palestinians (at least under the Rabin and Peres governments) had normalized their relations. Also, there was a gradual realization about the gains of cooperation in certain niche fields where Israel had a comparative advantage. Gowda had traditionally opposed any rapprochement with Israel in the opposition but shifted his position after travelling to Israel as chief minister. During his visit, he perceived the benefits of cooperation in the domain of agriculture for his state (as well as other states in need of irrigation infrastructure). Consequently, Weizman and Gowda signed four agreements, including one to set up a $3 million agricultural demonstration farm project at the Indian Agricultural Research Institute in Pusa (near New Delhi) and the Center for Agricultural Technological Assessment and Transfer

(*The Pioneer*, 9 January 1997). The purpose of the farm was to present Israeli technologies that focused on promoting the intensive and commercially viable cultivation of agricultural crops in India. Weizman was also accompanied by a delegation of 20 Israeli businessmen who had discussions with the CII and FICCI (*The Hindu*, 3 January 1997). The visit highly emphasized the commercial and cultural aspects of bilateral cooperation and notably what could be gained from Israel's experience and technology in agricultural production.[44]

The analysis of the 1992–8 period in Indo-Israeli relations demonstrates that the foreign policy change which occurred in 1992 was not consolidated. Normalization did not immediately lead to strategic collaboration between the two countries. Given the absence of any clear policy direction, it was difficult to create a consensus. While normalization had now become an accepted political fact, criticism at home and from the Arab world was mostly aimed at the development of defence ties. The initial domestic backlash against Minister of Defence Sharad Pawar's comments in February 1992 on military collaboration pushed the government to be very cautious in its dealings with Israel. As a result, the Indian government chose to mainly publicize commercial and cultural relations as well as the benefits gained from cooperating with Israel in the field of agriculture. The two major visits by Shimon Peres and Ezer Weizman to New Delhi were concluded by cultural, technological, educational, and agricultural agreements. Both countries also tried to create a favourable atmosphere for joint ventures between Indian and Israeli companies, between Israeli companies and Indian state governments, and between the Israeli government (or government-controlled firms) and Indian state governments. Many of these private and public actors did not have the same institutional and ideological obstacles the the central Indian government faced and could therefore more easily engage in specific economic projects. These multiple levels of interactions also created an ever-expanding group of private and public actors who had a direct stake in the political rapprochement between the two countries.

By contrast, the Indian government tried to keep discussions on defence matters with Israel limited and low key. For instance, Indian authorities regularly denied or reluctantly acknowledged the visits of Israeli and Indian defence delegations to New Delhi and Tel Aviv.[45] At some occasions, the Indian government sent mixed groups to visit Israel and only publicized the non-defence composition of the delegation. For instance, when Sharad Pawar visited Tel Aviv in 1993, he emphasized the agricultural dimension of the visit but he was also accompanied by representatives of India's security establishment. To limit internal and regional criticism, New Delhi also reportedly attempted to find indirect trading arrangements through third parties like Russia.[46] The issue of the nomination of the defence attaché was another example of the Indian government's initial reluctance to advertise any institutionalized defence contacts. Despite the opening of an Indian embassy in Israel in 1992, a defence attaché was named only in 1997. It therefore took five years of lobbying from the Indian military establishment to convince the political leadership in Delhi of the necessity to have a defence representative present on a regular basis in Tel Aviv. Indian diplomats also denied the signing of any substantial arms trade deal with Israel to their Arab partners. For instance, the ambassador of India to Israel, Shiv Shankar Menon, assured Palestinians in 1997 that while there were discussions between the two countries, there had been no purchase of Israeli weapons (Menon 1997).

The Formation of a Strategic Alliance? Assessing Change and Continuity in the BJP's Israel Policy (1998–2004)

It was within the context of gradual and cautious rapprochement with Israel that the BJP came to power in 1998. The UF government led by Gujral collapsed after the INC withdrew its support. Following the elections, the BJP, which was the strongest party in Parliament (254 seats), formed a governing coalition, the National Democratic Alliance (NDA), and Vajpayee was named prime minister.[47] Many authors have argued that while the INC was credited for passing the necessary step of establishing diplomatic relations with Israel, bilateral relations with Israel only gained substance and publicity under the BJP (Berman 2002; Gerberg 2008: 145–7; Inbar 2004; Jaffrelot 2003; Kapur 2006: 215–6; Kumaraswamy 2003; Pant 2004; Sherman 2003). These observers have argued that the BJP conducted a more unapologetic foreign policy towards Israel, which was less inhibited by the concerns of previous governments about Arab and domestic reactions.

The new pro-active Israel policy had two consequences. First, there were more high-level visits between the two countries. In 2000, both the Home Minister L. K. Advani and the Minister of External Affairs Jaswant Singh visited Israel. And in 2003, Ariel Sharon was the first Israeli prime minister to visit India. This visit was perceived as the high point of Indo-Israeli relations (Luce 2003; Waldman 2003). Second, it was argued that the BJP added a new strategic dimension to India's Israel policy. During their tenure, BJP leaders openly talked about strategic cooperation, and particularly counter-terrorism cooperation. Some observers have emphasized the ideological rapprochement between the Hindu right and Israel as an explanation for the emergence of a strong strategic axis.[48] The BJP government, through its National Security Advisor (NSA) Brajesh Mishra, even suggested a military and ideological alliance to fight terrorism.[49] However, BJP leaders also frequently clarified that India's foreign policy had not shifted regarding Israel and Palestine, and regularly reiterated India's support for a Palestinian state.[50]

As seen in previous chapters, the BJP (and its forerunner the Jan Sangh) had been a long-term supporter of Israel in the domestic political arena, and it had consistently advocated the establishment of diplomatic relations.[51] When the Jan Sangh was part of Moraji Desai's Janata government, it originally supported improving relations with Israel. Vajpayee, who had been a staunch supporter of Israel and who had supported the establishment of diplomatic relations, became minister of external affairs. However, given the fragility of the political coalition and the unfavourable political circumstances, the Jan Sangh was unable to bring about any radical changes in India's Israel policy. Instead, Vajpayee criticized Israel and supported the Palestinian movement (Vajpayee 1979: 85). This historical precedent demonstrated that while the BJP supported an increased cooperation with Israel, it had also adapted its policy given the existing political and institutional obstacles. In 1998–9, the BJP was again in a fragile governmental position and depended on the support of regional parties to stay in power. The BJP was also faced with a difficult regional context in West Asia with the Second Intifada which started in 2000.[52] Given these constraints, what led the BJP to openly engage Israel in 1998–2004?

1998–9 as a Critical Juncture for India's Israel Policy

The BJP came to power with a willingness to implement a foreign policy radically different from the one promoted by the INC. Unlike the Janata tenure, the BJP had a majority in Parliament and a stronger control of the NDA coalition. It had the means to actually implement a more 'realist' foreign policy alternative (Bajpai 2014; Chaulia 2002; Sagar 2009). While in the opposition, the BJP had regularly argued that India faced growing external threats and insisted on India's receding role in world affairs (Zaidi 1980: 690; Bharatiya Janata Party 1999: 25, 36). Consequently, the BJP's explicit aim was to gain India a global recognition, and what they considered to be a rightful place in the new multipolar system (Bharatiya Janata Party 1999: 2–4, 60–3; Singh 1999: 13). This approach did not break totally with the INC's own Nehruvian foreign policy perspective, which also wanted India to play a global role (Bajpai 2014). The important difference was in the choice of the actual means to become this global power. The party pledged for a 'strong India' which would be an 'autonomous power centre in the world', and for a more aggressive defence of India's borders (Chaulia 2002). The nuclear tests in May 1998 were framed as an example of a more realistic foreign policy initiative.[53] Vajpayee presented the test as the 'ultimate measure of national strength' that would earn India the respect of the world.[54]

In the context of a self-centred pursuit for national material power, the BJP had stated it was ready to engage with any state, including Israel, which could help bolster India's interests. This is why, unlike other opposition parties, the BJP welcomed the INC's decision to normalize relations with Israel in January 1992. A few weeks after the establishment of diplomatic relations, L. K. Advani wrote an op-ed reminding the BJP's long-standing pressure on the Indian government to establish full-fledged diplomatic relations with Israel, and calling for the need to increase defence cooperation with Tel Aviv.[55] Israel was considered an important partner to support BJP's massive military modernization effort. Going beyond discussions of technical cooperation, various BJP leaders even evoked sharing similar terrorist threats and encouraged intelligence sharing.[56] Some analysts have even argued that the strategic rapprochement between the BJP and Israel was due to common fears of radical Islam (Prasanvrajan 2003; Jaffrelot 2003).

Despite the BJP's rhetoric, the new Indian government mainly continued the already existing defence discussions. In the first few days of the BJP's tenure, India purchased $14 million of light ammunition and decided to upgrade the electronic warfare equipment of the INS Virat (Ved 1998). The visit of Chief of Army Staff General V. P. Malik to Israel in March 1998 demonstrated the enduring obstacles to the BJP's willingness to engage Israel on strategic issues. Malik was the first

Indian army chief to visit Israel.[57] During his visit, Malik revealed the Indian army's admiration for the Israeli army, and explained that the history of the Israeli conflicts was a compulsory study for all Indian officers.[58] However, the Malik visit raised concerns among India's Arab partners. The Arab states especially criticized the fact that the Indian army chief had visited the 'Israeli occupied' Golan Heights.[59] The ambassadors of Egypt, Syria, Lebanon, and the PLO in New Delhi officially asked for 'certain clarifications' from the Indian government. The BJP government explained that Malik had been sent to inspect the deployment of Israeli troops in the Tiberias and Metulla regions, well inside Israeli territories (Abadi 1999). In an apparent conciliatory gesture, General Malik was also sent to two other goodwill visits to Syria and Egypt in December 1998.[60] This diplomatic incident served as a reminder to the BJP that an open rapprochement with Israel was still contested in the Arab world.

The nuclear tests of May 1998 and their aftermath comforted the BJP in its desire to step up the strategic collaboration with Israel. On 6 June, the United Nations Security Council (UNSC) adopted Resolution 1172 to condemn the Indian nuclear tests (as well as the subsequent tests in Pakistan). The US immediately placed both India and Pakistan under economic sanctions.[61] The comprehensive sanctions included banning US economic assistance and the export of defence material and technologies. Of potentially greater economic consequence, the sanctions also required the US to oppose loans to the country by international lending agencies and US banks (except for food purchases). Unlike the US and Russia, Israel did not condemn the Indian nuclear tests conducted in May 1998, and did not join the weapons embargo against New Delhi.[62]

Instead, a few days after the tests, a delegation from the IAI toured India to accelerate the sale of Israeli-made UAVs (*International Herald Tribune*, 10 June 1998). A few weeks later, IAI also finalized a large-scale deal with India to sell advanced electronic equipment for India's warplanes. The fact that the equipment was solely developed and manufactured in Israel and contained no American technology helped circumvent the existing sanctions.[63] The US opposed the deal and argued that it violated international arms control treaties. Israel disagreed and honoured the deal that had been signed in 1996.[64] In fact, Tel Aviv assured India that all contracts and joint ventures which had been negotiated prior to the tests would be respected (*The Statesman*, 20 August 1998). Agricultural cooperation also continued in spite of the international sanctions.[65] Traditionally, the Soviet Republic had been India's all-weather military ally and supplier during times of crises and of international embargo. As the US, the UK, and the international community curbed exports to India, and as Russia criticized India's decision to test, the BJP welcomed Israel's willingness to resume its arms sales and its agricultural cooperation.

In November 1998, an important institutional obstacle to a rapprochement with Israel was equally removed. At the recommendation of a special task force, a new National Security Management System was put into place. The task force notably recommended the creation of the post of national security advisor (NSA) to the prime minister. The NSA was given the task to regularly advise the prime minister on matters related to internal and security threats to the country. The NSA also became the prime minister's special interlocutor in bilateral discussions with important partners like the US, China, Russia, and Israel. The institutional innovation proved to be a key factor as far as India's policy towards Israel was concerned, in particular during the tenure of the first NSA, Brajesh Mishra. A former Indian foreign service officer, Brajesh Mishra had joined the BJP and worked closely with Vajpayee. After the NDA's election, he became the principal secretary to the prime minister. It was under this status that Mishra first visited Israel in 1998 (MEA, *Annual Report*, 1998–1999: 44). In July 1999, Mishra was sent as NSA to Israel to meet with the newly elected Prime Minister Ehud Barak. The NSA office was a possibility to circumvent the MEA and to negotiate directly with the Israeli authorities.

In May 1999, large-scale military intrusions from Pakistan were detected by the Indian military and intelligence agencies in the Kargil– Dras sector of the disputed state of Jammu and Kashmir, a Pakistani provocation that escalated into the Kargil war.[66] It took more than a week for the Indian army to understand and estimate the scale of the infiltration, and subsequently to develop a course of action to drive the invaders out. Three weeks after the initial detection of incursion, the Indian army eventually started a counter-offensive, code-named Operation Vijay, which eventually drove the invaders behind the LoC by July 1999. The conflict was unique as it was one of the rare oppositions between two nuclear-weapon states. The Indian army had to promptly adapt to this new style of low-intensity warfare with all the doctrinal and technological changes it implied. In June–July 1999, the Indian forces restricted their military operations to the Indian side of the LoC to limit the potential of escalation of the conflict.

In spite of the final diplomatic and military victory, the Kargil crisis led to an important debate over India's defence and intelligence failures.[67] Pakistan's phased infiltration in forward outposts in inhospitable and elevated terrains revealed the Indian's military unpreparedness in both spotting and preventing the incursions across the LoC, as well the lack of training and experience in mountain warfare. It was in this enabling context of reforms that the BJP and especially India's security establishment chose to expand its cooperation with Israel. The Israeli army had an important experience (and the consequent technology) in coping with border-control, counter-terrorism, and limited wars. There is not enough evidence to claim that Israeli assistance helped India 'turn around' the situation during the Kargil war against Pakistan.[68] While Israel was one of the rare countries to directly help India during the short conflict, the short duration of the conflict did not result in an immediate increase in military supplies from Israel.[69] The qualitative changed happened after the crisis: the Kargil conflict revealed some important deficiencies in India's intelligence and military forces. In its efforts to remediate these problems, the Indian security establishment turned towards Israeli assistance and technologies.

In a first phase, Israel proved to be an important and reliable partner during the Kargil conflict by quickly providing India with necessary mortar ammunition and apparently also with laser-guided missiles for its fighter jets.[70] When trying to provide close air support to ground troops, the IAF faced problems of limited sight of the Pakistani bunkers, inaccurate unguided missiles, and the explicit instruction not to cross the LoC. To adapt to these constraints and specifically to correct the problem of accuracy in the Kargil heights, Air Chief Marshal Tipnis chose on 30 May to commit IAF Mirage 2000H fighters capable of delivering laser-guided bombs to ground attack operations (Lambeth 2012: 17–18). According to multiple accounts, India was promptly provided with laser-guided missiles for its Mirages from Israel (Bedi 2003; Inbar and Ningthoujam 2012; Pant 2004). In June 1999, the precision strikes from the upgraded Mirage 2000H limited the advantage of the Pakistani soldiers based on high positions, and helped turn around the conflict in India's favour. In addition, the shooting down of an IAF Canberra PR57 by a Chinese-made Anza infrared surface-to-air missile on 21 May had also exposed the limitations of India's traditional photo reconnaissance platforms (Lambeth 2012: 13). Despite pressures from the US and the international community, Israel agreed to speed up shipments of arms orders that had been submitted before the Kargil developments, including the delivery of Israeli Heron and Searcher UAVs.[71] UAVs for high-altitude surveillance represented a less costly and more effective alternative which provided more accurate imagery for ground troops and fighter jets.[72] At a time when India was still facing technological exports sanctions, Tel Aviv's quick reaction to India's request for military assistance further increased its credibility as a reliable arms supplier.

In a second phase, the Kargil crisis brought to light many structural problems in India's defence capabilities. The Kargil conflict created a favourable environment for key policy reforms. The first important lesson was the intelligence failure. The primary public document that addressed this issue was the India Kargil Review Committee Report which documented the shortfalls of Indian intelligence equipment and the inherent deficiencies of the Indian intelligence apparatus in anticipating the cross-border Pakistani infiltrations in Kargil. In the report, the intelligence agencies were described as relying too heavily on the notion that the inhospitable region and the lack of previous Pakistani infiltration in that area precluded any type of incursion into Kargil. There was hardly any surveillance in this part of the LoC. The conflict therefore precipitated military, intelligence, and technological efforts to prevent a new Kargil-like scenario. The second lesson was that India needed to improve the quality of its military arsenal in conjunction with the evolving regional threats and Pakistan's purchase of American material.

To address its surveillance and reconnaissance problems along the LoC, the Indian military establishment emphasized the need for drones. It was argued that the intrusions could have been spotted earlier if India had regular UAV surveillance of the border. By 1999, India's indigenous efforts to build UAVs for reconnaissance missions had yielded poor results. The Lakshya and Nishant UAV models were either produced in limited models and or were still undergoing flight tests.[73] Production delays and technical problems led the Indian army to consider the more sophisticated and higher range Israeli Searcher and Henron drones as an alternative to compensate for the delays. India had also been unsuccessful in developing an AWACS capability. An important setback occurred when an Avro aircraft with an indigenous airborne surveillance platform was tested and crashed in January 1999. Following the crash of this prototype, which killed eight scientists and the aircrew, the project was suspended.[74] In the absence of effective AWACS capabilities, the Indian army and the Indian navy relied on UAVs for airborne surveillance. The Indian military estimated it would need 100 tactical UAVs in the next five years, in addition to 200 UAVs for low- and high-altitude operations. In 2001, the Indian ministry of defence negotiated a fixed price deal with IAI at $7.2 million per UAV (Inbar 2008: 179). In 2003, India signed another $130 million contract with IAI for 18 Heron UAVs and ordered 16 additional ones. IAI also partnered with Hindustan Aeronautics Limited (HAL) for maintenance purposes (Inbar 2008: 179). The absence of AWACS technology also encouraged the Indian government to discuss with Israel the possibility of purchasing a Phalcon platform.[75] India also reportedly acquired from Israel sophisticated sensors to monitor cross-border infiltration.[76] In the aftermath of the Kargil war, the Indian army has maintained a constant surveillance of cross-border infiltration through its Israeli-made Searcher and Heron and sensing equipment.

While the Kargil conflict was mostly an air and ground battle, there were also some important navy manoeuvers in the Arabian Sea. While in the end there were no direct confrontations, the Indian navy was put on high alert as a result of Pakistan's build-up and prepared for a blockade of the Pakistani ports to cut off Pakistani supply routes and to force a Pakistani withdrawal from Kargil.[77] The preventive naval deployment apparently deterred Pakistan from embarking onto naval operations but also led to reflections within the Indian navy leadership over the implications of large-scale fighting. The Indian navy had apparently been concerned that Pakistan could have used its American-made Harpoon missiles if it felt threatened by a naval blockade.[78] The Indian navy also argued that there was urgency as the indigenous anti-missile defence (AMD) systems had failed to become operational. Consequently, a deal to purchase AMD system from Israel was negotiated by a committee headed by Vice-Admiral Arun Prakash, chief of naval personnel at naval Headquarters.[79] Kargil and its implications for future navy operation paved the way for the purchase of the nine Barak-I AMD systems and missiles from IAI and Rafael in February 2001 (Gupta 2001; Pandit 2012a).

The purchase by the NDA government of the Barak-1 vertically launched surface-to-air missiles from Israel in the late 1990s marked a significant technological and financial breakthrough in defence cooperation. The $270-million contract was also the biggest defence deal to date between the two countries. By the early 2000s, the Indian defence establishment had convinced the government that Israel could effectively meet India's emerging requirements in such niche technology areas like UAVs, surveillance systems, and anti-missile systems. In parallel, the DRDO had not been able to deliver operational UAVs, AWACS, and AMD systems to cope with emerging threats. Consequently, the Kargil conflict and its immediate aftermath were a decisive window of opportunity for the Indian defence establishment to present the Israel defence industry as a viable and positive alternative which could promptly deliver in the fields where India had pressing security concerns. The existing ideological and institutional obstacles to increased defence cooperation were gradually diluted.

An Attempt at an Ideological Rapprochement

The military and political victories for the NDA government in 1999 in Kargil and in the parliamentary elections also reinforced the Vajpayee government's legitimacy and policy leverage. This was an opportunity for the BJP to further publicize the rapprochement between the two countries. The upgrade of the bilateral relationship was illustrated by four important visits from 2000 to 2003. The first symbolic event was the visit of Home Minister (and Deputy Prime Minister) L. K. Advani to Israel in June 2000. Advani was the first senior cabinet minister to visit Israel and this was the first important political visit to reciprocate the Israeli President's visit in 1996.[80] The composition of Advani's delegation clearly indicated a focus on questions of internal security, counter-terrorism, and border control. Advani was accompanied by the home secretary, and the heads of the Central Bureau of Intelligence (CBI), the Intelligence Bureau (IB), and the Border Security Force (BSF).[81] Advani met the President Ezer Weizman, the Prime Minister Ehud Barak, the Minister for Regional Cooperation Shimon Peres, and the Minister of Internal Affairs Natan Sharansky. He also discussed with the heads of the Mossad and Shin Bet, as well as with Israeli arms manufacturers.[82] During his trip, Advani argued that India and Israel shared a 'common perception of terrorism' as a menace, especially if 'coupled with religious fundamentalism'. He added that the two countries "mutual determination to combat terrorism' was the basis for further discussion.[83] Advani's objective was to get Israel to provide India with technology, like UAVs, to deal with cross-border infiltration, as well as counter-terrorism training. Advani also visited Israel's northern border with Lebanon to study Israel's border management. He publicly discussed the possibility of nuclear cooperation with Israel. Concerned by the possible adverse reactions to this statement, Indian officials preferred to cancel his scheduled visit to a nuclear reactor. Advani also added that nuclear cooperation was not aimed against any other state (Melman 2000). In another conciliatory move to limit criticism at home and from the Arab states, the Home Minister met Yasser Arafat during his visit (*The Hindu*, 20 June 2000).

Just a few days after Advani's visit, India's Minister of External Affairs, Jaswant Singh, also visited Israel. Singh met with the Minister of Foreign Affairs David Levy and talked about cooperation in defence and counter-terrorism. Both ministers agreed on the creation of a joint working group (JWG) at the ministerial level for cooperation on terrorism (*Jerusalem Post*, 3 July 2000). Singh discussed defence purchases, including the possible acquisition of the Green Pine radar, which is an element of Israel's anti-ballistic system.[84] In addition, Jaswant Singh met with President Weizman and Prime Minister Barak. During his visit, Singh also made an important statement which illustrated the BJP's break with India's traditional approach towards West Asia and Israel. Indirectly referring to the domestic Muslim factor, Singh argued that India's Israel policy had been 'captive to domestic politics' and to an 'unstated veto' on India's 'larger West Asian Policy'.[85] Unlike previous governments, Jaswant Singh confirmed that the BJP's Israel policy was not constrained by criticism from Indian Muslims and from Arab states, especially if it was at the expense of cooperation with Israel on security matters. For instance, in August–September 2001, at the UN-sponsored conference against racism in Durban (South Africa), acting on Vajpayee's specific instructions, the Indian delegation refused to re-equate Zionism with racism, despite the appeals of the Arab countries and of Yasser Arafat who visited New Delhi just before the conference (Gaur 2005: 253).

Another decisive visit for the bilateral relationship that occurred in 2003 was not one from a minister, nor was it a visit which took place either to New Delhi or to Tel Aviv. In May 2003, India's NSA Brajesh Mishra visited the US and gave an important speech to the American Jewish Committee (AJC). Since Rajiv Gandhi's tenure, Indian policymakers had been conscious that contacts with pro-Israel organizations based in the US were necessary to improve relations with both Israel and the US. Narasimha Rao himself had met with representatives of US Jewish organizations in New York just a few days after the establishment of diplomatic relations (Gerberg 2008: 420). Since 1992, the American-Jewish community has tried to facilitate the development of India–Israel diplomatic relations. For instance, the AJC organized a conference in New Delhi in 1997 to celebrate the fiftieth anniversaries of independence of both India and Israel. Subsequently, a delegation of the AJC visited New Delhi in January 2004 (Pant 2004).

India also had an incentive in engaging the pro-Israel organizations in the US. Since 1992, India and Israel had been regularly discussing defence exchanges but India could only purchase weapons and technologies which were exclusively Israeli-made. There were institutional and legal obstacles to the purchase of the Phalcon AWACS and of ballistic missile defence systems as some of the technology originated from the US.[86] India was still targeted by US technological embargoes and sanctions which had been imposed after the nuclear tests of 1974 and 1998. Consequently, India actively engaged pro-Israel groups to improve Indo-US ties and to gain the approval of the US administration. The Indian government also encouraged Indian-American organizations like the US–India Political Action Committee to establish institutional links with the American–Israel Political Action Committee, and the AJC.[87]

Mishra's visit to the US and to the AJC must be seen within this objective of improving relations with both Israel and the US. The Indian NSA went beyond conveying India's security concerns to the Jewish-American community. In his speech, Mishra formulated the idea of a tripartite axis between the US, Israel, and India. Noting that all these countries were democracies which shared a 'common vision of pluralism tolerance and equal opportunities', he argued that stronger relations between the three countries had a 'natural logic'.[88] He added that the three democracies shared similar security threats and should form a 'viable alliance' to combat the common threat of 'global terrorism'.[89] While there has been no attempt to follow up on these declarations and to form an explicit alliance with Israel (and the US), both countries did start cooperating more closely on counter-terrorism. The BJP government had found it beneficial to learn from Israel's experience in dealing with terrorism. And the terrorism that both India and Israel faced was funded and assisted by neighbouring states. The BJP therefore perceived structural similarities in the kind of threats that India and Israel faced from terrorism.[90]

The peak of the Indo-Israeli rapprochement initiated by the BJP was the official visit from the Israeli Prime Minister Ariel Sharon to India in September 2003. This was the first visit from an active Israeli prime minister to New Delhi. Sharon was accompanied by the Minister of Justice Yossef Lapid; the Minister of Culture, Education, and Sport Limor Livnat; and the Minister of Agriculture Israel Katz. He was also accompanied by a large business delegation and by representatives from almost all of Israel's defence companies, including IAI, Elbit, Rafael, Israel Military Industries (IMI), and Tadiran. During his visit, Prime Minister Sharon met with the Indian President Abdul Kalam, the Prime Minister Vajpayee, the Minister of Home Affairs Advani, the Minister of Defence George Fernandes, the Minister of Finance Jaswant Singh, the Minister of External Affairs Yashwant Sinha, the NSA Brajesh Mishra, and even with the leader of the opposition and president of the INC, Sonia Gandhi (*The Statesman*, 9 September 2003).

In a speech at a banquet hosted for Sharon, Vajpayee qualified the visit as an important landmark in the bilateral relations between the two countries. While he did refer to trade relations, he mostly concentrated on counter-terrorism as a key area of cooperation. Prime Minister Vajpayee remarked that India and Israel were both 'victims of terrorism' and 'partners in the battle against this scourge' (*The Hindu*, 10 September 2003). Building on Mishra's earlier statements, Yossef Lapid told journalists in New Delhi that there was an 'unwritten, abstract' axis between India, Israel, and the US because there was mutual interest of the three countries in making the world a 'more secure place'.[91] Although the relationship was multifaceted, the BJP government decided to emphasize the menace of terrorism that afflicted both nations. The common theme of uniting against terrorism was again highlighted in the joint statement, the 'Delhi Statement on Friendship and Cooperation between India and Israel'. While there was no discussion on forming an 'alliance', the statement emphasized the fact both countries were 'open and democratic societies' jointly fighting a 'global threat' (*The Hindu*, 10 September 2003). The declaration signed during Sharon's visit also condemned states and individuals who aided and abetted terrorism across borders, harboured and provided sanctuary to terrorists besides giving financial support, training, or patronage. Both countries pledged both material and political support to each other in their struggle against terrorism. Interestingly, th e statement remained silent on the Palestine and Kashmir issues.[92] Beyond discussions on counter-terrorism, the two countries also signed four agreements of cooperation covering fields like health and medicine, combating illicit trafficking, and protection of the environment (Table 5.4).

Table 5.4 List of Bilateral Agreements (non-military) since 1992

Bilateral agreements	Agreement Date
Cultural agreement	18 May 1993
Economic Memorandum of Understanding (MoU)	
Agreement for Cooperation in the Field of Agriculture	24 December 1993
Air Transport Agreement	4 April 1994
Agreement concerning Cooperation in the Field of Telecommunication and Posts	20 November 1994
Agreement on Trade and Economic Cooperation	21 December 1994
Agreement for the Promotion and Protection of Investments	29 January 1996
Convention for the Avoidance of Double Taxation and for the Prevention of Fiscal Evasion with Respect to Taxes on Income and on Capital	29 January 1996
Bilateral Agreement regarding Mutual Assistance and Cooperation in Customs Matters	29 January 1996
Memorandum of Intent on a Joint High-tech Agricultural Demonstration Cooperation Project	30 December 1996
Umbrella Agreement on the Development of Cooperation in the Field of Industrial andTechnological Research and Development	30 December 1996
Agreement on Technical Cooperation	30 December 1996
Executive Agreement for a Program of Cooperation in the Field of Agriculture	17 October 1997
Agreement on Cooperation in Peace Uses of Outer Space	28 October 2002
Agreement on Cooperation in the field of Health and Medicine	9 September 2003 (Sharon visit)

(*Cont'd*)

Table 5.4 (Cont'd)

Bilateral agreements	Agreement Date
Agreement on Cooperation in combating illicit trafficking and abuse of narcotic drugs and psychotropic substances	9 September 2003 (Sharon visit)
Agreement on Cooperation in the field of Protection of the Environment	9 September 2003 (Sharon visit)
Agreement on Exemption of Visa requirement for holders of diplomatic, official, and service passports	9 September 2003 (Sharon visit)
Memorandum of Understanding (MoU) on India–Israeli Research and Development Fund Initiative	5 May 2005 (Sibal visit)
Indo-Israeli Industrial Initiative for R&D	July 2005
Agreement on Economic Cooperation	November 2005
Inter-Governmental three-year Work Plan on Agriculture Cooperation	10 May 2006
Extradition Treaty	10 January 2012
Agreement for Transfer of Sentenced Prisoners	10 January 2012
Free Trade Agreement	November 2013 (Third round of negotiations)

Source: Information compiled from different sources, including the Indian embassy in Israel (http://www.indembassy.co.il), and various Indian and Israel newspapers.

The growing political rapprochement was seconded by institutionalized dialogues between the bureaucracies and the services of the two countries. The two countries set up a JWG to discuss counter-terrorism issues during the Jaswant Singh visit.[93] The two countries also established a regular dialogue between their national security councils on September 2001 on the occasion of the Israeli NSA Uzi Dayan's visit (Sherman 2003). During the visit of the Israeli Minister of Foreign Affairs, Shimon Peres, in January 2002, a mutual agreement on counter-terrorism was discussed between the two countries (Gerberg 2008: 372). Discussions continued in 2002 with several visits from Amos Yaron, the director-general of Israel's ministry of defence.[94] Reportedly, the Indian ministry of defence, which was in the middle of an international diplomatic crisis with Pakistan, asked Yaron about using imagery on Kashmir from Israel's Ofek-5 spy satellite, and about the purchase of the Arrow anti-ballistic missile (ABM) system. Yaron could not commit on either of these two demands but offered the possibility to acquire two Green Pine Radars from Israel.[95] The decision to launch an Israeli spy satellite from India was taken during one of Yaron's visits (Katz 2008). The head of the Indian IB, K. P. Singh, visited Israel and met with the heads of the Israeli security services in March 2004. These meetings strengthened the intelligence collaboration between the two countries, especially with regards to sharing information on terrorist organizations (*Times of India*, 19 March 2004). The different military services from the two countries have also organized an institutionalized dialogue and regular bilateral visits (Tables 5.5 and 5.6).

At the economic level, business and trade delegations have continued to organize visits and discussions. For instance, in 1999, the Small Business Authority of Israel and the Federation of Israel Chamber of Commerce visited India, and the Indian Trade Promotion Organization held an event called the 'India Week' to showcase India's industrial strength in Tel Aviv in May 2000. In September 2003, the CII and the Israel Export and International Cooperation Institute as well as the Manufacturers Association of Israel set up a forum to promote trade and economic relations (Gerberg 2008: 379). In addition, the two countries had institutionalized a scientific dialogue since the creation of the joint Indo-Israeli fund in 1993. Representatives from various research organizations in India and Israel met once a year to agree on joint research projects. In November 1999, both sides agreed on a Protocol of Cooperation on joint research and development between the office of the chief scientist of Israel and the Indian Department of Scientific and Industrial Research.[96] In November 2002, the Indian Space Research Organization (ISRO) and the Israel Space Agency (ISA) signed an agreement on cooperation with regard to peaceful uses of outer space. Both agencies had complementary interests: Israel was attracted by India's launch vehicles while India was drawn to Israel's dual-use small satellite technology (Inbar 2004). In August 2003, the chairperson of ISRO visited Israel and signed an agreement which included collaboration in the area of small and micro satellites. One month later, Sharon announced in New Delhi the future launch of an Israeli space telescope, on top of the Indian polar satellite launch vehicle (Pant 2004). In February 2001, the MFA also sent an Israeli army medical team to the state of Gujarat, following a devastating earthquake, to help restore the state's medical facilities (Gerberg 2008: 356).

Table 5.5 Indian Military Visits to Israel since 1992

Year	Nature of visit	Outcome/deal/signal
1993 (May)	High-level military team travelling with Indian delegation led by CM Pawar	Military team visited Israeli military facilities including the Israeli Anti-Terror Unit
1993 (June)	G. S. Iyer, joint secretary in the defence ministry	Led a 16-member National Defence College (NDC) team
1995 (July)	High-level Indian team, led by Defence Secretary K. A. Nambiar	Talks on the upgrade of the MIG-21, Russian T-72 tank, and interest for remotely piloted vehicles (RPVs)
1995 (October)	Ashok Tandon, director-general of the National Security Guard (NSG)	Reportedly to look for cooperation on training and upgrading the skills of commandos and purchase of weaponry
1995 (November)	INS Gomati and INS Subhadra	First Indian naval goodwill visit to an Israeli port
1995 (December)	Air Vice-Marshal V. K. Bhatia, Assistant Chief of Air Staff Operations	Led a four-member delegation to Israel to discuss flight safety measures
1996 (June)	Dr A. P. J. Abdul Kalam, scientific adviser to the defence minister	Reportedly discussed ABM projects and purchase of airborne early warning (AEW) systems
1996 (July)	Air Chief Marshal S. K. Sareen	Guest of Air Force Commander Major General Eitan Ben-Eliyahu
		Reportedly discussed purchase of AWACS and UAVs
1996 (September)	Deputy Air-Chief Marshal M. S. Vasudev	
1997 (February)	India's Defence Secretary T. K. Banerjee	Led a high-level defence delegation to discuss the exchange of technology
1997 (January)	Dr A. P. J. Abdul Kalam, Head of DRDO	Undisclosed
1998 (March)	Chief of Army Staff General V. P. Malik	First visit by a serving Indian chief of army staff
		Indian governmental initative

(Cont'd)

Table 5.5 (Cont'd)

Year	Nature of visit	Outcome/deal/signal
		Discussed field formation, military training, UAVs, and radio communication
		Visited border facilities
2000	INS SHAKTI, INS GOMTI, and INS RANVEER visited Port Eilat	Senior Indian naval officers held talks with Israeli defence officials
2004 (March)	Head of IB K. P. Singh	Met with the heads the Israeli security services to strengthen intelligence collaboration
2005	Lieutenant-General Shantonu Choudhary and Vice-Admiral Arun Prakash	Announced that India intends to purchase 18 Israeli-made SPYDER anti-aircraft missile systems to bolster its defences
2006	Chief of Air Staff, Air Chief Marshal S. P. Tyagi, and the Vice-Chief of the Navy, Vice-Admiral Venkat Bharathan	
2006	Two Indian warships docked in the Israeli port of Haifa	Goodwill visit to enhance diplomatic relations
2007 (March)	Army Chief General J. J. Singh	Reviewed military projects like the upgrade of 300 T-72 MI tanks, BMP2 infantry combat vehicles, and the induction of UAVs
		Purchased Israeli night vision equipment
2008 (January)	Indian navy chief and chairman of the Indian Joint Chiefs of Staff, Admiral Suresh Mehta	Met his Israeli naval counterpart and senior defence officials for discussions on weapons project (including Barak-2 missile defence) and joint training

(*Cont'd*)

Table 5.5   (Cont'd)

Year	Nature of visit	Outcome/deal/signal
2008 (November)	Indian Secretary of Defence Vijay Singh and delegation composed of IAF deputy chief Air Marshal N. A. K. Browne, Army deputy chief (planning and systems) M. S. Dadwal, Navy assistant chief (policy and plans) Rear Admiral Girish Luthra, and DRDO chief controller Prahlada	JWG on defence cooperation Discussed the sale of three Phalcon aircraft radar systems, as well as missiles, helicopters, maintenance equipment, and UAVs
2009 (November)	Chief of Army Staff to the Indian Army, General Deepak Kapoor	Discussed the Barak-8 tactical air-defence system purchase Sent to allay fears that corruption investigations in India would disrupt defence links
2010 (October)	India's Naval Chief, Admiral Nirmal Kumar Verma	Met with his Israeli counterpart Eliezer Marom, Defence Minister Ehud Barak, Chief of Staff Gabi Ashkenazi Discussed the expansion of defence relations, especially on joint manufacturing of defence equipment
2013 (January)	Chief of Air Staff N. A. K. Browne	Held strategic talks with Israel Air Force Chief Amir Eshel, Israeli defence Minister Ehud Barak, and Israel Defence Forces (IDF) Chief Benny Gantz

Note: The vice-chief of the Indian Army, the Indian Navy chief, and the chief of the Indian Air Force have all visited Israel since the new Congress government assumed office in May 2004. All three serving chiefs have visited Israel between 2009 and 2011.

Source: Information compiled from various Indian and Israel newspapers.

Table 5.6 Israeli Military Visits to India since 1992

Year	Nature of visit	Outcome/deal/signal
1992 (June)	Six-member Israeli defence team	Came at the invitation of the ministry of defence
		Held meetings with several ministry officials
1994 (August)	Defence ministry's Director-General David Ivry	Led a high-level delegation, reciprocating Iyer's visit a year earlier
1995 (March)	Israeli Air Force Chief, Major General Helz Bodinger	First serving defence chief to visit India
		Offered a package deal, which included airborne warning and control systems, remotely piloted vehicles, access to an air platform for anti-detection and anti-jamming manoeuvre, and specialized weapons
1996 (November)	Israeli naval chief Vice-Admiral Alex Tal	Held talks with Indian officials including junior Defence Minister N. V. N. Somu
2001 (September)	Visit of an Israeli counter-terrorism team led by Eli Katzir of the Counter-Terrorism Combat Unit in the Prime Minister's Office	Official launch of an Indo-Israeli joint working group (JWG) on counter-terrorism
2001 (September)	Visit of head of the National Security Council General Uzi Dayan	Met his Indian counterpart NSA Brajesh Mishra to discuss cooperation in dealing with terrorism and developments in West Asia
2001 (November)	Director-General of Israeli Defence Ministry, Major-General (retd) Amos Yaron	Led a seven-member military delegation
		Met Defence Secretary Yogendra Narain to establish a JWG for defence which would meet every year alternatively in New Delhi and Tel Aviv and would be headed by the respective defence secretaries

(Cont'd)

Table 5.6 (*Cont'd*)

Year	Nature of visit	Outcome/deal/signal
2002 (June)	Director-General of Israeli Defence Ministry Amos Yaron	Israel supplied hardware through special planes as part of 'Operation Parakram', discussed the purchase of the Green Pine radars
2004 (November)	Visit of an Israeli delegation to discuss counter-terrorism, composed of high-level Israeli defence ministry officials and high-level executives from major armament manufacturers	Indo-Israeli Joint Working Group (JWG) on Counter-Terrorism Discussed new joint ventures and purchases
2007 (March)	Israeli delegation was led by Miriam Ziv, deputy director-general, strategic division, ministry of foreign affairs	Sixth meeting of Indo-Israeli Joint Working Group (JWG) on Counter-Terrorism Met Indian delegation headed by K. C. Singh, additional aecretary (international organizations), ministry of external affairs
2008 (January)	Israeli Defence Ministry Chief, Brig Gen (retd) Pinchas Buchris	Held talks with NSA M. K. Narayanan Met Defence Secretary Vijay Singh, Army Chief General Deepak Kapoor, Naval Chief Admiral Suresh Mehta, and Air Force Chief Fali Homi Major Discussed the setting up of a mechanism for intelligence sharing
2008 (September)	Chief of Staff of the Israeli ground forces command, Brig-General Avi Mizrahi	Sharing of military intelligence, equipment, conducting joint training and exercises, and 'interoperability' Visited the Line of Control (LoC) in Jammu and Kashmir
2008 (September)	Israeli Deputy Chief of General Staff, Major General Moshe Kaplinsky	Visited Kashmir, including the 16 Corps headquarters in Nagrota to help India with 'counter-insurgency' operations

Table 5.6 (Cont'd)

Year	Nature of visit	Outcome/deal/signal
2009 (December)	Chief of the General Staff of the Israeli Defence Forces, Lt Gen. Gabi Ashkenazi	First official visit to the country by an Israeli military chief
		Met with his Indian counterpart, Chief of Army Staff to the Indian Army, General Deepak Kapoor, NSA M. K. Narayanan, and the chiefs of Indian Navy and Air Force
2009 (December)	High-level delegation from the Israel defence establishment, led by Brigadier General (retd) Pinchas Buchris	Meetings of JWGs on defence cooperation and counter-terrorism
		Met with defence minister A. K. Antony, Defence Secretary Pradeep Kumar, NSA M. K. Narayanan, the chiefs of the armed forces, and DRDO chief V. K. Saraswat
2010	Display by the Israel national pavilion at Aero India 2011, notably Rafael chairman Major General (retd) Herzle Bodinger	
2010 (January)	Israeli navy chief Vice-Admiral Eliezer Marom	Held discussions with Defence Minister A. K. Antony and the three service chiefs, and visited the South-Western Army Command at Jaipur and the Western Naval Command at Mumbai
2012 (December)	Director General of Israel's defence ministry Major General Udi Shani	Met with Defence Secretary Shashi Kant Sharma
2013 (November)	Israeli chief of land forces Major General Guy Zur	Held talks with Defence Minister A. K. Antony, Army Chief General Bikram Singh, Navy Chief Admiral D. K. Joshi, and IAF Chief Air Chief Marshal N. A. K. Browne

Source: Information compiled from various Indian and Israel newspapers.

Both the defence reforms induced by the Kargil crisis and the publicized political rapprochement between the BJP and the Likud from 2001 to 2004 facilitated the acceleration and conclusion of ongoing military deals, and especially joint ventures. In September 2002, HAL and IAI signed a contract to jointly manufacture advanced light helicopters for the Indian army. The two companies also set up a division in Hyderabad for the maintenance services.[97] IAI also signed another contract in February 2003 with Nelco Limited to develop, manufacture, and market a range of electronic products primarily for the Indian defence forces.[98] The Indian ministry of defence concluded an estimated $20 million agreement with IMI for the acquisition of assault and sniper rifles. Rafael signed a contract in 2003 for the transfer of technology to produce the Spike anti-armour and the advanced Python-4 air-to-air missiles (Raghuvanshi 2003a, 2003c). A $40 million deal was signed in April 2003 for an additional Barak missile system and for 10 more over the next five to seven years, to bring to the total of 20 in the Indian navy (Raghuvanshi 2003b).

The major deal the BJP government negotiated with Israel during this period was the $1.1 billion purchase of the Phalcon AWACS system in 2003. This was a game-changing agreement for two reasons. First, the Phalcon system brought a new qualitative edge to Indo-Israeli defence operations. The system was an airborne and mobile force-multiplier which put India's air force in an unparalleled advantage in case of a new type of Kargil face-off against either Pakistan or China (Blarel 2006). Second, the deal marked the evolution of the US position on technology transfer between Israel and India. Weary of the Chinese precedent, India and Israel coordinated their efforts with high-ranking US officials during the Phalcon negotiations. After four years of negotiations, Washington finally authorized the Phalcon sale in 2003.[99] The political lobbying efforts from the BJP in Washington facilitated this approval and marked a new phase of defence and technological engagement with Israel.[100]

Remaining Oppositions to India's Israel Policy

The new publicized and active engagement of Israel under the BJP was not consensual. The high-profile visits and the new rhetoric led many observers to suspect a radical change in India's West Asia policy which was considered to be more pro-Israel and anti-Islam (Blarel 2006; Jaffrelot

2003; Karat 2002). At the domestic level, the BJP-led government was accused of no longer supporting the Palestinian cause. The critics of the BJP's policy were representatives of the old orthodoxy and of the historical legacy of unconditional support for the Palestinian cause. The criticism came from the INC and especially from the Indian Left parties who were concerned that the growth of the bilateral relationship could destabilize India's relations with other West Asian states. INC leader Natwar Singh said that India should maintain good relations with Israel but not at the expense of India's relations with the Palestinian people (*The Hindu*, 22 October 2000). The CPI(M) regularly criticized the BJP for not supporting Yasser Arafat during the Second Intifada and for not condemning the confinement to his Ramallah house in the early 2000s (Cherian 2004; Gopal and Sharma 2007: 360). In September 2003, during the Sharon visit, there were widespread protests and demonstrations, mostly organized by the Indian Left parties but also by Indian Muslim organizations.[101] The CPI(M) directly accused the government of inviting a 'war-criminal' (Jayaprakash 2003).

There was also an opposition from the Arab states against growing Indo-Israeli ties. Egypt, Syria, and Jordan expressed their concerns over the visit of Chief of Army Staff General V. P. Malik to Israel in 1998. In 2001, the Arab League expressed its 'deep concern' over the military and security cooperation between India and Israel which could 'create tension in the Middle-East'. The Arab League also warned New Delhi that Arab states could reconsider their commercial interests with India.[102] Arab diplomats were also disappointed that India did not vote in favour of the UNGA resolution condemning Israel's excessive use of force against Palestinian civilians. The statements issued by the Indian government on the Intifada apportioned blame to both sides and urged them to restore normalcy. Arab diplomats stationed in the country tried to convince New Delhi to change its position and argued that India's permanent interests lay in the Arab world. After a meeting with the MEA, the Arab diplomats were convinced that the old guard at the MEA supported continuity in India's pro-Arab policy and that the new policy direction mainly came from the BJP ministers (Cherian 2000; Katyal 2000; Mohan 2000).

There were also institutional and ideological obstacles to the BJP's ambition to actively engage Israel in counter-terrorism cooperation. For instance, there were some important perceptual differences on the definition of terrorism.[103] Cooperation on counter-terrorism and intelligence-sharing efforts were limited. India did not totally identify with Israel's definition of terrorism, and India does not focus on the same kind of coercive apparatus Israel advocated. Finally, Indian decision-makers were conscious that Israeli tactics of building walls and waging punitive wars had proved to be successful to limit terrorist attacks in the short term but only entrenched further hatred in the Arab world.[104] Consequently, Israel's training of Indian forces in counter-terrorism has been limited. Cooperation has focused on the purchase of specialized technology and equipment, and on intelligence cooperation. In fact, given the domestic compulsions, there have not been any joint military exercises during the BJP tenure. Israeli–Indian counter-terror talks have mostly been done at a non-governmental level and between research institutions (Peraino 2008).

To limit criticisms at home and abroad against its West Asian policy, the BJP made some diplomatic gestures to demonstrate its continuing support for the Palestine national movement. Arafat was greeted in Delhi in April 1999 for a working visit. Prime Minister Vajpayee assured the Palestinian leader of India's continued strong support to the Palestinian people's 'legitimate and inalienable' right to a homeland.[105] Following their visits to Israel in 2000, Advani and Singh also met with Arafat. The Indian government and the Palestinian National Authority (PA) also encouraged direct trade, which reached $20 million in 2001 (Gerberg 2008: 408). During Israeli Prime Minister Sharon's visit, the Indian government made it clear that it would not dilute its traditional support for Palestine.[106] The Indian government also offered the PA a diplomatic enclave for their embassy in 2003 in a prized real estate area of New Delhi (Sirohi 2008b). In 2003, the Indian government supported the transfer of the case of Israel's security fence to the International Court of Justice (ICJ).[107] Alongside its increased engagement with Israel, the BJP also actively courted other key regional players like Iran and Saudi Arabia (Mohan 2001). The Minister of External Affairs Jaswant Singh travelled to both countries in 2001 and the Prime Minister Vajpayee travelled to Tehran in April 2001 (Khana 2001). In January 2003, India hosted the Iranian President Mohammed Khatami as a guest for the Republic Day celebrations (Fair 2009).

In addition, the attitude of actors within the old orthodoxy has been increasingly ambiguous vis-à-vis Israel, especially in the ranks of the

Communist Party. For instance, in the summer of 2000, the chairperson of the Israel Parliamentary Friendship League and a leader of the CPI(M), Somnath Chatterjee, and the then chief minister of West Bengal and member of the CPI(M) Jyoti Basu, led a 20-member business delegation to Israel to look for investment opportunities for their home state.[108] The visit demonstrated that even important communist leaders were no longer opposed to ties with Israel (Silyer 2000). It was an important diplomatic coup for Israel. However, the Second Intifada limited the effects of this initial rapprochement and pushed the Indian Left back to its pro-Palestinian stand.

The BJP tenure marked a qualitative change in Indo-Israeli relations. The BJP government's quasi-uninhibited Israel policy opened doors for further cooperation in some traditionally sensitive fields like defence procurement and satellite and space collaboration. Nevertheless, while the BJP's political willingness was a decisive factor, other events like the nuclear tests of 1998 and the following sanctions as well as the Kargil crisis created a policy window to further engage Israel in certain niche fields where India's needs were urgent. The BJP's role in removing the US veto to defence acquisitions was decisive. However, it is equally important to note that many of the areas of cooperation and defence deals which were negotiated and secured in the 1998–2004 period had already been identified and discussed between 1992 and 1996. The military establishment was already conscious of the benefits of collaboration with the Israeli defence industries. However, there were important political and institutional obstacles, remnants of the previous policy compromise, which limited any substantial rapprochement. The BJP therefore built on existing efforts and on previous mil-to-mil links.

The Consolidation of India's New Israel Policy? (2004–13)

Ariel Sharon became the first serving Israeli Prime Minister to visit India in September 2003. By then, the two countries had already built strong defence relations and were progressively developing trade relations which had reached $1.27 billion in 2002, compared to the meagre $202 million exchange when both countries established full diplomatic relations in 1992 (Table 5.3). This symbolically rich visit also confirmed the important political dialogue that had been engaged under the NDA/BJP government. However, exactly a year after the highly publicized Sharon visit, the Indo-Israeli partnership was apparently challenged by the return to power of the INC. The INC had been the architect of normalization with Israel but there were initial doubts about the endurance of this new privileged partnership as the UPA's electoral programme had evoked a new beginning in relations with West Asia, including a reassertion of India's support of the Palestinian cause.[109] Since 2004, there have been very few senior cabinet-level visits and Prime Minister Manmohan Singh shied away from visiting Israel or from making any public comments on India's relations with Israel (Table 5.2).[110]

Yet, despite initial doubts following the return of the INC to power, the INC unambiguously resumed and even increased defence cooperation and economic relations with Tel Aviv. The signing of various specialized trade agreements after 2004 has paved the way for a substantial increase in the volume of bilateral trade, which stood at over $5 billion in 2011 (see Table 5.3). Hence, after the INC came back to power, bilateral trade was multiplied by five, and is expected to double if the two nations sign an FTA.[111] India has also become Israel's largest arms export market in the world over the last five years (replacing Turkey and China), and Israel is today India's second largest arms supplier (behind the traditional Russian partner).[112] As a result, the government led by Manmohan Singh after 2004 did not reverse the new Israel policy. In fact, today, almost all Indian parties (with the exception maybe of the communists)[113] realize the strategic benefits of cooperation with Israel and have encouraged this new orientation of India's West Asia policy.

There were, however, important differences with the BJP's Israel policy over the last decade. Parallel to the thriving defence cooperation and to a rapidly developing bilateral commercial relationship, the post-2004 Indian government also took strong pro-Palestinian, if not anti-Israel, positions in most multilateral fora. For example, Manmohan Singh explicitly supported the Palestinian demand for an observer status before the UNGA in September 2011 (Rajiv 2011). India also co-sponsored the resolution favouring the Palestinian request for upgrading its status to non-member observer status at the UNGA in November 2012.[114] As a consequence, the INC government attempted to diversify its alliances in the region, engaging Israel alongside its traditional Arab and Muslim partners.

Return to a More Cautious Israel Policy?

With the parliamentary elections of May 2004, the INC was able to come back to power by putting together a comfortable majority coalition (UPA) of more than 335 members. The INC President Sonia Gandhi surprised observers by declining to become the new prime minister, and by instead asking former finance minister Manmohan Singh to head the new government.[115] After six years of BJP rule and four years of publicized engagement with Israel, it was expected that the new government would renew its traditionally friendly foreign policy with the Arab world and project itself again as a supporter of the Palestinians' quest for an independent state. Some analysts originally considered this could mark a return to the traditional zero-sum game which had prevailed for decades where India would privilege its support for the Arab states at the expense of better relations with Israel (Kumaraswamy 2004b, 2004c; Pant 2004). In fact, the old guard of the Congress (Natwar Singh, Mani Shankar Aiyar) and parties like the CPI(M), which supported the UPA, expected a return to previous policies and a decrease of the military deals and imports.

Given the need for the parliamentary support of the communists, the INC government lacked leverage in its West Asia policy.[116] Before the elections, the INC had agreed with the CPI(M) on a common minimum programme which guaranteed a rebalancing of India's West Asia policy and a reaffirmation of India's support of Palestine. In June 2004, the UPA's new policy was expressed by President Abdul Kalam to Parliament. He stated that 'traditional ties with the countries of West Asia' would be given a fresh thrust. While he said that ties with Israel which had been developed 'on the basis of mutually beneficial cooperation' were important, he also added that this relationship would in no way dilute India's 'principled support for the legitimate aspirations of the Palestinian people'.[117]

Subsequently, there were further signs that India would modify its West Asia policy. After 2004, there were indeed very few senior cabinet-level visits (Table 5.2) and public statements made about India's dealings with Israel. Natwar K. Singh was designated as India's new minister of external affairs. While in opposition, he was critical of the BJP's efforts to promote relations with Israel at the expense of the Palestinians (*The Hindu*, 22 October 2000). After his nomination, Singh said India valued its relationship with Israel and that it would not affect its relations with

Palestine (*The Times of India*, 12 July 2004). In 2005, Natwar Singh added that India had 'civilizational links' with the Arab world and reasserted India's support for the 'just aspirations of the Palestinian people' (Gerberg 2008: 410). The new government also appointed E. Ahamed, the representative of the Indian Union Muslim League (in the state of Kerala), as Union minister of state for the ministry of external affairs. In September 2004, Ahamed visited the PA where he met Yasser Arafat and other Palestinian officials (Gaur 2005: 14 September 2004, 270–1). This visit was meant to demonstrate India's strong support for Palestinian independence while also calling on Israel to lift the siege imposed on the Arafat's headquarters in Ramallah. Following the visit, Ahamed said he wanted to reassure the Arab–Muslim world that India had not been 'drifting away from its decades-long ties with the Arabs, especially on the issue of Palestine'.[118] There were also changes in India's voting behaviour at the UN on issues related to Israel and Palestine. In July 2004, India voted in favour of a UNGA resolution calling on Israel to comply with the advisory opinion of the ICJ which had deemed the West Bank fence to be contrary to international law (MEA, *Annual Report*, 2004–2005: 57). Likewise, the India–EU joint statement of November 2004 called for Israel's withdrawal of the Gaza settlements.[119]

A series of visits during the next two years also seemed to demonstrate a desire to repair ties with Arab and Palestinian partners. An Indian official delegation headed by Natwar Singh attended the funeral of Yasser Arafat in Cairo on 12 November 2004.[120] In the post-Arafat period, India tried to get actively engaged in the West Asian peace process. India sent observers to the general elections of the PA in January 2005 and congratulated Mahmoud Abbas upon his election as the new leader of the PA.[121] In January 2005, the diplomat Chinmay Gharekhan was appointed special envoy of the prime minister to West Asia. Gharekhan visited Israel and the PA in February, March and November 2005.[122] During his visit to Israel in March, he met the Vice-Prime Minister Shimon Peres and the Minister of Foreign Affairs Silvan Shalom, and through his visit to the PA, he met with the newly elected PA Chairman Mahmoud Abbas. Mahmoud Abbas visited New Delhi in May 2005 where he met with the new Indian President Abdul Kalam and the Prime Minister Manmohan Singh as well as the INC President Sonia Gandhi.[123] For the first time, India sent a delegate as an observer to the eighteenth Arab League Summit in Algeria in March 2006 in the person of Minister E. Ahamed.[124]

Following the Sharm-El-Sheikh summit of February 2005, the MEA published a statement in support of the Israeli–Palestinian peace process, urging an end to violence from all sides and a 'just and peaceful solution within a reasonable time-frame, leading to a sovereign, independent state of Palestine with well-defined and secured borders, living at peace with the state of Israel'.[125] The MEA also officially saluted in a statement the Israeli withdrawal from settlements in Gaza and the northern West Bank as part of the unilateral Disengagement Plan.[126] Following this statement, Ambassador Gharekhan visited Israel in November 2005 and met with several Israeli leaders. In a statement, Gharekhan said that India supported the Agreement on Movement and Access concluded between Israel and the PA which involved the opening of the Rafah border crossing and the building of a seaport in the Gaza strip (MEA, *Annual Report* 2005–2006: 53).

These statements from the INC government marked a clear return to the traditional rhetoric encouraging progress in the West Asian peace process. India also tried to re-balance its relations with Palestine and the Arab states after an impression of deviation from the traditional pro-Palestine policy during the BJP years. Despite these renewed overtures to the Arab world, India did not get any immediate diplomatic dividends at the OIC. In July 2005, another resolution on Kashmir passed by the foreign ministers of the OIC in Yemen criticized India. Once more, New Delhi argued that the OIC had no legal and political authority over an internal matter (Naqvi 2005). While the INC government had toned down the rapprochement with Israel both at the public level and within multilateral fora, it did not revise the military or trade deals the BJP had negotiated or started negotiating with Israel. Despite the government's prudence in publicly discussing its policy vis-à-vis Israel, defence and economic relations continued and even increased dramatically (see Table 5.3).

There were various factors that explained the INC's decision to not drastically reverse the policy trend. First, there were elements of a new orthodoxy supporting an increased engagement with Israel within the new INC government. For instance J. N. Dixit, who had been one of the architects of the establishment of diplomatic relations, was a co-chair of the External Affairs Committee of the Congress party and was nominated to the post of NSA after the elections. In his memoirs, Dixit qualified the establishment of relations with Israel as one of 'the most significant developments in India's foreign policy' (Dixit 1996: 315). Even the president of the INC, Sonia Gandhi, did not seem to have a fixed position on Israel. For instance, she met with Shimon Peres, who visited India in February 2002, and then with Prime Minister Sharon when he visited New Delhi in September 2003. This last meeting took place in spite of the fact that an important section of the Congress had opposed the meeting (*The Hindu*, 6 September 2003). While Sonia Gandhi did not openly support an engagement with Israel, she did not seem inflexible to the idea of keeping a channel of communication open with Tel Aviv.

Second, the political parties and the MEA, which had traditionally defined the parameters of India's Israel policy, no longer dictated alone the direction of this relationship. The international and domestic shocks of the 1990s durably reversed the old ideological and institutional arrangements from the previous policy compromise. Given the increasing costs of preserving the existing policy, the defenders of the existing policy had to accept normalization. After 1992, the policy towards Israel was in flux and exposed to new ideas, preferences, and actors. New players adroitly exploited political events and opportunities to offer new policy prescriptions and to redefine the basic dimensions of the policy process in their favour. As a result, issue re-definition and opportunities to redraw institutional arrangements interacted in the 1990s to modify India's Israel policy in a durable way. I argue that after a few years of a renewed and open-ended debate around India's Israel policy (1992–2004), a new policy compromise emerged by 2004 which was defined around narrower defence and economic interests. Two main groups of actors, which had historically envisaged the long-term benefits of engaging Israel, supported a redefinition of India's Israel policy. The Indian military had already sporadically and discreetly collaborated with the Israelis and had encouraged further cooperation. Similarly, certain economic actors, who had both directly and indirectly suffered from the economic boycott against Israel, saw in normalization a profitable opportunity.

A Military–Technical Cooperation Based on India's 'Security Requirements'

The Indian military had always admired the experience and expertise of the Israeli army in its different successful military campaigns, and had already lobbied for more cooperation with its Israeli counterpart. The study of the 1967 Israeli military operations has, for instance, been made compulsory for all officers of the Indian army.[127] Indian soldiers and also scientists particularly appreciated the advances the Israel had made in the field of defence technology. However, the subordination to the political authorities had kept the military from translating their professional appreciation of Israel's military into actual cooperation. Traditionally, the Indian military has had little say in the making of India's foreign policy, with probably the exception of technical issues like the procurement of military equipment necessary to deal with India's immediate security problems.

Even before normalization, there had been an urgent need to diversify India's military procurements given India's over-dependence on Soviet equipment and the increasing obsolescence of Soviet acquisitions.[128] The internal solution was not an alternative as the indigenous military industry had not yet been able to deliver new operational defence systems (Hoyt 2006: 61–6). A change in India's arms procurement strategy became even more pressing following the collapse of the USSR and the division of the Soviet military industry in 15 different states. As a consequence, the Narasimha Rao government had openly acknowledged that it had taken the security factor into consideration when deciding to establish full and normal diplomatic relations with Israel. This was a first opportunity structure for military actors to play a greater role in India's Israel policy.

The influence of military interests in policy-making vis-à-vis Israel increased in the 1990s after the normalization of bilateral relations and the opening up of the decision-making process. In a first phase, the Indian military establishment mostly discussed with its Israeli counterparts and representatives from Israeli defence industries to identify areas of potential complementary cooperation. Because politicians feared opposition at the domestic and regional levels, most subsequent defence exchanges and visits were not disclosed until they had happened. They were then presented as 'goodwill' visits, and no details of the discussions were publicized.[129] Due to internal reluctance, it also took many years for the military establishment to convince the MEA and the political class for the need to have a defence attaché based in Israel. In addition, there was the DRDO's informal veto against defence acquisitions. The niche fields where the Israeli defence industries had comparative advantages were systems that the DRDO was itself attempting to develop (UAVs, AWACS, and ABM systems). Finally, there was the US opposition to technology transfer to India which limited or undermined imports as well as attempts to form joint ventures with Israeli firms.

Military exchanges only became substantial in the early 2000s (see Tables 5.7 and 5.8). The Indian military establishment insisted on the technical benefits of collaboration with Israel. In certain high-technology niche fields such as surveillance equipment (UAVs, electronic sensor equipment, night-vision equipment, airborne early warning system) and ballistic missile defence, where India (and especially the DRDO) had failed to develop robust indigenous capabilities, Israel could offer important equipment and expertise (Blarel 2006: 85–6; Hoyt 2006: 66). The return of the INC to power in 2004 did not stop or even slow the new momentum in defence cooperation. For instance, the cooperation on drones continued under the Congress government as IAI secured in 2012 a $958 million contract from India's military to upgrade 150 IAI-built Heron and Searcher UAVs.[130] Negotiations with Israel also proved to be

Table 5.7   India's Arms Procurement from Israel since the 1999 Kargil War (in US$ million)

Years	Annual arms procurement	Cumulative arms procurement
1999		770
2000	144	914
2001	274	1,189
2002	259	1,448
2003	70	1,508
2004	1,100	2,608
2005		2,608
2006	660	3,268
2007	30	5,000*
2008	325	5,325
2009	3,228	8,553
2010		8,553
2011	2,200	10,753
2012	958	10,511

Source: Information compiled from various Indian and Israel newspapers.
Note: *The Government of Indian openly announced in 2007 that the bilateral military trade had reached 5 billion dollars.

Table 5.8 Major Indo-Israeli Defence Deals since 1992

Year	Nature	Vendor
1993	Fire-control systems for Vijayanta tanks, artillery equipment and ammunition for T-72 tanks	Tamam
1996	32 Searcher-II UAVs	IAI
	Artillery (155 mm self-propelled guns)	Soltam
1996	Electronic upgrade to India's MiG-21s	Elta (IAI subsidiary)
1997	2 Super-Dvora Mark II fast attack crafts and licence to build another four	IAI
1998	Advanced Electronic Equipment	IAI
1999	8 Heron-1 drones	IAI
1999	40,000 rounds of 155 mm ammunition, 30,000 rounds of 160 mm mortars, 50,000 rounds of 130 mm artillery gun ammunition, 100,000 rounds of 125 mm shells (for tanks)	IAI
2000	Upgrade of 180 130-mm M-46 field guns	Soltam
2000	20 Heron-1 drones	IAI
2000	Israeli electronic warfare system for INS VIRAT (aircraft carrier)	IAI
2000–1	7 Barak-I ship defence system	IAI and Rafael
2001	3 Super-Dvora Mark II fast attack craft (FACs)	IAI
2002	2 Green Pine radars (component Arrow Ballistic Missile Defence System)	Elta (IAI)
2003	3,400 Tavor assault rifles, 200 Galil sniper rifles, Star Night Technologies night vision goggles, laser range finding and targeting equipment	IMI
2003	Integrate IAI's avionics into the advanced light helicopter (ALH) platform	IAI–HAL
2003	Supply of advanced Israeli avionic systems for the Indian Air Force's new MiG-27 combat aircraft	IAI
2003	Additional Barak missile system	IAI
2004	3 Phalcon early warning aircraft	IAI/Elta
2005	50 Heron MALE UAVs	IAI
2005	acquisition of third Green Pine radar	Elta
2006	70-km-range Barak-2 medium range surface-to-air missile (MR-SAM), also known as Barak NG	IAI (joint production with India's DRDO)
2006	Medium power radars for the IAF	Elta

(Cont'd)

Table 5.8 *(Cont'd)*

Year	Nature	Vendor
2007	Night vision equipment	Star Night Technologies
2008	Spyder anti-aircraft missile systems	Rafael/Elbit Systems Ltd
2008	Agreement to cooperate on the development, manufacturing, and sale of defence products in India	IAI/Tata group
2008	Launch of the RISAT-2 satellite	IAI/ISRO
2009	9 EL/M-2083 radars to be installed on aerostats	Elta (IAI)
2009	Advanced Barak-8 tactical air-defence system or LR-SAM, primarily for use aboard warships	IAI /Elta/Rafael
2009	18 Spyder surface-to-air missile systems	Rafael/IAI
2009	16 Heron UAVs	IAI
2009	Harpy 'killer'; drones	IAI
2011	8,356 Spike anti-tank missiles with 321 launchers, 15 training simulators, and associated equipment	Rafael
2011	Derby air-to-air missile to equip on at least 200 Tejas Light Combat Aircraft (LCA) jets	Rafael
2011	44,618 close-quarter battle (CQB) carbines and 33.6 million rounds of ammunition	Possibly IMI
2011	2 advanced versions of the Phalcon AWACS (in addition to the three procured earlier)	IAI/Elta
2012	Upgrade of 150 IAI-built Heron and Searcher UAVs	IAI

Source: Information compiled from various Indian and Israel newspapers.

an indirect way to access Western, and especially US, defence technology (such as sub-elements of the Arrow system like the Green Pine radar) (Koshy 2003).

Under the INC, Israel also continued to provide qualitative upgrades to some of India's ageing Soviet equipment. A new qualitative edge was attained with the $1.1 billion purchase of the Phalcon systems which were finally delivered when the INC was in power.[131] In spite of delivery delays and some operational difficulties, the Congress government was planning on buying two more Phalcon AWACS (Pandit 2011). After it came back to power, the INC also had its share of important defence deals with Israel. In 2006, India bought from Rafael 18 Spyder low-level quick reaction anti-aircraft missile systems for $325 million. Given the delays in the production of the indigenous Akash and Trishul missile systems, the IAF had been pushing for this purchase which was announced by Air Chief Marshal S. P. Tyagi in 2006 (Melman 2006). In December 2006, Elta (a subsidiary of IAI) signed another $180 million deal with India to develop medium power radars for the IAF.[132] In 2008, Rafael was awarded a $325 million contract to supply IAF with Spyder missile systems armed with Python and Derby missiles (*The Economic Times* 2012).

In addition, Israel was also gradually presented by the Indian security establishment as a potential facilitator to reach self-sustaining indigenous defence capabilities. The Israel military industry had demonstrated its disposition to transfer technology and to collaborate with the Indian defence industry in joint ventures, production, and research and development in high-technology military equipment. For instance, since September 2002, HAL and IAI have been jointly producing advanced light helicopters. In February 2003, IAI and Nelco Limited signed an agreement to develop, manufacture, and market electronic equipment for Indian defence forces together. There was also an agreement signed between IMI and India's Ordnance Factory Board (OFB) to jointly manufacture ammunitions.[133] IAI has also been assisting India's state-owned Aeronautical Development Establishment (ADE) to develop indigenous UAVs since 2005 (Pandit 2007). India and Israel have pursued their space and satellite cooperation under the INC tenure. In January 2008, an Indian space launch vehicle put into space Israel's Polaris satellite (Riedel 2008).

Israeli defence industries have also been in discussions with the DRDO since 2005 on various programmes, including the development of medium- and long-range surface-to-air missiles systems.[134] This is an interesting development since Israeli industries and the DRDO previously competed on similar projects and have now been cooperating. This joint venture was accepted by the Cabinet Committee on Security (CCS), along with the purchase of Spyder systems, to replace the ageing Pechora missiles.[135] In 2010, India and Israel tested the Indo-Israeli Barak LR-SAM both in Israel and in India (*Economic Times* 2012; Unnithan 2010). While most of the tests have been made, India has reportedly expressed concerns at the two-year delay in the delivery of the IAI missiles for the joint SAM system (Pandit 2012c). In spite of these concerns, Bharat Electronics Ltd and IAI signed a MoU in December 2012 for the joint development and indigenous production of LR-SAMs to defend Indian warships.[136] India has also started discussing with Israel the supply of the 'Spike' third-generation anti-tank guided missiles (ATGMs), a missile project worth around $1 billion. India had originally considered buying the US-made 'Javelin' missiles but the negotiations stalled because of Washington's reluctance to share technology with India and to not allow India to then indigenously manufacture the 'tank killer' missiles.[137] This latest development has confirmed Israel's unparalleled flexibility in technology transfer and its imposition of very minimal political conditions in its dealings with India.

The special mil-to-mil relationship which began secretively in the early 1990s also continued and accelerated after 2004 (Tables 5.5 and 5.6). The routine reciprocal visits between chiefs of various wings of the defence forces of the two countries are now publicized and actively followed by the Indian media. Additionally, institutional consultation mechanisms have been established between the two foreign ministries (like the JWG on counter-terrorism) and between the two defence ministries (through the JWG on defence cooperation). For instance, the tenth JWG on defence cooperation and the eighth JWG on counter-terrorism met in New Delhi, respectively, in December 2012 and in February 2013.[138] Indian and Israeli vessels also made regular visits to ports in the two countries (Tables 5.5 and 5.6). Service chiefs of the two armies also make regular visits. The vice-chief of the Indian army, the Indian navy chief, and the chief of the IAF all visited Israel since the new INC government assumed office in May 2004. Furthermore, all three serving chiefs have now visited Israel since 2008 (Table 5.5). The year 2010 particularly marked an expansion in India–Israel naval discussions as the naval chiefs from both countries made reciprocal visits.[139] The visit in January 2013 of IAF Chief of Air Staff N. A. K. Browne was symbolical as Browne had been named India's first defence attaché at the Indian embassy 16 years earlier (Lappin 2013). There are very few other security establishments with which the Indian army has had such a regular and ongoing military dialogue. The evolution and institutionalization of this military diplomacy is all the more impressive as until the late 1990s, bilateral visits were either limited or kept secret.

Because of the technical nature of this collaboration, most political decision-makers have deferred to the defence bureaucrats for the negotiations.[140] Actors within the Indian defence establishment have managed to frame Israeli military-technical assistance as the solution to their crucial security requirements like the need to offset cross-border infiltration and potential ballistic missile threats (from both Pakistan and China). In addition, military-technical cooperation with Israel has been presented by India's defence establishment as indirectly enabling India's quest for self-reliance. First, joint ventures and transfer of technology from Israel were presented as a way to develop India's own indigenous defence production. Second, since most of Israel's sophisticated weapons have been developed indigenously, there are fewer risks of external pressures on Israel to stop supplying India with military equipment, especially during military crises. For example, Israel did not interrupt the export of its military provisions to India during the two Indo-Pakistani crises of 1999 and 2001–2. As a result, strategic collaboration with Israel was perceived positively by politicians across the political spectrum as a way to preserve India's strategic autonomy. Both these two self-reinforcing factors ensured deference to the Indian military in dealings with Israel.

The more a policy area is complex and dominated by technical considerations, the more it is insulated from political intervention. The difficulties in reversing the new Israel policy have been directly observable since the return of the INC to power in 2004. While expressing strong anti-Israeli rhetoric during the electoral campaign, the INC was more prudent after it came to power.[141] The INC even declared it would not review its diplomatic relations with Israel which had now been framed as a 'strategic imperative'.[142] The first minister of defence in the UPA government, Pranab Mukherjee, made it clear in 2004 that there would be 'no change in the existing defence ties between India and Israel' (*The Indian Express*, 1 July 2004). After three years of discreet military exchanges (2004-2007), the Minister of Defence A. K. Antony for the first time announced in May 2007 that the total amount of the defence procurements from Israel had attained 'US$5 billion'.[143] In July 2007, Antony further argued to Parliament that 'successive governments since 1992 have had defence ties with Israel. This is not new. And the relation is not ideological, but purely based on our security requirements.'[144] Finally, the increase in expenditures in very specific high-technological sectors such as missile defence since 2005 (see Table 5.8) has confirmed the

INC's tacit approval of this military-technical collaboration. As a result, there is a bipartisan political consensus behind a new Israel policy based on more narrow, military-technical terms.[145]

Far from developing into a political or strategic partnership, Indo-Israeli military relations seem to have evolved into a 'focused' cooperation in certain high-technology fields which meet India's growing defence requirements and quest for technical autonomy. A strategic partnership would imply a long-term commitment for joint military cooperation which would be institutionalized by important bilateral treaties and joint statements by the respective defence ministers. For example, India signed a strategic agreement with the USSR in 1971 (Indo-Soviet Treaty of Peace, Friendship and Cooperation). The relationship with Israel is not a privileged and exclusive military relationship similar to the Indo-Soviet partnership where India would get most of its military equipment on favourable rates from the USSR. Most of India's purchases of Israeli equipment have been done through competitive tenders, where the Israeli defence industries have offered high-quality material at reasonable costs.[146] India and Israel have also not held joint military exercises, another visible indicator of a substantial strategic partnership. The formation of a strategic partnership would also suggest that the two states share a common view of world politics and of their respective positions in the international arena (Kandel 2009). Repeated disagreements over the Palestine, Syria, and Iran issues have revealed two very different worldviews in the two capitals (Abhyankar 2012; Blarel 2011; Jha 2013; Komireddi 2012).

In Parallel, the Development of an Economic and Trade Relationship

Similar to the dynamics observed in the strategic-military sphere, certain economic actors have also exploited the shocks and openings of the 1990s to influence the direction of India's Israel policy. There had been early frustrations from some economic sectors with India's pre-1992 Israel policy. For instance, Prime Minister Nehru had always indicated India could learn much from Israel's achievements in agriculture and especially from drip irrigation systems.[147] On Nehru's initiative, limited technical assistance had, for example, happened in the management of water resources in the Rajasthan desert (Rafael 1981: 90). However, agricultural assistance remained limited as other demands of advice from Israeli experts on irrigation projects (often at the India state-level initiative) were not approved by the Government of India.[148] Other specific sectors were disadvantaged by the lack of diplomatic relations such as the diamond trade business. Prior to normalization, most of the limited $200 million trade between the two countries concentrated on the diamond industry, with most exchanges with Israeli companies having to circumvent the Indian government's boycott and happening through third countries (Gerberg 1996: 36). Many Indian companies were also indirectly negatively affected by the no-relationship policy because of the Arab boycott blacklist. Even firms that were not directly trading with Israel but that had links with Western companies trading with Israel were sanctioned. The early 1990s were a structural opportunity for these actors to engage Israeli partners and to diversify Indo-Israeli bilateral trade beyond the traditional diamond and chemicals trade (which constituted about 83 per cent of Israel's exports to India in the early 1990s) (Naaz 2000). Normalization of relations also happened a few weeks after the economic liberalization and opening up of India's economy to the global economy. India's continuing economic expansion since 1996 was another important factor in building political self-confidence for stepping up relations with Israel. This was a major factor in reducing the importance of the Muslim factor.

The first set of economic actors to take advantage of the opening of the policy-making process were local governments from Indian states facing drought and water shortage issues, and which were looking for Israeli assistance in the production of high-yield crops and irrigation systems. Indian state governments, free from the political and institutional constraints inhibiting the central government, started directly discussing with the Israeli government and Israeli firms. Several joint ventures, agricultural projects, and MoUs were signed between state governments and Israel, notably during the visits of Indian chief ministers to agricultural exhibitions in Israel (see Table 5.9) and following the visits of Israeli President Weizman and Prime Minister Sharon in 1996 and 2003, respectively. In addition, active participation in trade fairs and exhibitions enhanced the awareness regarding business opportunities and promoted contact between Indian and Israeli firms. Traditionally, the international agricultural exhibitions in Israel have attracted a large number of delegations and high-level officials from India, including state ministers, resulting in increased collaboration in the field of agriculture.

Table 5.9 Visits from Indian Chief Ministers and Other State Government Officials to Israel since 1992

Year	Nature of visit	Outcome
1993 (May)	Maharashtra CM Sharad Pawar	Indian delegation to attend Agritech in Tel Aviv
		Accompanied by a high-level military team
1993 (September)	Gujarat CM Chimanbhai Patel	Signed a MoU between Gujarat and the Israeli company Eisenberg Group
1994 (June)	Rajasthan CM Bhairon Singh Shekhawat	Discussed cooperation in water management systems
1995 (February)	Karnataka CM H. D. Deve Gowda	Discussed cooperation in agriculture
1995 (April)	CMs of several Indian states	Discussed cooperation in agriculture, dry land farming, horticulture, and conservation of water resources
1996 (May)	Ministers and officials from several Indian state governments	Visited Agritech exhibition
1996 (October)	Maharashtra CM Manohar Joshi	Participated in the Global Marathi Conference organized in Israel in October 1996 by Israelis of Indian origin having migrated from Marathi-speaking areas
		The Joint Business Council was upgraded to India–Israel Business Alliance
		Signed a MoU between Maharashtra and Israel on agriculture cooperation
2000	CM of West Bengal Jyoti Basu	Accompanied by senior colleague Somnath Chatterjee
		25-member business delegation to solicit Israeli investment in West Bengal
2005 (July)	CM of Andhra Pradesh Y. S. Rajasekhara Reddy	Pilgrimage

(Cont'd)

Table 5.9 *(Cont'd)*

Year	Nature of visit	Outcome
2006 (May)	Agriculture Minister Pawar led a delegation comprising the CMs of Rajasthan, Gujarat, and Nagaland, and included senior officials from other Indian states (notably ministers of agriculture)	Three-year Work Plan for Cooperation in the Field of Agriculture was signed by the two governments
2006 (October)	Rajasthan CM Vasundhara Raje and Rajasthan Agriculture Minister Prabhula Saini	Bilateral agreement between the Rajasthan State Agricutlural Marketing Board and the Nan Den Agro Company of Israel
2007 (January–February)	CM of Madhya Pradesh, Shivraj Singh Chouhan, led a 16-member delegation to Israel	At the invitation of Minister of Agriculture & Rural Development of Israel Shalom Simhon
		Visited various institutes at Volcani Centre and companies involved in irrigation and agricultural projects as well as water treatment and management
2009 (May)	CM of Andhra Pradesh Y. S. Rajasekhara Reddy	Pilgrimage
2009 (November)	CM of Punjab Prakash Singh Badal and CM of Himachal Pradesh Prem Kumar Dhumal	Led high-level delegations to visit WATEC Israel 2009 Exhibition
		In addition, delegations from FICCI, CII, IMC, and many businessmen also visited the exhibition
2010 (August)	Minister of State for Agriculture, Government of Haryana	Visited Israel on an exposure visit on the cultivation technology and post-harvest management of citrus, olives, and mango under the Indo-Israel Project of National Horticulture Mission
		Indo-Israeli Center of Excellence to be established in Haryana
2011 (April)	CM of Haryana Bhupinder Singh Hooda	Looked for assistance in techniques of drip and sprinkler irrigation for water-deficit southern Haryana

(Cont'd)

Table 5.9 *(Cont'd)*

Year	Nature of visit	Outcome
		Agreed to constitute working groups to further agricultural cooperation
2013 (April–May)	CM of Rajasthan Ashok Gehlot	Discussed ways of enhancing cooperation in agriculture in arid areas; water management; and management of extension network. The delegation met senior executives of Israeli companies to discuss possibilities of cooperation in agriculture and water technologies.

Source: Information compiled from different sources, including the Indian embassy in Israel (http://www.indembassy.co.il), and various Indian and Israel newspapers.

Likewise, when Agriculture Minister Sharad Pawar visited Israel in 2005 and 2006, he discussed various agricultural agreements and was accompanied by various delegates from state governments.[149] In addition, some leading Indian corporate groups and cooperatives, including the National Cooperative Union of India, Mahindra & Mahindra, Yes Bank, Amul Dairy, and Sumul Dairy, also visited Israel to build direct ties with Israeli companies in the field of agriculture, horticulture, irrigation, and dairying.[150] Sharad Pawar signed with his Israeli counterpart, the Minister of Agriculture and Rural Development Shalom Simhon, a three-year work plan for cooperation in agriculture. The plan included the development of joint agri-business projects, transfer of technology and techniques from Israel in post-harvest management, value addition for certain products, greenhouse structures, and water management (*The Hindu*, 12 May 2006). Following Pawar's visit, other chief ministers visited Israel to look for agricultural cooperation and training. For instance, the Chief Minister of Rajasthan Vasundhara Raje visited Israel in 2006 and supervised the signing of a bilateral agreement between the Rajasthan State Agricultural Marketing Board and the Nan Den Agro Company of Israel to establish a farm near Jaipur for the training of farmers in the Israeli techniques of irrigation and management of crops (*The Hindu*, 12 may 2006). This decentralized economic relationship between Israel, sub-national governments, and private companies has further insulated the direction of India's Israel policy from political decision-makers in New Delhi.

Israeli diplomats have closely observed this new political development and the advantages of directly reaching out to local governments to develop business opportunities and general goodwill. The Israeli government's Action Plan 2008–2010 for agricultural collaboration focused, for instance, on the states of Haryana, Maharashtra, Rajasthan, and Gujarat, and the 2012–2015 Action Plan has been expanded to include three more states: Tamil Nadu, Punjab, and Karnataka (Rajiv 2013). These plans included, for instance, the creation of Indo-Israeli centres of excellence for various agricultural projects.[151] The former Israeli ambassador, Alon Ushpiz, also actively engaged state governments and met with the chief ministers of other states like West Bengal, Andhra Pradesh, Bihar, and Karnataka.[152] In fact, an Israeli consulate was opened in the hi-tech hub of Bangalore in 2012. The direct courting of chief ministers and local governments has two advantages for Israeli diplomacy. First, it is possible to create joint ventures in the fields of agriculture, solar energy, and water harnessing at a more local and manageable level. It is a way to directly publicize the contributions Israel can make to the development of certain states. Second, given the increasing reliance of the INC and BJP on coalitions with regional parties to govern, it is also possible for Israel to generate political understandings with key regional players, whether parties or individuals, who could hold national roles in the future. For instance, Narendra Modi visited Israel in 2006 as the chief minister of Gujarat and became the Prime Minister in 2014. It is an indirect way of generating political goodwill and increasing the number of stakeholders in the current relationships.

Economic relations have continued and accelerated after the return of the INC to power in 2004. As India's economic profile has risen over the last decade, Indian private actors have explored certain complementary niche fields where collaboration with Israel could bring benefits such as in the pharmaceutical, IT software, telecommunications, clean energy technologies, biotechnology, nanotechnology, and space technology (notably satellites) sectors.[153] Beyond receiving technical advice from Israeli companies, Indian firms have also been trying to attract Israeli investments. Israel's FTAs with the US and EU also presented an opportunity for India to take advantage of Israel's position as a bridge to export Indian products to these markets. This is another level of dialogue which is rarely discussed by state-centred approaches of Indo-Israeli relations: many deals and MoUs have directly been signed between industry associations.[154] For instance, business forums like the CII, FICCI, and the PHD Chamber of Commerce have bilateral agreements with their Israeli counterparts and have been organizing trade delegation visits.

Political action has been mostly that of following and encouraging these private Indian initiatives, notably by negotiating various specialized agreements facilitating investments, and MoUs to promote further research and development cooperation. Approximately 150 bilateral agreements were reportedly signed during the first 15 years of bilateral diplomatic relations (Kumaraswamy 2010: 255). Israel's Finance Minister, Benjamin Netanyahu, met his Indian counterpart, P. Chidambaram, in Washington in October 2004 in order to discuss monetary guarantees for Indian states for projects carried out by Israeli enterprises (Gerberg 2008: 379). A few weeks later, the Israeli Minister of Industry Trade and Employment, Ehud Olmert, visited India with representatives from 45 Israeli companies.[155] This was the first visit by an Israeli minister since the INC had won the elections in June 2004. At a meeting organized by FICCI, the Israeli minister agreed with the Indian Commerce and Industry Minister Kamal Nath on setting up a joint study group (JSG) to make recommendations on mechanisms and targets for expanding trade and economic cooperation (*The Hindu*, 6 December 2006). Several steps followed like the opening of a branch of the Bank of India in Israel in 2005. And in 2006, Israel's Minister of Industry Eli Yishai visited India and agreed with Nath on a preferential trade agreement (PTA) based on the recommendations of the JSG (*The Hindu*, 6 December 2006). The INC government has also encouraged further scientific cooperation. During the visit of India's Minister of Science and Technology Kapil Sibal in May 2005, the two countries signed a MoU on Israel–India Industrial, Research and Development Initiative Cooperation, and agreed upon setting up a joint research and development fund.[156]

In spite of the diversification of the bilateral trade, diamonds still constituted about 56.4 per cent of the total bilateral trade in the year 2011.[157] Other major areas of cooperation were agriculture, chemicals, and pharmaceuticals. While there has been a growing interest from other sectors and new agreements in other industries, the bilateral economic relationship has concentrated on a few narrow and technical areas. Furthermore, while trade has been multiplied by five over the last decade and India stood at the sixth place in terms of Israel's trade partner countries (third-largest trade partner in Asia) in 2010, Israel represented only 0.85 per cent of India's total trade in 2011.[158] Israel was only India's fourth-largest trading partner in West Asia.[159] This situation could evolve with the negotiations for an FTA which has the potential to change the composition of trade and to give opportunities for more sectors, such as IT and biotechnology, to invest in India. However, talks on the FTA were on their seventh round in June 2013 with no clear expectation of when they will be concluded.[160] Until now, this economic relationship has been limited to specific collaboration on niche fields with various sub-national actors (private economic actors and state governments) taking their own initiatives and managing its policy direction. Given the decentralized nature of this new economic partnership, it will also be difficult for political actors to reverse the existing policy.

A Stable Policy Compromise

Rather than looking at India's Israel policy over the last decade as contradictory or duplicitous, as some observers have labelled it,[161] one needs to look at it more like a segmented foreign policy-making process with different actors, levels of analysis, and nested interests. At the political-state level, the Indian government has argued that it needs to follow its pro-Palestinian policy (even if it is at odds with its Israeli partner) in West Asia to satisfy historically held ideological principles, domestic constituencies, and its Arab and Muslim partners in the region. While this rationale has been publicly expressed and is well known, it does not cover all the dimensions of interactions between India and Israel and the fact that other military and economic actors have their own nested interests. The current Israeli policy is not an overarching plan decided by a few key political players at the top but the aggregative outcome of debates and bargaining between different groups. The new policy compromise is now more narrowly defined by an emerging 'coalition' of technical-military experts who appreciate the Israeli military industry's unique expertise and assistance, and of domestic sub-national economic actors who benefit from specialized joint ventures with Israeli private actors.[162] Their expert input deeply affects the image of this policy and the current positive feedback Indian politicians perceive. As a result, this policy compromise explains the Indian government's intention to support the current state of bilateral relations despite the possible ideological and diplomatic ambiguities this policy can create at the public level. Indo-Israeli ties are of a somewhat unique nature given the high-level military interactions which contrast with the lack of important bilateral political visits.[163]

The redefinition of India's policy from a strongly politicized issue (and therefore dependent on regional events and domestic electoral cycles) to a more narrow, selective, and technical partnership has two important implications for the future of Indo-Israeli relations. First, since there is a new policy compromise insulated from the fluctuations of political events, controlled by informed bureaucrats, and reinforced by positive feedback, it is likely that the current state of relations will not be reversed in the short term. There is now a new solid equilibrium which can only be modified by new external shocks and the inflow of new participants and policy proposals. The current policy compromise has already been tested by different regional–diplomatic shocks such as the 2006 Lebanon conflict, the 2008 and 2014 Gaza crises, and the Palestinian statehood bids in 2011 and in 2012. Until now, bilateral defence and economic relations have been relatively unaffected by these different diplomatic events. Indian politicians have publicly condemned Israeli actions but have not attempted to reverse the current policy.[164] External shocks are not a sufficient condition for the policy to change.

There is, however, a possibility that the current positive feedback from Israel's military assistance could change if cooperation does not deliver and if scandals linked to some important defence purchases become more publicized and politicized (Kundu 2012; Melman 2009; Samanta 2011). The bribery scandals affecting important Israeli companies like IMI or even IAI in the Barak missile deal could seriously delay or limit future defence deals. Incriminated companies could either be blacklisted or tenders prove to be longer processes in the future.[165] Recent reports have also revealed lack of progress in joint ventures as well as absence of transparency and lack of transfer of technology by Israeli partners. These problems have notably stalled the cooperation between the DRDO and IAI in their joint production of SAMs (Kaur 2013). Some other observers have also noticed a perverse and unexpected effect of India's privileged defence partnership with Tel Aviv: India's growing dependence on Israel for cutting-edge technology (*The Economic Times* 2012). Such image reversal would make it more difficult for advocates of Indo-Israeli military-technical collaboration to prevent political deci·ion-makers from reassessing the technical advantages of engaging Israel in this field.

India could also revise its privileged military partnership if there is evidence of substantive sales of Israeli weapons to China and/or Pakistan. For instance, there were concerns in India over a report released by Britain's Department for Business, Innovation and Skills (which oversees security exports) in June 2013 that Israel had exported military technology to Pakistan.[166] In 2010 and 2011, Israel reportedly sought to purchase electronic warfare systems and aircraft parts from Britain for systems that would then be exported to Pakistan. Israel immediately denied the report and reiterated its policy of not exporting defence equipment to Pakistan.[167] Similarly, Sino-Israeli relations have also been improving for the past decade. Like India, China established diplomatic relations with Israel only in January 1992, but it had already developed military ties with Tel Aviv in the 1980s. In fact, the development of strategic relations between the two countries was closely monitored by Indian policymakers and was a factor in the decision to normalize relations. There was a severe setback in bilateral defence ties in 2000 when Israel had to cancel its sale of the Phalcon radar system plane to China (Blarel 2006). However, the two countries have again explored the possibility of military cooperation over the last three years. In June 2011, the Israeli Defence Minister Ehud Barak visited China. This was the first visit by a defense minister to the country in 10 years. On 14 August 2011, the chief of the People's Liberation Army (PLA) General Staff Department visited Israel for the first time.[168] On 13 August 2012, vessels from the PLA Navy's eleventh escort fleet anchored at Israel's Haifa naval base for a four-day goodwill visit to mark 20 years of cooperation between the Israel Defence Forces and the PLA.[169] India closely observes these moves by China and Pakistan to normalize ties with Israel as it could lose out the edge it enjoys over its neighbours due to its previously exclusive access to certain Israeli defence equipments. However, Israeli authorities are also conscious that India is Israel's largest buyer of defence equipment and that reports of defence sales to China and/or Pakistan could prove damaging to the strategic relations between the two countries.

The second conclusion and finding of this new policy compromise is that the current narrow policy understanding leaves little prospects for radical developments and the emergence of a stronger political and strategic partnership between the two countries. The wide differences between Indian and Israeli worldviews, notably on Iran, and the absence of common enemies (except maybe for the Pakistani nuclear problem but with varying threat intensity) limit any possibility of a stronger strategic rapprochement. For example, despite multiple rounds of discussions through a joint working group on counter-terrorism, cooperation and intelligence-sharing efforts have only been limited. For instance, Israel promptly offered technical assistance to India during the 2008 Mumbai terrorist attacks which had also targeted Israelis and Jewish Americans. Some observers interpreted the targeting of the Jewish Community Centre in Mumbai as a direct attack on Indo-Israeli ties (Sloman 2011). Israeli Defence Minister Ehud Barak qualified the attacks as 'part of the global wave of terror' (McGirk 2008). However, India declined the offer of assistance and preferred to deal independently with the crisis.[170]

Any move towards a closer ideological partnership, similar to the one the BJP had publicly advocated, would witness a strong counter-mobilization from the old guard composed of MEA bureaucrats and some elements of the Congress-led UPA (beholden to India's 130 million Muslims for part of its political support) which still resolutely defend the Palestinian cause.[171] Furthermore, India is also engaging other actors in the region for energy requirements and will need to manage these different relationships. While mil-to-mil collaboration will continue to grow, it will never evolve into a strong exclusive strategic partnership as India also purchases different types of weapons from other countries such as Russia, the US, France, the UK, or Sweden. The bilateral economic relationship has more potential to expand and to open up to new interests with the prospect of an FTA in the coming years. However, the partnership will still be dependent on technical and industrial collaboration in key fields like diamond processing and agro-technologies. Given the narrow parameters and the positive feedback of bilateral cooperation, the current policy compromise is consolidated for the long term.

Finally, the new policy compromise also marked a shift in India's foreign policy from a one-sided position in favour of the Arabs in their dispute with Israel, to a more balanced stance. It is misleading to consider and interpret India's changing relationship with Israel as the only example of change in India's approach to West Asia. After the regional shocks of 1992 and the disappointment with the negatives votes at the OIC, there was a shift in India's foreign policy from a zero-sum approach—or what the former Indian ambassador to Israel Shiv Shankar Menon had termed an 'either-or-situation'—to a policy of multi-engagement of all relevant regional actors (Menon 1997). Over the last two decades, India has engaged various actors in the region such as Iran, Saudi Arabia, and the Gulf Cooperation Council (GCC) for geopolitical, economic, and energy reasons. India has developed relations with each country in a bilateral fashion. Learning from previous failed policies in the region, and given the current degree of political division in the region, India no longer attempts to take sides in inter-Arab disputes. Since 1992, successive Indian governments have realized that doing business with all the protagonists in West Asia, on the one hand, without ignoring India's economic and political interests in the region, on the other hand, has been the most beneficial course of action for its national strategic interests.

Notes

1. *Business and Social Observer*, 7 November 1992.

2. 'India–Israel Trade Rises to $6 Billion in 2012–13', *The Hindu Business Line*, 7 July 2013.

3. Only in the last decade have Israeli defence sales surpassed $10 billion (Table 5.7). See also Inbar and Ningthoujam (2012).

4. See NSA Brajesh Mishra's speech at the AJC dinner (Mishra 2003).

5. 'Visits by Indian Leaders were Better under BJP: Israel', *The Indian Express*, 14 June 2011.

6. The UPA is the INC-led coalition of political parties which headed the Government of India from 2004 to 2014. For reference to the Palestinian issue, see the *National Common Minimum Programme of the Government of India*, 23 May 2004 (available at http://pmindia.nic.in/cmp.pdf, accessed on 15 March 2013).

7. Some analysts have even portrayed the Indo-Israeli partnership as running on 'autopilot'. See Ganguly (2011).

8. The exceptions are two articles by Kumaraswamy written in the late 1990s. See Kumaraswamy (1996b, 1998).

9. 'Diplomatic Ties with Israel', *The Statesman*, 31 January 1992.

10. On 6 December 1992, the Babri Masjid in Ayodhya was demolished by a crowd of 150,000 militants. Riots then broke out in many major Indian cities, including Mumbai, Delhi, and Hyderabad, killing more than 2,000 people. For more details on the Ayodhya incident and riots, read Guha (2008: Chapter 27); Jaffrelot (1998: Chapter 13); Rao (2006).

11. The Anti-Defamation League strongly condemned the Indian treatment of the Orchestra. See 'India Criticized for Treatment of Jerusalem Symphony Orchestra', *Jewish Telegraphic Agency*, 22 August 1993.

12. Every contact should also have first been officially approved by the higher political authorities. Dixit (1996: 313).

13. See 'Summary of a Visit to India by Foreign Minister Peres—18 May 1993' in Israel, Ministry of Foreign Affairs (1992–1994); *Times of India*, 20 May 1993.

14. Table 5.3 demonstrates how these figures were not attained until 2000.

15. His visit was, however, interpreted by Muslim personalities as a dilution of his earlier positions on Israel; Pasha (1995: 52–3).

16. Both India and Israel were not members of the Non-Proliferation Treaty (NPT), and therefore preferred not to vote on nuclear issues, for fear of creating a reputational precedent which could be held against them and their own nuclear programmes. Because of shared security and diplomatic concerns, the two countries had some similarities in their nuclear strategies and voting behaviours in multilateral fora.

17. 'India Reassures Arafat on Ties with Israel', *India News Network Digest* 2:64, 28 May 1993.

18. Saudi Arabia even suggested making India an observer at the OIC in January 2006.

19. By 1991, Israel was even structurally forced to export and to share technology. Following the end of the Cold War and the signing of peace treaties with several of its Arab neighbours, its defence industry needed to look for new markets and partners if it wanted to maintain its technological edge. See Lewis (2003).

20. Although when asked about the meeting, Yegar explained that he did not know of any 'Indian needs in the areas of defense'. See *The Hindu*, 26 March 1992. See also *Foreign Affair Record* 38:3, 23 March 1992 and 24 March 1992.

21. The delegation met senior officials in the ministry of defence's department of defense production and supplies. See *Foreign Affair Record* 38:3, 24 May 1992; *TheTelegraph*, 29 May 1992.

22. Although Ramesh Thakur reported that the sale of UAVs was discussed during that meeting. See Thakur (1994: 291).

23. The IAI Searcher is a reconnaissance UAV developed in Israel in the 1980s. This was an interesting offer as India was still the target of Western technology controls at that time. Thakur (1994: 291).

24. The Ranger is a tactical UAV system for use in extreme weather conditions for surveillance, reconnaissance, target acquisition, artillery adjustment, and damage assessment. See Kumaraswamy (1998: 14).

25. The Hunter is a heavy tactical UAV system for surveillance, reconnaissance, target acquisition, artillery adjustment, and damage assessment that was developed by IAI. Raghuvanshi (1994); *Jane's Defense Weekly*, 5 March 1994, p. 29.

26. The IAI Harpy is a UAV produced by IAI that is specifically designed to attack radar systems. It notably carries a high explosive warhead. Kumaraswamy (1998: 16).

27. This prolonged the cooperation between the NSG and its Israeli equivalent, which had started after Indira Gandhi's assassination.

28. India and Israel have both had historical communities specialized in diamond cutting and polishing. See Gerber, 'India developing trade', *Israel-Asia Trade* (1996: 8).

29. In an article, Advani actively promoted defence cooperation between the two countries (Advani 1993).

30. India became the fourth country with which Israel had such an arrangement after France, Germany, and the US. See *Hindustan Times*, 19 May 1993.

31. *Israel Today* 3 (1997): 8.

32. In fact, the Chief Minister of Rajasthan, Bhairon Singh Shekhawat, who visited Israel in 1995, commissioned Tahal Consulting to conduct a statewide survey of the state's surface and underground water resources and to design an efficient water management system for the growing needs of the state's population. See Khan (2000: 158, 163).

33. *Israel Today* 3(1997): 5.

34. *Israel Today* 3(1997): 13.

35. A cotton demonstration farm was set up in Akola in Maharashtra during President Weizman's visit (Gopal and Sharma 2007: 323).

36. In 1995, the bilateral trade stood at $430 million. This was the optimistic figure presented by the president of the Israeli Federation of Chambers of Commerce Danny Gillerman in 1993. See also Feiler (2012).

37. Diamonds and chemicals still constituted in 1997 about 83 per cent of Israel's exports to India, and diamonds and cotton accounted for approximately 76 per cent of India's exports to Israel. See *Israel Today* 3(1997): 4, 9.

38. The election delivered an unclear mandate and resulted in a hung Parliament. A weak INC declined to attempt to form a government and instead chose to support a coalition headed by the Janata Dal, and chose Karnataka Chief Minister H. D. Deve Gowda to assume the prime minister's post. See Pai (1997).

39. Kalam's visit to Israel was only disclosed a few weeks later. Ameer (1996); Kumaraswamy (1998: 17). There were also reports that he travelled a second time to Israel in January 1997. See *Haaretz*, 4 June 1998.

40. Israel's IAI had lost the tender for the MIG upgrade to the Mikoyan Design Bureau of Russia but managed to secure the sub-contract for avionics. See *Globes*, 11 July 1996.

41. Interestingly, Nak Browne visited Israel again in January 2013 as India's air force chief. See 'IAF Chief Visits Israel', *Deccan Herald*, 20 January 2013; Lappin (2013).

42. During his stay, Weizman briefly visited Bangalore where he had been stationed during World War II as a pilot in the Royal Air Force. *The Tribune*, 7 January 1997.

43. *Times of India,* 28 December 1996; *The Hindu,* 3 January 1997; *The Tribune,* 7 January 1997; *The Pioneer,* 9 January 1997.

44. Defence deals were also signed during the visit. The IAI subsidiary Elta reportedly signed a $100 million agreement with India to provide electronic warfare systems for India's MIGs.

45. For example, the Indian government originally refused to confirm the visit of Israeli ministry of defence Director General David Ivry to New Delhi in August 1994, of Abdul Kalam to Tel Aviv in June 1996, and the visit of the Indian Defence Secretary T. K. Banerjee to Israel in February 1997.

46. India had previously already relied on third parties when it had purchased mortar ammunitions from Israel before normalization. See Datta (1997).

47. The BJP government eventually collapsed in late 1998 when the AIADMK (a regional party from Tamil Nadu) withdrew the support of its 18 MPs, leading to new elections in September–October 1999. The results, however, confirmed the BJP and the NDA in power (269 seats).

48. Louise Tillin, 'US-Israel-India: Strategic Axis?' *BBC News,* 9 September 2003, available at http://news.bbc.co.uk/2/hi/south_asia/3092726.stm (accessed on 15 March 2013).

49. See Mishra's speech at the AJC dinner (Mishra 2003).

50. 'Unequivocal Support for Palestinian Cause, Says PM', *The Hindu,* 25 September 2003; Baruah (2003).

51. In October 1991, the BJP All India National Conference had even made the establishment of diplomatic relations with Israel part of its electoral platform.

52. The Second Intifada, sometimes called the Al Aqsa Intifada, was the second Palestinian uprising against Israel which started in September 2000 and ended in 2005.

53. To read more about the decision-making process leading to the nuclear tests and its international consequences, see Perkovich (1999); Tellis (2001).

54. 'Hawkish India', *India Today,* 1 June 1998; Bajpai (2009). Some other authors have argued that the nuclear tests did not represent a break from the nuclear policies of earlier governments. The weaponization of the nuclear programme had begun in the 1980s and there have been multiple reports indicating that Narasimha Rao had himself envisaged a nuclear test in 1995. Rao was persuaded by the US, which threatened economic sanctions, not to carry out the test. In fact, Rao had briefed Vajpayee, who he thought would be his successor in 1996, about the nuclear test plans. See Jain (2013); Samanta (2013); Subrahmanyam (2004).

55. Advani (1993). While in opposition, Advani also visited Israel.

56. See Luce (2003); Jaffrelot (2003).

57. MEA, *Annual Report,* 1997–1998: 54; Interview with V. P. Malik, 3 November 2011, New Delhi.

58. Ved (1998); Interview with Malik.

59. Abadi (1999); Interview with Malik.

60. Ironically, General Malik visited the disputed Golan Heights on both sides of the border in 1998. See MEA, *Annual Report*, 1998–1999; Interview with Malik.

61. 'Clinton Imposes Full Sanctions on India', *Business Standard*, 14 May 1998.

62. *Haaretz*, 17 May 1998. On 3 June 1998, however, as there had been rumours about nuclear cooperation between India and Israel, the Israeli Deputy Minister of Defence, Silvan Shalom, explained to the Knesset that Israel had played no role in the nuclear tests. See Gerberg (2008: 377). A visit of the Israeli Chief of Staff, Lt General Amnon Lipkin-Shahak, scheduled for June 1998, was even cancelled to limit any further speculation on nuclear cooperation. See Kumaraswamy (1998).

63. Both the countries had been engaged in negotiations for a year and an Indian delegation had even visited Israel to inspect the equipment.

64. *Asian Recorder* 45: 22, 28 May–3 June 1999, p. 28151; Naaz (2000).

65. The agro-exhibition Advantage Maharashtra was, for instance, inaugurated in Bombay on 6 November 1998. A panel of Israeli firms from the agricultural sector and the Israeli Export Institute participated. The former Israeli Minister of Agriculture Yaakov Tsur was also present to give a speech. See Naaz, 'Indo-Israel Military Cooperation'.

66. For more details on the causes and developments of the conflict, read Lavoy (2009); Malik (2006); Tellis et al. (2001).

67. *From Surprise to Reckoning: The Kargil Review Committee Report* (2000).

68. The statement about Israel helping India reversing the situation on the ground in Kargil came from the former Israeli ambassador to India, Mark Sofer (2008–11). See Sirohi (2008a).

69. The US, China, Russia, France, England, and Saudi Arabia all pressured both India and Pakistan to draw back their forces and to put an end to the military confrontation. Interview with Malik. V. P. Malik was chief of staff of the Indian Army during the Kargil conflict.

70. Israel supplied the Indian Army with about 40,000 rounds of 155 mm ammunitions and 30,000 rounds of 160 mm mortars at the cost of $400 each during this war. Pant (2004); *Economic Times* (2012); Inbar and Ningthoujam (2012); Interview with Malik.

71. The IAI Heron is a medium altitude long endurance UAV developed by the Malat (UAV) division of IAI. The Heron is capable of medium altitude long endurance (MALE) operations of up to 52 hours' duration at up to 35,000 feet. See *Haaretz*, 12 August 1999; *The Indian Express*, 3 July 2000.

72. Given the short duration of the conflict, it is again not clear if Israel provided UAVs in May–July 1999. However, Israel had already sold surveillance

UAVs to India before the conflict and had signed contracts to provide additional ones in the following years.

73. Lakshya is a high-speed target drone system developed by the Aeronautical Development Establishment (ADE) of DRDO. It is used to perform discreet aerial reconnaissance of battlefield and target acquisition. The Nishant is a UAV developed by India's ADE. The Nishant UAV is primarily tasked with intelligence-gathering over enemy territory and also for reconnaissance, training, surveillance, target designation, artillery fire correction, and damage assessment.

74. 'Avro Crash Victims' Bodies Flown Home', *The Indian Express*, 13 January 1999.

75. The Phalcon is an AEW&C radar system developed by IAI and Elta Electronics Industries. Its primary objective is to provide intelligence to maintain air superiority and to conduct surveillance. As there were important delays in the delivery of an indigenous AWACS system, India had already started discussing the purchase of the Israeli Phalcon system in the mid-1990s. See Ameer (1996).

76. Following the Kargil conflict, India has also shown interest in the counter-infiltration devices Israel uses on the Golan Heights and in the Negev Desert. Luce (2003).

77. General Ashok K. Mehta, 'The Silent Sentinel', *Rediff*, 5 August 1999; Interview with Vice-Admiral Arun Prakash, 4 December 2011, New Delhi.

78. Interview with Vice-Admiral Arun Prakash.

79. Ibid.

80. The only two other ministers to have visited Israel were the Minister of Human Resource Development Arjun Singh in 1994 and the Minister of Urban Affairs, Health, and Welfare Ram Jethmalani in 1999.

81. The CBI and the IB are respectively India's main domestic investigative and intelligence agencies. The BSF is a paramilitary force in charge of guarding the borders of India. See 'Seeking Israel's Help', *The Hindu*, 20 June 2000.

82. Mossad is Israel's external intelligence agency while Shin Bet is the internal security agency. The daily *Haaretz* noticed that it was rather unusual that a foreign home minister gets to meet the prime minister and the directors of Israel's intelligence agencies. Melman (2000).

83. Quoted in *India Today*, 26 June 2000.

84. "'India Shops for Israeli Air Defence', *Far Eastern Economic Review*, 13 July 2000.

85. Quoted in Malhotra (2000); Varadarajan (2005); Interview with Jaswant Singh, 25 November 2011, New Delhi.

86. The Chinese precedent influenced India's military negotiations with Israel and the US. Since the 1980s, Washington and Tel Aviv have often diverged over the transfer of Israeli weapons and technology to China. This culminated in an important diplomatic showdown in 2000. Under intense pressure from the

Clinton administration, Israel was forced to cancel the sale of the Phalcon radar system to China despite talks that began in 1996 and the loss of a billion-dollar contract. See 'Israel's Sale of Airborne Early Warning Aircraft to China', *CRS Report RS20583*, 18 May 2000.

87. The US–India Political Action Committee, created in September 2002, explicitly expressed its ambition to emulate the lobbying strategies of American Jewish organizations. See Blarel (2006).

88. See the NSA Brajesh Mishra's speech at the AJC dinner (Mishra 2003).

89. While the NSA did not refer to Islamic fundamentalism as a common threat, he discussed the impact of 11 September 2001 and Al Qaeda. This impression that India, Israel, and the US were the victims of a similar terrorist threat emerged in 2001. Coincidentally, on 11 September, the Israeli head of the National Security Council, Major General Uzi Dayan, met with Brajesh Mishra to discuss cooperation on national security. Both watched together on television the events in New York unfold. See Sherman (2003); Blarel (2006).

90. The period of May 2003 also coincided with the US operations in Iraq and the peak of the neo-conservative moment and global war on terror. The rhetoric used by the Indian NSA was aimed at the US audience and at the George Bush administration whose support India was courting. It is in this logic that the BJP government had also considered sending troops to Iraq at this time. See Blarel and Pardesi (2012).

91. 'Unwritten, Abstract US–India–Israeli Axis to Fight Terror', *The Indian Express*, 10 September 2003.

92. During the Sharon visit, there were reportedly attempts by Israel to change its position on Kashmir and to move away from the unconditional support Peres had guaranteed to India during his visit to Delhi in 1993. There were at the time reports of talks between Israel and the Pervez Musharraf government which could have led to this modification of Israel's position. Given the absence of an understanding on a common statement, the two countries decided not to mention the Kashmir dispute. 'Musharraf Opens Debate on Israel Relations', *BBC News*, 3 July 2003, available at http://news.bbc.co.uk/2/hi/south_asia/3040632.stm (accessed on 15 March 2013); Yegar (2007); Interview with a senior Indian diplomat, New Delhi, 24 June 2010.

93. The discussions in the JWG have diversified and moved beyond counter-terrorism. There have been seminars dealing with subjects such as border security, suicide bombers, aviation security, and the financing of terrorism as well as information security including digital and cyber warfare. *Times of India*, 30 May 2005.

94. A few months later, Yaron was the senior defence representative in the Sharon delegation which visited New Delhi. Yaron was accompanied by representatives from all of Israel's defence companies.

95. Israel could not sell the Arrow technology because it was being jointly developed with the US, under an agreement between Boeing and IAI. However, the Green Pine radar was just a ground-based sub-system of the Arrow and Israel had persuaded the US that it did not breach the MTCR. See Bagchi (2002); 'India Acquires Green Pine Radars from Israel', *Times of India*, 28 June 2002.

96. The agreement provided a framework for the exchange of researchers and for the organization of conferences. See Gerberg (2008: 382).

97. 'India, Israel to Jointly Market Advanced Light Helicopter', *The Rediff*, 21 January 2003.

98. 'IAI, Indian Firm Start Venture', *Defense News*, 17 February 2003.

99. 'US Approves Israeli Phalcon Sale to India', *The Indian Express*, 23 May 2003; Guttman (2003); O'Sullivan (2004).

100. For a discussion of Indo-US relations under the BJP, read Talbott (2006).

101. 'Imam Leads Muslims in Protest against Sharon's Visit', *Times of India*, 9 September 2003; 'Leftspeak: Visit Tel Aviv, But Slam Sharon Trip', *Economic Times*, 10 September 2003; 'Discreet Friends', *The Telegraph*, 15 September 2003.

102. 'Arab League Concerned over India's Military, Security Cooperation with Israel', *Albawaba News*, 13 June 2001, available at http://www.albawaba.com/news/arab-league-concerned-over-india%E2%80%99s-military-security-cooperation-israel (accessed on 3 March 2013).

103. See Rushda Siddiqui, 'India and Israel's Counter-Terrorism Policy', in *West Asia and the Region*; Priyedarshi (2010).

104. Siddiqui, 'India and Israel's Counter-Terrorism Policy'.

105. 'Palestine: India Assures Arafat of Support', *The Indian Express*, 11 April 1999.

106. 'Unequivocal Support for Palestinian Cause, Says PM', *The Hindu*, 25 September 2003; Baruah (2003).

107. Interestingly, India voted to refer the construction of the barrier to the ICJ despite its concurrent cooperation on cross-border infiltration barriers with Tel Aviv. Press Release GA/10216, General Assembly Plenary, 10th Emergency Special Session, 23rd Meeting. Available at http://www.un.org/News/Press/docs/2003/ga10216.doc.htm (accessed on 3 March 2013).

108. 'Leftspeak: Visit Tel Aviv, But Slam Sharon Trip', *Economic Times*, 10 September 2003.

109. *National Common Minimum Programme of the Government of India*, 23.

110. There were, for instance, only two cabinet-level visits under the first UPA government (2004–2009), and many scheduled visits were reportedly called off. For instance, Minister of Defence Pranab Mukherjee apparently cancelled his visit of July 2006 because of domestic political concerns. See Pandit (2006). Reportedly, a visit of the Indian minister of external affairs was also cancelled in 2007 at the last minute. Senior officials at the Israeli MFA have lamented the

lack of high-level visits under the UPA government. See 'Visits by Indian Leaders were Better under BJP: Israel', *The Indian Express*, 14 June 2011.

111. 'Free Trade Agreement may Double India–Israel Trade to $10 bn in 5 Years', *Economic Times*, 7 October 2013.

112. Srivastava (2009); 'Israel Eyes Big Arms Deals with Longtime Buyer India', *United Press International*, 2 December 2013.

113. 'Snap the Growing Ties with Israel, Says Karat', *Rediff India Abroad*, 5 March 2008.

114. Yoshita Singh, 'Palestine Wins Historic UN General Assembly Vote', *Outlook*, 30 November 2012.

115. Manmohan Singh had previously served in the INC government of Prime Minister Narasimha Rao in the early 1990s. As finance minister, he had met with Shimon Peres and negotiated with the Israeli Minister of Finance Avraham Shochat an important trade agreement in 1996.

116. The CPI(M) did not join the government and coalition but supported the government in Parliament.

117. 'President Kalam's Address to the Joint Session of Parliament', Office of The President of India, New Delhi, 7 June 2004.

118. Interview of Minister of State for External Affairs E. Ahamed in 'Old Wine. New Bottle', *Times of India*, 12 October 2004.

119. *Fifth India–EU Summit Joint Press Statement* 14431/04 (Presse 315), The Hague, 8 November 2004, 7.

120. Natwar Singh was accompanied by Union ministers Laloo Prasad Yadav, Ghulam Nabi Azad, and E. Ahamed, along with CPM politburo member Sitaram Yechury. Although some observers noticed that the Prime Minister did not go himself to the funeral. See Bidwai (2004); Kumaraswamy (2005).

121. 'Mahmoud Abbas to Arrive on Thursday', *Times of India*, 18 May 2005.

122. 'Gharekhan Visit can Push Forward Peace Process: Palestine', *Outlook*, 18 November 2005.

123. The Palestinian President Mahmoud Abbas then visited India again in 2008, 2010, and 2012. The visits in 2008 and 2010 were state visits.

124. 'Mr. E. Ahamed, Minister of State for External Affairs Attends 18th Arab League Summit', *MEA Press Release*, 30 March 2006.

125. *MEA Press Release*, 13 February 2005.

126. *MEA Press Release*, 13 September 2005.

127. See General V. P. Malik's statement on his visit to Israel in 1998 in Ved (1998). This was confirmed in interviews with various Indian military officials in fall 2011 and summer 2012.

128. By 1991, 70 per cent of India's military equipment was of Soviet origin. According to some analysts, the rapid defeat of Iraqi forces which had depended on Soviet military support had forced the Indian military establishment to reconsider patterns of defence acquisitions before the fall of the USSR. See

Chari, 'India's weapons acquisition decision-making process and Indo-Soviet military cooperation'; Gupta (1995); Thakur and Thayer (1992).

129. For example, Indian diplomats were initially reluctant to acknowledge the visits of military officials to Israel.

130. 'Israel's IAI Wins $958M India Drone Deal', *United Press International*, 12 October 2012.

131. 'Israeli Phalcon to Land in India Today', *The Hindu*, 25 May 2009.

132. Elta was the first Israeli firm to make mandatory investments in India under the 2006 offset clause. Elta invested 30 per cent of the amount of the deal into the Indian industry. See 'Out of Rs 833-cr Deal, Israel's Elta to Invest 250 cr in India', *The Indian Express*, 21 December 2006.

133. Although this deal has recently led to accusations of graft and to a 10-year ban for IMI on Indian defence contracts. See Kundu (2012).

134. 'DRDO to Get Israel Help for Missiles', *The Indian Express*, 13 July 2007.

135. The Isayev S-125 Neva/Pechora was a Soviet surface-to-air missile system which India had purchased. Interestingly, there was no tendering process and the long range surface-to-air missile (LR-SAM) joint development programme between DRDO and IAI was briefly debated and promptly approved because of the perceived urgent need to replace the ageing Russian defence systems. See 'Indo-Israel Missile Deal: All Sides of the Story', *The Indian Express*, 29 April 2010.

136. 'BEL, Israel's IAI Ink MoU on Naval Missiles', *The Hindu*, 11 December 2012.

137. However, the Spike deal with IAI, which was scheduled to be signed on a 'single vendor basis' in November 2013, has been kept pending, despite the military pressing for these 'critical operational requirements'. Some have argued that this could be due to renewed US efforts to sell the Javelin ATGMs to India with an offer to jointly manufacture the next generation of the missiles. See Pandit (2012b, 2013); Raghuvanshi (2013).

138. Pandit (2012c); 'Israeli Diplomat Attackers be Brought to Book', *Times of India*, 22 February 2013.

139. In January 2010, Israeli navy chief Vice-Admiral Eliezer Marom visited India, and the Indian navy chief Admiral Neermal Virmal made a reciprocal visit to Israel in October 2010.

140. Interestingly, some of the contracts that Israel has won have not been contested processes. Either there was no tendering process (like for the LR-SAM joint venture between IAI and the DRDO) or the tender was in a niche field where Israel had a competitive edge.

141. 'India Should Initiate Action Against Israel: Antony', *The Hindu*, 27 April 2004.

142. *The National Herald*, 10 March 2004; 'Israel Ties Won't Affect Palestine Ties: Natwar', *The Indian Express*, 12 July 2004.

143. *Rajya Sabha*, Unstarred Questions 4481, 16 May 2007.

144. 'Relation with Israel Based on Our Security Requirements, Says Antony', *Financial Express*, 23 July 2007.

145. An interview with the BJP leader of the opposition Sushma Swaraj, on a visit to Israel as the chairperson of the Indo-Israel Parliamentary Friendship Group, illustrated well this new bipartisan consensus. She lauded Israel for 'demonstrating its reliability during the Kargil war' and the ruling Congress-led government for not compromising on the 'continuity in the foreign policy' with regard to military ties with Israel despite pressures from Left. See 'Israel a Reliable Partner: Sushma Swaraj', *Economic Times*, 2 April 2008. The lack of change in India's Israel policy and the impression of a new consensus was criticized by CPI(M) leader Sitaram Yechury in 'Aggression by Israel Condemned', *People's Democracy* 30:30, 23 July 2007.

146. As both military establishments have set up various institutional linkages through joint working groups and multiple bilateral visits, there is a temporary momentum which could create conditions for an expansion of military ties. There are, however, remaining obstacles (language difference, different worldviews) for this relationship to develop into a robust strategic partnership.

147. Similarly, Prime Minister Shastri also spoke highly about Israel's achievements and did not rule out the possibility of Israeli technical cooperation with India in agricultural development. See *The Jerusalem Post*, 14 January 1966.

148. Projects in Rajasthan in 1964, Mysore in 1970 could not go through because of New Delhi's opposition. See Shimoni (1991).

149. Pawar had already visited Israel in May 1993 as chief minister of Maharashtra to discuss agricultural cooperation.

150. Information recovered from the Indian embassy in Israel website (http://www.indembassy.co.il/Bilateral%20Trade%20Relations.htm, accessed on 11 December 2013).

151. '3 Israel Centers of Excellence Coming Up', *Times of India*, 5 September 2012.

152. 'Israel Eyes Business Ties with West Bengal', *The Hindu Business Line*, 19 June 2011; Salomi (2012).

153. Information on India–Israel relations recovered from the ministry of external affairs website (http://mea.gov.in/meaxpsite/foreignrelation/israel.pdf, accessed on 11 December 2013).

154. 'Israel Signs High-Tech Deal with India', *United Press International*, 6 June 2011.

155. 'Govt Change in India has not Altered Relations: Israel', *Times of India*, 9 December 2004.

156. 'India, Israel Ink R&D Fund Pact', *Economic Times*, 31 May 2005.

157. Indian embassy figures available at http://www.indembassy.co.il/Bilateral%20Trade%20Relations.htm (accessed on 4 March 2013).

158. Information recovered from the Indian Department of Commerce (http://commerce.nic.in, accessed on 15 March 2013).

159. This is due to the fact that India imports a lot of its crude oil from West Asian states.

160. 'Free Trade Agreement may Double India–Israel Trade to $10 bn in 5 Years', *Economic Times*, 7 October 2013.

161. See, notably, the American embassy in Delhi criticizing the UPA's position as duplicitous in a leaked embassy cable, quoted in Hasan Suroor, 'MEA's Team's Visit Incensed Israel', *The Hindu*, 15 March 2011. For another criticism of India's ambiguous position, see Dhume (2011).

162. Here I define the term 'coalition' as consisting of members who share policy stakes in engaging Israel and do not necessarily engage in a planned and concerted cooperation but in an indirect and nontrivial degree of coordination to push for a certain policy direction.

163. The exception being the symbolic visit by Minister of External Affairs S. M. Krishna to Israel in January 2012. See 'Timing of Krishna's Maiden Trip to Israel Holds the Key', *Times of India*, 8 January 2012.

164. In fact, India and Israel seem to have reached some informal understanding on the separation between India's international and multilateral positioning on the Israeli–Palestinian issue and its bilateral interactions with Israel. See Blarel (2011); Clary and Karlin (2009); Suroor (2011).

165. Some suspect that the Indian Navy's scheduled acquisition of 262 Barak-I missiles to arm the Israeli-made ABMS (Anti-Ballistic Missiles) on Indian warships was delayed in November 2013 because of the pending probe in the Barak kickbacks case. See Pandit (2012a, 2013).

166. 'Israel Not to Supply Weapon Systems to Pakistan', *Times of India*, 15 September 2013.

167. 'Israel Denies Exporting Military Equipment to Pakistan', *Business Standard*, 12 June 2013.

168. Williams (2011); 'China, Israel Vow to Improve ties', *Xinhua*, 15 August 2011; Katz (2011).

169. 'Chinese Navy Ships Visit Israel's Haifa Port', *Xinhua*, 14 August 2012.

170. Interestingly, while the Indian government declined the offer, the government of Maharashtra (of which Mumbai is the capital) sent an Indian delegation to Israel to learn from the Israeli experience. This is another example of the separate bilateral dynamic directing Israel to sub-national actors, circumventing the central Indian government. See Sarin (2009).

171. Komireddi (2011). Some have argued that only substantial progress in the peace negotiations will help upgrade the India–Israel relationship. See Primor (2011).

Conclusion

2012: Three Events, Three Dimensions of India's Israel Policy

THE YEAR 2012 was eventful for Indo-Israeli relations. In January 2012, S. M. Krishna became the first Minister of External Affairs in 12 years to visit Israel. His visit also coincided with the twentieth anniversary of the establishment of diplomatic relations. A month later, a bomb blast injured the wife of an Israeli diplomat in New Delhi. The attack and the consequent investigation (which reportedly revealed an Iranian involvement) demonstrated India's difficulties in maintaining a fine balance between its relations with Israel on one hand and with Iran (and other regional partners) on the other (Chauhan 2012). Finally, in November 2012, India voted at the United Nations General Assembly (UNGA) to give Palestine the non-member observer state status, 65 years after voting for the independence of Palestine (and against partition). Although it did not publicly criticize India's vote, the government of Israel strongly contested the Palestinian move at the UNGA.

These different events illustrate three important findings from this study. First, the Krishna visit marked the public confirmation of what had mostly been a secretive but robust relationship between India and Israel over the last decade (Rajiv 2012b). The theoretical framework discussed in the preceding chapters helped explain how a substantial bilateral partnership emerged without an explicit political backing until the Krishna visit. Second, the bomb attack in New Delhi is another illustration of the difficulties for India to maintain a neutral and even-handed approach to West Asian affairs over the last 60 years. India has always walked on a tightrope in the Arab–Israeli, inter-Arab, and intra-Islam conflicts in the region. The nature of these disputes has shaped

India's different policy compromises vis-à-vis Israel. Third, the Indian vote in favour of granting Palestine the observer status at the UNGA is one more example of India's historical and constant support for Palestinian nationalism. As Palestine's political and national entity has evolved over the years, India's support has also taken various forms. Continuity and change in India's position towards the evolving Palestinian question has also informed its Israel policy.

Celebrating 20 Years of Indo-Israeli Relations: The Disclosure of the Affair

The January 2012 trip to Israel by the Minister of External Affairs S. M. Krishna was considered by many observers as a historic moment. The visit celebrated the twentieth anniversary of the establishment of diplomatic relations between the two countries ('Timing of Krishna's Maiden Trip to Israel Holds the Key'). Furthermore, prior to Krishna's visit, only two high-level Cabinet Ministers (Sharad Pawar and Kamal Nath) had travelled to Israel since the Indian National Congress (INC) came back to power in 2004. Some had compared the low number of ministerial visits during the tenure of the United Progressive Alliance (UPA) with the important and highly publicized visits that took place during the Bharatiya Janata Party's (BJP) rule, and concluded that the relationship had downgraded.[1] However, I have demonstrated in Chapter 5 that this bilateral relationship must not be evaluated on the basis of high-level political visits but rather in the light of the frequent interactions, visits, and agreements between sub-national actors. There have been regular visits by Indian state chief ministers, military service chiefs, and private economic actors over the last decade. Consequently, the Krishna visit must not be interpreted as a re-engagement or a course correction after years of neglect but as the confirmation of a burgeoning and consolidated relationship (Bagchi 2012). In spite of the absence of high-level contacts, the volume of bilateral (non-defence) trade had more than doubled in the last eight years (Table 5.1) while the defence trade has been multiplied by five since the INC came back to power. These numbers are set to grow even more as the two governments negotiate a free trade agreement (Rajiv 2012a).

India's Israel policy has consolidated around a new policy compromise since 2004. The new policy was redefined from a strongly politicized issue, which was highly dependent on regional conjunctures and domestic politics, to a more specialized collaboration. The new policy compromise has effectively been insulated from fluctuations of political events in the region and in India. This new dimension of India's Israel policy helped explain why Krishna visited Israel at an uncertain political period in the West Asian region.[2] The Arab Spring revolts and the increasing tensions between Israel and Iran did not lead to a cancellation or a rescheduling of the visit.[3] Insulated from political considerations, the new policy direction has been shaped concurrently by the security establishment which appreciated the Israeli military industry's unique expertise, by private economic actors who benefitted from specialized joint ventures with Israeli firms, and finally by Indian state governments which have directly sought agricultural assistance from the state-owned and private companies in Israel. Already in the 1950s, Nehru had not hesitated to engage Israel to get agricultural assistance, and even sought military equipment in 1962. Despite political disagreements, notably after the Suez crisis, the first Indian prime minister had kept diplomatic channels open and asked Israel for help when it abetted India's national interests. Consequently, the UPA government's selective engagement with Israel was hardly unprecedented.

In addition, the consolidation of the policy compromise helps explain why successive Indian governments (whether it is the UPA or the NDA) have supported the development of good bilateral relations despite the ideological and diplomatic ambiguities the policy has created at the public level. In fact, the Indian government and the MEA do no longer seem to be guiding the policy towards Israel. Their role is to 'manage' relations with both Arab countries and Israel in order to mobilize all resources, whether military or energetic, from the region to satisfy India's national interests. For instance, Krishna visited not only Tel Aviv but also Jordan, the Palestinian territories and the UAE in January 2012. This West Asian tour was illustrative of India's new multi-engagement policy in West Asia. Following his Israeli trip, Krishna notably paid the customary visit to Ramallah to meet the PA president Mahmoud Abbas and reaffirmed India's long-standing support to the Palestinian cause. Similarly, Prime Minister Narendra Modi (who was elected in May 2014) resumed the balancing act between India's traditional support for Palestine and its friendly ties with the Israel during the escalation in violence in Gaza in July-August 2014 (Katyal 2014). The desire to maintain good relations with all West Asian nations is not a new dimension of India's Israel policy.

India's Multi-Engagement in West Asia: A Not So Fine Balance?

The terrorist attack against an Israeli diplomat in New Delhi in February 2012 revealed the limits of India's balancing game. Over the past decade, India has adroitly managed to develop relations with various different actors such as Israel, Palestine, Iran, and Saudi Arabia. Contrary to the conventional wisdom on India's West Asia policy, moral and ideological considerations have never been a decisive factor. For instance, the policy of limited recognition of Israel with deferment of diplomatic relations in 1950, and then to normalize relations in 1992, was indicative of careful pragmatism and diplomatic prudence on India's part. The cryptic recognition, which acknowledged the existence of the state of Israel but remained vague on the subsequent establishment of diplomatic relations, was a carefully weighted decision. The compromise of the 1950s was a policy of studied aloofness towards Israel and of consistent support of the Arab line. This approached helped India to maintain a certain measure of judicious restraint towards Israel. However, this policy of skilful ambiguity was regularly tested in the following decades.

In the 1960s and 1970s, the asymmetry in diplomatic support between India and the Arab countries created a policy dilemma for the Indira Gandhi government. One of the main criticisms was that India's West Asia policy had become too Cairo-centred, up to a point where support for Egypt directly conflicted with India's regional and national interests. India's pro-Egypt bias also led New Delhi to unconditionally condemn Israel's actions. Indian policymakers, who faced adverse feedback from West Asia and criticism at home in 1967, were confronted with a difficult choice between loss-inducing, long-term policy commitments in the region and the choice for policy change that also incurred potential losses. India's West Asia policy was therefore modified in the mid-1970s and a new policy compromise emerged. To adapt to new regional developments, India moved closer to the Palestine Liberation Organization (PLO) and no longer exclusively deferred to Cairo's judgement on West Asian affairs. India also engaged other regional actors who shared strategic and economic interests like Iran and Iraq. The realignment of India's West Asia policy also broke with India's previous efforts at trying to uphold a balanced policy towards Israel and the Arab states. The pro-Arab bias was deemed necessary in order to preserve Arab support or to the least to cancel out anti-India propaganda efforts from both Pakistan and China in the region.

The UPA government attempted during its decade-long tenure to return to Nehru's pragmatic and even-handed approach to the region. The new policy compromise of 2004 marked a shift in (or a return to) India's foreign policy from a one-sided position in favour of the Arabs in their dispute with Israel to a more balanced stance. Over the last two decades, India has engaged various actors in the region such as Iran and Saudi Arabia, for geopolitical and economic reasons. India has developed relations with each country separately. New Delhi has progressively acknowledged the pragmatism of the Arabs themselves, most of whom did not really object to India's normalization of relations with Israel. The successive Indian governments since 1992 have also noticed that most Arab states would not risk hurting their economic and political relationship with a rising India for the defence of the Palestinian cause (Mohan 2005: 226–7).

India has therefore increased its economic and political relations with various regional actors. The Gulf and the Arab countries are no longer just a source of oil and destination for Indian labour; they have also become economic and political partners.[4] Countries like Saudi Arabia have also been willing to promote deepened economic relations and to invest in India. While there has been an important literature focusing on the recent upgrade of Indo-Israeli relations, the other important and overlooked change of the last decade has been the Indo-Saudi political rapprochement. While bilateral relations were significant in the 1950s, the two countries were estranged for the next three decades. During that period, Saudi Arabia developed a privileged relationship with Pakistan. The Saudi King Abdullah visited India in 2006 after a gap of 50 years. Manmohan Singh was then the first Indian prime minister to visit Saudi Arabia in 28 years in February 2010.[5] These two visits marked a change in Indian and Saudi perceptions of each other. Very much like with Israel, India and Saudi Arabia have come to an informal agreement to separate Saudi Arabia's behaviour in international fora and its bilateral relations with India. While Saudi Arabia will continue to provide firm rhetorical support to Pakistan on the Kashmir issue at the Organisation of Islamic Cooperation (OIC), it will continue to provide India with oil. Both countries have maintained their historical energy partnership and economic cooperation, but have also added a new strategic dimension by agreeing to enhance collaboration in counter-terrorism. The recent deportation of Indian terrorist Abu Jundal by Saudi Arabia to India seemed to signal a major strategic shift in bilateral relations.[6]

Since the mid-1990s, India has also improved its relations with the Islamic Republic of Iran. India has tried with relative success for the last 20 years to balance its relations with Iran on one hand and Israel and the US on the other hand (Pant 2007). In the early 1990s, India wanted to counter growing Pakistani influence in Afghanistan and to obtain an indirect access to the newly independent Central Asian countries. Prime Minister Rao visited Tehran in September 1993 and reassured Iranian leaders on the Babri Masjid incidents. In response, the Iranian government said that it considered Kashmir an internal Indian matter. Both countries developed convergent interests in Afghanistan, notably in opposition to the Taliban regime (Fair 2009). The election of the moderate President Mohammed Khatami further strengthened ties and led to the visit to Tehran by Jaswant Singh in May 2000 and by Prime Minister Vajpayee in April 2001. The Iranian President Khatami then visited Delhi in January 2003. The two countries signed a strategic partnership agreement, the Delhi Declaration. Within a span of nine months, the BJP had welcomed both the Iranian President and the Israeli Prime Minister in Delhi. This had proved to be a diplomatic *coup de force*.

Nevertheless, India's balancing act proved to be increasingly difficult to sustain as the Israeli–Iranian rivalry escalated in recent years. Until 2012, India had maintained an economic and political partnership with Iran despite US pressure and Israeli concerns (Abhyankar June 2012; Timmons 2012). India has historically been one of Iran's largest crude oil buyers and has also had eyes on Iran's natural gas reserves (Bagchi 2011). During his visit to Israel, Krishna also indirectly supported Iran by emphasizing the 'consistent stance' of India at the International Atomic Energy Agency (IAEA) regarding Iran and restated that 'every country has the right [to a peaceful nuclear energy programme] but that right is within the parameters which the IAEA sets up' (Rajiv 2012a). However, the attack against an Israeli diplomat in New Delhi in February 2012 strained the relationship (Sharma 2012). The Israeli Prime Minister Benjamin Netanyahu and the Defence Minister Ehud Barak immediately accused Iran of orchestrating the attack (Bronner 2012). Indian intelligence agencies also reportedly found enough evidence to confirm that Iranian elements were involved in the bombing (Chauhan 2012, 2013; Ravid 2012). Nevertheless, India's investigation has tried to play down the Iranian role to avoid a rift with Tehran. While the Israeli ambassador to Delhi, Alon Ushpiz, thanked India for the probe and the support it offered to Israel, it is not clear how long India will maintain this studied but fragile equidistance from Iran and Israel (Chauhan 2013). The nuclear deal struck between the US and Iran in November 2013 might further complicate the equation as Tehran again becomes a legitimate international partner and as international sanctions ease.[7]

India's Unwavering Support for Palestinian Nationalism Since 1922

In November 2012, Palestine sought to become a non-member United Nations (UN) state with observer status. India co-sponsored the UNGA resolution 67/19 which effectively upgraded the PA to observer status. India had also supported the PA President Mahmoud Abbas' previous September 2011 bid for Palestine to become a full UN member on the basis of the June 1967 borders (Blarel 2011). India's position at the UNGA must be understood in the context of its historical and unrelenting support for an independent Palestinian state. India's support for Palestinian nationalism cannot be dissociated from the story and evolution of India's Israel policy.

The INC made its first statement on the Palestine question in 1922. Before independence, India voiced its sympathy with the struggle of the Palestinian nationalist movement. In the late 1930s and in the United Nations Special Committee on Palestine (UNSCOP) deliberations, India defended the formation of an independent Palestine with a federal system which would guarantee the Jewish minority's religious rights in Palestine. After the partition of Palestine, sanctioned by the UN in November 1947, India decided to not recognize the newly created All Palestine Government (APG). The Indian government was sceptic at the time of the movement's political legitimacy and autonomy. India therefore maintained a vague support for Palestinian nationalism as there was no functioning or legitimate Palestinian leadership with which New Delhi could directly interact with. However, the Indian government did support Palestinian refugees through financial assistance. India's vague position towards the Palestine movement during that period facilitated the recognition of Israel in 1950, which had an established political leadership and which had been recognized by an important number of international actors.

The situation drastically changed in the mid-1970s as India began to directly engage the PLO. India was the second non-Arab country (after China) to recognize the PLO's authority as the sole legitimate representative of the Palestinian people in 1974, and a PLO office was set up in the Indian capital in 1975. Full diplomatic relations were then established in March 1980. India was then the first non-Arab country to recognize Palestine when it was proclaimed in November 1988. India had therefore a well-established and longstanding position on the issue of Palestinian statehood before the normalization of diplomatic relations with Israel. The rapprochement with Tel Aviv did not change this historical stance. Even the BJP respected this position when it was in power. India's privileged relations with Palestine must also be interpreted in light of its multi-engagement policy over the last two decades. India has engaged many actors in the region. All these countries supported the Palestinian bid in 2012, and India has traditionally sided with its West Asian partners on the Arab–Israeli conflict in multilateral fora.

To date, India's position on Palestine has not led to any negative public reactions from the Israeli political authorities or the Israeli media. For example, following the 2011 vote on Palestinian UN membership, the Israeli ambassador to India, Alon Ushpiz, did not express any regrets. He categorically remarked that it was 'not about disappointment...Israel and India are tremendously intimate friends. We face same challenges. We hold friendly, frank and transparent dialogue on all issues' (Tuteja 2011). When asked if Israel officially complained about the vote, Ushpiz explained that 'friends should not protest against each other' (Roy 2011). The Israeli ambassador also remarked that Israel was not taken by surprise in view of India's well known historical position on the Palestinian issue, and that it would not hurt their collaboration on other issues. He clearly stated that 'relations between India and Israel are one of the most intimate, frank and important Israel has. When two countries reach this kind of intimacy, one should be able not to isolate specific issues—even if you have differences of opinion' (Das 2011).

A later editorial in *The Jerusalem Post* (2012) also noted that 'India's foreign policy is proof that a strong pro-Palestinian stance is not an obstacle to robust and mutually advantageous relations with Israel'. In the last 20 years, defence and economic relations between India and Israel have indeed thrived in spite of India's strong pro-Palestine positions at the UN and other international fora.[8] India and Israel seemed to have found an informal understanding on the Israeli–Palestinian issue. Israeli decision-makers understand that it is not a zero-sum relationship and India wants to engage different actors in the region. Noting that India has full diplomatic relations with Israel since 1992, the Indian ambassador to the UN Hardeep Puri observed that these different relationships would not influence each other nor modify India's traditional position on Palestinian statehood (Mozumder 2011). India for instance supported along with China and Russia a Palestinian-drafted UN Human Rights Council resolution to launch a probe into Israel's offensive on Gaza in August 2014. The Israeli Ambassador to India, Daniel Carmon stated that his country would have appreciated a better understanding of their security concerns in Gaza from its international interlocutors, including India, but also added that he 'hoped' that India's stand would not impact Indo-Israeli military ties ('Israel Hopes India's UN Vote Decision Won't Impact Ties', rediff.com, 2014).

Empirical and Theoretical Implications

The new theoretical framework introduced in this book makes some important empirical contributions to the study of India's policy towards Israel. I also argue that the model of policy change within a subsystem could be applied to similar cases of dynamic and gradual foreign policy change. More tests will be necessary to evaluate this theory's explanatory scope. In this book, I have assessed and exposed the limits of the static binary narrative which had concentrated on 1992 as the sole benchmark to understand the evolution of India's Israel policy. Because of the exaggerated focus on the January 1992 decision, there has been a general impression that India's no-relationship policy with Israel and its support for the Palestinian cause had been continuous and consensual from 1948 to 1992. Likewise, there has been an impression that the sudden change in India's Israel policy after January 1992 was complete and unchallenged. The objective of this book was to demonstrate that India's Israel policy was actually contested from the start and that various actors competed and agreed at different crucial junctures on compromise positions.

Building on work in the public policy literature, as well as on recent studies on foreign policy change, this book offered a new theoretical framework which presented a more dynamic narrative of the evolution of India's Israel policy, insisting on important critical junctures and policy compromises. The subsystem framework helped identify important policy debates behind the formation of India's Israel policies. For instance, the first policy debate happened in the pre-independence period as the INC was forming its initial position on the Palestine issue. This first policy was then tested in 1947–8 with the concurrent partitions of South Asia and Palestine. The creation of Israel led to a second important policy debate which ended with the partial recognition of 1950. For the next decades, Israel continued to figure prominently in foreign policy debates in New Delhi. India's position towards Israel was again severely criticized during the 1967–73 time period. While India did not establish diplomatic relations with Tel Aviv, it changed its policy compromise towards West Asia, and new interests and priorities redefined India's position towards the region. The study of the policy debates in the 1950s and in the 1967–73 period has been decisive to understand the subtle modifications of India's Israel policy over the years, and to explain the delayed establishment of diplomatic relations until the early 1990s. This framework has helped identify and separate continuities and actual changes that took place in Indian foreign-policy-making vis-à-vis Israel *before* 1992.

In addition, the theoretical framework helped identify the main actors involved in policy-making vis-à-vis Israel over the years. Before independence, the INC and Nehru were the main architects of India's position towards the Palestine issue, but a close analysis of the domestic debate demonstrated how other actors like the British colonial administration and the Muslim League also indirectly shaped India's position. Following independence, it was also important to discern the various influences on Nehru which delimited the parameters of India's Israel policy. A personality like Maulana Azad had a decisive influence on the initial delay of normalization in the 1950s. The changing role of the ministry of external affairs (MEA) is another important finding of this historical study. Originally, some individual Indian diplomats had supported the establishment of diplomatic relations with Israel. The professionalization of the ministry and the repeated interactions with Arab diplomats in the 1950s gradually modified the perception of Israel among Indian diplomats. From the mid-1950s up to the late 1990s, the MEA had been the most reluctant actor to adjust to the policy change vis-à-vis Israel. For three decades, the MEA and the INC had then been the major advocates of the no-relationship policy.

A close analysis of the different debates on India's Israel policy has also helped determine the alternative ideas to the no-relationship policy before 1992. There were opposition parties which had criticized the Indira Gandhi government's pro-Arab approach in 1967. For instance, the Praja Socialist

Party (PSP) had traditionally supported the possibility of agricultural cooperation with Israel. Another party in the opposition, the Bharatiya Jana Sangh (BJS) (and future BJP), also explicitly expressed its desire to engage Israel in the security domain. Progressively, other interests—like the military, economic actors, state governments—also publicized their interest in cooperating with Israel. The events of 1991–2 created an opportunity structure for these actors to redefine the existing Israel policy. The theoretical framework presented in this book has helped delineate the new policy compromise on Israel that is narrowly defined by technical-military experts who appreciate the Israeli military industry's unique expertise and assistance, and by sub-national economic actors who benefit from specialized joint ventures with Israeli private actors. This policy towards Israel has now been consolidated and will prove difficult to reverse, even if there is a strong political willingness. There is a now a solid policy equilibrium which can only be restructured by a combination of shocks, adverse policy feedback, and the proposition of alternative policy options.[9]

At the theoretical level, this framework attempted to answer some of the problems in the foreign policy change literature. Many theoretical frameworks studying the specific phenomenon of policy change still concentrate on exogenous shocks as necessary conditions to bring about radical re-evaluation of foreign policy behaviour. As a result, the literature has had difficulties in differentiating and separating the causal pertinence of long-term, incremental factors from the more immediate factors. This study of the various debates and policy compromises has demonstrated how policy change is the result of shocks and propitious conditions, but also of debates, framing strategies, and negotiations between the old orthodoxy and a more or less coordinated and unified new orthodoxy. The consolidation of a new policy might also take time and further shocks. The outcomes of debates can be perceived as negotiated stalemates between various actors involved in the policy debate. An interesting finding is that the negotiated policy compromises create higher levels of threshold for future policy change. Since a vast array of actors is satisfied in the existing policy compromise, it will be difficult to reverse the existing policy. Both in 1977 and in the mid-1980s, the Janata government and Rajiv Gandhi tried to change India's Israel policy but were confronted with strong entrenched interests and stakeholders in the existing policy compromise. Only a series of shocks and an increasingly shared perception of painful costs can lead to change, like in 1992.

Additionally, the literature has often overlooked the significance of policy direction in explaining change and the consolidation of change. The literature has generally considered policy alternatives as 'floating ideas' which are only relevant when defended by efficient and skilled policy entrepreneurs. In the case of India's Israel policy, the debates of 1967–73 and of the early 1990s have demonstrated that the nature of the new policy is crucial to explain its entrenchment into a sustainable policy compromise. Policy change is not a sudden, clear-cut process. Shocks and negative policy feedback first create a permissive condition for policy change, what I have defined as a stage of policy flux. This second phase is one of debates between various actors, including the old orthodoxy (which defends the previous policy compromise) and pro-change actors. I argue that a new orthodoxy does not have to be united for policy change to happen and to consolidate.

Various actors promote change, and in the case of India's engagement with Israel, for different reasons. Through minimal core policy beliefs— the need to keep certain narrow technical channels of cooperation open with Israel—various Indian actors have jointly pushed for a new policy direction. There is not a policy consensus but a minimal common ground which indirectly pushes these actors to coordinate. The disparate coalition which defines India's Israel policy today is happy to settle for less than a strategic partnership, for example. The new policy compromise is focused on technical cooperation and perceives Israel mostly as a 'supplier' (and not a political-strategic partner). India's Israel policy is effectively insulated from regional and domestic politics. Given the nature of the policy compromise, it is likely that the current state of relations will not be reversed in the short term.

Change in leadership in India and Israel, and the deterioration of the security situation in West Asia were not sufficient conditions to initiate major changes. The election of Narendra Modi as India's Prime Minister and the escalation of violence in Gaza in July-August 2014 are illustrative of the long-term tendencies identified in this book. Following the election of Modi, who was the BJP's candidate, many evoked a strengthening of the India-Israel relationship. These accounts mostly build from the previous BJP government (1999-2004) which had openly embraced cooperation with Tel Aviv, as well as from pro-Israel statements made by Modi during his campaign. (Ghitis 2014 ; Gupta 2014; Tharoor 2014). Additionally, in the new Modi government, Sushma Swaraj, who served as chairwoman of the Indo-Israel Parliamentary Friendship Group from 2006 to 2009 and had called Israel a 'reliable partner' in 2009, was named Minister of External Affairs. (Newman 2014). As a result, the Israeli press has speculated on an expansion of the India-Israel relationship. (Frantzman 2014; Haaretz 2014; Moskowitz 2014). However, in spite of an early statement of a 'desire to deepen and develop' ties with Israel, India's Israel policy has not evolved much. (*The Hindu*, May 18, 2014). There have been no discussions of elevating the technical collaboration to a strategic partnership. Instead, Modi, who has travelled to Gujarat as Chief Minister and who has actively encouraged cooperation at the state-level with Israeli agriculture, pharmaceutical, alternative energy, and information technology companies, appreciates Tel Aviv's technical support in these particular areas (along with defence) (Moskowitz, 2014). This confirms the decisive input of state governments in the formation and direction of India's Israel policy.

Moreover, most accounts of strengthened Indo-Israeli relations have mainly discussed the developing of a sturdier civil trade and not the emergence of a political relationship (Lipsky 2014; *The Indian Express*, June 13, 2014). Similarly, the Modi government's balancing act during the Gaza confrontation between the Israeli defence forces and Hamas has demonstrated that India has not decisively tilted towards an unconditional pro-Israel position. (http://www.rediff.com/news/report/israel-hopes-indias-un-vote-decision-wont-impact-ties/20140810.htm; Pant, July 30, 2014). In fact, India has both voted against Israel at the UN Human Rights Council and purchased 262 Barak-I anti-ship missile systems and spares from Israel in August 2014 (Gupta 2014; *The Hindustan Times*). As a result, India will maintain a solid buyer-seller relationship with Israel, separate and insulated from its open political support to Palestinian grievances. Only an image reversal and a perception of painful costs emanating from the cooperation on military and economic matters could push political decision-makers to seriously reassess the relationship with Israel.

Notes

1. 'Visits by Indian Leaders were Better under BJP: Israel', *The Indian Express*, 14 June 2011; P. R. Kumaraswamy, 'Warming Up to Israel', *The New Indian Express*, 8 January 2012.

2. 'Middle East Turmoil: Indian Foreign Minister Visits Israel After a Decade', *Times of India*, 9 January 2012.

3. Because of regional tensions, previously scheduled high-level UPA visits had regularly been cancelled at the last minute. See Pandit (2006); 'Visits by Indian Leaders were Better under BJP: Israel', *The Indian Express*, 14 June 2011.

4. The Indian expatriate population in the Gulf Cooperation Council (GCC) countries is estimated to be between 4 million and 5 million, depending on different estimates. See Prakash Jain, 'Indian Diaspora in West Asia', in *West Asia and the Region*, p. 199.

5. 'PM Manmohan Singh's Visit Dominates Headlines in Saudi Media', *The Times of India*, 28 February 2010.

6. During the visit of Prime Minister Manmohan Singh to Saudi Arabia, the two countries had signed a new extradition treaty. Colonel (retd) Athale (2012). For more on Indo-Saudi cooperation, read Pradhan (2013).

7. It is not clear if India has made a choice. While India's oil imports have substantially decreased in 2012 and 2013 due to the American embargo and its growing energy relationship with the Gulf states, India has also been negotiating new energy deals with Tehran. Iran has also become gradually more dependent on India's oil purchases and has hardly been in a situation to criticize the evolution of Indo-Israeli relations. Some have also argued that India could benefit from the recent nuclear deal to increase its oil imports from Iran. See Bagchi (2013); Daly (2013); Kumar and Verma (2013).

8. India has, for instance, officially supported the PA's demand for East Jerusalem to become the future capital of a Palestinian state. See P. R. Kumaraswamy, 'Jerusalem Isn't Chandigarh', *The Pioneer*, 30 September 2011.

9. For instance, India would have to identify possible defence procurement alternatives to Tel Aviv.

Bibliography

Interviews

Mani Shankar Aiyar, 29 November 2011, New Delhi
Inder Malhotra, 19 July 2012, New Delhi
V. P. Malik, 3 November 2011, New Delhi
Lalit Mansingh, 12 October 2011, New Delhi
Arun Prakash, 4 December 2011, New Delhi
Ronen Sen, 16 July 2012, New Delhi
Jasjit Singh, 11 October 2011, New Delhi
Jaswant Singh, 25 November 2011, New Delhi
Subramaniam Swamy, 21 October 2011, New Delhi

Primary Source Documents

Official Documents, Speeches, Party Documents, Correspondence, First-Hand Accounts, and Autobiographical Works

Anti-Defamation League (ADL) (1987), *India's Campaign Against Israel* (New York: Anti-Defamation League of B'nai B'rith).

The Aga Khan (1954), *The Memoirs of Aga Khan* (New York: Simon and Schuster).

Ahma, Jamil-ud-din (ed.) (1952), *Some Recent Speeches and Writings of Mr. Jinnah* (Lahore: Sh. Muhammad Ashraf).

Allon, Yigal (1981), *A Curtain of Sand* (Tel Aviv: Hakibutz Hameuchad).

Appadorai, A. (1948), *Asian Relations: Report of the Proceedings and Documentation of the First Asian Relations Conference*, New Delhi, March–April 1947 (New Delhi).

Avimor, Shimon (ed.) (1991), *Relations between Israel and Asian and African States: A Guide to Selected Documentation* (Jerusalem: Maor-Wallach Press Ltd: Jerusalem).

Aynor, H. S. and S. Avimor (eds) (1990), *Thirty Years of Israel's International Technical Assistance and Cooperation: Documents* (Jerusalem: Haigud).

Aynor, H. S., Shimon Avimor, and N. Kaminer (eds) (1989), *The Role of the Israel Labour Movement in Establishing Relations with States in Africa and Asia (Documents 1948–1975)* (Jerusalem: The Hebrew University of Jerusalem).

Azad, Abul Kalam (1989 [1959]), *India Wins Freedom* (New Delhi: Orient Longman).

Ben-Gurion, David (1972), *Israel: A Personal History* (London: New English Library Ltd).

Bharatiya Jana Sangh (1956–73), *Party Documents*, 5 Volumes (New Delhi: Jana Sangh).

——— (1967), *Election Manifesto* (New Delhi, Bharatiya Jana Sangh).

Bharatiya Janata Party (1999), *BJP Foreign Policy Resolutions and Statements 1980–1999* (Delhi: BJP Office).

Buber, Martin (2005 [1954]), 'We Need The Arabs, They Need Us!' in Paul Mendes-Flohr (ed.), *A Land of Two Peoples* (Chicago: University of Chicago).

——— (1999 [1957]), *Pointing the Way Collected Essays*, edited by Maurice Friedman (New York: Humanity Books).

Buber, Martin and J. L. Magnes (1939), *Two Letters to Gandhi* (Jerusalem: Rubin Mass).

Chagla, M. C. (1973), *Roses in December: An Autobiography* (Bombay: Bharatiya Vidya Bhavan).

Dayan, Moshe (1978), *Breakthrough, A Personal Account of the Egypt–Israel Peace Negotiations* (New Delhi: Vikas Publishing House).

Desai, Moraji (1974–9), *The Story of My Life*, 3 Volumes (New Delhi: Macmillan India).

Dixit, J. N. (1996), *My South Block Years: Memoirs of a Foreign Secretary* (New Delhi: UBS Publishers).

——— (1998a), *Assignment Colombo* (New Delhi: Konark Publishers).

——— 2003, *India's Foreign Policy 1947–2003* (New Delhi: Picus).

——— (2004), *Makers of India's Foreign Policy* (New Delhi: HarperCollins).

——— (2005), *Indian Foreign Service: History and Challenge* (New Delhi: Konark Publishers).

Documents of the 8th Congress of the CPI (1968) (New Delhi: CPI Publications).

'Exchange of Letters between the Prime Minister of India and the President of Sri Lanka', 29 July 1987, in *Indo-Sri Lanka Agreement to Establish Peace and Normalcy in Sri Lanka*

Eytan, Walter (1958), *The First Ten Years: A Diplomatic History of Israel* (London: Weidenfeld and Nicolson).

Fifth India–EU Summit Joint Press Statement 14431/04 (Presse 315) (2004), The Hague, 8 November.

Final communiqué of the 20th Islamic Conference of Foreign Ministers (Istanbul), 4–8 August, 1991, ICFM/20-91/FC/FINAL.

From Surprise to Reckoning: The Kargil Review Committee Report (2000) (New Delhi: Sage).

Gandhi, Mohandas Karamchand (1958–99), *The Collected Works of Mahatma Gandhi*, 98 Volumes (New Delhi: Publications Division).

Gaur, Mahendra (2005), *Foreign Policy Annual, 2004: Events and Documents* (New Delhi: Gyan Publishing House).

Hadawi, Sami (ed.) (1967), *United Nations Resolutions on Palestine 1947–1966* (Beirut: The Institute for Palestine Studies).

Goldmann, Nahum (1969), *Sixty Years of Jewish Life* (New York: Holt, Rinehart and Winston).

Gopal, Sarvepalli (ed.) (1972–94), *Selected Works of Jawaharlal Nehru*, 16 Volumes (New Delhi: Orient Longman).

Government of India, *Census of India*, 1941.

Hacohen, David (1963), *Burmese Diary 1953–1955* (Tel Aviv: Am Oved Ltd Publishers).

India (1947–9), *Constituent Assembly Debates*, 12 volumes (New Delhi: Parliamentary Publications).

———, *Election Commission of India*, 'General Election of India 1967, 4th Lok Sabha'.

———, *Election Commission of India*, 'General Election of India 1971, 5th Lok Sabha'.

———, *Election Commission of India*, 'General Election of India 1977, 6th Lok Sabha'.

——— (1952–), *Lok Sabha Debates* (New Delhi, Lok Sabha Secretariat).

———, Lok Sabha (1959), *Foreign Policy of India: Texts of Documents, 1947–1959* (New Delhi: Lok Sabha Secretariat).

——— (1950–2), *Provisional Parliament Debates*, 2 volumes (New Delhi).

——— (1952–), *Rajya Sabha Debates* (New Delhi, Rajya Sabha Secretariat).

——— (1956), *The Suez Canal Crisis and India* (New Delhi: Information Service of India).

Israel, Ministry of Foreign Affairs, *Israel's Foreign Relations since 1947* (1992–4), Vols 13–14.

——— (1992–1994), 'Summary of a Visit to India by Foreign Minister Peres—18 May 1993', *Israel's Foreign Relations since 1947*, Vols 13–14.

'Israel's Sale of Airborne Early Warning Aircraft to China', *CRS Report RS20583*, 18 May 2000.

Janata (1956). Vol 11, pp. 40–41, 11 November.

——— (1966) Vol 21, N. 39, p. 11, 16 October.

Jha, C. S. (1983), *From Bandung to Tashkent: Glimpses of India's Foreign Policy* (London: Sangam Books).

Lall, Arthur (1967), *The UN and the Middle-East Crisis* (New York: Columbia University Press).

Leibler, Isi J. (1991), *Winds of Change in the Asia Pacific* (Victoria, Australia: WJC Report).

Middle East Records (1960) (Jerusalem: George Weidenfeld & Nicolson Limited).

Ministry of Commerce, (2005), *Israel-India Final Report of the Joint Study Group, 10 November 2005*. (New Delhi: Ministry of Commerce).

Ministry of External Affairs (1947–), *Annual Report* (New Delhi: External Publicity Division of the Ministry of External Affairs).

———, Bilateral/Multilateral Documents, 'Simla Agreement, 2 July, 1972'.

——— (1981), *Documents on the Gatherings of Non-Aligned Countries 1961–1979* (New Delhi: Ministry of External Affairs, Government of India).

——— (1947–), *Foreign Affairs Record* (New Delhi: External Publicity Division of the Ministry of External Affairs).

——— (1963–88), *Indian and Foreign Affairs* (New Delhi: External Publicity Division of the Ministry of External Affairs).

——— (1968), *India and Palestine: The Evolution of a Policy* (New Delhi: External Publicity Division of the Ministry of External Affairs).

Monthly Public Opinion Surveys (1967) (New Delhi: The Indian Institute of Public Opinion, July).

National Common Minimum Programme of the Government of India, 23, May 2004.

Nehru, Jawaharlal (2004[1934]), *Glimpses of World History* (New Delhi: Penguin).

——— (1942), *The Unity of India: Collected Writings 1937–1940* (New York: John Day Company).

——— (1954), *Press Conference: 1953* (New Delhi: Information Service of India).

——— (1958), *A Bunch of Old Letters* (New Delhi: Asia Publishing House).

——— (1961), *India's Foreign Policy: Selected Speeches, September 1946–April 1961* (New Delhi: The Publications Division, Ministry Information and Broadcasting).

Nielsen, Jorgen S. (ed.) (1977), *International Documents on Palestine, 1974* (Institute for Palestine Studies).

Mishra, Brajesh (NSA) (2003), Speech at the American Jewish Committee dinner, 5 May. Available at http://www.ajc.org/site/apps/nlnet/content3.aspx?c=ijI TI2PHKoG&b=851361&ct=1118743 (accessed on 8 March 2013).

Panikkar, K. M. (1955), *In Two Chinas: Memoirs of a Diplomat* (London: G. Allen & Unwin).

Parthasarathy, G. (ed.) (1985–90), *Jawaharlal Nehru, Letters to Chief Ministers 1947–1964*, 5 Volumes (Delhi: Oxford University Press).

Pearlman, Moshe (1965), *Ben Gurion Looks Back* (London: Weidenfeld and Nicolson).

Pirzada, Syed Sharifuddin (1969–70), *Foundations of Pakistan: All-India Muslim League Documents, 1906–1947*, 3 volumes (Karachi: National Publishing House).

Prasad, Bimal (ed.) (2000–10), *Jayaprakash Narayan: Selected Works*, 10 Volumes (New Delhi: Manohar).

'President Kalam's Address to the Joint Session of Parliament', Office of The President of India, New Delhi, 7 June 2004.

Rabinovich, Itamar and Jehuda Reinharz (eds) (2008), *Israel in the Middle East: Documents and Readings on Society, Politics, and Foreign Relations, Pre-1948 to the Present* (Hanover, NH: University Press of New England).

Rafael, Gideon (1981), *Destination Peace: Three Decades of Israeli Foreign Policy/ A Personal Memoir* (New York: Stein and Day).

Rao, Narasimha (2006), *Ayodhya: 6 December 1992* (New Delhi: Penguin).

'Resolution Adopted by All India Working Committee of the BJS, Rajkot, 3–4 November 1973' (1974), *Annual Register of Indian Political Parties Volume 2* (New Delhi: Michiko & Panjathan).

Singh, Jaswant (1999), *Defending India* (New York: St. Martin's Press).

Singh, V. P. (1993), *Selected Speeches and Writings 1989–90* (New Delhi: Publications Division, Ministry of Information and Broadcasting, Government of India).

Suffot, Zev E. (1997), *A China Diary: Towards the Establishment of China–Israel Diplomatic Relations* (London: Routledge).

Swatantra Party (1967), *Election Manifesto* (Bombay: Swatantra Party).

Tendulkar, D. G. (1961), *Mahatma: 1934–1938* (New Delhi: The Publications Division).

United Nations, United Nations General Assembly (UNGA) (1947–8), *Official Record of the First Special Session of the General Assembly* (New York).

—— (1947–), *Official Records of Annual Session of the General Assembly* (New York).

—— (1947), *Second Session, Ad Hoc Committee on the Palestinian Question* (New York).

—— (1948), *Third Session, Ad Hoc Committee on the Palestinian Question* (New York).

United Nations Security Council (1948), *Official Records. Third Year* (New York).

United Nations (United Nations Special Committee on Palestine [UNSCOP]) (1947), *Report to the General Assembly*, 5 Volumes (New York).

United States, Department of State (1956), *Foreign Relations of the United States, 1955–1957, Suez Crisis, July 26–December 31, 1956*, vol. 16 (Washington: G.P.O.).

Vajpayee, Atal Bihari (1979), *India's Foreign Policy: New Dimensions* (New Delhi: Ministry of External Affairs, External Publicity Division).

Weizmann, Chaim (1949), *Trial and Error* (London: Hamish Hamilton).

—— (1983–93), *Letters and Papers of Chaim Weizmann*, 23 volumes (New Haven: Transaction Publishers).

Yegar, Moshe (2010a), 'The Normalization of Relations Between India and Israel: I', *Indian Defence Review*, 14 November.

—— (2010b), 'The Normalization of Relations Between India and Israel: II', *Indian Defence Review*, 16 November.

Yunus, Mohammed (1980), *Persons, Passions, and Politics* (New Delhi: Vikas).

Zaidi, A. G. (ed.) (1980), *Annual Register of Indian Political Parties* (Delhi: Institute of Applied Political Research).

Zaidi, A. G. and S. G. Zaidi (eds) (1977–85), *The Encyclopedia of the Indian National Congress*, 25 volumes (New Delhi: S. Chand).

Secondary Sources

Electronic Sources

Interview with Arthur Lall (1990), United Nations Oral History Project, 27 June. available at: http://www.unmultimedia.org/oralhistory/2011/10/lall-arthur-samuel/ (accessed on 9 March 2013).

Menon, Shiv Shankar (1997), 'Indian Foreign Policy in the Middle-East', *Palestinian Academic Society for the Study of International Affairs*, 7 May 1997. Available at http://www.passia.org/meetings/97/meet04.htm (accessed on 9 March 2013).

Savarkar, Vinayak (2012) 'Glad to Note that Independent Jewish State is Established', *Historic Statements—Veer Savarkar*. Available at www.docstoc. com (accessed on 6 May 2012).

Newspapers and Periodicals

The Asian Age (New Delhi)
Asia Times (Online) (Hong Kong)
Asian Recorder (New Delhi)
Business Standard (New Delhi)
The Christian Science Monitor (Boston)

The Diplomat (Tokyo)

Daily News and Analysis (Bombay)

Dawn (Karachi)

Deccan Herald (Bangalore)

Defense News (Springfield, Virginia)

The Economic Times (Bombay)

Express Tribune (Karachi)

Far Eastern Economic Review (Hong Kong)

Financial Express (New Delhi)

Financial Times (London)

Frontline (Madras)

Globes (Tel Aviv)

The Guardian (London)

Haaretz (Tel Aviv)

Hindu (Madras)

The Hindu Business Line (Madras)

Hindustan Times (New Delhi)

India and Israel (Bombay)

Indian Defense Review (New Delhi)

India Today (Noida)

The Israel Digest (Tel Aviv)

Jane's Defense Weekly (Coulsdon, Surrey)

Jerusalem Post

Jewish Agency's Digest (Tel Aviv)

The Indian Express (Bombay)

Los Angeles Times

The National Herald (New Delhi)

Newsweek (New York)

New York Times

Outlook (New Delhi)

The Patriot (Calcutta)

People's Democracy (New Delhi)

The Pioneer (New Delhi)

Rediff (Bombay)

The Statesman (Calcutta)

Sunday Observer (Bombay)

Telegraph (Calcutta)

Times (London)

Times of India (Bombay)
Tribune (Chandigarh)
UN Monthly Chronicle (New York)
The Wall Street Journal (New York)
The Week (Cochin)
World Politics Review

Papers/Reports

Abhyankar, Rajendra (2012), 'The Evolution and Future of Indo-Israeli Relations', *Tel Aviv University Research Paper* 6, March. Available at http://www.tau.ac.il/humanities/abraham/india-israel.pdf (accessed on 26 August 2013).

Bitzinger, Richard A. (2013), 'Israeli Arms Transfers to India: Ad Hoc Defence Cooperation or the Beginnings of a Strategic Partnership?' *Policy Brief S. Rajaratnam School of International Studies*, April. Available at http://www.rsis.edu.sg/publications/policy_papers/Israeli%20Arms%20Transfers%20to%20India_27052013%20FINAL.pdf (accessed 17 November 2013).

Blarel, Nicolas (2011), 'The Palestinian Quest for Statehood at the United Nations: International Reactions and India's Position', *Institute for Defence and Strategic Analyses Issue Brief*, 20 October.

Brecher, Michael (1957), *India's Foreign Policy* (New York: Institute of Pacific Relations).

Calabrese, John (2009), 'The Consolidation of Gulf–Asia Relations: Washington Tuned In or Out of Touch?' *Middle East Institute Policy Brief*, 25 June.

Chari, P. R. (1995), 'India's Weapons Acquisition Decision-making Process and Indo-Soviet Military Cooperation', *SIPRI Arms Procurement Decision Making Project*, Working Paper 19.

Feiler, Gil (2012), 'India's Economic Relations with Israel and the Arabs', *Mideast Security and Policy Studies* 96 (Tel Aviv: Begin-Sadat Center for Strategic Studies Bar-Ilan University).

Gerberg, Itzhak (1996), 'India Developing Trade', *Israel–Asia Trade* No. 8 (Tel Aviv: Israel Asia Chamber of Commerce).

Inbar, Efraim and Alvite Singh Ningthoujam (2012), 'Indo-Israeli Defense Cooperation in the Twenty-First Century', *Mideast Security and Policy Studies* 93, Begin-Sadat Center for Strategic Studies, Bar-Ilan University, January.

Israel-India Final Report of the Joint Study Group, 10 November 2005 (New Delhi: Ministry of Commerce, 2005).

Kapila, Subhash (2003a), 'Israeli-Indian Strategic Cooperation and Prime Minister Sharon's Visit: The Added Dimensions', *SAAG Paper* 777 (New Delhi: South Asia Analysis Group).

Kapila, Subhash (2003b). 'India-Israel: The Imperatives for Strategic Cooperation', *SAAG Paper 131* (New Delhi: South Asia Analysis Group)

Khemlani, Brijesh (2010), 'India–Israel: A Robust Strategic Partnership', *RUSI Newsbrief*, 20 May.

Khilnani, Sunil, Rajiv Kumar, Pratap Bhanu Mehta, Lt Gen. (retd) Prakash Menon, Nandan Nilekani, Srinath Raghavan, Shyam Saran, and Siddharth Varadarajan (2012), *Non-Alignment 2.0: A Foreign and Strategic Policy for India in the Twenty-First Century* (New Delhi: Centre For Policy Research).

Kumaraswamy, P. R. (2000), *Beyond the Veil: Israel–Pakistan Relations* (Tel Aviv: Jaffee Center for Strategic Studies, Tel Aviv University).

——— (2005), 'Indo-Israeli Ties: The Post-Arafat Shift', *The Power and Interest News Report* (PINR), March.

Lambeth, Benjamin (2012), *Airpower at 18,000: The Indian Air Force in the Kargil War* (Washington DC: Carnegie Endowment for International Peace report).

Rajiv, S. Samuel (2012a), 'Foreign Minister Krishna's Visit to Israel: Adding Political Content to a Robust Partnership', *IDSA Issue Brief*, 16 January.

——— (2012b), 'The Delicate Balance: Israel and India's Foreign Policy Practice', *Strategic Analysis*, 36: 128–44.

Riedel, Bruce (2008), 'Israel and India: New Allies', *Middle East Bulletin Brookings Institute*, 21 March.

Articles in Newspapers and Periodicals

Abhyankar, Rajendra (2012), 'Israel, Iran, and India', *Haaretz*, 22 June.

Advani, L. K. (1993), 'Should Indo-Israel Ties be Strengthened? A Defence Tie-Up will Benefit India', *Indian Express*, 24 May.

Aiyar, Mani Shankar (1993), 'Chutzpah', *Sunday*, 6 June.

Ameer, P. S. (1996), 'Indo-Israeli Tie-Up Likely for AWACS', *The Pioneer*, 4 November.

Athale, Colonel (retd) Anil (2012), 'India, US and Saudi Arabia: The "New" Great Game!' *Rediff*, 27 June.

Bagchi, Indrani (2002), 'Israel—India's Latest Defence Chum', *Economic Times*, 28 June.

——— (2008), 'Why India Didn't Make It to OIC', *Times of India*, 25 February.

——— (2011), 'Post-Iran Deal Fiasco, India Gets Israel's Gas Offer', *Times of India*, 19 December.

——— (2012), 'India–Israel Relations Come Out of Arab World Shadow', *Times of India*, 13 January.

——— (2013), 'India Likely to Fast-Track Iran Port, Oil Plans', *Times of India*, 28 November.

Baruah, Amit (2003), 'We Fully Support Palestinian Cause, Says Vajpayee', *The Hindu*, 16 November.

Bedi, Rahul (1993), 'India Eyes Israeli Arms Upgrades', *Jane's Defense Weekly*, 13 November.

——— (2003), 'Moving Closer to Israel', *Frontline*, 20: 4, February.

Bidwai, Praful (2004), 'Giving Arafat His Due', *Frontline*, 20 November–3 December.

Brilliant, Joshua (2003), 'Why India and Israel Joined Forces', *United Press International*, 7 September.

Bronner, Ethan (2012), 'Israel Says Iran Is Behind Bombs', *New York Times*, 13 February.

Burns, John (1990), 'Flow of Asian Fleeing Iraq has Eased, Jordan Reports', *New York Times*, 13 September.

——— (1994), 'Return to India: A Mehta Triumph', *New York Times*, 6 December.

Chauhan, Neeraj (2012), 'Cops Name Iran Military Arm for Attack on Israeli Diplomat', *Times of India*, 30 July.

——— (2013), 'Security Cover for Israelis on Car Blast Anniversary', *Times of India*, 13 February.

Cherian, John (2000), 'India's Changing Stand', *Frontline*, 10 November.

——— (2004), 'A Breach of Trust', *Frontline*, 4–17 December.

Clary, Christopher and Mara E. Karlin (2009), 'A Fine Balance: India's Middle East Policy', *Indian Express*, 9 May.

Cowell, Alan (1990), 'Jordan Attacks Pace of Refugees' Exit', *New York Times*, 1 October.

Dagoni, Ran (2004), 'There Won't be Another Phalcon Affair: Dr Joseph Draznin on Scandal Versus Reality in Israel-US Defense Relations', *Globes*, 20 October.

Daly, John (2013), 'Iranian Sanctions Easing to Benefit India', *The Diplomat*, 7 December.

Das, Srijana Mitra (2011), 'The UN is Quite a Difficult Arena for Us to Operate In', *Times of India*, 28 September.

Datta, Rahul (1997), 'Israeli Arms for India through Russia', *The Hindustan Times*, 13 February.

Desai, Ronak D. (2012), 'India's Israeli–Palestinian Balancing Act', *The Diplomat*, 18 September.

Dhume, Sadanand (2011), 'India Fumbles on Palestine', *The Wall Street Journal*, 14 October.

Economic Times (2012), '$ 10 Billion Business: How Israel Became India's Most Important Partner in Arms Bazaar', 24 September.

Fontaine, Richard and Daniel Twining (2011), 'India's Arab Spring Opportunity', *The Diplomat*, 24 August.

Ford, Peter (1992), 'Israelis Scramble to Keep Up with Pace of New Diplomatic Ties', *The Christian Science Monitor*, 12 February.

Frantzman,Seth J. (2014). 'Terra Incognita: Why Modi Matters', *The Jerusalem Post*, May 15.

Ganguli, Bodhisatva (2012), 'UP Elections 2012: The Contrasting Styles of Rahul Gandhi, Akhilesh Yadav and Mayawati', *Economic Times*, 21 February.

Ganguly, Sumit (2011), 'A Foreign Policy Adrift', *The Asian Age*, 7 September.

Gargan, Edward (1992), 'India Announces Full Israeli Ties', *New York Times*, 30 January.

Ghildiyal, Subodh (2008), 'Mayawati Uses N-deal to Win Over Muslim Vote', *Times of India*, 17 July.

Ghitis, Frida (2014), 'India-Israel Ties Set to Blossom Under Modi', *World Politics Review*, May 22. Available at : http://www.worldpoliticsreview.com/articles/13801/india-israel-ties-set-to-blossom-under-Modi.

Gupta, Kanchi (2014), 'Indo-Israeli Relations Set to Improve', *The Diplomat*, June 19, 2014. Available at : http://thediplomat.com/2014/06/indo-israeli-relations-set-to-improve/

Gupta, Sekhar (1992), 'Indo-Israeli Relations: A Pragmatic Peace', *India Today*, 29 February.

——— (2013), 'National Interest: Conscience and Cowardice', *Indian Express*, 9 November.

Gupta, Shishir (2001), 'India to Buy Missile Defense Systems from Israel', *The Hindustan Times*, 11 February.

——— (2014), 'Weeks after UN vote, India Seeks Israel Missile Deal', *The Hindustan Times*, August 7.

Guttman, Nathan (2003), 'US Formally Announces Permission for Phalcon Sale to India', *Haaretz*, 11 August.

Hijaz, Ishan A. (1990), 'P.L.O. and Iraq Cooperate on Hard-Line Strategy', *New York Times*, 13 May.

Hoodboy, Pervez (2012), 'The Bomb: Iran, Saudi Arabia, and Pakistan', *The Express Tribune*, 22 January.

Ibrahim, Youssef M. (1990), 'Arafat's Support of Iraq Creates Rift in P.L.O.', *New York Times*, 14 August.

Jain, Bharti (2013), 'Narasimha Rao Had Asked Kalam to be Ready for Nuclear Test', *Times of India*, 25 January.

Janmohamed, Zahir (2003), 'Golwalkar, Savarkar...and Jews', *Outlook*, 17 July.

Jayaprakash, N. D. (2003), 'Ariel Sharon: Profile of a Zionist Killer', *People's Democracy* 27:36, 7 September.

Jha, Saurav (2013), 'India–Israel Ties Complicated by Iran Opening, Shifting Defense Priorities', *Work Politics Review*, 6 December.

Kapadia, Payal (2008), 'Tears and Sackcloth', *Outlook*, 15 December.

Karat, Prakash (2002), 'The Bush–Sharon Axis of Evil', *People's Democracy* 26:18, 12 May.

Katyal, K. K. (2000), 'West Asia Crisis Tells on Foreign Policy Consensus', *The Hindu*, 18 October.

Katyal, Anita (2014), 'Modi Govt's Dilemma over Israel-Palestine Conflict', Rediff Online, Jul 16, available at: http://www.rediff.com/news/report/modi-govts-dilemma-over-israel-palestine-conflict/20140716.htm.

Katz, Yaakoov (2008), 'Spy Satellite Launched from India', *Jerusalem Post*, 21 January.

——— (2011), 'Chinese Army Chief Here to Talk Defense Cooperation', *The Jerusalem Post*, 15 August.

Kaur, Jatinder (2013), 'India–Israel Joint Venture to Manufacture Missiles Fails to Take Off', *Times of India*, 14 November.

Komireddi, Kapil (2011), 'India and Israel: A Friendship Deepened by Prejudice', *The Guardian*, 25 October.

——— (2012), 'Israel, Use India to Pressure Iran', *Haaretz*, 20 June.

Koshy, Ninan (2003), 'US Plays Matchmaker to India, Israel', *The Asia Times*, 10 June.

Kumar, Manoj and Nidhi Verma (2013), 'Iran, India Meet to Discuss Oil Exports, Payments', *Reuters*, 10 December.

Kumaraswamy, P. R. (2004b), 'Uncertainties about Indo-Israeli Ties', *The Deccan Herald*, 15 June.

Kundu, Rhik (2012), 'Banning Foreign Defence Contractors is a Loss for Both Country and Firms: Experts', *Times of India*, 9 August.

Lappin, Yaakov (2013), 'Indian Air Force Chief Visits Israel', *The Jerusalem Post*, 21 January.

Lipsky, Seth (2014), 'Will Modi be the Most Pro-Israel PM in India's History?', *Haaretz*, May 19.

Luce, Edward (2003), 'India and Israel Ready to Consummate Secret Affair', *The Financial Times*, 4 September.

Malhotra, Jyoti (2000), 'Arab Diplomats Sore with Jaswant, Advani', *Indian Express*, 17 July.

McGirk, Tim (2008), 'Israel Reacts to the Mumbai Massacre', *Time*, 28 November.

Melman, Yossi (2000), 'India's Visiting Strongman Wants to Expand Nuclear Cooperation with Israel', *Haaretz*, 16 June.

—— (2009), 'Media Allege Corruption in Massive Israel–India Arms Deal', *Haaretz*, 29 March.

—— (2006), 'India to Purchase Israeli-Made Anti-Aircraft Missile Systems', *Haaretz*, 7 October.

Mohan, C. Raja (2000), 'India's West Asian Stakes', *The Hindu*, 16 October.

—— (2001), 'India Woos Saudi Arabia', *The Hindu*, 18 January.

Moskowitz, Jeff (2014), 'Is Narendra Modi, India's New Prime Minister, Israel's New Best Friend?', *Tablet*, May 23, available at: http://www.tabletmag.com/jewish-news-and-politics/173767/modi-israels-new-best-friend

Mozumder, Suman Guha (2011), 'India to Back Palestine's UN Bid, Reassures PM', *Rediff*, 22 September.

Naqvi, Jawed (2005), 'India Rejects OIC Stand on Kashmir', *Dawn*, 18 July.

Newman, Marissa (2014) 'India's New Foreign Minister a Strong Fan of Israel', *The Times of Israel*, May 27, 2014, available at: http://www.timesofisrael.com/indias-new-foreign-minister-a-strong-fan-of-israel/#ixzz3A4RBgIvl

Noorani, A. G. (1969), 'Rabat: Religion and Diplomacy', *Indian Express*, 4 December.

—— (1994), 'Living with the OIC', *Frontline*, 2 December.

O'Sullivan, Arieh (2004), 'Phalcon Deal Signed with India', *The Jerusalem Post*, 6 March.

Pant, Harsh (2014), 'India's Israel Dilemma', *The Jerusalem Post*, July 30.

Pandit, Rajat (2013), 'Antony defers decision on critical but controversial missile deals with Israel', *Times of India*, 11 November.

—— (2006). 'Pranab "forced" to defer Israel visit', *Times of India*, 1 July.

—— (2007), 'After Jets, UAVs are on Shopping List', *Times of India*, 10 February.

—— (2011), 'IAF will Add Two More Israeli AWACS to Its Fleet', *Times of India*, 8 November.

—— (2012a), 'Navy's Critical Requirement for Israeli Barak Missiles Stalled Due to CBI Case', *Times of India*, 27 August.

—— (2012b), 'Israel Pips US in Anti-Tank Guided Missile Supply to India', *Times of India*, 29 November.

—— (2012c), 'India Urges Israel to Speed Up Defence Projects', *Times of India*, 5 December.

Peraino, Kevin (2008), 'Why Israel Isn't Angry?' *Newsweek*, 2 December.

Prasanvrajan, S. (2003), 'States of Survival: Why India and Israel Should be Partners in an Existential Trauma', *India Today*, 22 September.

Primor, Adar (2011), 'The Potential of Israel's Relationship with India', *Haaretz*, 1 November.

Raghuvanshi, Vivek (1994), 'India Buys UAVs from Israeli Firm', *Defense News*, 21 March.

——— (2003a), 'India Strives for Missile-Building Hub', *Defense News*, 24 February.

——— (2003b), 'India Imports Naval Missile Defences', *Defence News*, 23 May.

——— (2003c), 'India's Ordinance Board Looks Overseas', *Defense News*, 26 May.

——— (2013), 'India Again Considers Buying Israeli-Made ATGM', *Defense News*, 11 November.

Rajiv, Samuel (2011), 'Palestine's Strongest UN Ally', *The Diplomat*, 21 September.

Rajiv, Samuel C. (2013), 'India Blots Out Israeli Issues', *Asia Times*, 18 March.

Ravid, Barak (2012), 'Israeli Officials: India Playing Down New Delhi Attacks to Avoid Rift with Iran', *Haaretz*, 26 February.

Rediff.com (2014), 'Israel Hopes India's UN Vote Decision Won't Impact Ties', August 10, 2014. Available at http://www.rediff.com/news/report/israel-hopes-indias-un-vote-decision-wont-impact-ties/20140810.htm).

Roy, Shubhajit (2011), 'Palestine's UN Bid a Negative Development, Says Israel', *Indian Express*, 23 September.

Salomi, Vithika (2012), 'Israel to Aid Bihar's Development Bid', *Times of India*, 30 August.

Samanta, Pranab Dhal (2011), 'Blacklist Effect: Tank Ammo at Critical Low Levels, MoD Waives Policy to Buy', *Indian Express*, 4 October.

——— (2013), 'Cable Thickness, Personnel Activity "Gave Away" India's 1995 N-Test Plan to US', *Indian Express*, 26 February.

Sandler, Neal (1993), 'Trade Winds', *The Jerusalem Report*, 6 May.

Sarin, R. (2009), 'From Israel, Lessons of Fighting Terror', *Indian Express*, 21 July.

Sharma, Amol (2012), 'New Delhi Attacks Tests India's Relations with Iran', *Wall Street Journal*, 15 February.

Sherman, Martin (2003), 'From Conflict to Convergence: India and Israel Forge a Solid and Strategic Alliance', *The Jerusalem Post*, 28 February.

Shukla, Rajiv (1993), 'Talking Too Much', *Sunday*, 13 June.

Silyer, Eric (2000), 'For India, Israel is Now a Different Ball Game', *The Statesman*, 6 July.

Sirohi, Seema (2008a), 'The Secret Part of Indo-Israel Defence Ties will Remain a Secret', *Outlook*, 18 February.

——— (2008b), 'Li'l Homeland', *Outlook*, 13 October.

Sloman, Mark (2011), 'After Mumbai Attack, Indo-Israel Ties Stronger Than Ever', *Jerusalem Post*, 23 November.

Sneh, Ephraim (1990), 'PLO–Iraq Alliance Clouds Peace Hopes', *The Christian Science Monitor*, 20 July.

Srivastava, Siddharth (2009), 'Israel Rushes to India's Defense', *Asia Times Online*, 2 April.

Suroor, Hasan (2011), 'West Asia Policy Hostage to "Muslim" Vote', *The Hindu*, 15 March.

Swamy, Subramaniam (1982), 'The Secret Friendship Between India and Israel', *Sunday*, 28 November.

Tillin, Louise (2003), 'US–Israel–India: Strategic Axis?' *BBC News*, 9 September.

The Jerusalem Post (2012), 'India's Delicate Balance', 10 January.

Time Magazine (1969), 'The Burning of Al-Aqsa', 29 August.

Times of India (2012), 'Timing of Krishna's Maiden Trip to Israel Holds the Key', 8 January.

Timmons, Heather (2012), 'India–Iran–Israel: A Fine Balance', *New York Times*, 15 February.

The Indian Express (2014), 'Israel to Expand ties with Modi govt, offers help in Ganga Clean-up', June 13.

Triparthi, Salil (1988), 'A Discernible Thaw', *India Today*, 30 September.

Tuteja, Ashok (2011), 'Palestine Issue: Israel Rules Out Third-Party Intervention', *The Tribune*, 26 September.

Unnithan, Sandeep (2010), 'Indo-Israeli Missile Successfully Test-Fired: DRDO Chief', *India Today*, 28 May.

Varadarajan, Siddharth (2005), 'When Jaswant Took Indian Politics to Foreign Shores', *The Hindu*, 16 September.

Ved, Mahendra (1998), 'Slow and Steady: Growing Security Ties with Israel', *Times of India*, 30 March.

Waldman, Amy (2003), 'The Bond between India and Israel Grows', *The New York Times*, 7 September.

Williams, Dan (2011), 'Chinese Military Chief Makes First Visit to Israel', *Reuters*, 14 August.

Winraub, Bernard (1974), 'Israel and India: Long-Unhealed Rift; Lifted a Similar Ban', *New York Times*, 22 December.

Yadav, Yogendra (2009), 'Five Myths about the Muslim Vote', *The Hindu*, 20 April.

Journal Articles

Abadi, Jacob (1991), 'Israeli–Indian Relations: Futile Attempts at Rapprochement', *Journal of Third World Studies*, 8: 161–74

————, 'The Bitter Harvest of Indo-Egyptian Relations', *Journal of South Asian and Middle Eastern Studies*, 23: 38–64.

Adams, John (1971), 'The Impact of the Suez Canal on India's Trade', *Indian Economic & Social History Review*, 8: 229–40.

Agwani, M. S. (1963a), 'The Reactions of West Asia and the UAR', *International Studies*, 5: 75–9.

———— (1963b), 'India and West Asia', *International Studies*, 5: 169–71.

———— (1963c), 'Islam and Modernism in the Arab East', *India Quarterly*, 19: 266–75.

———— (1966), 'India, Pakistan and West Asia', *International Studies*, 8: 158–66.

———— (1973a), 'India and the Arab World, 1947–1964', *Indian Horizon*, 22.

———— (1973b), 'Ingredients of India's Arab Policy', *Indian and Foreign Affair*, 10: 12–13.

Ahmad, Syed Barakat (1973), 'India and Palestine 1896–1947: The Genesis of a Foreign Policy', *India Quarterly: A Journal of International Affairs*, 29.

Ahmad, Talmiz (2013), 'The Arab Spring and Its Implications for India', *Strategic Analysis*, 37: 119–27.

Andersen, Walter K. (1991), 'India's 1991 Elections: The Uncertain Verdict', *Asian Survey*, 31: 976–89.

Bajpai, K. Shankar (1992), 'India in 1991: New Beginnings', *Asian Survey*, 32: 207–16.

Baral, J. K. and J. N. Mohanty (1992), 'India and the Gulf Crisis', *Pacific Affairs*, 65: 368–84.

Berman, Ilan (2002), 'Israel, India and Turkey: Triple Entente?' *Middle East Quarterly*, 9: 33–40.

Bishku, Michael (1987), 'Personalities and Perceptions: Political and Economic Factors Which Led to India's Involvement in the Suez Crisis of 1956', *Journal of South Asian and Middle Eastern Studies*, 10: 17–32.

Blyth, Mark (2003), 'Structures Do Not Come with an Instruction Sheet: Interests, Ideas and Progress in Political Science', *Perspective on Politics*, 1: 695–703.

Brecher, Michael (1961), 'Israel and Afro-Asia', *International Journal*, 16: 107–37.

———— (1975), 'India's Decision to Remain in the Commonwealth', *Journal of Commonwealth and Comparative Politics*, 12: 69–90.

Boquerat, Gilles (2001), 'Indian Response to the Gulf Crisis of 1990–91', *International Studies*, 38: 427–40.

Byman, Daniel L. and Kenneth M. Pollack (2001), 'Let US Now Praise Great Men: Bringing the Statesman Back In', *International Security*, 25: 107–46.

Caplan, Neil (2002), 'The 1956 Sinai Campaign Viewed From Asia', *Israel Studies*, 7: 81–103.

Chaulia, Sreeram S. (2002), 'BJP, India's Foreign Policy and the "Realist Alternative" to the Nehruvian Tradition', *International Politics*, 39: 215–34.

Chen, Yiyi (2012), 'China's Relationship with Israel, Opportunities and Challenges: Perspectives from China', *Israel Studies*, 17: 1–21.

Clarke, Duncan (1995), 'Israel's Unauthorized Arms Transfers', *Foreign Policy*, 99: 89–109.

Cooley, John K. (1972), 'China and the Palestinians', *Journal of Palestine Studies*, 1: 19–34.

Dasgupta, Punyapriya (1992), 'Betrayal of India's Israel Policy', *Economic and Political Weekly*, 27: 767–72.

Dastur, Aloo J. (1988), 'India and the West Asian Crisis', *West Asia*, 20: 27–31.

Decalo, Samuel (1967), 'Israeli Foreign Policy and the Third World', *Orbis*, 11: 724–45.

Dhamji, Ram (1969), 'The Rabat Episode', *Indian and Foreign Affair*, 1 November, pp. 11–12.

Dueck, Colin (2004), 'Ideas and Alternatives in American Grand Strategy, 2000–2004', *Review of International Studies*, 30: 511–35.

Eagleton, Clyde (1950), 'The Case of Hyderabad before the Security Council', *The American Journal of International Law*, 44: 277–302.

Gangal, S. C. (1979), 'Major Developments in India's Foreign Policy and Relations July–December 1977', *International Studies*, 18: 70.

Ghosh, Partha and R. Panda (1983), 'Domestic Support for Mrs. Gandhi's Afghanistan Policy: The Soviet Factor in Indian Politics', *Asian Survey*, 23: 261–79.

Glucklich, Ariel (1988), 'Brahmins and Pharisees: The Roots of India's Anti-Zionism', *Midstream*, 34: 12–15.

Goldberg, Ellen S. (1995), 'Leaving Mother India: Reasons for the Cochin Jews' Migration to Israel', *Population Review*, 39: 35–53.

Goldstein, Jonathan (2004), 'The Republic of China and Israel', *Israel Affairs*, 10: 223–53.

Gordon, Leonard A. (1975), 'Indian Nationalist Ideas About Palestine and Israel', *Jewish Social Studies*, 37: 221–34.

Gupta, Amit (1995), 'Determining India's Force Structure and Military Doctrine', *Asian Survey*, 35: 441–58.

Haas, Peter M. (1992), 'Introduction: Epistemic Communities and International Policy Coordination', *International Organization*, 46: 1–35.

Hadass, Joseph (2002), 'Evolution of the Relations Between India and Israel', *India Quarterly*, 58: 15–32.

Hall, Peter A. (1993), 'Policy Paradigms, Social Learning, and the State: The Case of Economic Policymaking in Britain', *Comparative Politics*, 25: 275–96.

Han, Xiaoxing (1993), 'Sino-Israeli Relations', *Journal of Palestine Studies*, 22: 62–77.

Hasan, Najmul (1982), 'Multi-Faceted Indo-Arab Cooperation', *Indian and Foreign Affair*, 19: 10–11.

Hermann, Charles F. (1990), 'Changing Course: When Governments Choose to Redirect Foreign Policy', *International Studies Quarterly*, 34: 3–21.

Hermann, Margaret G., Thomas Preston, Baghat Korany, and Timothy M. Shaw (2001), 'Who Leads Matters: The Effects of Powerful Individuals', *International Studies Review*, 3: 83–131.

Hirshi, Christian and Thomas Widmer (2010), 'Policy Change and Policy Stasis: Comparing Swiss Foreign Policy toward South Africa (1968–94) and Iraq (1990–91)', *The Policy Studies Journal*, 38: 537–63.

Inbar, Efraim (2004), 'The Indian–Israeli Entente', *Orbis*, 48: 89–104.

Jaffrelot, Christophe (2003), 'Inde-Israël, le Nouvel Elément-Clé de l'Axe du Bien?' *Critique internationale*, 21: 24–32.

Jansen, G. H. (1966), 'The Limits of Lobbying: The Zionist Failure with Mahatma Gandhi', *Middle East Forum*, 42: 27–37.

Jenkins, Rob (2003), 'India's States and the Making of Foreign Economic Policy: The Limits of the Constituent Diplomacy Paradigm', *Publius*, 33: 63–82.

Kandel, Arielle (2009), 'The Significant Warming of Indo-Israeli Relations in the Post-Cold War Period', *Middle East Review for International Affairs*, 13. Available at http://www.gloria-center.org/2009/12/kandel-2009-12-07/ (accessed on 17 November 2013).

Kember, James (1976), 'India in International Affairs, 1944–1947: The Prelude to Independence', *International Studies*, 15: 365–91.

Khana, Naseem (2001), 'Vajpayee's Visit to Iran: Indo-Iranian Relations and Prospects of Bilateral Cooperation', *Strategic Analysis*, 25: 765–79.

Kohn, Leo (1959), 'Israel and the New Nation States of Asia and Africa', *Annals of the American Academy of Political and Social Science*, 324: 96–102.

Kozicki, Richard (1958), 'India and Israel: A Problem in Asian Politics', *Middle Eastern Affairs*, 9: 162–72.

——— (1967), 'Indian Policy towards the Middle-East', *Orbis*, 11: 786–97.

Kumar, Bharat (1982), 'India's Policy towards the Arab–Israeli Conflict', *United Services Institution of India*, 112: 138–49.

Kumaraswamy, P. R. (1994), 'The Star and the Dragon: An Overview of Israeli–PRC Military Relations', *Issues and Studies*, 30: 36–55.

——— (1995a), 'India's Recognition of Israel, September 1950', *Middle Eastern Studies*, 31: 124–38.

Kumaraswamy, P. R. (1995b), 'Sardar K. M. Panikkar and India–Israel Relations', *International Studies*, 32: 327–37.

——— (1996a), 'Israel, China and the United States: The Patriot Controversy', *Israel Affairs*, 3: 12–33.

——— (1996b), 'The Limitations of Indo-Israeli Military Cooperation', *Contemporary South Asia*, 5: 75–84.

——— (2002), 'India, Israel and the Davis Cup Tie 1987', *Journal of Indo-Judaic Studies*, 5: 29–39.

——— (2004c), 'Are Indo-Israeli Deals Doomed?', *Bulletin of the Atomic Scientist*, November/December.

Laufer, Leopold (1972), 'Israel and the Third World', *Political Science Quarterly*, 87: 615–30.

Legro, Jeffrey (2000), 'The Transformation of Policy Ideas', *American Journal of Political Science*, 44: 419–32.

Levi, Werner (1958), 'India, Israel and the Arabs', *Eastern World*, 12: 14–18.

Lieberman, Robert C. (2002), 'Ideas, Institutions, and Political Order: Explaining Political Change', *American Political Science Review*, 96: 697–712.

Madhok Balraj (1967), 'India's Foreign Policy: The Jana Sangh View', *India Quarterly*, 23: 3–7.

Malik, Mohan (1991), 'India's Response to the Gulf Crisis: Implications for Indian Foreign Policy', *Asian Survey*, 31: 847–61.

Manchanda, S. L. (1966), 'An Islamic Pact?' *Afro-Asian and World Affairs*, 3.

Medzini, Meron (1972), 'Reflections on India's Asian Policy', *Midstream*, 18: 25–35.

Mehta, Pratap Bhanu (2009), 'Still Under Nehru's Shadow? The Absence of Foreign Policy Frameworks in India', *India Review*, 8: 209–33.

Mehrish, B. N. (1975), 'Recognition of the Palestine Liberation Organization (PLO): An Appraisal of India's Policy', *The Indian Journal of Political Science*, 36: 137–60.

Mishra, Upendra (1982), 'India's Policy towards the Palestinian Question', *International Studies*, 21: 101–15.

Mittchell, David (2007), 'Determining Indian Foreign Policy: An Examination of Prime Ministerial Leadership Styles', *India Review*, 6: 251–87.

Muni, S. D. (1991), 'India and the Post–Cold War World: Opportunities and Challenges', *Asian Survey*, 31 (9).

Naaz, Farah (1999), 'Indo-Israel Relations: An Evolutionary Perspective', *Strategic Analysis*, 23: 241–54.

——— (2000), 'Indo-Israel Military Cooperation', *Strategic Analysis*, 24: 969–85.

Narang, Vipin and Paul Staniland (2012), 'Institutions and Worldviews in Indian Foreign Security Policy', *India Review*, 11: 76–94.

Onley, John (2009), 'The Raj Reconsidered: British India's Informal Empire and Spheres of Influence in Asia and Africa', *Asian Affairs*, 40: 44–62.

Pant, H. V. (2004), 'India–Israel Partnership: Convergence and Constraints', *MERIA Middle East Review of International Affairs*, 8: 60–73.

Pant, Harsh (2007), 'A Fine Balance: India Walks a Tightrope between Iran and the United States', *Orbis*, 51: 495–509.

Pai, Sudha (1997), 'Transformation of the Indian Party System: The 1996 Lok Sabha Elections', *Asian Survey*, 36: 1170–83.

Porath, Yehoshua (1971), 'Al-Haji Amin al-Hussayni, Mufti of Jerusalem: His Rise to Power and Consolidation of His Position', *Asian and African Studies*, 7: 212–56.

Pradhan, Prasanta Kumar (2013), 'India's Relationship with Saudi Arabia: Forging a Strategic Partnership', *Strategic Analysis*, 37: 231–41.

Qureshi, I. H. (1945), 'The Purpose of Tipu Sultan's Embassy to Constantinople', *Journal of Indian History*, 24: 77–84.

Ramana Murti, V. V. (1968), 'Buber's Dialogue and Gandhi's Satyagraha', *Journal of the History of Ideas*, 29: 605–13.

Rangaswami, K. (1969), 'India and West Asian Situation', *Indian and Foreign Affair*, 15 December.

Retzlaff, Ralph J. (1963), 'India: A Year of Stability and Change', *Asian Survey*, 3: 96–106.

Rivkin, Arnold (1959), 'Israel and the Afro-Asian World', *Foreign Affairs*, 37: 486–95.

Rubinoff, Arthur G. (1995), 'India's Normalization of Relations with Israel', *Asian Survey*, 35: 487–505.

Sagar, Rahul (2009), 'State of Mind: What Kind of Power Will India Become?' *International Affairs*, 85: 801–16.

Saliba, Najib E. (1972), 'Impact of the Indo-Pakistani War on the Middle-East', *World Affairs*, 135: 129–37.

Sayigh, Yezid (1989), 'Struggle Within, Struggle Without: The Transformation of PLO Politics Since 1982', *International Affairs*, 65: 247–71.

Schechtman, Joseph (1966), 'India and Israel', *Midstream*, 12: 48–71.

Shichor, Yitzhak (1998), 'Israel's Military Transfers to China and Taiwan', *Survival*, 40: 68–91.

Shlaim, Avi (2004), 'Israel between East and West, 1948–1956', *International Journal of Middle Eastern Studies*, 36: 657–73.

Singh, Anita Inder (1995), 'Keeping India in the Commonwealth: British Political and Military Aims, 1947–49', *Journal of Contemporary History*, 20: 469–81.

Singh, Gurbachan (2006), 'Oral History: India at the Rabat Islamic Summit (1969)', *Indian Foreign Affairs Journal*, 1.

Singh, K. R. (1963), 'India, the Middle-East and the Chinese Aggression', *United Asia*, 11: 759–64.

Singh, Surjit (1979), 'Indo-Israel Relations: A Study of Some Aspects of India's Foreign Policy', *Journal of Indian History*, 57: 387–99.

Somaratna, G. P. V. (1989), 'Renewal of Ties Between Sri Lanka and Israel', *Jerusalem Journal of International Relations*, 11: 74–86.

Sorkhabi, Rasoul (2005), 'Einstein and the Indian Minds: Tagore, Gandhi and Nehru', *Current Science*, 88: 1187–91.

Srivastava, R. K. (1967), 'Indo-Israeli Relations: Pulls and Pressures', *Mainstream*, 9 December.

——— (1968), 'India and the West Asian Crisis', *Foreign Affair Reporter*, 17: 43–52.

Subrahmanyam, K. (2004), 'Narasimha Rao and the Bomb', *Strategic Analysis*, 28: 593–5.

Syed, Abu (1964), 'India and the Arab World', *Indian and Foreign Affair*, 1.

Tharoor, Kansihk (2014) 'Why Modi's India aligns more closely with Israel than with Palestinians', *Aljazeera America*, August 3, 2014, available at: http://america.aljazeera.com/articles/2014/8/3/modi-israel-relations.html

Tsur, Jacob (1957), 'Les Fondements de la Politique Etrangere d'Israel', *Politique Etrangere*, 22: 14.

Turck, Nancy (1977), 'The Arab Boycott of Israel', *Foreign Affairs*, 55: 472–93.

Wriggins, Howard (1976), 'Changing Power Relations Between the Middle East and South Asia', *Orbis*, 20: 785–804.

Yegar, Moshe (2007), 'Pakistan and Israel', *Jewish Political Studies Review*, 19: 125–41.

Zartman, William (1991), 'Conflict and Resolution: Contest, Cost and Change', *Annals of the American Academy of Political and Social Science*, 518: 11–22.

Books and book chapters

Aaron, Sushil J. (2003), *Straddling Faultlines: India's Foreign Policy Toward the Greater Middle East*, CSH Occasional Paper 7 (New Delhi: French Research Institute).

Agwani, M. S. (1995), *Contemporary West Asia* (New Delhi: Har-Anand Publications).

Ahmad, Maqbul (1969), *Indo-Arab Relations* (Bombay: Indian Council for Cultural Relations).

Alimi, Eitan Y. (2007), *Israeli Politics and the First Palestinian Intifada* (Abingdon: Routledge).

Allen, Richard (1974), *Imperialism and Nationalism in the Fertile Crescent* (New York: Oxford University Press).

Alterman, Jon B. and John W. Garver (2008), *The Vital Triangle: China, the United States, and the Middle East* (Washington, D.C.: Center for Strategic & International Studies).

Ansari, Hamid (2007), 'India and the Persian Gulf', in Atish Sinha and Madhup Mohta (eds), *Indian Foreign Policy: Challenges and Opportunities* (New Delhi: Foreign Service Institute/Academic Foundation).

Aziz, Ahmad (1967), *Islamic Modernism in India and Pakistan, 1857–1964* (London: Oxford University Press).

Baba, Noor Ahmad (2008), 'OIC and Pakistan's Foreign Policy: The Indian Dimension', in Rajendra N. Abhyankar (ed.), *West Asia and the Region: Defining India's Role* (New Delhi: Academic Foundation), pp. 669–73.

Baghavan, Manu (2012), *The Peacemakers: India and the Quest for One World* (New Delhi: HarperCollins).

Bhagwati, Jagdish (1993), *India in Transition: Freeing the Economy* (New York: Clarendon).

Bahadur, Kalim (1998), 'Pakistan as a Factor in Indo-OIC Relations', in Riyaz Punjabi and A. K. Pasha (eds), *India and the Islamic World* (New Delhi: Radiant).

Bajpai, Kanti (2002), 'Indian Strategic Culture', in Michael R. Chambers (ed.), *South Asia in 2020: Future Strategic Balances and Alliances* (Carlisle: Strategic Studies Institute, US Army War College).

——— (2009), 'The BJP and the Bomb', in Scott Sagan (ed.), *Inside Nuclear South Asia* (Stanford, CA: Stanford University Press).

——— (2010), 'India and the World', in Niraja Gopal Jayal and Pratap Bhanu Mehta (eds), *The Oxford Companion to Politics in India* (New Delhi: Oxford University Press).

——— (2014), 'Indian Grand Strategic Thought: Six Approaches in Search of a Core?' in Kanti Bajpai, Krishnappa Venkatshamy, and Saira Basit (eds), *India's Grand Strategy: History, Theory, Cases* (New Delhi: Routledge).

Ball, George W. and Douglas B. Ball (1992), *The Passionate Attachment: America's Involvement with Israel, 1947 to the Present* (New York: W. W. Norton).

Bandyopadhyaya, J. (1970), *The Making of India's Foreign Policy: Determinants, Institutions, Processes, and Personalities* (New Delhi: Allied Publishers).

Barr, James (2011), *A Line in the Sand: Britain, France and the Struggle That Shaped the Middle East* (London: Simon & Schuster).

Basham, A. L. (2005 [1954]), *The Wonder That Was India* (New Delhi: Picador).

Bass, Gary (2013), *The Blood Telegram: Nixon, Kissinger, and a Forgotten Genocide* (New York: Knopf).

Bass, Warren (2003), *Support Any Friend: Kennedy's Middle East and the Making of the US–Israel Alliance* (New York: Oxford University Press).

Baumgartner, Frank and Bryan Jones (2009), *Agendas and Instability in American Politics 2nd edn* (Chicago: The University of Chicago Press).

Bethell, Nicholas (1979), *The Palestine Triangle* (London: A. Deutsch).

Bialer, Uri (1981), '"Our Place in the World," Mapai and Israel's Foreign Policy Orientation 1947–1952', *Jerusalem Papers on Peace Problems* 33 (Jerusalem: The Magnes Press, The Hebrew University).

Blarel, Nicolas (2006), *Inde et Israel: Le Rapprochement Stratégique, Pragmatisme et complémentarité* (Paris: L'Harmattan).

——— (2009), 'Indo-Israeli Relations: Emergence of a Strategic Partnership', in Sumit Ganguly (ed.), *India's Foreign Policy: Retrospect and Prospect* (New Delhi: Oxford University Press), pp. 143–61.

——— (2014), 'Redefining India's Grand Strategy? The Evolving Nature of India's Israel Policy', in Kanti Bajpai, Krishnappa Venkatshamy, and Saira Basit (eds), *India's Grand Strategy: History, Theory, Cases* (New Delhi: Routledge).

Blarel, Nicolas and Manjeet S. Pardesi (2012), 'Indian Public Opinion and the War in Iraq', in Richard Sobel, Peter Furia, and Bethany Barratt (eds), *Public Opinion and International Intervention: Lessons from the Iraq War* (Dulles: Potomac).

Blyth, Robert (2003), *The Empire of the Raj. India, Eastern Africa and the Middle East 1858–1947* (New York: Palgrave).

Bose, Sugata (2006), *A Hundred Horizons: The Indian Ocean in the Age of Global Empire* (Cambridge, MA: Harvard University Press).

Brecher, Michael (1959), *Nehru: A Political Biography* (Bristol: Oxford University Press).

——— (1963), *The New States of Asia: A Political Analysis* (London: Oxford University Press).

——— (1968), *India and World Politics: Krishna Menon's View of the World* (Bristol: Oxford University Press).

——— (1972), *The Foreign Policy System of Israel* (London: Oxford University Press).

——— (1974), *Israel, the Korean War and China: Images, Decisions and Consequences* (Jerusalem: Academic Press).

——— (1976), 'Israel and China: An Historic "Missed Opportunity"', in Michael Curtis and Susan Aurelia Gitelson (eds), *Israel in the Third World* (New Brunswick, NJ: Transaction Books).

Bregman, Ahron (2002), *Israel's Wars: A History Since 1947* (London: Routledge).

Burke, S. M. (1973), *Pakistan's Foreign Policy: An Historical Analysis* (London: Oxford University Press).

—— (1974), *Mainsprings of Indian and Pakistani Foreign Policies* (Minneapolis: University of Minnesota Press).

Buzan, Barry and R. J. Barry Jones (eds) (1981), *Change and the Study of International Relations: The Evaded Dimension* (London: Frances Pinter).

Chandra, Kanchan (2004), *Why Ethnic Parties Succeed: Patronage and Ethnic Head Counts in India* (Cambridge: Cambridge University Press).

Chatterjee, Kingshuk (ed.) (2012), *India and the Middle East: Problems and Prospects* (Kolkata: University of Calcutta).

Chatterjee, Margaret (1992), *Gandhi and His Jewish Friends* (London: Macmillan).

Chawla, Sandeep (1981), 'The Palestine Issue in Indian Politics in the 1920s', in Mushirul Hasan (ed.), *Communal and Pan-Islamic Trends in Colonial India* (New Delhi: Manohar).

Checkel, Jeffrey (1997), *Ideas and International Political Change: Soviet/Russian Behavior and the End of the Cold War* (Yale University Press).

Cobb, Roger and Charles Elder (1983), *Participation in American Politics: The Dynamics of Agenda-Building* (Baltimore: Johns Hopkins University Press).

Cohen, Michael J. (1982), *Palestine and the Great Powers; 1945–1948* (Princeton: Princeton University Press).

Cohen, Stephen P. (2001), *India: Emerging Power* (New Delhi: Oxford University Press).

—— (2004), *The Idea of Pakistan* (Washington: Brookings Institution Press).

Curzon, George Nathaniel (1907), *Frontiers*, The 1907 Romanes Lecture, delivered at the University of Oxford on November 2 (Oxford: Clarendon Press).

Darwin, John (2009), *The Empire Project: The Rise and Fall of the British World-System, 1830–1970* (Cambridge: Cambridge University Press).

Davidson, Christopher (2010), *The Persian Gulf and Pacific Asia: From Indifference to Interdependence* (London: Hurst & Co).

Devine, Michael J. (ed.) (2009), *Harry S. Truman, The State of Israel, and the Quest for Peace in the Middle East* (Kirksville: Truman State University Press).

Devotta, Neil (2004), *Blowback: Linguistic Nationalism, Institutional Decay, and Ethnic Conflict in Sri Lanka* (Stanford: Stanford University Press).

Devji, Faisal (2013), *Muslim Zion: Pakistan as a Political Idea* (Cambridge: Harvard University Press).

Dietl, Gulshan (2000), 'The Security of Supply Issue: The Growing Dependence on the Middle East', in Pierre Audinet, P. R. Shukla, and Frederic Grare (eds), *India's Energy: Essays on Sustainable Development* (New Delhi: Manohar).

Dixit, J. N. (2003), 'Jawaharlal Nehru—Architect of India's Foreign Policy', in M. V. Kamath (ed.), *Nehru Revisited* (Mumbai: Nehru Centre).

Dueck, Colin (2008), *Reluctant Crusaders: Power, Culture, and Change in American Grand Strategy* (Princeton: Princeton University Press).

Eayrs, James (1964), *The Commonwealth and Suez, A Documentary Survey* (London: Oxford University Press).

Ehrlich, Avrum (ed.) (2008), *The Jewish-Chinese Nexus: A Meeting of Civilizations* (London: Routledge).

Engelmeier, Tobias F. (2009), *Nation-building and Foreign Policy in India: An Identity-Strategy Conflict* (Delhi: Foundation Books).

Fabry, Mikulas (2010), *Recognizing States: International Society and the Establishment of New States Since 1776* (New York: Oxford University Press).

Fair, Christine (2009), 'Indo-Iranian Relations—What Prospects for Transformation?' in Sumit Ganguly (ed.), *India's Foreign Policy: Retrospect and Prospect* (New Delhi: Oxford University Press).

Feifer, Gregory (2009), *The Great Gamble: The Soviet War in Afghanistan* (New York: Harper).

Feiler, Gil (1998), *From Boycott to Economic Cooperation: The Political Economy of the Arab Boycott of Israel* (London: Psychology Press).

Fischer, Louis (1947), *Gandhi and Stalin: Two Signs at the World's Crossroads* (New York: Harper).

Freedman, Lawrence and Efraim Karsh (1993), *The Gulf Conflict: Diplomacy and War in the New World Order* (Princeton, NJ: Princeton University Press).

Gandhi, Arun (1983), *The Moraji Papers: Fall of the Janata Government* (New Delhi: Vision Books).

Gandhi, Rajmohan (1986), *Eight Lives: A Study of the Hindu–Muslim Encounter* (New York: State University of New York Press).

Ganguly, Sumit (1997), *The Crisis in Kashmir: Portents of War, Hopes of Peace* (Cambridge: Cambridge University Press).

——— (2002), *Conflict Unending* (New York: Columbia University Press).

Garver, John W. (2001), *Protracted Contest: Sino-Indian Rivalry in the Twentieth Century* (Seattle: University of Washington Press).

Gayer, Laurent and Christophe Jaffrelot (eds) (2012), *Muslims in Indian Cities: Trajectories of Marginalisation* (London: Hurst & Company).

George, Alexander and Andrew Bennett (2005), *Case Studies and Theory Development in the Social Sciences* (Cambridge, MA: MIT Press).

Gerberg, Itzhak (2008), *The Changing Nature of Israeli–Indian Relations: 1948–2005* (Pretoria: University of South Africa).

Ghosh, Anjali (2009), *India's Foreign Policy* (New Delhi: Pearson Education India).

Gilpin, Robert (1981), *War and Change in World Politics* (Cambridge: Cambridge University Press).

Goldmann, Kjell, *Change and Stability in Foreign Policy: The Problems and Possibilities of Détente* (Princeton: Princeton University Press).

Goldstein, Jonathan (ed.) (1999), *China and Israel, 1948–98: A Fifty Year Retrospective* (Westport, CT: Praeger).

Goldstein, Judith and Robert Keohane (1993), *Ideas and Foreign Policy: Beliefs, Institutions and Political Change* (Ithaca: Cornell University Press).

Gopal, Krishan and Sarabjit Sharma (2007), *India and Israel: Towards Strategic Partnership* (New Delhi: Authorspress).

Gopal, Sarvepalli (1979), *Jawaharlal Nehru: A Biography, Vol. 2: 1947–1956* (London: Cape).

——— (1989), 'India, the Crisis, and the Non-Aligned Nations', in W. M. Roger Louis and Roger Owen (eds), *Suez 1956: The Crisis and Its Consequences* (New York: Oxford University Press).

——— (2013) 'Israel Diary' in Raghavan, Srinath (ed.) *Imperialists, Nationalists, Democrats: The Collected Essays* (New Delhi: Orient Blackswan).

Guha, Ramachandra (2008), *India After Gandhi: The History of the World's Largest Democracy* (New Delhi: HarperCollins).

——— (2013), *Gandhi Before India* (New Delhi: Allen Lane).

Hasan, Hadi (1928), *A History of Persian Navigation* (London: Methuen).

Hasan, Mushirul (1994), *Nationalism and Communal Politics in India, 1885–1930* (New Delhi: Manohar).

Hasmi, Sohail H. (2009), 'Islam, the Middle East and the Pan-Islamic Movement', in Barry Buzan and Ana Gonzalez-Pelaez (eds), *International Society and the Middle East: English School Theory at the Regional Level* (London: Palgrave).

Heikal, Muhammad Hasanayn (1973), *The Cairo Document: The Inside Story of Nasser and His Relationship with World Leaders, Rebels, and Statesmen* (New York: Doubleday).

——— (1975), *The Road to Ramadan* (London: Collins).

Heptullah, Nejma (1991), *Indo-West Asian Relations: The Nehru Era* (New Delhi: Allied Publishers).

Herzog, Chaim ([1975]2003), *The War of Atonement: The Inside Story of the Yom Kippur War* (London: Greenhill Books).

Hoffman, Steven A. (1990), *India & China Crisis* (Berkeley and Los Angeles: University of California Press).

Holsti, Kal J. (ed.) (1982), *Why Nations Realign: Foreign Policy Restructuring in the Postwar Period* (London: Allen & Unwin).

Horn, Robert C. (1982), *Soviet–Indian Relations: Issues and Influence* (New York: Praeger).

Hoyt, Thimothy D. (2006), *Military Industry and Regional Defense Policy: India, Iraq and Israel* (London: Routledge).

Hudson, Valerie (2007), *Foreign Policy Analysis: Classical and Contemporary Theory* (Boulder, CO: Rowman and Littlefield).

Hudson, Valerie and Eric Singer (eds) (1992), *Political Psychology and Foreign Policy* (Boulder: Westview Press).

Inbar, Efraim (2008), *Israel's National Security: Issues and Challenges Since the Yom Kippur War* (New York: Routledge).

Jaffrelot, Christophe (1998), *The Hindu Nationalist Movement in India* (New York: Columbia University Press).

Jain, Prakash (ed.) (2007), *Indian Diaspora in West Asia: A Reader* (New Delhi: Manohar).

——— (2008), 'Indian Diaspora in West Asia', in *West Asia and the Region: Defining India's Role* (ed.). Rajendra N. Abhyankar (New Delhi: Academic Foundation,), 177-202.

Jalal, Ayesha (2000), *Self and Sovereignty: Individual and Community in South Asian Islam since 1850* (London and New York: Routledge).

James, Lawrence (2000), *Raj: The Making and Unmaking of British India* (New York: St. Martin's Griffin).

Jansen, G. H. (1971), *Zionism, Israel and the Asian Nationalism* (Beirut: Institute for Palestinian Studies).

Jbara, Taysir (1985), *Palestinian Leader, Hajj Amin Al-Husoyni, Mufti of Jerusalem* (Princeton, N.J.: Kingston Press).

Jervis, Robert (1976), *Perception and Misperception in International Politics* (Princeton, N.J.: Princeton University Press).

Kaplan, Robert D. (2010), *Monsoon: The Indian Ocean and the Future of American Power* (New York: Random House).

Kapur, Ashok (2006), *India: From Regional to World Power* (New York: Routledge).

Kapur, Harish (1994), *India's Foreign Policy, 1947-92: Shadows and Substance* (New Delhi: Sage).

——— (2009), *Foreign Policies of India's Prime Ministers* (New Delhi: Lancer).

Katz, Nathan (2000), *Who Are the Jews of India?* (Berkeley: University of California Press).

Keay, John (2000), *India: A History* (New York: Grove Press).

Keddie, N. R. (1968), *An Islamic Response to Imperialism: Political and Religious Writings of Sayyid Jamal ad-Din 'al-Afghani'* (Berkeley and Los Angeles: University of California Press).

Kemp, Geoffrey (2010), *The East Moves West: India, China and Asia's Growing Presence in the Middle East* (Washington D.C.: Brookings Institution Press).

Kennedy, Andrew Bingham (2012), *The International Ambitions of Mao and Nehru* (New York: Cambridge University Press).

Khan, Javed Ahamed (2000), *India and West Asia: Emerging Markets in the Liberalisation Era* (New Delhi: Sage).

Khosla, I. P. (2009), 'Introduction', in I. P. Khosla (ed.), *India and the Gulf* (New Delhi: Konark Publications).

Kingdon, John (1984), *Agendas, Alternatives, and Public Policies* (Boston: Little, Brown).

Klieman, Aaron S. (1988), *Statecraft in the Dark: Israel's Practice of Quiet Diplomacy* (Jerusalem: Westview Press).

Kochan, Ran (1976), 'Israel in Third World Forums', in Michael Curtis and Susan Aurelia Gitelson (eds), *Israel in the Third World* (New Brunswick, NJ: Transaction Books).

Kowert, Paul and Jeffrey Legro (1996), 'Norms, Identity and Their Limits: A Theoretical Reprise', in Peter Katzenstein (ed.), *The Culture of National Security* (New York: Columbia University Press).

Kramer, Martin (1986), *Islam Assembled: The Advent of the Muslim Congresses* (New York: Columbia University Press).

Kumar, Ravinder (1966), *India and the Persian Gulf Region 1858–1907: A Study in British Imperial Policy* (New York: Asia Publishing House).

Kumaraswamy, P. R. (1998), *India and Israel: Evolving Strategic Partnership* (Ramat-Gan, Israel: The Begin-Sadat Center for Strategic Studies, Bar Ilan University).

—— (1999), *China's Quest for Power and Influence in the Middle East* (New Delhi: Sage).

—— (2003), 'India and Israel: Emerging Partnership', in Sumit Ganguly (ed.), *India as an Emerging Power* (London: Frank Cass).

—— (2004a), 'Israel–India Relations: Seeking Balance and Realism', in Efraim Karsh (ed.), *Israel: The First Hundred Years: Israel in the International Arena* (London: Frank Cass), pp. 254–73.

—— (2010), *India's Israel Policy* (New York: Columbia University Press).

—— (2012), *Reading the Silence: India and the Arab Spring* (Jerusalem: The Leonard Davis Institute for International Relations, The Hebrew University of Jerusalem).

Kyle, Keith (2011), *Suez: Britain's End of Empire in the Middle East* (London: I.B Tauris).

Landau, Jacob M. (1990), *The Politics of Pan-Islam: Ideology and Organisation* (Oxford: Clarendon).

Laqueur, Walter (2009), *A History of Zionism: From the French Revolution to the Establishment of the State of Israel* (New York: Random House).

Laufer, Leopold (1967), *Israel and the Developing Countries: New Approaches to Cooperation* (New York: The Twentieth Century Fund).

Lavoy, Peter R. (ed.) (2009), *Asymmetric Warfare in South Asia: The Causes and Consequences of the Kargil Conflict* (Cambridge: Cambridge University Press).

Legrenzi, Matteo and Bessma Momani (eds) (2011), *Shifting Geo-Economic Power of the Gulf: Oil, Finance and Institutions* (Surrey, UK: Ashgate).

Legro, Jeffrey (2005), *Rethinking the World: Great Power Strategies and International Order* (Ithaca, NY: Cornell University Press).

Lelyveld, Joseph (2011), *Great Soul: Mahatma Gandhi and His Struggle with India* (New York: Knopf).

Levi, Werner (1952), *Free India in Asia* (Minneapolis: University of Minnesota Press).

Lewis, D. A. (2003), 'Diversification and Niche Market Exporting: The Restructuring of Israel's Defense Industry in the Post–Cold War Era', in A. Markusen, S. DiGovianna, and M. Leary (eds), *From Defense to Development? International Perspectives on Realizing the Peace Dividend* (London: Routledge).

Lifton, Robert (2012), *An Entrepreneur's Journey: Stories from a Life in Business and Personal Diplomacy* (Bloomington: AuthorHouse).

Madfai, Madiha Rashid al (1993), *Jordan, the United States and the Middle East Peace Process, 1974–1991* (Cambridge: Cambridge University Press).

Majumdar, Ramesh Chandra (ed.) (1968), *The Age of Imperial Unity: History & Culture* (Bombay: Bharatiya Vidya Bhavan).

Malik, V. P. (2006), *Kargil: From Surprise to Victory* (New Delhi: HarperCollins).

Malone, David (2011), *Does the Elephant Dance? Contemporary Indian Foreign Policy* (New York: Oxford University Press).

Mansingh, Surjit (1984), *India's Search for Power: Indira Gandhi's Foreign Policy 1966–1982* (New Delhi: Sage Publications).

Mattar, Philip (1992), *The Mufti of Jerusalem: Al-Hajj Amin al-Husayni and the Palestinian National Movement* (New York: Columbia University Press).

Maxwell, Neville (1970), *India's China War* (New York: Random House).

Mazower, Mark (2009), *No Enchanted Palace: The End of Empire and the Ideological Origins of the United Nations* (Princeton: Princeton University Press).

McGarr, Paul (2013), *The Cold War in South Asia: Britain, the United States and the Indian Subcontinent, 1945–1965* (New York: Cambridge University Press).

Mehrish, B. N. (1972), *India's Recognition Policy Towards New Nations* (New Delhi: Oriental Publishers).

Menon, V. P. (1956), *The Story of the Integration of the Indian States* (New York: Macmillan).

——— (1957), *The Transfer of Power in India* (Princeton: Princeton University Press).

Metcalf, Thomas R. (2007), *Imperial Connections: India in the Indian Ocean Arena, 1860–1920* (Berkeley and Los Angeles: University of California Press).

Minault, Gail (1982), *The Khilafat Movement: Religious Symbolism and Political Mobilization in India* (New York: Columbia University Press).

Mishra, Pankaj (2012), *From the Ruins of Empire: The Intellectuals Who Remade Asia* (New York: Farrar, Straus and Giroux).

Misra, K. P. (1966), *India's Policy of Recognition of States and Government* (New Delhi: Allied Publishers).

Mohan, C. Raja (2005), *Crossing the Rubicon: The Shaping of India's Foreign Policy* (London: Penguin).

Moore, John Norton (ed.) (1974), *The Arab Israeli Conflict Volume 2* (Princeton: Princeton University Press).

Moravcsik, Andrew (1997), *The Choice for Europe: Social Progress and State Power from Messina to Maastricht* (Ithaca: Cornell University Press).

Morris, Benny (1993), *Israel's Border Wars, 1949–1956: Arab Infiltration, Israeli Retaliation, and the Countdown to the Suez War* (New York: Oxford University Press).

——— (2003), *The Birth of the Palestinian Refugee Problem Revisited* (Cambridge: Cambridge University Press).

Mudiam, Prithvi Ram (1994), *India and the Middle East* (London: British Academic Press).

Naaz, Farah (2005), *West Asia and India: Changing Perspectives* (New Delhi: Shipra Publications).

Nadkarni, Vidya (forthcoming), 'India and Russia: A Special Relationship?' Sumit Ganguly (ed.), in *Engaging the World: India's Foreign Policy Since 1947* (New Delhi: Oxford University Press).

Nair, Sreekantan (2004), *Dynamics of a Diplomacy Delayed: India and Israel* (New Delhi: Kalpaz Publications).

Nanda, B. R. (ed.) (1976), *Indian Foreign Policy: The Nehru Years* (Honolulu: University Press of Hawaii).

Nanda, Prakash (2008), *Rising India: Friends and Foes* (New Delhi: Lancer Publishers).

Nandy, Ashis (2002), *Time Warps: Silent and Evasive Pasts in Indian Politics and Religion* (New Brunswick, NJ: Rutgers University Press).

Narizny, Kevin (2007), *The Political Economy of Grand Strategy* (Ithaca: Cornell University Press).

Niemeijer, A. C. (1972), *The Khilafat Movement in India, 1919–1924* (Seattle: University of Washington Press).

Olimat, Muhamad S. (2012), *China and the Middle East: From Silk Road to Arab Spring* (New York: Routledge).

Oliver-Dee, Sean (2009), *The Caliphate Question: The British Government and Islamic Governance* (Lanham: Lexington Books).

Onley, James (2007), *The Arabian Frontier of the British Raj: Merchants, Rulers and British in the Nineteenth-Century Gulf* (Oxford: Oxford University Press).

Panagariya, Arvind (2010), *India: The Emerging Giant* (New York: Oxford University Press).

Pant, Harsh V. (2008a), *Indian Foreign Policy in a Unipolar World* (London: Routledge).

——— (2008b), *Contemporary Debates in Indian Foreign and Security Policy: India Negotiates Its Rise in the International System* (New York: Palgrave Macmillan).

Panter-Brick, Simone (2008), *Gandhi and the Middle East: Jews, Arabs and Imperial Interests* (London: I.B Tauris).

Pasha, Aftab Kamal (1995), *India and OIC: Strategy and Diplomacy* (New Delhi: Center for Peace Studies).

Perkovich, George (1999), *India's Nuclear Bomb: The Impact on Global Proliferation* (Berkeley: University of California Press).

Prasad, Bimal (1960), *The Origins of Indian Foreign Policy: The Indian National Congress and World Affairs, 1885–1947* (Calcutta: Bookland).

——— (1985), 'Foreign Policy in the Making', in B. N. Pande (ed.), *History of National Congress (1885–1985)* (New Delhi: Vikas).

Prasad, Birendra (1979), *Indian Nationalism and Asia, 1900–1947* (New Delhi: B.R. Publishing Corporation).

Prasad, Bisheshwar (1965), *Our Foreign Policy Legacy: A Study of British Indian Foreign Policy* (Delhi: People's Publishing House).

Pigato, Miria (2009), *Strengthening China's and India's Trade and Investment Ties to the Middle East and North Africa* (Washington D.C.: World Bank).

Priyedarshi, Vinita (2010), *Typology of Counter-Terrorism Strategies: A Comparative Study of India and Israel* (New Delhi: KW Publishers).

Quandt, William B. (2001), *Peace Process, American Diplomacy and the Arab–Israeli Conflict Since 1967* (revised edn) (Washington, DC: Brookings Institution Press).

Qureshi, Naeem M. (1999), *Pan-Islam in British Indian Politics: A Study of the Khilafat Movement, 1918–1924* (Liedan: Brill).

Raghavan, Srinath (ed.) (2013), *Imperialists, Nationalists, Democrats: The Collected Essays* (New Delhi: Orient Blackswan).

——— (2013), *1971: A Global History of the Creation of Bangladesh* (Cambridge, MA: Harvard University Press).

Rajan, M. S. (1964), *India in World Affairs, 1954–1956* (London: Asia Publishing House).

Raj Nayar, Baldev and T. V. Paul (2003), *India in the World Order: Searching for Major Power Status* (Cambridge: Cambridge University Press).

Rajkumar, Nagoji Vasudev (ed.) (1952), *The Background of India's Foreign Policy* (New Delhi: AICC).

Raman, B. R. (2008), *The Kaoboys of R&AW: Down Memory Lane* (New Delhi: Lancer Publishers & Distributors).

Rao, Sudha V. (1972), *The Arab–Israeli Conflict: The Indian View* (New Delhi: Orient Longman).

Ratnagar, Shereen (2004), *Trading Encounters: From the Euphrates to the Indus in the Bronze Age* (New York: Oxford University Press).

Raviv, Dan and Yossi Melman (1990), *Every Spy a Prince: The Complete History of Israel's Intelligence Community* (Boston: Houghton Mifflin Company).

Rikhye, Indar Jit (1980), *The Sinai Blunder: Withdrawal of the United Nations Emergency Force Leading to the Six Day War, June 1967* (London: Frank Cass).

Roger Louis, W. M. and Avi Shlaim (eds) (2012), *The 1967 Arab–Israeli War: Origins and Consequences* (Cambridge: Cambridge University Press).

Roland, Joan G. (1989), *The Jewish Communities of India: Identity in a Colonial Era* (Hanover, N.H.: Brandeis University Press).

Rosati, Jerel, Joe D. Hagan, and Martin Sampson (eds) (1994), *Foreign Policy Restructuring: How Governments Respond to Global Change* (Columbia, SC: University of South Carolina Press).

Rosenau, James (1981), *The Study of Political Adaptation: Essays on the Analysis of World Politics* (MY: Nichols Publishing).

Sabatier, Paul and Hank C. Jenkins-Smith (1993), *Policy Change and Learning: An Advocacy Coalition Approach* (Boulder: Westview).

Safran, Nadav (1988), *Saudi Arabia: The Ceaseless Quest for Security* (Ithaca: Cornell University Press).

Sarna, Aaron J. (1986), *Boycott and Blacklist: A History of Arab Economic Warfare against Israel* (Totowa, NJ: Rowman & Littlefield).

Sareen, T. R. (1999), 'Indian Response to the Holocaust', in Anil Bhatti and J. H. Voigt (eds), *Jewish Exile in India, 1933–1945* (New Delhi: Manohar).

Shani, Ornit (2007), *Communalism, Caste and Hindu Nationalism: The Violence in Gujarat* (Cambridge University Press).

Shimoni, Gideon (1977), *Gandhi, Satyagraha and the Jews: A Formative Factor in India's Policy Towards Israel* (Jerusalem: The Leonard Davis Institute for International Relations, The Hebrew University of Jerusalem).

Shimoni, Yaacov (1991), 'Introduction', in S. Avimor (ed.), *Relations between Israel and Asian and African States: A Guide to Selected Documentation*, No. 6 (Jerusalem: The Hebrew University of Jerusalem, Maor-Wallach Press).

Schneer, Jonathan (2010), *The Balfour Declaration: The Origins of the Arab–Israeli Conflict* (New York: Random House).

Schottli, Jivanta (2012), *Vision and Strategy in Indian Politics: Jawaharlal Nehru's Policy Choices and the Designing of Political Institutions* (New York: Routledge).

Simpfendorfer, Ben (2009), *The New Silk Road: How a Rising Arab World is Turning Away from the West and Rediscovering China* (New York: Palgrave Macmillan).

Siddiqui, Rushda, (2008), 'India and Israel's Counter-Terrorism Policy', in *West Asia and the Region: Defining India's Role*, (ed.). Rajendra N. Abhyankar (New Delhi: Academic Foundation,), 107-130.

Singh, Gurcharan (1975), *The Middle East and Indian Diplomacy* (Pearl River, NY: Alovar Press).

Singh, K. R. (1968), 'India and the West Asia Crisis', in M. S. Agwani (ed.), *The West Asian Crisis 1967* (Meerut: Meenakshi Prakshan).

Singh, Ravinder Pal (1998), 'India', in Ravinder Pal Singh (ed.), *Arms Procurement Decision Making Volume 1* (Oxford: Oxford University Press).

Sisson, Richard and Leo E. Rose (1991), *War and Secession: Pakistan, India, and the Creation of Bangladesh* (Berkeley and Los Angeles: University of California Press).

Smith, Charles D. (2010), *Palestine and the Arab–Israeli Conflict* (Boston: Bedford/St. Martin's).

Smolansky, Oles M. (1991), *The USSR and Iraq: The Soviet Quest for Influence* (Durham, NC: Duke University Press).

Snyder, Jack (1991), *Myths of Empire: Domestic Politics and International Ambition* (Ithaca: Cornell University Press).

Sofer, Sasson (1998), *Zionism and the Foundations of Zionist Diplomacy* (Cambridge, UK: Cambridge University Press).

Somaratna, G. P. V. (1993), 'Sri Lanka's Relations with Israel', in Shelton U. Kodikara (ed.), *External Compulsion of South Asian Politics* (New Delhi: Sage).

Soz, Saifuddhin (1998), 'The OIC and Indian Muslims', in Riyaz Punjabi and A. K. Pasha (eds), *India and the Islamic World* (New Delhi: Radiant).

Sridharan, Eswaran (2012), 'Coalitions and Democratic Deepening in India', in Eswaran Sridharan (ed.), *Coalition Politics and Democratic Consolidation in Asia* (New Delhi: Oxford University Press).

Stein, Janice Gross and David A. Welch (1997), 'Rational and Psychological Approaches to the Study of International Conflict: Comparative Strengths and Weaknesses', in Nehemia Geva and Alex Mintz (eds), *Decision-Making on War and Peace: The Cognitive-Rational Debate* (Boulder: Lynne Rienner).

Stein, Kenneth (1999), *Heroic Diplomacy: Sadat, Kissinger, Carter, Begin, and the Quest for Arab–Israeli Peace* (London: Taylor & Francis).

Talbott, Strobe (2006), *Engaging India: Diplomacy, Democracy, and the Bomb* (Washington, DC: Brookings Institution Press).

Taliaferro, Jeffrey, Steven E. Lobell, and Norrin M. Ripsman (eds) (2009), *Neoclassical Realism, the State, and Foreign Policy* (Cambridge: Cambridge University Press).

——— (2012), *The Challenge of Grand Strategy: The Great Powers and Broken Balance between the World Wars* (Cambridge: Cambridge University Press).

Tan, Seng and Amitav Acharya (eds) (2008), *Bandung Revisited: The Legacy of the 1955 Asian–African Conference* (Singapore: NUS Press).

Tarrow, Sydney (1994), *Power in Movement: Social Movements, Collective Action and Politics* (Cambridge: Cambridge University Press).

Tellis, Ashley J. (2001), *India's Emerging Nuclear Posture: Between Recessed Deterrent and Ready Arsenal* (Santa Monica, CA: RAND Corporation).

Tellis, Ashley J., C. Christine Fair, and Jamison Jo Medby (2001), *Limited Conflicts Under the Nuclear Umbrella: Indian and Pakistani Lessons from the Kargil Crisis* (Santa Monica, CA: RAND Corporation).

Tessler, Mark A. (1994), *A History of the Israeli–Palestinian Conflict* (Bloomington: Indiana University Press).

Thakur, Ramesh (1994), *The Politics and Economics of India's Foreign Policy* (New York: Palgrave Macmillan).

Thakur, Ramesh and Carlyle A. Thayer (1992), *Soviet Relations with India and Vietnam, 1945–1992* (New York: St. Martin's Press).

Thapar, Romila (2002), *The Penguin History of Early India: From The Origins to AD 1300* (New Delhi: Penguin Books).

Thomas, Raju (1993), *South Asian Security in the 1990s* (Brassey, UK: Adelphi Paper 278).

Thomas, Richard (1982), *India's Emergence as an Industrial Power: Middle Eastern Contracts* (London: C. Hurst and Co.).

Valiani, Arafat (2011), *Militant Publics in India: Physical Culture and Violence in the Making of a Modern Polity* (New York: Palgrave MacMillan).

Venn, Fiona (2002), *The Oil Crisis* (London: Longman).

Wakefield, Bryce and Susan Levenstein (eds) (2011), *China and the Persian Gulf: Implications for the United States* (Washington, DC: Woodrow Wilson International Center for Scholars).

Waltz, Kenneth (1979), *Theory of International Politics* (Boston: McGraw-Hill, Inc.).

———— (1986), 'Reductionist and Systemic Theories', in Robert O. Keohane (ed.), *Neorealism and Its Critics* (New York: Columbia University Press).

Ward, Richard E. (1992), *India's Pro-Arab Policy: A Study in Continuity* (New York: Praeger).

Wasey, Akhtarul (2003), 'India–West Asia Interaction', in N. N. Vohra (ed.), *History, Culture, and Society in India and West Asia* (New Delhi: Shipra Publications).

Weiner, Myron (1967), *Party Building in a New Nation: The Indian National Congress* (Chicago: University of Chicago Press).

Welch, David A. (2005), *Painful Choices: A Theory of Foreign Policy Change* (Princeton: Princeton University Press).

Wilkinson, Steven (2004), *Votes and Violence: Electoral Competition and Ethnic Riots in India* (Cambridge: Cambridge University Press).

Wilson, Evan M. (1979), *Decision on Palestine: How the United States Came to Recognize Israel* (Stanford: Hoover Press).

Yunus, Mohammed (2011), *Bhutto and the Breakup of Pakistan* (Karachi: Oxford University Press).

Index

About the Author

Nicolas Blarel is Assistant Professor of International Relations at the Institute of Political Science, Leiden University, Netherlands. He studies foreign policy issues, with a focus on security issues in South Asia.

His current research focuses on why rising powers choose to redefine their strategic objectives and means. Building on work in the public policy literature, and especially on theories of advocacy coalitions, he suggests a new understanding of the sources and dynamics of foreign policy change and indirectly of the evolution of a state's grand strategy.

Blarel has published book chapters and articles on India's nuclear policies, and more specifically on terrorism and nuclear escalation; India's relations with the US; the evaluation of India's soft power potential; and India's insurgent movements and state-making. He has worked for the French Foreign Ministry's policy planning staff (the Centre d'Analyses et de Prévisions) on questions related to Afghanistan, South Asia, and nuclear proliferation. Blarel has also been a visiting fellow at the Institute for Defence Studies and Analyses (IDSA) in New Delhi. He was an editorial assistant with the peer-reviewed academic journal, *International Studies Quarterly*.

Before coming to Leiden, Blarel studied at l'Institut d'Etudes Politiques in Strasbourg, Sciences Po Paris, and Indiana University, Bloomington. He can be contacted at n.r.j.b.blarel@fsw.leidenuniv.nl.